Nandita Haksar is a human rights lawyer, teacher, activist and writer. She has been instrumental in setting up the country's first human rights courses at several universities. In 1983, she became the first person to challenge the infamous Armed Forces (Special Powers) Act (AFSPA) in the Supreme Court. She successfully led the campaign for the acquittal of one of the people framed in the Indian Parliament attack case, and has been working for and with migrant workers from the Northeast.

Nandita's published works include *Demystification of Law for Women* (1986); *Framing Geelani, Hanging Afzal: Patriotism in the Time of Terror* (2009); *Rogue Agent: How India's Military Intelligence Betrayed the Burmese Resistance* (2010); *The Judgement That Never Came: Army Rule in North East India* (with Sebastian Hongray, 2011); *ABC of Naga Culture and Civilization* (2011); *Across the Chicken Neck: Travels in North East India* (2013); *The Many Faces of Kashmiri Nationalism: From the Cold War to the Present Day* (2015; revised edition, 2020); *The Exodus Is Not Over: Migrations from the Ruptured Homelands of Northeast India* (2016); *The Flavours of Nationalism: Recipes for Love, Hate and Friendship* (2018) and *Kuknalim: Naga Armed Resistance* (with Sebastian Hongray, 2019).

Nandita lives in Delhi, Goa and, sometimes, Ukhrul.

THE MANY FACES OF KASHMIRI NATIONALISM

FROM THE COLD WAR TO THE PRESENT DAY

NANDITA HAKSAR

SPEAKING
TIGER

SPEAKING TIGER BOOKS LLP
4381/4, Ansari Road, Daryaganj
New Delhi 110002

First published in India by Speaking Tiger 2015
This revised edition published 2020

Copyright © Nandita Haksar

ISBN: 978-93-85288-18-0

10 9 8 7 6 5 4 3 2 1

Typeset by SÜRYA, New Delhi

CONTENTS

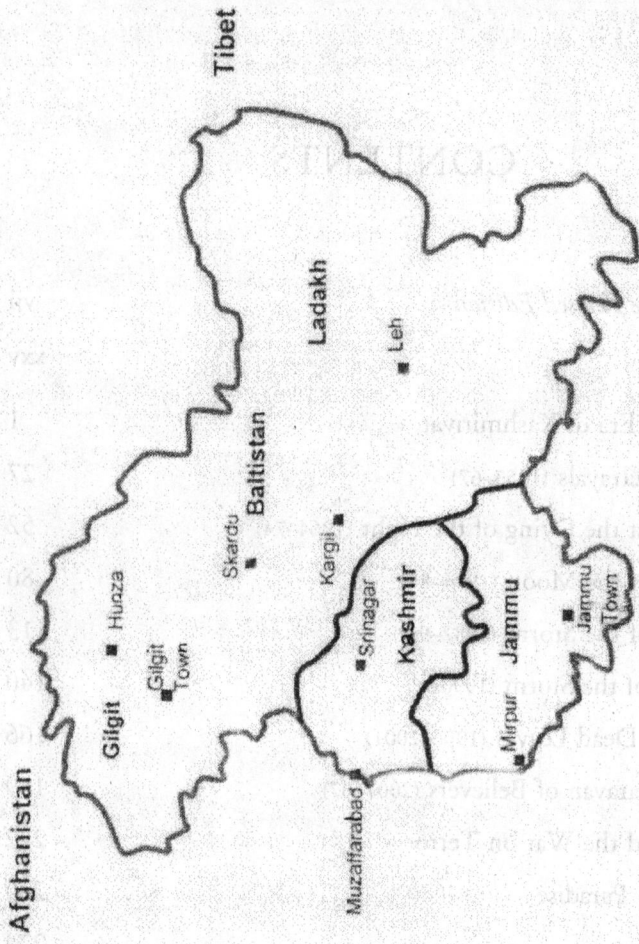

Map of the Princely State of Jammu and Kashmir, 1946.

Tibet

Afghanistan

Ladakh

Leh

Baltistan

Skardu

Gilgit

Hunza

Gilgit
Town

Kargil

Srinagar

Kashmir

Jammu

Muzaffarabad

Mirpur

Jammu
Town

PREFACE TO THE
REVISED EDITION

KASHMIR: SEA OF SUPPRESSED SENTIMENTS

Pooraa bachpan jung mein palaa hai
Dehshat ka samaa jo gheebat se badaa hai
Haarna mere khoon mein kahaan hai
Junoon ye gawaah hai, main maut se ladaa hai.

(I was brought up in war
The season of terror and slander
Losing is not in my blood
My passion is witness, I have fought death.)

—Ahmer Javed, 23-year-old Kashmiri rapper
(translated by Akhil Sood)

This book was first published in August 2015, exactly four years
before Jammu and Kashmir was stripped of its special status in the
Indian Union and of its statehood. It is the story of Kashmiri
nationalism told mainly through the life and work—and in one case,
the death—of two men: Sampat Prakash, a communist trade union
leader and a Kashmiri Pandit; and Afzal Guru, a Kashmiri Muslim,
and a militant disillusioned with Pakistan who surrendered and then
got caught in a complex web of politics that eventually led to his
execution.

Even though the book is critical of political leadership across the ideological spectrum, it has been welcomed by both Kashmiri Pandits and Kashmiri Muslims. In Delhi the book was released at an event attended by many Kashmiri Pandits, including members of the RSS and the Panun Kashmir movement; in Srinagar it was released in the presence of trade union leaders and Tabassum, the widow of Afzal Guru.

As I was writing the book, I knew that some, perhaps many, readers, especially those outside Kashmir, would be critical of my choice of Afzal Guru as one of its protagonists. But I was convinced they needed to be shown truths that would make them recognize their bias.

With the recent arrest of Davinder Singh, a senior officer of the Jammu and Kashmir Police, and the man who admitted to torturing Afzal, this book has attracted wider public attention. On 11 January 2020 Davinder Singh, Deputy Superintendent of Police, was arrested on the Jammu-Srinagar National Highway along with two militants of the banned Hizbul Mujahideen, whom he was ferrying out of the Valley in his car. It has been reported that they were on their way to Delhi. This was the same officer who had asked Afzal to accompany Mohammad, one of the five men who attacked the Indian Parliament in December 2001, to Delhi. Some news reports say that Davinder Singh is a rogue agent who was being used by the Indian intelligence agencies. But did these agencies also allow him to carry on his terrorist activities? There have been strong indications of Davinder Singh's links with terrorists for well over two decades.

Was Davinder Singh involved in the Parliament attack and later in the Pulwama case? What was the mission that he was part of in January 2020, escorting terrorists to Delhi just days before Republic Day? When he was arrested, Davinder Singh is reported to have told the senior officer who ordered his arrest, 'Sir, this is a game, don't spoil it.' What 'game' was he playing, and for whom? These are the questions that are being asked and need to be answered.

Most readers would have encountered the murky world of spooks and agents only in books or movies. But Kashmiris actually inhabit such a world and many, like Afzal, become pawns in cynical games. During Afzal's trial in various courts, not a shred of evidence was produced by the prosecution linking him to any terrorist organization, and the Supreme Court acquitted him of these charges; he was not directly involved in killing anyone; the Supreme Court rejected his confession because it was found to have been extracted by torture. And yet he was hanged.

Sunil Gupta, the Tihar jail official who was with Afzal at the time of his execution, has written about those last hours in his book *Black Warrant: Confessions of a Tihar Jailer* (2019). Gupta says that before carrying out an execution the prisoner is given two weeks, but in Afzal's case only six days were given. Even this much, he writes, was 'definitely enough time to inform Afzal's family and to allow for a last meeting'. But the authorities decided not to inform his family. Gupta then describes the jail staff's last hour with Afzal:

> We sat down with him and asked if he wanted tea. As we sipped it slowly, Afzal spoke calmly about his case. He told us he was not a terrorist... All he wanted, he said, was to fight against corruption, but 'who listens in India?... This was never my fight. I never wanted or even intended to be a Kashmiri separatist. All that I did was to fight against corrupt politicians.'
>
> And then he started singing a song from the 1960s' movie *Badal*: 'Apney liye jiye toh kya jiye, tu ji ae dil zamane ke liye.' (What is the point of a life lived for ourselves, my heart lives for others.)
>
> ...There was no fear in his voice. There was just something about the way Afzal sang it, that I could not help myself. I sang along with him until he stopped and asked for more tea. Unfortunately, the man who serves tea in prison had already left so this wish of his remained unfulfilled.

Gupta goes on to say that when he shared the experience with his family, he broke down before them. He remembers Afzal as a quiet man who would read books of all faiths, and when he was not reading, he would be saying his prayers five times a day. 'I think about Afzal a lot,' Gupta writes. 'I know that anyone who refers to him is called an "anti-national", but I think he was a good man who wanted to work with the NGO People's Union for Civil Liberties. All he wanted was to serve humanity and for his people to live peacefully.'

Reading Sunil Gupta's account, I felt my stand had been vindicated. People needed to know the person who had been demonized, condemned and sentenced to death—the Supreme Court ruled that 'his life should become extinct', so that 'the collective conscience of the society' was 'satisfied'.[1]

Not only Afzal, but all those who believe that his execution was wrong have also been demonized; they're branded as the 'tukde-tukde gang', enemies of the nation. In February 2016, some students of Jawaharlal Nehru University decided to observe a meeting to commemorate Afzal Guru's hanging; they were ruthlessly persecuted, and are still facing charges of 'sedition'. The authorities do not see that acts of solidarity of the kind that those brave JNU students attempted can build bridges between individuals and communities across the abyss of alienation. Watching the manner in which the students were hounded by the authorities and the mainstream media, it seemed to me that my book, like most other books, would change nothing.

But there were also reactions that made me feel that I hadn't failed entirely. In his review of the first edition of *The Many Faces of Kashmiri Nationalism*, the outspoken Kashmiri journalist Shujaat Bukhari[2] wrote: 'The book is another reminder about how various powers-that-be have played with Kashmir. It is an incisive account of a bruised past and present and probably points to the future, as well, of a society that has shown resilience to onslaughts.'

An email I received from an anguished Kashmiri Muslim said:

Dear Ma'am,
Greetings of the Day.
I would like to thank you profusely for the analysis and honest version put forth in your book 'The Many Faces of

Kashmiri Nationalism'. I have spent a great deal of my growing years studying in different parts of the country and it sure doesn't look like the country I used to reside in. After abrogation of Article 370, witnessing the rhetoric made me feel sad about the condition of the country made by the valiant Gandhiji & Nehruji and other freedom fighters…

[*The Many Faces of Kashmiri Nationalism*] is very right in saying the we weren't always right and India wasn't wrong always… The bridges between the two have been broken far from repair.

It still brightens my day hoping that few continue to highlight the oppression of the fascist government. It won't be the first mail of appreciation and surely won't be the last but I as a Kashmiri wanted to [say] I am really thankful.

God bless you ma'am.

There were also positive reactions from and serious discussions with people I met in Kashmir as well as in other parts of the country who had read the book. These gave me hope that the book could create space for different conversations on Kashmir. In a small but significant way, perhaps it could open up the possibility of alternative political discourse.

Central to the spirit of the book are the exuberant optimism of Sampat Prakash, the efforts of thousands of Kashmiris over the decades to preserve the unique ethos of Kashmiri nationalism, and the dark forebodings expressed by Afzal Guru about the future. The stories in the book also show that there is an ever-present danger of destructive political forces crushing any hope of an alternative political discourse which could lead to a resolution to the Kashmir conflict. And in August 2019 the possibility of any resolution was extinguished when the central government decided to do away with the special status of Jammu and Kashmir under the Constitution of India. It all but scrapped Article 370, which made specific provisions for the applicability of the Indian Constitution in the state—a special concession made for the accession of Jammu and Kashmir to India.

The Government of India claimed that this revocation of the special status would help integrate Kashmir with India; it would bring development to the Kashmir Valley; and it would bring peace, security and stability to the conflict-ridden region. Many academics, experts and security analysts have questioned this assumption. Some have even challenged the revocation in the Supreme Court. Whatever the judgement, the revocation of the special status of Jammu and Kashmir is a politically significant step with long-term consequences for India and the rest of South Asia.

This book shows that the special status of Jammu and Kashmir under the Constitution—specifically, the protection of the identity of its people under Article 370—is the bridge which linked Kashmir with the rest of India. Now, with that link gone, what connects India and Kashmir?

—

When we examine, carefully and objectively, the arguments put forward for the revocation of the special status of Jammu and Kashmir, they are all shown to be false and against the weight of historical evidence.

Greater Integration with the Indian Union

The Indian government's Constitutional Order (C.O.) 272 dated 5 August 2019 nullified Article 370 (it has not been abrogated yet) and allowed the government to introduce The Jammu and Kashmir Reorganization Bill, 2019, which was then passed by the Parliament. By this Act of Parliament, the state of Jammu and Kashmir was reconstituted, effective 31 October 2019, into two union territories, one to be called Jammu and Kashmir, and the other Ladakh. While Jammu and Kashmir will have a legislative assembly, Ladakh will be a union territory under a lieutenant governor without a legislative assembly.

The passage of the Bill in Parliament was possible because it was supported by political parties who have usually opposed BJP's

Hindutva ideology, such as the Aam Aadmi Party, Bahujan Samaj Party, and even some prominent members of the Congress Party which is officially opposed to the revocation of the special status. They justified their support in the belief that the nullification of Article 370 would help integrate Jammu and Kashmir with the rest of the country and help bring an end to militancy and proxy war.

The Union Home Minister, Amit Shah, while announcing the nullification of Article 370, said this step would bring everlasting peace to Jammu and Kashmir and 'completely eradicate' Pakistan-sponsored terrorism from the Kashmir Valley. Before the announcement of the bifurcation of the state, there was a clampdown in Kashmir. Seven million people living in the Valley were imprisoned in their own land, within their own homes. Telephone and internet services were cut off. Kashmiri students living outside the Valley could not contact their families; schools were closed down; public assembly was banned; political leaders, including those who had risked their lives supporting India for decades, were detained; even children were arrested. The average loss of business per day in Kashmir during the clampdown has been to the tune of at least Rs 175 crore, according to the Kashmir Chamber of Commerce and Industry (KCCI). Bakeries and animal herders have been hit particularly badly, as have fruit growers.

Greater than the discomfort of the curfews, the arbitrary arrests and detentions and the loss of trade, has been the impact of the feeling of helplessness, humiliation, injustice and repression among the Kashmiri people. The unprecedented triumphalism in the rest of the country has only added to the alienation and anger in Kashmir.

Kashmiris are not new to military repression. As the young Kashmiri rapper Ahmer Javed has sung: *Crackdown as manz zaamit, curfew manz maraan... Bunker yeti gharan manz, bha qabrah khanaan* (We're born in crackdowns, we die in curfews... They turned our homes into bunkers, and I'm digging graves). Even in the midst of this latest clampdown, the Kashmiris found a unique way of protesting. They sent boxes of their famous apples with slogans written across the fruits. When traders in Kathua District opened the wooden boxes, they found apples with slogans like 'Azadi', 'Burhan Wani', 'Zakir Musa Zindabad' and 'Go India Go Back' on them. People in Kargil too have protested and demanded that they should be part of the Muslim majority Kashmir Valley rather than Buddhist majority Ladakh.

Militant elements have found violent ways of making their displeasure known; their target: migrant workers, the most vulnerable section of our society. Militants have killed workers from Bengal and Rajasthan, truck drivers, and a trader from Punjab. Now it will not be 'guest militants' from outside who will use guns, but Kashmiri youth too might take to the gun to avenge their humiliation.

It is not only human rights activists and opposition leaders who are warning of the consequences of this alienation. Police officers, officers of the Indian security forces and defence experts too fear that the repercussions of revoking Article 370 and keeping an entire people under lockdown will lead to greater militancy. Ashok Bhan, the former Director General of Police in Jammu and Kashmir has warned: 'The abrogation of the special status accorded to J&K and re-organization of the state will add to alienation, mistrust and the questioning of the government's democratic credentials in the Valley. While it will be hailed in large parts of Jammu province and in Leh district, both condemnation and appreciation will be along religious lines.'[3] Alok Joshi, Member, National Security Advisory Board (NSAB) and former Secretary of the country's main espionage agency, Research and Analysis Wing (RAW), has warned that the nullification of Article 370 could lead to greater involvement of Pakistan. He has said: 'With the talks with the Taliban reaching a critical point and the Pakistani establishment leveraging these talks, would Pakistan be encouraged towards adventurism on the Kashmir front? Prudence demands that we prepare for a more active involvement of the Pakistani deep state in Kashmir and beyond.'[4]

The BJP-led central government has argued that the nullification of Article 370 ensures that Jammu and Kashmir is fully integrated with the Indian Union. In order to achieve this integration, the Constitution of India and the law have been used in a way that undermines the integrity of legal processes. The government has cleverly, perhaps too cleverly, added a sub clause to Article 367—which is the interpretation clause of the Constitution—in order to give itself Constitutional and legal validity in revoking Jammu and Kashmir's special status under Article 370.

This is how it was done: Article 370(1)(d) says that provisions of the Indian Constitution can be made applicable to Jammu and Kashmir with such modifications as the President of India 'may by order specify'; but it also requires that the President secure the concurrence of the Jammu and Kashmir government before issuing such an order. There is also Article 370(3), which states that via a Presidential order, the entire Article 370 can cease to be operative, provided that a recommendation to this effect is made by the Jammu and Kashmir Constituent Assembly, an elected body set up in 1951 to formulate the Constitution of the state. The Jammu and Kashmir Constituent Assembly had dissolved itself on 26 January 1957, without making any recommendation for a change in or abrogation of Article 370, thus, in effect, making the Article permanent. To get around this legal position, in the Indian government's Constitutional Order 272 of 5 August 2019, a modification was made to Article 367, inserting a sub-clause which states that the words 'Constituent Assembly' in Article 370(3) must be read as 'legislative assembly'. Since the Jammu and Kashmir legislative assembly did not exist in August 2019 (President's rule had been imposed in the state in June 2018 and extended for another six months in July 2019), the recommendation of the governor was deemed analogous to the recommendation of the legislative assembly and C.O. 272, nullifying Article 370, was passed by the central government.

Lawyers are asking whether an amendment to Article 367 can be done in this manner, and if so, whether the governor, as a representative of the President of India, can replace an elected legislative assembly for giving consent to cease operation of Article

370. Retired military officers and bureaucrats have filed a petition in the Supreme Court challenging the Presidential order by which Article 370 was made un-operational, saying that the order was constitutionally invalid. The petitioners have also challenged the Jammu and Kashmir Reorganization Act, 2019. The petitioners include former Air Vice Marshal Kapil Kak, Retired Major General Ashok Mehta, former IAS officers Hindal Haidar Tyabji, Amitabha Pande and Gopal Pillai, and former member of the Home Ministry's Group of Interlocutors for J&K, Radha Kumar.

The central government's revocation of the special status of Jammu and Kashmir has consequences beyond the state. There are special provisions for other parts of the country, mainly in the Northeast region, such as Nagaland and Sikkim. What will become of *those* provisions now? In fact, the claim that only Jammu and Kashmir was given a special status under the Indian Constitution is itself incorrect. At the time of Indian independence when the Government of India was negotiating with more than 500 princely states like Jammu and Kashmir (the biggest such state), Manipur, Junagarh and Hyderabad, among others, they were asked to accede only on three subjects—defence, foreign affairs and communications. While the other princely states finally decided to accept the Indian Constitution's applicability to themselves, Jammu and Kashmir reserved the right to formulate its own constitution and laws—especially related to citizenship and property rights—and accept only some parts of the Indian Constitution.

The BJP and its affiliate organizations have long argued that Article 370 was the brainchild of Jawaharlal Nehru and that Sardar Patel was against its provisions. Historical documents and records show clearly that this was not so. Article 370 was a way to provide space, in matters of governance, to the people of a state who felt deeply vulnerable about their identity and insecure about the future. Both Nehru and Patel felt this understanding was necessary.

Quoting in detail the discussion around the provisions of Article 370, Amitabh Mattoo, an academic from Kashmir, wrote in 2013 in response to Narendra Modi's 'lalkar rally' in Jammu that year:

Indeed, the synergy that Patel and Nehru brought to governing India is evident in the negotiations over Article 370. Consider this: In October 1949, there was a tense standoff between Sheikh Abdullah and Ayyangar over parts of Article 370 (or Article 306A, as it was known during the drafting stage). Nehru was in the United States, where—addressing members of the U.S. Congress—he said, 'Where freedom is menaced or justice threatened or where aggression takes place, we cannot be and shall not be neutral.' Meanwhile, Ayyangar was struggling with the Sheikh, and later even threatened to resign from the Constituent Assembly. 'You have left me even more distressed than I have been since I received your last letter... I feel weighted with the responsibility of finding a solution for the difficulties that, after Panditji left for America...have been created...without adequate excuse,' he wrote to the Sheikh on October 15. And who did Ayyangar turn to, in this crisis with the Sheikh, while Nehru was abroad? None other than the Sardar himself. Patel, of course, was not enamoured of the Sheikh, who he thought kept changing course. He wrote to Ayyangar: 'Whenever Sheikh Sahib wishes to back out, he always confronts us with his duty to the people.' But it was Patel finally who managed the crisis and navigated most of the amendments sought by the Sheikh through the Congress Party and the Constituent Assembly to ensure that Article 370 became part of the Indian Constitution.[5]

Historical records clearly show that Patel and Gopalaswami Ayyangar (minister without portfolio in the first Union Cabinet and a former Diwan to Maharaja Hari Singh of Jammu and Kashmir) rather than Nehru were the chief architects of Article 370.

However, as this book shows, successive governments from the time of Jawaharlal Nehru himself undermined the spirit and intent of Article 370 by extending various laws made by the Indian Parliament to Jammu and Kashmir, by getting the approval of pliant state legislatures. New Delhi argued that since the constituent assembly of Kashmir had wound up in 1957, the powers granted to that body should be vested in the state legislature.

In fact, Article 370 of the Indian Constitution was already a dead letter by the time the present BJP-led government decided to make it un-operational. What was the need, then, to nullify the Article by a convoluted and questionable legal process and impose a crackdown which has served only to alienate the people of Kashmir completely?

Economic Development

The government says de-operationalizing Article 370 will lead to economic development for Jammu, Kashmir and Ladakh. Members of the BJP, including cabinet ministers, have said that once the special status of Jammu and Kashmir has gone, everyone will be able to buy land and use it for the development of the state. At present only 'permanent residents' of the state can buy and own land in the state of Jammu and Kashmir under Article 35A, which was added to the Indian Constitution, under Article 370, through a Presidential order called 'The Constitution (Application to Jammu and Kashmir) Order, 1954'. This order was adopted by the Jammu and Kashmir constitution in 1956, and defines a permanent resident as a person who was a state subject on 14 May 1954, or one who has lived in the state for ten years and has legally bought immovable property there. This definition can only be changed if the Jammu and Kashmir legislature passes an amendment with a two-thirds majority.

It was this provision which allowed the state of Jammu and Kashmir to carry out extensive land reforms. The land reforms were a part of the Naya Kashmir programme inspired by socialist ideals and is largely responsible for the fact that Jammu and Kashmir is ahead of many states in India in almost all economic indicators, despite the years of insurgency. These land reforms along with a massive debt write-off undertaken over two decades, from 1951 to 1973, transformed the lives of Jammu and Kashmir's rural masses. Economists such as Hasib Drabu have pointed out that the absolute level of poverty in Jammu and Kashmir—households living below the poverty line—is 10%, against the all India average of 22%. The income inequality coefficient for rural households in the state is 0.221, making it one of the most egalitarian sub-national economies in India. Households in Jammu and Kashmir have the second lowest incidence of indebtedness in the country.

A survey of India's states by the Delhi-based PHD Research Bureau in December 2011 stated that Jammu and Kashmir stands 8th on the basis of various socio economic parameters, viz. macro economy, investment environment, infrastructure, agriculture, primary education and consumer markets. The survey showed that the state has been ranked first in primary health, 3rd in macro economy, 4th in industrial investments and primary education, 6th in consumer markets, 10th in infrastructure and 11th in agriculture. The state has been ranked 4th in labour regulations, 9th in overall economic freedom, 13th in legal systems and 14th in terms of size of the government.[6]

So, how will the repeal of Article 35A help in the development of the people in Jammu, Kashmir or Ladakh? The government says land can now be bought by anyone, i.e., corporations. But private investment has been coming into Jammu and Kashmir despite the restrictions on land ownership imposed by Article 35A. Land for industrial development is available to outsiders and foreigners like elsewhere in the country. The government of Jammu and Kashmir offers land for industry for a 90-year lease, which is further renewable; that too at lower prices and on better terms than in many other states.

However, corporations have not been able to take over the pristine lands of the state; the protection of Article 35A has ensured that the mountains, forests and rivers of Kashmir are still preserved from wanton destruction which corporations and unregulated tourism have wrought in other parts of the country.

Return of the Kashmiri Pandits

During Prime Minister Narendra Modi's September 2019 trip to the USA given the moniker 'Howdy Modi', Kashmiri Pandits settled in that country welcomed him as a hero who had given them justice by finishing the special status of Kashmir. But no one said anything about giving up their American citizenship and returning to Kashmir.

Responsible Kashmiri Pandits have not only condemned the revocation of the special status but have even challenged the changes to the law before the Supreme Court of India. Former Air Marshal Kapil Kak, a Kashmiri Pandit, has warned that the community is being used as an instrument of the Hindutva project and its brazen majoritarianism.

This does not mean that the Kashmiri Pandits have not suffered deeply because of the insurgency in the Kashmir Valley, and this book has dealt extensively with the question.

The Kashmiri Muslim

This book shows how the Kashmiri identity was defined as an inclusive one, embracing the diversity of the erstwhile province of Jammu, Kashmir and Ladakh. However, over time it has become almost synonymous with the Kashmiri Muslim identity.

With the passing of the contentious Citizenship Amendment Act 2019, which gives special protection to non-Muslim migrants in India, the idea of citizenship itself has been communalized by the BJP-led central government, and there have been nationwide protests against the undermining of the secular nature of the Constitution of India. The Kashmir question has now converged with the question of the future of Muslims in India. Despite assurances by Prime Minister Modi, the Muslim citizens feel deeply threatened by the unfolding of the Hindutva agenda of making India a Hindu homeland, and Muslims either stateless or second-class citizens. The Kashmiri Muslim will be further, and perhaps irrevocably, alienated.

The Dalit Question

It is true that members of the scheduled castes in Jammu have suffered discrimination under Article 35A. There is a historical context to their grievance which needs to be noted—not as a justification for the discrimination but to understand its historical origins.

In 1957, the local sweepers' union went on an indefinite strike demanding regularization of their jobs and a salary hike.[7] The protest continued for months, resulting in the stagnation of municipal work in the state, which led to several towns becoming garbage dumps. The state government led by Bakshi Ghulam Mohammad— then the Prime Minister (Sadr-e-Riyasat) of Jammu and Kashmir— took the decision to bring in safai karamcharis from nieghbouring Punjab. After negotiations with the Punjab government, Valmikis from Gurdaspur and Amritsar were invited to the state specifically to be employed as sweepers. The number of families that migrated to Jammu at that time differs in records; the numbers range between 206 and 272.

Since the men and women who were invited from Punjab to work in Jammu municipality were not permanent residents of the state, modifications were made in the Jammu and Kashmir Civil Service Regulations to accommodate them. The mandatory condition of obtaining a permanent residence certificate (PRC) was relaxed for them. These families left their homes in Punjab to settle in Jammu only because of the promise that they would have the same rights as others and that they would be granted 'permanent resident' status. The Valmikis were also allotted land for the construction of houses and some were given residential accommodation in different areas of Jammu city.

While relaxing the PRC condition for Valmikis, a clause was inserted in the Jammu and Kashmir Civil Service Regulations that clarified that the rules were relaxed only to the point of the community members getting appointed as safai karamcharis. Though that was not an issue for the first generation of Valmikis, who were happy to get regular jobs and accommodation, the newer generation have been unable to venture into other fields of employment in the state as they could not prove their domicile. They also do not get the right to special educational and employment reserved for permanent residents.

None of the political parties, national or regional, have ever made any attempt to redress this grievance. Since the Valmikis do not have the right to vote in the state assembly, they do not constitute a vote bank and are excluded entirely from state-level politics.

In this book, Sampat Prakash describes the strike of the Corporation Safai Karamcharis, and shows that their condition has continued to be bad over the years. The 1957 strike did lead to some improvement in the working conditions of the safai karamcharis, according to Sampat Prakash, but he did not speak of the problem of discrimination suffered by the Valmikis under Article 35A. While writing this new preface, I tried to call him in Srinagar, where he now lives, to discuss this issue, but communications have yet to be restored in the Valley.

I am sure Sampat Prakash would say the solution is to give permanent resident status to the erstwhile Valmiki safai karamcharis so that their children can take advantage of both educational and employment opportunities reserved for permanent residents. The matter does not need, and cannot justify, the repeal of Article 35A.

By not redressing the genuine grievance of the Jammu Valmiki community, all the political parties of the state have allowed the Hindutva forces to take advantage of the situation.

The International Context

The virtual abrogation of Article 370, the re-organization of the state of Jammu and Kashmir and the repeal of Article 35A will have international consequences which will fuel militancy. It will make the position of those Kashmiri leaders who have risked their lives for decades to defend the accession to India, entirely untenable.

Kashmiri youth who have lived through this clampdown, who have been in jails and who have been witness to the humiliation of their people and the triumphalism of the Indian government and much of its public, will seek justice—and they won't do this only by painting a few slogans on apples.

Internationally, the Indian prime minister may find support among many of the world's leaders today, but the militant, too, will find money and arms to fuel his resentment.

Repurcussions in the Northeast

The events unfolding in Kashmir have been closely watched by people in the Northeast, most especially the National Socialist Council of Nagalim (IM), which has been involved in a peace process with the Government of India since 1997. N. Ravi was credited with persuading the NSCN (IM) to sign the Framework Agreement in August 2015 and it was said that the talks were in their final stages. But the nullification of Article 370 showed the Nagas that any promises made by the Indian government are easily broken.

There is now an increased presence of the Indian armed forces in Nagaland, with helicopters hovering over the NSCN (IM) camp near Dimapur.

Meanwhile, new alliances are being forged between militants; and there is a growing sense of alienation in the Northeast. How does the present government hope to bring greater peace to India when the citizens living on our most vulnerable borders are feeling alienated and betrayed?

Is there any hope?

The number of citizens all over India who have reacted against the nullification of Article 370 is far more than ever before; the interest in Kashmir, the need to reach out to the people of Kashmir, is real. When S.A.R. Geelani, the man who was acquitted of charges of being a part of the conspiracy to attack the Indian Parliament in 2001, died recently, the large gathering at the funeral was a sharp contrast to the time when he and his family were virtually boycotted.

However, the reactions to the events in Kashmir also show massive ignorance about the complexity of the political situation in the erstwhile state of Jammu and Kashmir, and a lack of knowledge of its history.

There is an urgent need to understand the situation and books can be valuable sources of information. At least that is what I try to believe. Books like this one have been written in harsh and dispiriting times, but always with the hope that the reader might find some answers in, perhaps even derive comfort and inspiration from, the past; from histories which would otherwise be lost, or deliberately obliterated from our collective memories. I believe that the stories of the Kashmiri people recorded within the covers of this book deserve to be remembered; perhaps they can still shine a light in these dark times. Present events have made these histories even more relevant than before.

NANDITA HAKSAR
January 2020

INTRODUCTION

ALONG THE SILK ROUTE AGAIN

Bahar Kashmiri, a poet from the Valley, wrote in the 1940s:

> From all sides I am assaulted,
> The English, the Indians, the Afghans, the Pakistanis,
> To whom should I complain, to whom should I tell my fate?
> Capitalists, tyrants, oppressors, and friends, all want me
> To become their accomplice,
> With whom should I agree, with whom should I disagree?
> To whom should I complain, to whom should I tell my fate?[1]

These words reflect the agony of the Kashmiri people who have been caught in the web of political machinations and intrigue throughout the history of the Valley. This book traces the tortured history of Kashmiri nationalism, primarily through the lives of two men: Sampat Prakash, a Kashmiri Pandit and Communist trade union leader who became active in politics during the Cold War years, and Mohammad Afzal Guru, a Kashmiri Muslim who became politically active at the beginning of the Kashmir insurgency, coinciding with the end of the Cold War, the defeat of Soviet Union, and the start of the War on Terror. The stories of many other Kashmiris are also woven into this account.

The book also examines how Kashmiri nationalists have to negotiate the rivalries between superpowers, the competing nationalisms of India and Pakistan, which invariably translates into

Hindu-Muslim antagonisms. The results of the latest elections of 2014 show how deeply divided the people of Jammu and Kashmir are along communal lines. The controversies surrounding the government formation reflect the long history of mobilization of people along religious lines and, more recently, the competing communalism of Hindu and Muslim extremism.

The two parties who have formed the government in Jammu and Kashmir, the Jammu and Kashmir People's Democratic Party (PDP) and the Bharatiya Janata Party (BJP), are as different as the North Pole is from the South Pole.[2] The Valley-based PDP was formed in 1998 and is committed to self-rule by Kashmiris without disturbing the sovereignty of either India or Pakistan. The BJP was created in 1980 but its origins lie in the Bharatiya Jana Sangh, formed in 1951 to contest the special status accorded to Kashmir under the Indian Constitution. The BJP base is entirely in Hindu-dominated Jammu.[3]

Some public leaders have hailed this alliance as a triumph of Indian democracy and an opportunity for reconciliation between the Hindus of Jammu and the Muslims of the Kashmir Valley. But there are those who warn that this could well be the beginning of the 'partitioning of the state's peoples by two colluding communal blocks'.

In the collective memory of the Kashmiris, their land has been under continuous foreign rule ever since the Mughal emperor Akbar invaded the Valley in 1586 and imprisoned Yusuf Shah Chak and later sent him to Bihar where he died in anonymity. He was the last independent king of Kashmir.

The Mughal rule in Kashmir ended with the invasion of the Valley by Ahmad Shah Durrani in 1751. There are innumerable stories about the brutalities committed by the Afghans during their rule which ended in 1819 when the Sikhs conquered Kashmir. The Sikh rule is remembered for the harsh treatment meted out to the Muslim subjects. The Jama Masjid at Srinagar was closed to the public for prayers and Muslims were forbidden to say Azan. Sikh rule came to end with the coming of the Dogra Raj in 1846.

It was the Dogras who united the entire Province of Jammu and Kashmir. One of Maharaja Ranjit Singh's most able generals, Gulab Singh (1792–1858)[4], joined the Lahore court in 1809 and in 1821 Maharaja Ranjit Singh gave him the estate of Jammu. Gulab Singh sent his loyal general, Zorawar Singh, to conquer Baltistan and Western Tibet. In September 1842, a Treaty of Friendship was signed between the ruler of Jammu, the emperor of China and the lama guru of Lhasa by which the boundary between Ladakh and Tibet was established.[5] This treaty assured Gulab Singh that the trade in wool, shawls and tea would not be interfered with.

The Sikhs, and later the Dogras, controlled the lucrative overland Indo-Central Asian trade through Ladakh. Between 1919 to 1931, goods worth about Rs 285 million were exported through Ladakh to Xinjiang in present-day China, while merchandise valued at about Rs 330 million was imported from Xinjiang into Ladakh during the same period. However, the Indo-Central Asian trade through Ladakh, which scaled an unprecedented height of over Rs 68 million during the financial year 1920–21, finally ceased to flow after 1949 following the Communist takeover of Xinjiang.[6] Even though the trade link was broken when the British imposed restrictions on exports of essential commodities from India to Central Asia during the height of Anglo-Soviet tensions, the influence of Central Asia on the culture is visible everywhere in the Kashmir Valley.

The Yarkandi Serai on the left bank of the Jhelum river near the Safa Kadal Bridge in Srinagar is a standing reminder of the ancient connections between Kashmir and Central Asia. This was where travellers from Central Asia rested, and their yaks and ponies laden with delicate porcelain grazed in the grounds surrounding the Eidgah.

Now the possibilities of reviving these old links through trade are opening up with the global shift from Europe to Asia. The ancient Silk Routes are being revived and railway lines, bridges and roads are being constructed to link Asia with Europe again. Pakistan-occupied

Kashmir (PoK) shares borders with several countries: Pakistan, the Wakhan Corridor of Afghanistan and Tajikistan to the west, and the Xinjiang province of the People's Republic of China to the north. Ever since the Karakoram highway (KKH) was built to connect Pakistan with China via PoK, the geopolitical significance of PoK has increased manifold. PoK is a gateway to the Central Asian republics and to their expanding markets.

What would the impact of this opening up of trade routes to Central Asia through Gilgit-Iskardu-Kargil be on the Kashmir Valley? The people of Kashmir could once again be linked to international trade routes, but for the India-Pakistan and India-China tensions. For the time being, the only reminder of the past connections with Central Asia can be seen in the culture of the Kashmiris—from the pheran that they wear to the kangri (earthen pot containing burning coals) that they carry, and the samovars filled with tea throughout the year.

All through the colonial period, the British and the Russians eyed the trade routes. The British East India Company had already established itself and was at that time engaged in a war with the Sikhs. In this war, Gulab Singh remained neutral. The British defeated the Sikhs and, in 1846, the independent Sikh kingdom became a protectorate in accordance with the Treaty of Lahore. The British then took away the territories of Jammu and Kashmir from the Sikhs on the excuse that they could not pay the indemnity and it was handed over to Gulab Singh by the Treaty of Amritsar signed on 16 March 1842.

Thus, Gulab Singh became the maharaja of the Princely State of Jammu and Kashmir. The Dogra kingdom consisted of three administrative areas—the Jammu Province, the Kashmir Province and the Frontier Ilaquas consisting of Ladakh Wazarat, the Gilgit Agency and the vassal states of Hunza and Nagar. Before Indian Independence, the Princely State of Jammu and Kashmir was the largest princely state and culturally, too, the most diverse.

The Dogras united a large territory inhabited by a population speaking a variety of languages, ranging from Shinaki, Burushaski and Wakhi to Dogri, Kashmiri and Bodhi. The people practised different religions as well and among the subjects were Moravian Christians, Buddhists, Shias, Sunnis, Ahmadiyyas, Jains and Hindus.[7]

The origins of Kashmiri nationalism lie in the movement against the oppressive Dogra rule which began in 1846 and ended in 1947.

The condition of the ordinary people has been described by many writers who visited Kashmir; all have documented the terrible poverty in which the majority of the people lived. For instance, Sir Albion Banerji, the Foreign and political minister of the State, made this observation:

> Jammu and Kashmir State is labouring under many disadvantages, with a large Muhammadan population absolutely illiterate, labouring under poverty and very low economic conditions of living in the villages and practically governed like dumb driven cattle. There is no touch between the Government and the people, no suitable opportunity for representing grievances and the administrative machinery itself requires overhauling from the top to bottom to bring it up to the modern conditions of efficiency. It has at present little or no sympathy with the people's wants and grievances.[8]

The Kashmiri people did rebel against Dogra oppression. The most famous was the protest by the shawl weavers (shawl-bafs) in April 1865.

Kashmiri shawls came to be known in Europe in the late eighteenth century, after Napoleon Bonaparte of France presented a Kashmiri shawl to his wife, Josephine. Her use of the shawls set off a Europe-wide fashion trend, and French dealers soon began descending on Srinagar to feed the growing demand at home.

European demand ensured that the shawl industry continued to flourish. Between 1860 and 1870, according to the economic historian D.N. Dhar, exports of shawls ranged between Rs 2.5 million and Rs 2.8 million annually.

Maharaja Ranbir Singh's administration now set up the Dagshawl Department, which was charged with raising Rs 1.2 million each year from the trade. Pandit Raj Kak Dhar, the department's daroga, or inspector, set about doing so with great enthusiasm—and great brutality.

The shawl-bafs faced enormous hardship. Each weaver was expected to pay Rs 49 a year towards the new tax, which meant over half of his average wage of Rs 7 a month was now being expropriated. In addition, the staff of the Dagshawl Department extracted illegal levies.

Faced with starvation, Srinagar's shawl-bafs chose to fight. On the morning of 29 April 1865, the weavers and their khandwaws, or apprentices, peacefully marched through the streets of Srinagar towards the palace of Kripa Ram, the governor of Kashmir. Effigies of Raj Kak Dhar were burned by the protesters, and slogans raised against the Dagshawl Department.

Kripa Ram was determined to teach Srinagar's workers a lesson they would not forget. As the protesters reached the old city neighbourhood of Zaldagar, troops under the command of Colonel Bijoy Singh surrounded the procession and demanded that the workers disperse. They refused. What followed was horrific. The unarmed men were fired on at point-blank range and then as they fled, were charged at with spears. Hundreds jumped off the bridge of Haji Rather Sum at Zaldagar, hoping to hide in the marshes along the Dal Lake.

Historians have not been able to record the names of all those who were killed on 29 April 1865, but the fate of the leaders of the uprising is well recorded. Sheikh Rasool and Abli Baba were tortured to death in a dungeon in the Shergarhi Palace, while Qudda Lal and Sona Shah were imprisoned in the Bahu Fort at Jammu after they failed to pay a fine of Rs 50,000 each to the Maharaja. Hundreds of other protesters were held in prison at Habak, where many died of cold and hunger.[9]

The weavers' strike failed because they did not have a leader to take their agitation forward. At the time there were no newspapers, no political parties and even social organizations were banned. It would take more than six decades before the Kashmiris would rise as a people against Dogra Raj. This time they would rise under the leadership of a charismatic Kashmiri leader, Sheikh Mohammad Abdullah.

The greatest challenge before the Sheikh was to build an organization and a movement in which both Kashmiri Hindus and Muslims could feel an equal sense of belonging. He was deeply influenced by ideas of Socialism and Communism. It was during this time that Sampat Prakash and his comrades in the trade union movement began their political activism.

I was introduced to Sampat Prakash by Balraj Puri,[10] whom I had asked to find a Kashmiri Pandit willing to testify as an expert witness. I was representing Syed Abdul Rehman Geelani, a Delhi University lecturer, one of the four people accused of being a part of the conspiracy to attack the Indian Parliament on 13 December 2001. Later I was involved in the campaign to save Mohammad Afzal Guru from the gallows.

Sampat Prakash testified in the court as a defence witness in the Parliament attack case and throughout the trial, he and his comrades in the trade union movement were active in the campaign for justice for the accused. It was the first campaign in which Kashmiris and non-Kashmiris jointly fought for justice and it finally led to the acquittal of three of the accused. But the campaign could not save Afzal Guru from the gallows. He was secretly hanged in Tihar Jail on 9 February 2013. Now the PDP, along with other parties and organizations, is demanding that his mortal remains be given to his family so he can be buried in the martyrs' graveyard, but it was the BJP which had carried out a vicious campaign to hang Afzal Guru whom they looked upon as a Pakistan-trained terrorist.

Sampat Prakash and Mohammad Afzal Guru seem to have nothing much in common; they belong to two different generations and two different communities. Sampat was born in a typical Kashmiri Pandit family, barely two decades after the Russian Revolution. He grew up when Kashmiris, Hindu and Muslim, were inspired by the revolutionary ideas of Communism. Afzal Guru grew up at a time when Russians were seen as the enemies of Islam, and the heroes of his time were the freedom fighters like the Taliban who successfully defeated the Russians in Afghanistan.

Sampat was born as a subject of the Princely State of Jammu and Kashmir; Afzal was born as a citizen of independent India. While Sampat Prakash was growing up, the hero of the people was Sheikh Abdullah—the man who was called the Lion of Kashmir, the leader who would lead his people to freedom. But by the time Afzal Guru grew up, the Sheikh was seen as a traitor by many Kashmiri nationalists—a man who had betrayed the dream of Kashmiri independence.

However, there were similarities between the two men which gave me a glimpse into the complexities defining Kashmiri nationalism. Both men were deeply committed to the idea of an independent Kashmir, free from the dominance of both India and Pakistan. Both were, at an important juncture of their life, members of the militant Jammu and Kashmir Liberation Front or the JKLF. The JKLF projected itself as a secular organization fighting for Jammu and Kashmir, independent of both India and Pakistan, with the same boundaries as the Princely State under the Dogras.

The idea of an independent Kashmir, free from the hold of both India and Pakistan, appeals to a vast number of Kashmiris but they are aware that in order to realize their dream, they would have to successfully fight the three nuclear states who lay claim to the territory of Jammu and Kashmir.

Today, the territory of the erstwhile Princely State of Jammu and Kashmir is divided and administered by three sovereign states—India, Pakistan and China. At present, China holds about 20 per cent,[11] Pakistan 35 per cent[12] and India the remaining 45 per cent.[13] The United Nations referred to this region as Jammu and Kashmir, a disputed territory, until November 2010, when it was removed from the list of disputes under the observation of the Security Council. Both Sampat Prakash and Afzal Guru look upon Jammu and Kashmir as disputed territory.

Sampat and Afzal equally felt that their only real home was the Kashmir Valley. Both the men, however, could not return to live in the Valley because of the threat to their lives. Sampat continues to be threatened by the militants and condemned by his own community for supporting Kashmiri separatists; Afzal was threatened by the Indian security forces, even though he was a surrendered militant but not an approver.

Despite being Kashmiri nationalists, they both gave their sons names that were not Kashmiri—Sampat named his son Lenin; Afzal's son is called Ghalib. Both Sampat Prakash and Afzal Guru struggled with the ideological conflicts between universal ideals and conflicting nationalisms.

Sampat Prakash does not and Mohammad Afzal Guru did not characterize the struggle for Kashmiri independence as a religious war. Afzal, in a letter to me, wrote: 'When Naga conflict is not Christian why conflict in Kashmir is branded as Islamic [?] Fundamentally, it is political, social and historical in nature.'

But Sampat Prakash now concedes that religion has become an important factor in the Kashmir movement. The ascendancy of the Hindutva factor and the rise of political Islam cannot be wished away. He is grappling with redefining the meaning of Kashmiri nationalism.

Sampat Prakash and Afzal Guru have both expressed concern about the growth of radical Islam. Afzal expressed his concern in his letters to friends and to me. Sampat Prakash and his comrades have done much to stem the tide of Islamic fundamentalism; they have managed, against all odds, to continue to fight for better living and working conditions for government employees in Jammu, Kashmir and Ladakh, despite the risk to their lives. Their stories are inspirational and they have never been told.

The growth of Hindutva ideology and political Islam makes it

increasingly difficult for Sampat Prakash or his comrades to dream
of a future in which Kashmiri Hindus and Kashmiri Muslims can
live together with mutual respect.

Sampat Prakash has asked me more than once: 'What more could
we have done to bring the two communities together?'

It is not a question that only Sampat Prakash should be asking.

BORN IN THE ERA OF KASHMIRIYAT[1]

Sampat Prakash was born on 26 June 1939, two weeks after Sheikh Mohammad Abdullah changed the name of his party from the All Jammu and Kashmir Muslim Conference to the All Jammu and Kashmir National Conference.

Sampat was born in a typical Kashmiri Pandit family in the Kralyar neighbourhood of Rainawari in Srinagar. His mother, Leelavati, died when he was barely two, while giving birth at the Mission Hospital. Sampat's father, Neelkanth Kundu, was a school teacher at the C.E. Tyndale Biscoe School in Rainawari, a branch of the first school run by Christian missionaries in Kashmir.

In the beginning, the school attracted children from Kashmiri Pandit families because Muslims could not afford its fees. When Tyndale Biscoe first came to Srinagar in 1890, he observed that the Kashmiri Pandits had 'lost their self-respect' and a 'slave mentality had been well stamped on them by the heels of their conquerors'.[2] The school aimed to turn 'these high caste conceited Brahman sons of the ruling class into men'. The motto of the school was: 'In All Things Be Men'.

The missionary was shocked to find that the boys did not know how to swim, even though they lived by the Dal Lake, and that they did not climb mountains because they were too scared of going into the home of the gods. It was only on the threat of expulsion that the boys learnt to swim and trek. The missionary observed that his task was made easier because of the Kashmiri sense of humour.

1

At the time, Kashmiri Pandit men wore 'tight bandage-like pugaree (turban), golden ear and nose rings, wooden clogs and a long nightgown garment reaching from neck to ankles, called a pheran'.[3]

By the time Sampat was old enough to enter school, Neelkanth was the Headmaster of the Tyndale Biscoe School. Sampat remembers his father wearing Western clothes, a suit and, on occasion, a tie with a tight pugaree on his head when he went out visiting. However, at home, he continued to wear the pheran so he could warm his hands around a kangri held inside the garment.

Neelkanth named his son Bansi Lal. It was strange for a staunch Shaivite family to name their son after Krishna. Perhaps Neelkanth too had doubts. He asked a famous astrologer, who was staying at the home of a family where he went to tutor the children, about the appropriateness of his son's name.

The astrologer looked at the baby's astrological charts and declared that Bansi Lal was not an auspicious name for the boy and suggested another name, Samvith Prakash, the 'First Ray of the Sun'. He predicted that the child would go a long way in politics. Accordingly, the father changed the name of his son. Subsequently, his name was changed to Sampat Prakash, but that was many years later, when he joined college.

After his wife died, Neelkanth was distraught. At that time, he met an elderly English woman missionary. She invited him to stay with her and promised to adopt both Neelkanth and his son. She said she would treat Sampat as her grandson and send him to London for higher studies when the time came. Neelkanth accepted the offer, converted to Christianity and moved out of his newly built home in Rainawari, taking his son with him.

Neelkanth's brothers were outraged. They put pressure on their wayward brother to return to the family fold. After a year of pressure and persuasion Neelkanth returned, and three days of special prayers were held to purify him before he could be accepted back into the Kashmiri Pandit society. Sampat always teased his father that he had deprived his son of an English education.

Neelkanth's brothers also found him a new wife, a schoolgirl called Prabhawati. Sampat always called her his 'new mother'. Prabhawati was from Habba Kadal where she was still studying at the Kashyap Girls' School, the only girls' school where Kashmiri Pandits sent their daughters. She was barely fourteen years old when she was married to Neelkanth.

Many years later, in February 2008, Sampat took me to meet his stepmother in Najafgarh, an ugly, crowded colony on the outskirts of southwest Delhi, her home ever since the events in Kashmir forced her to leave the Valley. She greeted me with a warm Kashmiri embrace as she would any Kashmiri woman.

Clad in a pheran, she laughed with a young girl's delight when she recalled her life in Rainawari. Sampat urged her to remember the good old days when Hindus and Muslims lived together in harmony.

I asked her to describe how she would spend an average day.

She used to get up at five in the morning, even in the winter, to prepare breakfast for her husband and children; by ten she was again in the kitchen to prepare a light lunch; by four in the evening she had to make some snacks for the family and by eight she busied herself with the evening meal. On an average, she had to cook three to four different dishes, apart from rice, every day.

Prabhawati had seven children. Sampat was the eighth, but considered him her eldest son. The cooking and caring for the children kept her so occupied and tied down that she rarely had any time for outings, and festivals meant extra cooking and work.

The air in the room was thick with memories and resentment. Many of the relatives had come into the room and were listening intently. They were wondering why I was asking all these questions about the past; Sampat had already warned me that his relatives were not at all happy with the fact that he had gone to court to give testimony for a Kashmiri Muslim who had been accused of attacking the Indian Parliament. They knew that I was responsible for involving him in the case. And they were even more bitter that the man had been acquitted. To lighten the mood, I asked Prabhawati to describe how Shivratri was celebrated in Kashmir—it is the biggest festival for the Pandits.

Prabhawati's expression changed and there was again delight as she recalled how they observed Shivratri. The festival lasted many days. Before the actual day the house had to be thoroughly cleaned, utensils polished and earthenware pots thrown away.

On each day of the festival, she would have to cook special vegetables like knol khol and lotus stems instead of the usual collard greens or haak. She would prepare cottage cheese dishes as well as fish and meat. The day after the special puja was called Salaam, when poor Muslims would come with their pots and she would fill them with the food she had cooked. Friends, relatives and neighbours would come to wish them and exchange greetings and invitations to feasts. Elders would give money to the younger members of the family like the Muslims do during Id.

I told Prabhawati that we, the Kashmiris of Delhi,[4] also celebrate Shivaratri and even today eat dishes made out of goat liver for breakfast on that day. I thought this might build a bridge between us. But Sampat's brother's wife, Asha, looked at me with cold eyes and said: 'We do not eat non-vegetarian food any more. We are vegetarians.' Later, Sampat told me that she was a hardcore member of the Rashtriya Swayamsevak Sangh, the RSS.[5]

I asked Prabhawati whether she visited Sufi dargahs. Sampat had emphasized how it was a tradition in Kashmir that Hindus visited the Sufi shrines and temples. Sampat had said his mother would visit Sharika Devi temple on the western slope of Hari Parbat and then offer prayers at the Muslim shrines of Khwaja Makhdoom Sahib and Akhund Mullah Shah on the southern slope. Sampat had stressed that it was a part of the syncretic culture of Kashmir which he called Kashmiriyat.

Prabhawati said that she had no time to go out visiting any place. But she remembered the annual visits of the travelling minstrel called

Ladi Shah. When Ladi Shah arrived, the family would collect together and listen to his songs and enjoy the humour and satire. She remembered that Ladi Shah had an iron rod with iron rings which he jingled as he told his stories. But she could not remember the stories, she only knew that they were satires on the political and social situation of the time.

She appeared to be unaware that the daily routine she described seemed to be one of endless grind. But not once did she express any resentment. The only pain she expressed was the loss of her home. She remembered Kashmir as a home she missed; with no nostalgia for Kashmiriyat. She left behind all her belongings and a home full of memories. There was no time to take even the most precious reminders of her past when she packed her bags on 19 January 1990.

Prabhawati never returned to her home, or to Kashmir. She died quietly on 20 June 2013 in the house in Delhi—a house she never learnt to call home. Neelkanth never went to Delhi; he died in his son's home in Jammu in April 1992.

Sampat Prakash was disappointed that his mother had not been able to affirm his memory of growing up in Kashmir in harmony with their Muslim neighbours. I asked him about his schooldays.

Sampat studied at the Tyndale Biscoe School till the seventh standard. He recited the school motto with pride: 'In All Things Be Men'. On the day he joined school, two other boys from Rainawari joined as well—Jawaharlal Dhar and Jawaharlal Koul Bira. The three were to remain friends all their lives. Sampat's childhood memories of Kashmiriyat are linked to his memories filled with picnics. In spring everyone—Hindus and Muslims—went to the Badamwari,[6] a sprawling garden below the Hari Parbat to sit amidst the delicate purple and white almond blossoms all day, filling their glasses with kahwa from the traditional samovars, and roasting water chestnuts over small fires.

Sampat egged his mother to tell me about her relations with their Muslim neighbours. Prabhawati was enjoying the attention. She said the relations with their Muslim neighbours were cordial and they were especially close to the Baqaals, who were like family. During her daughter's marriage it was one of the Baqaals who put the first garlanded the groom's party.

Yes, it was true that the Baqaals and the Kundus would go for picnics together, each carrying their own stoves and carpets. They would sit side by side and the children would play together. Prabhawati, like most Kashmiri Pandit women, did not eat food from a Muslim home, not because she did not eat meat but because she did not eat onions or garlic. But she could eat dry fruits and the fruit of the lotus offered to her by her Muslim neighbours. During Id, the Baqaals would send raw meat since she would not eat meat cooked in their home.

Sampat Prakash forgot to mention that Muslim samovars were made of copper and they drank pink-coloured salty tea which they called noon chai and Kashmiri Pandits call sheer chai. Better-off Kashmiri Pandits usually drank kahwa, brewed in their brass samovars. For Sampat these were minor details; the important thing was that the two families together enjoyed the almond blossoms and the warmth of the spring air.

Foolishly, I asked her whether she would like to return to Kashmir, and it was only then that I glimpsed her suppressed anger: 'Am I fool to have left Kashmir? My home, my belongings and my memories have been left behind. Now where would I go and stay—with the Baqaals?'

Once again Sampat reminded his mother that the Baqaals had taken the trouble to visit them when the whole family had been forced to leave the Valley in the wake of the insurgency. She conceded that her neighbours did visit them when they lived in Jammu and even now they exchanged news over telephone, but the calls had become less frequent over the years.

Sampat said that the recent events had wiped out the memories of those days when Hindu and Muslim Kashmiris lived together in peace and friendship. He insisted that in his childhood the boys of both communities shared much more than the elders.

He described the picnics on the Dal Lake which he went to with his friends from school. Sampat said the boys of both communities ate food together and did all the things little boys do when they want to have fun. They would cook and eat together, clamber on the roof of the boat and jump into the lake and swim in its clean waters. Swimming was a compulsory subject at school, as were excursions. Sampat remembered how the boys had to swim across the Dal Lake before they were promoted into the seventh standard and, as they swam, the teachers would throw them kulchas filled with meat to give them energy.

When I asked how many Muslim boys studied in his class, he named just one, Ghulam Mohammad, who was the son of the peon and was exempt from paying fees. During Sampat's time the fee was Rs 25 annually, a sum which his neighbours, the Baqaals, could not afford. The Baqaal boys went to the Hari Singh High School, which was free.

Sampat was keenly aware of the poverty around him. And then there was the terrible poverty of the Muslim peasants which he saw whenever Prabhawati took him to Nowgam and Natipora, villages in Budgam where his mother's sisters lived. There were only three Kashmiri Pandit families living there in houses which were made of brick and cement; there were carpets on the floor and enough coal for the kangris.

They were beautiful villages full of pomegranate trees, walnut and almond trees but in the midst of the beauty was the ugly reality of the poverty of the homes where the Muslim families spread out reed mats instead of carpets, wore torn pherans and the children wandered around wearing a single sweater even in winter.

Although he was treated with affection by his aunts, it is the love of the Muslim women Sampat remember most vividly till this day. Under those thatch roofs of small, single-storey homes, he was treated like a prince so that he would not miss the love of his dead mother. The Muslim women always found something from their bare kitchens to put in his mouth, warm water to bathe him with, and the warmth of their embraces to hold him in. He, in turn, never forgot to invite them for every family function and subsequently, his two sons, too, have spent many months basking in the love of the Muslim community.

There was one thing that disturbed young Sampat from early childhood and that was the differences between the rich and the poor. In the same compound where Sampat lived, his father's brothers also had their own houses. One of the brothers, Balajee Kundu, was much richer. He owned five liquor shops and a hotel in Sonawar, a posh neighbourhood of Srinagar. The wealthy businessman bought his children expensive clothes, good food and they even had money to hire a tonga. But this uncle never thought of helping Neelkanth who struggled every day, cycling miles even in severe winter to take extra tuitions to support his large family. Sampat felt angry that the uncle never helped his father or even gave gifts on festivals.

Sampat said Kashmiris love a tamasha or spectacle; they come out in the hundreds to see any spectacle, whether a political leader or a camel. He was barely four years old when his father took his little son to the Tattoo Ground in Batmaloo, in Srinagar, to see the strange animal called the camel. The Kashmiris were excited to see the animal that Prophet Mohammad had ridden through the desert. But when the camel farted, they were shocked, and lots of stories were concocted around this event, reflecting the Kashmiri humour which is not easy to render into English.

As he grew up, Sampat began to understand that Kashmir was at war against the oppression of a king. But in school he did not learn much about the history of Kashmir—neither in Tyndale Biscoe nor later when he studied in the DAV school[7] where his father was headmaster after the Biscoe School was nationalized.

When Sampat was still a child, he heard folk stories and Kashmiri songs from Kungmal, his beloved Ded,[8] the matriarch of the family who had been widowed when she was barely thirteen years old. Sampat would sleep in her bed and she would spread out her pheran to keep him warm and tell him stories.

Neelkanth, the history teacher, would tell his son about ancient Kashmiri culture and that Kashmir was the oldest civilization, even older than Mohenjo-Daro. His father instilled a sense of Kashmiri nationalism in his son. He also told his son that Sheikh Abdullah was the first Kashmiri leader to emerge after seven centuries of oppression.

Neelkanth told his son how Kashmir had once been an independent land of great beauty. The last Kashmiri king was Yusuf Shah[9] who was defeated by the Mughals who annexed Kashmir in 1586. The Mughals laid out more than 700 gardens but Kashmiris were forbidden from entering them at that time. Then came the Afghans who conquered Kashmir in 1739 and let loose a reign of terror. The Afghans were defeated by the Sikhs in 1819 and thus began the Sikh rule which turned out to be as oppressive for the Kashmiris. In 1846, the British defeated the Sikhs and gave the Kashmir Valley to the Dogras for supporting them in the Anglo-Sikh war. Neelkanth had told his son that Kashmir would be an independent country once again.

Neelkanth Kundu was a staunch Kashmiri nationalist and he made sure that his son, too, became one. He took him for meetings addressed by Sheikh Abdullah, the most popular leader of the time; even if little Sampat did not understand the speeches, he joined in shouting the slogans: 'Sheikh Asia ka buland sitara' (The Sheikh is Asia's exalted star), 'Sher-e-Kashmir hamara' (Our Lion of Kashmir). And when the Sheikh converted his Muslim Conference into the National Conference, Neelkanth gave his whole-hearted support to the Party.

Throughout Sampat's childhood, momentous events were happening around him and even if he was too young to understand their significance, his consciousness was influenced by them. They shaped his political views and instilled in him a desire to be a part of something he knew was greater than his family or the community in which he was born.

Sampat still remembers standing at the edge of crowds, listening to animated discussions, impassioned speeches by Communists addressing meetings in Rainawari and being stirred by the resounding slogans.

—

The hope of Kashmiri independence was embodied in the person of Sheikh Muhammad Abdullah.

Sheikh Abdullah was born in the village of Soura on 15 December 1905, fifteen days after the death of his father. Khair-un-Nisa, his mother, managed to give him Quranic education in a nearby Maktab. He did his matriculation from State High School, Fateh Kadal, and graduated in 1924 from S.P. College, Srinagar.

From Srinagar, he went to Lahore where he joined the Islamia College. Here he met many intellectuals across the ideological divide, from the poet Mohammad Iqbal to Communist leaders. In Lahore he saw how poorly Kashmiri Muslims were treated by the Punjabis.

After finishing college in Lahore, he studied for his postgraduation in chemistry at the Aligarh Muslim University. His stay at Aligarh helped him broaden his vision and understanding of politics. He returned to Kashmir in April 1930. Sheikh Abdullah did not get a job in the administration even though he was the first and only postgraduate in chemistry amongst Kashmiri Muslims. In February 1931, Sheikh Abdullah joined as a second teacher in the government school, Bagh-i-Dilawar Khan, Srinagar. A month later he was transferred to the government school in Muzaffarabad. In April 1931, he decided to resign and went back to Srinagar.

In Srinagar, the Sheikh was approached by the Reading Room Party that had been organized by some educated Muslim men. These young met in a room where they would read Urdu and English newspapers, discuss the French and Russian revolutions as well as the possibilities of finding jobs. The newspapers were published in the thousands and smuggled in through trucks and cars entering Srinagar form Rawalpindi.[10]

The youth used to go to the house of Muhammad Sikander, Post and Telegraph Master who was a patron of these unemployed but educated Muslim young men. The Party had also set up an underground political cell since the maharaja had banned all political activities. The Reading Room Party was the forerunner to the All Jammu and Kashmir Muslim Conference.

After Sheikh Abdullah joined the Reading Room Party, the office was shifted to the house of Mufti Zia-ud Din at Fateh Kadal. The Party was re-organized as well and Sheikh Muhammad Abdullah was elected president. Standing six foot four inches tall and speaking with a beautiful voice, he soon attracted many followers and emerged as the voice of the oppressed and downtrodden Kashmiri Muslims.

The first significant political mobilization of Kashmiri Muslims happened in 1931 when Sheikh Abdullah was to address a meeting organized by the Young Men's Muslim Association.[11] It was his first mass meeting of more than 7,000 men at the Khanqah-i-Moula, one of the oldest mosques in Srinagar, built on the banks of the Jhelum River.[12]

The meeting was organized on 21 June 1931 to express concern over two specific incidents reported from Jammu where police officers had insulted Islam. In one incident, Lakha Ram had thrown the Holy Quran from which a Muslim employee was reciting; the other took place on 29 April when Khem Chand, a police officer, ordered an imam to stop his sermon.[13]

In his speech, Sheikh Abdullah asked all Muslims to unite and demand their rights. He also appealed to the Pandits to join hands with Muslims for redressal of their grievances as well as for independence.[14]

Just as the meeting was ending, a well-built Pathan, about thirty-five years of age, with a large mustache on a big face, stood up and delivered a fiery speech instigating the people against the tyranny of the Dogra Maharaja.

He said,

> The honour, respect and reverence of the Holy Quran are dearer to the Muslims than earthly kingdoms. They can never tolerate any interference in their religion or defilement of their Holy Book. The government of the maharaja does not care for

his subjects. It has no touch with the people, or any sympathy for the downtrodden. Oh, Muslims arise! Time has come when you should retaliate bricks with stones. I warn you that your representatives and memorials won't rescue you, nor will these papers remove injustice and misery. You must stand on your own legs and fight against the autocratic force. Even if you have no arms, fight with sticks and stones.

The people and their leaders listened to his speech in complete silence and amazement. At the end of his speech, the fiery speaker pointed towards the Shergarhi Palace of the maharaja and shouted: 'Demolish this edifice of injustice, cruelty and subjugation.'[15]

The man's name was Abdul Qadeer Khan Ghazi[16] and he was arrested on 25 June 1931 on charges of sedition. The Kashmiri Muslims were outraged and gathered outside the courtroom in large numbers.

In his speech, in the Jama Masjid, Srinagar, on 10 July 1931, Sheikh Abdullah said that, 'Maulana Abdul Qadeer Khan Ghazi has been prosecuted for the cause of Islam and for the Kashmiri Muslims.' He asked the people to pray for his acquittal and show complete solidarity with him.[17]

The public presence forced the judge to hold the trial inside the jail premises on 11 July 1931. This trial was the first case of a political nature and the people had gathered in defiance of a ban on political rallies.

On 13 July 1931, the people had, as usual, assembled outside the court, and when the Sessions Judge ordered them to disperse, they requested for permission to offer prayers. The police arrested five men and this incensed the crowd further. One of them stood up and recited the Azan loudly. A policeman shot him dead. The people were angry and they started pelting stones at the police. The police fired around 200 rounds in which twenty-two men died. Later, six more succumbed to their wounds. The bodies of the men were buried at the Martyrs Graveyard in Srinagar and for nineteen days there was a hartal in Kashmir

13 July 1931 was a landmark in the history of Kashmir—it was the first time in the history of Kashmir that the entire Muslim population in the Valley rose as one and took up the task of securing for themselves the right of democratic self-rule.[18]

It was during this uprising that Sheikh Mohammad Abdullah emerged as an undisputed leader of his people. Women composed songs in Kashmiri in his praise, conferring on him the title Sher-e-Kashmir, the Lion of Kashmir.

However, in the aftermath of the firing, there were tensions between Hindus and Muslims. The public opinion among the Muslims was that since all the officials and the rulers were Hindus, the firing was motivated by anti-Muslim sentiments. Hindu shops were looted, and serious rioting took place in which three Hindus were murdered and 163 wounded.

Maharaja Hari Singh[19] passed an ordinance and handed over the city of Srinagar to the military. The Muslims continued their agitation and they were joined by the Muslims of Jammu who had formed a Kashmir Committee. This Committee gave a call to Muslims all over India to observe 14 August as Kashmir Day.

The Maharaja, perhaps because of pressure from the British, appointed a committee to look into the grievances of the people. The Commission was headed by a European, B.J. Glancy. The four non-official members were: G. A. Ashahi, Prem Nath Bazaz,[20] Ghulam Abbas and Lok Nath Sharma.

Many of the Hindus opposed the Commission because they thought it would only serve Muslim interests and launched an agitation asking the Hindu members to resign from the committee. Sharma, a Hindu from Jammu, resigned but Bazaz, a Kashmiri Pandit, refused.

The Commission submitted its report in April 1932. The recommendations included land ownership rights to all, return of Muslim religious shrines to the community, ban on the forced labour system, suspension of grazing tax and doing away with the higher minimum qualification for recruitment in government services.

The Pandit community felt threatened by the Glancy Commission's recommendations, particularly the doing away of the higher minimum qualification. They were reluctant to share education and jobs with Muslims on equal terms and thus launched a 'Roti Agitation' against the Glancy Commission's recommendations.

From here on, it became evident that the politically active Kashmiri Pandits had split into two camps—the communal minded Hindus who opposed the legitimate aspirations of the Kashmiri Muslims organized themselves around the Yuvak Sabha, also called Kashmiri Pandits' Conference; and those who like Prem Nath Bazaz thought, 'The progress and prosperity of Kashmiri Pandits is synonymous with the complete political, social and economic freedom of Kashmir and the liberation of the Muslim masses.'[21]

The Glancy Commission recommended that people be allowed to form political parties and to publish newspapers. Sheikh Abdullah immediately took advantage of this and founded the All Jammu and Kashmir Muslim Conference in October 1932.

The Muslim Conference focused on the dominance of the Kashmiri Pandits and suggestions were made that the community were the enemies of the Kashmiri Muslims.[22] Although Kashmiri Pandits were approximately 15 per cent of the population as opposed to 85 per cent of Kashmiri Muslims, they held most jobs in the lower bureaucracy—the senior officers were either Dogras or Punjabis. In rural areas, the Kashmiri Pandits were the petty revenue officers and in the factories they were the managers.

Many Kashmiri Muslims wondered why they were so poor and why the Pandits had been able to do better than them even though it was the Muslims who did all the hard work.

In his autobiography, *Aatish-e-Chinar*, published posthumously in 1982, Sheikh Abdullah says: 'I started to question why Muslims were singled out for such treatment. We constituted the majority, and contributed the most towards the state's revenues, still we were continuously oppressed. Why? Was it because the majority of government servants were Non-Muslims, or, because most of the low grade officers who dealt with the public were Kashmiri Pandits? I concluded that the ill treatment of Muslims was an outcome of religious prejudice.'[23]

The Sheikh came to this conclusion on the basis of the empirical reality he saw all around him. For instance, when he took up the cause of the striking workers of the State Silk Factory once again, he was confronted with the ugly reality of Kashmiri Pandits oppressing the Muslim workers. He documented in a report, presented in 1932, the conditions of the workers, all of whom were Muslims, and the high-handed manner in which the managerial staff treated the workers; except for a small number of European managers, the rest were Kashmiri Pandits. The report exposed how the management had been responsible for embezzlement, withholding of wages and pension funds, and expulsion of many workers. Even though the factory was owned by the government, the agitation was directed largely against the management who were Kashmiri Pandits.[24]

However, Sheikh Abdullah did not apologize for those Kashmiri Muslims who exploited their own people. On one occasion he was asked to accompany officials to attach the moveable property of a weaver in Ganderbal against whom court decrees had been obtained for owing money to the Sheikh's family. When he saw the pitiable condition of the weaver who had just a few mats and kitchen utensils, he refused to enforce the court order.

In his autobiography the Sheikh recalls: 'We were living a good life thanks to these wretched workers...not only had this man lost his job but thanks to us was due to lose his meagre possessions as well. I set fire to court decrees and returned home with a heavy heart. When my brothers demanded the money, I narrated my experience.'[25]

Sheikh Abdullah was deeply influenced by ideas of Socialism and Communism. Bazaz was able to convince the Sheikh that his dream of empowerment of Kashmiri Muslims could not be realized unless the Dogras' autocratic rule was replaced by a responsible secular government, and that was possible only with the support of the non-Muslims of the state, most of whom were living in the Jammu province. The Sheikh was convinced, but was apprehensive as there were strong religious forces in the Kashmir Valley who would oppose the running of the political movement on a secular basis. Bazaz then proposed the need to raise public awareness and build public opinion by jointly bringing out a Urdu weekly called *Hamdard*.[26]

Further, Sheikh Abdullah started preparing the ground for changing the name of his Jammu and Kashmir Muslim Conference to the Jammu and Kashmir National Conference. In his Presidential Address at the Sixth Annual Session of the Muslim Conference on 26 March 1938, he said:

> Like us the large majority of Hindus and Sikhs in the state have immensely suffered at the hands of the irresponsible government...The main problem, therefore, now is to organize joint action and a united front against the forces that stand in our way in the achievement of our goal. This will require re-christening our organization as a non-communal political body...I reiterate today what I have often said. Firstly, we must end communalism by ceasing to think in terms of Muslims and non-Muslims when discussing our political problems. Secondly, there must be universal suffrage on the basis of joint electorates. Without these two, democracy is lifeless...You complain that the Hindus belonging to the vested interests are reactionary and stand in the way of our progress. But have we not had the same experience in the case of capitalist Muslims also?[27]

It was against this background that the historic session of the All Jammu and Kashmir Muslim Conference was held at Pathar Masjid on 10 and 11 June 1939. The name of the party was changed to All Jammu and Kashmir National Conference, but it took a long and intense debate which lasted fifty-two hours.

The flag of the Party was a bright red with a white plough in the middle. It was a flag designed to appeal to the vast majority of Muslim peasants who were living in utter poverty and had to bear the brunt of official corruption and exploitation by absentee landlords.

The colours and symbol of the flag reflected the influence of Communist ideas and ideals: the Russian Revolution had taken place barely twenty-three years earlier and the proximity of the Soviet Asian Republics to Kashmir was a source of inspiration to young Kashmiris who yearned to liberate themselves from an oppressive monarchical system.

Sheikh Abdullah welcomed the Communists and counted many of them as personal friends. Among them was Professor M.D. Taseer, a Punjabi Marxist from Lahore, who was invited to be the Principal of S.P. College in Srinagar. He was married to an English woman, Christobel, and their nikahnama had been drawn by Allama Iqbal.

Christobel invited her sister Alys George and her fiancé, the poet Faiz Ahmed Faiz, to Srinagar. The couple stayed in the Maharaja's summer palace. Alys converted to Islam and took the name Kulsoom and their marriage rites were performed by none other than Sheikh Mohammad Abdullah in October 1941.[28]

The Communist Party of India (CPI) had been legalized in 1942 and so Communist literature was available in the Valley. The CPI opened a bookshop called the New Kashmir Book Shop run by Niranjan Nath Raina in Srinagar, and it ran a paper called *Azad*. In Jammu another Communist, Dhanwantri, ran a bookshop and published a daily called *Shamsher*. By the summer of 1945, the party's official organ, *People's War*, sold 270 copies every week; this was in addition to the 100 sold to subscribers.[29]

However, the Communist Party did not work under its own banner; its members worked through the National Conference and influenced its social and economic programmes. They organized several trade unions which were affiliated to the National Conference, as a result Kashmiri nationalists and trade unions had a strong alliance.[30]

The Communists helped shape Sheikh Abdullah's campaign against princely rule. In 1944, the Sheikh asked them to put forward a vision for the future. It is believed that the manifesto, which was called Naya Kashmir, was largely drafted by Baba Pyare Lal Bedi and his English wife, Freda Bedi;[31] they had based their manifesto on a Soviet Central Asian publication. The National Conference presented it to Maharaja Hari Singh and later adopted it formally at a session in Sopore in 1944.

The proposed constitution promised single citizenship to all inhabitants of Jammu, Kashmir and Ladakh. It had a workers' charter, a peasants' charter and a women's charter (Appendix I). In his introduction to the Naya Kashmir manifesto, Sheikh Abdullah wrote:

> Soviet Russia has demonstrated before our eyes not merely theoretically but in her actual day to day life and development, that real freedom takes birth only from economic emancipation.[32]

When Sheikh Abdullah became the prime minister of Jammu and Kashmir in 1948, he renamed Srinagar chowk as 'Lal Chowk' after Moscow's Red Square, the name by which it is still called. Even though the Sheikh was attracted to Communist ideals, he never questioned the tenets of his religion.

———

By the time Sheikh Abdullah launched his Quit Kashmir movement in 1946, Sampat was seven years old.

He recalls that throughout his childhood, Rainawari was electrified by a politically charged atmosphere. Even now, when he recalls the slogans of the time, he feels a thrill. 'Bynaamaa Amritsar Tordo Kashmir chhor do' (Break the Amritsar Treaty Leave Kashmir).

On 12 May 1946, the Cabinet Mission sent to India declared that when the British left the subcontinent, their paramountcy would lapse and the rights of the Princely States would return to the local monarchs. This would mean a return of Dogra autocracy in Kashmir after India became independent and the British left. It was against such a possibility Sheikh Abdullah called for a Quit Kashmir movement. He declared that the Amritsar Treaty by which the

British sold the Valley of Kashmir to the Dogras for a sum of 750,000 Nanakshahi rupees was illegal and demanded that Maharaja Hari Singh hand over sovereignty to the people. He tried to rally the support of the Kashmiri Pandits against the Dogras by appealing to their nationalism.

At that time, the contradictions between Kashmiri nationalism, Indian nationalism and religious beliefs had submerged in the anti-monarchy, anti-colonial and pro-democracy movement. But the conflicts and contradictions were always there, below the surface, even in those days. Sometimes the Pandits would rally together in the name of saving their religious identity; sometimes the Kashmiri Muslims would respond to the slogan of Islam in danger.

The National Conference made a special effort to appeal to the Kashmiri Pandits. However, the Pandits and Dogras saw the anti-Dogra slogans as anti-Hindu, and the Kashmiri Pandit National Conference leader, Kashyap Bandhu,[33] lamented that the National Conference members had not been consulted before the Quit Kashmir movement was launched.[34]

Sheikh Abdullah was arrested and detained at the Badami Bagh cantonment in Srinagar. The Communists organized a solidarity movement with lectures, meetings, road barricades and many were arrested, sentenced and fined. Quit Kashmir was the biggest organized political mobilization the Kashmir Valley had seen.

The Sheikh's trial was attended by the well-known British Communist, Rajani Palme Dutt,[35] who had been invited to Srinagar by Sheikh Abdullah. But by the time the journalist arrived in Srinagar in July 1946, the Sheikh had been arrested and was on trial for sedition. Palme Dutt met Sheikh Abdullah in court and praised the Kashmiri leader warmly in his journal, *Monthly Review*: 'Kashmir is the strongest and most militant of any Indian State...its leader Sheikh Abdulla (sic) impressed me as one of the most honest, courageous and able political leaders I had the pleasure of seeing in India.'[36]

The Sheikh was sentenced to nine years of imprisonment for

challenging the Maharaja's right to rule over Jammu and Kashmir. It was only after India became independent and Nehru became prime minister that Abdullah was freed on 29 September 1947.

—

Colonial rule had ended in British India but freedom had come at a terrible price—the Partition, the mass exodus of people, the carnage and communal conflagration which engulfed the subcontinent.

In almost every speech that I have heard, Sampat Prakash never fails to remind his audience that during the Partition of India, when Hindus, Sikhs and Muslims were butchering each other, when homes and hearths were burnt to cinders, Kashmir alone remained an oasis of peace and communal harmony. This, for him, is proof of Kashmiriyat, the unique syncretic culture of the Kashmir Valley.

The reality was much more complex, and uglier than what Sampat Prakash had described. Even though there was no communal violence in the Kashmir Valley, the Muslims in Jammu were targets and the inter-religious violence led to significant migrations which resulted in a change in demography in both Jammu and Kashmir. An estimated 200,000 Muslim men, women and children were murdered by the Dogra troops (who were Hindus), RSS stormtroopers and Hindu and Sikh civilians.[37] There are reports of 22,000 Hindus and Sikhs killed while crossing from West Jammu in newly formed Pakistan to Uri in the Kashmir Valley.

The number of non-Muslims in Pakistan-administered 'Azad' Kashmir was reduced from 12.5 per cent to less than 2 per cent. The Muslim population here strongly favoured joining Pakistan, unlike the Kashmiri-speaking Muslims of the Valley who supported the secular leadership of Sheikh Abdullah.[38]

The Communists in Kashmir Valley knew of the massacres in Jammu and had sent their people to intervene; it was heroic but not very effective. Many of them died in the process, and one of them was Sampat's best friend's brother, Som Nath Bira. Sampat still vividly remembers how his school friend Jawahar Koul's elder brother,

Somnath Bira, had joined the People's Militia. He was a part of a group that had been sent to Jammu to intervene in the communal situation. Bira died on the way at Regi Nallah between Bhadarwah and Doda.[39]

Bira's body was never found. But Sampat remembers attending a memorial meeting held at Saraf Park where the Deputy Prime Minister, Bakshi Ghulam Mohammad, himself came to offer condolences and honour the martyr who had given up his life for the cause of Kashmir.

I met Jawahar Koul in his home in Gurgaon. I had gone there to interview him regarding his thoughts on Kashmiriyat. Koul was a gentle and soft-spoken philosopher surrounded by books. But the home was enveloped in melancholy, and life in exile had taken its toll. Every corner reminded one of some aspect of Kashmir—the curtains, the walnut furniture and, most of all, the garden he had so carefully created. But he did not once mention Kashmiriyat as an aspect of the life he left behind in Kashmir. He complained he had no one to talk to except a Kashmiri Muslim neighbour with whom he could converse in Kashmiri about things of mutual interest.

When I told Sampat that his friend had not once mentioned the word Kashmiriyat to describe his life in Kashmir, he reacted: 'He is not a political person.' So did that mean that Kashmiriyat is a political invention, not a cultural tradition?[40]

Sampat pointed out the solidarity shown by the people of Kashmir in the face of the raiders who invaded the Valley in October 1947.

I asked Sampat what his reaction was to the claims by Kashmiri Muslims that the raiders were actually liberators. This was the reason why they had initially welcomed the invaders and provided them with food and shelter, but it was when the liberators turned into looters, arsonists and rapists that the Kashmiris had turned against them. Sampat felt disturbed when I raised such questions and he lapsed into silence.

In 1947, Kashmir was vulnerable and the Maharaja had asked Nehru to send in the Indian Army. But Nehru replied that since the Maharaja had not signed the Instrument of Accession, India sending its army in would be viewed as a foreign invasion. It was under these conditions that the Maharaja signed the Instrument of Accession on 26 October 1947. There has been serious controversy over whether such an Instrument was actually signed. However, in 2005, the Home Ministry put the text on its website and put the controversy to rest.

Sheikh Abdullah, however, criticized the Instrument of Accession: 'If forty lakhs of people living in Jammu and Kashmir are bypassed and the State declares accession to India or Pakistan, I shall raise a banner of revolt and we face a struggle.'[41]

Before the Indian troops arrived, the raiders backed by the Pakistani army had entered the Kashmir Valley. It was cold and the situation was grim. Kashmiri Hindus and Muslims together fought the invasion with exemplary courage. In the history of official India, this was the moment when India proved her secular credentials. A Muslim-majority state had not only decided to join the Indian Union but the people were willing to fight against Pakistan, a nation based on religious identity.

The Communists contributed to the resistance against the tribal raiders during this first war between India and Pakistan over Kashmir. They too believed that the raiders had been sent by the Pakistani army, encouraged by the British.

The situation was very serious. Pakistan stopped supplies of essential items into Kashmir and at the time the only access to the Valley from the Indian side was a dirt road connecting Pathankot with Jammu, and from there a road over the Banihal Pass to Srinagar which was not an easy route then.

But the Kashmiris were ready to defend their land. An eye-witness describes the atmosphere of the time in these words:

Within a few hours the whole atmosphere in the Valley changed. Young and old started marching, and offering for guard duties on bridges and in bazaars, banks, telephone and telegraph exchanges. All the refugees who had been coming into Srinagar were disarmed. A large number of swords, axes, shot-guns and other arms were collected. The exhibition ground was used for training and lodging of volunteers, many of whom were from Srinagar factories, schools and colleges. Gole Bagh was used for training lady volunteers. There were few among the Kashmiris who knew much about arms. Soon enough we had Mohammad Akram of Baug tehsil, Poonch, Salar of Muslim National Guard in his home district, teaching workers to fight the invaders. There were ex-servicemen like Shamjee, Mahmuda Begum's bother, Gurbux Singh, leader of the Defence Industry Workers from Rawalpindi, Sher Jung, a famous revolutionary from Delhi, and several others providing expertise.[42]

Women—Hindu and Muslim—formed the women's militia and learnt to fire .303 rifles and throw hand grenades. Children, too, were organized and were armed with sticks. Even though Srinagar was without power after the invaders blew up the hydro-electrical plant at Mahura, and the winter was cold, the spirit of the Kashmiris never dampened. K.A. Abbas, the filmmaker, said that the atmosphere was like when the Communists joined the international brigade against fascism in Spain. He said: 'Poets have come to die for their poetry.'[43]

The Communists organized a cultural front and wrote plays based on the heroes and heroines of the resistance. The most famous, of course, was Maqbool Sherwani of Baramullah who was arrested, tortured and killed by the tribal marauders; then there was Sara, the Kashmiri woman, who offered to cook for the invaders and collected information from their camp and passed it on to the resistance.

Sampat Prakash was barely eight years old then but he recollects the mood in those days. He was a part of the children's militia. Children were given training with wooden rifles. But more than the wooden rifle, Sampat remembers the excitement of shouting the slogans of the time; even now, five decades later, when he chants them his voice has the pride of a Kashmiri nationalist:

Hamlevar khabardaar
Hum Kashmiri hain tayyaar
(Beware, invaders
We Kashmiris are ready)

And there is another which he remembers shouting loudly and with great feeling:

Sher-e-Kashmir ka hai irshaad
Hindu Muslim Sikh ithaad
Kadam kadam ladenge hum...
Her mahaaz per ladenge hum
(The Lion of Kashmir has ordered
Unity of Hindu-Muslim-Sikhs
We will resist at every step
We will fight every battle)

The first Indo-Pakistan war ended with the Pakistan Army occupying Gilgit-Balstistan and the area which Pakistan now calls 'Azad' Kashmir.

The five-member United Nations Commission on India and Pakistan (UNCIP) brokered a ceasefire between India and Pakistan in Janury 1949. A UN Resolution was passed recognizing the right of the Kashmiri people to a plebiscite to decide whether they wanted to be a part of India or Pakistan. The Resolution did not recognize the third option: the possibility of Jammu and Kashmir becoming an independent state.[44]

In accordance with the UN Resolution, the UN Military Observer Group in India and Pakistan (UNMOGIP) was established to oversee the ceasefire. The offices of UNMOGIP were opened in Srinagar and Muzaffarabad; in India they occupied a government bungalow in Delhi.[45] Sampat Prakash, like hundreds of thousands of Kashmiris, has been marching to their office in Srinagar and on every occasion they have organized protests to demand azadi; it is a symbol that Kashmir remains a disputed territory.

By the time Sampat was about to finish school, Sheikh Abdullah had already become the Prime Minister of Jammu and Kashmir. The

Indian Constituent Assembly had in October 1949 included Article 370 in the Indian Constitution granting the state of Jammu and Kashmir special status.[46]

Immediately there was a reaction to this special provision by the Hindu nationalists. The Praja Parishad Party[47] had launched a movement against the special status for Kashmir with a slogan: 'Ek desh main do vidhan, do pradhan aur do nishan.' They asked how one nation could have two heads, two legislatures and two flags. They expressed their outrage that Sheikh Abdullah was called Prime Minister of Kashmir, which had its own Constituent Assembly, its own flag.

Syama Prasad Mukherjee,[48] minister of industry and supply in Nehru's Cabinet, posed a question on 21 May 1952 to Nehru in Parliament: 'Are Kashmiris Indians first and Kashmiris next, or are they Kashmiris first and Indians next, or are they Kashmiris first, second and third and not Indian at all?'

In defiance of the special provisions, when Syama Prasad Mukherjee tried to enter Jammu to support the movement against the special status for Kashmir, he was arrested and detained. He died under mysterious circumstances in a prison in Srinagar on 26 June 1953.[49]

Sampat Prakash has no memory of the death of Syama Prasad Mukherjee. He just remembers that there was some agitation in Jammu. At the time he was already in his final year of school and had not been able to decide on what he should do next. His friends advised him to seek the advice of Professor Hridaynath Durrani who lived virtually next door to Sampat's home in Rainawari.

Durrani had become a Communist while studying in Lahore and had returned to Kashmir just before the tribal invasion and had joined the People's Militia. In fact he was in the same group as Bira but had to turn back because of ill health. Durrani taught English in a college but he put an equal amount of energy into nurturing and guiding the youth who gathered around him every evening.

Sampat started going regularly to Professor Hridaynath Durrani's home. It was there that Sampat was introduced to Communist literature, including classics such as Liu Shaoqi's *How to be a Good Communist* and Lenin's *One Step Forward, Two Steps Back*. Sampat did not understand these writings and Durrani would patiently explain their intent and meaning.

Sampat was inspired by the stories of the Russian Revolution and the successes of the Chinese Revolution. Mao and Lenin were his heroes. The thought that these revolutions had succeeded in backward parts of the world opened up vast possibilities for work in Kashmir. Sampat felt an inner turbulence he could hardly understand.

The most exciting part of this new world was that Sampat met the top Communist leaders, including Motilal Misri, Pran Nath Jalali and N.N. Raina, who visited Durrani; a disproportionate number were from the Kahmiri Pandit community.

He also met Roop Krishna Watal, who later worked at the Chinese embassy in New Delhi and was in contact with the Naxalites. Sampat felt a new sense of belonging and enjoyed listening to the leaders discuss politics late into the night.

By the time Sampat had finished school, he felt a deep urge to involve himself in political change. It was a time when it seemed that the world could become a better place if only one could work towards that change. Sampat Prakash did not find any contradiction in his love of Communism and his fiery commitment to Kashmiri nationalism. For him, both nationalism and Communism were twin bridges which united Hindus and Muslims, Jammu and Kashmir, and perhaps Kashmir and India.

But America and Britain saw the attraction to Communist ideologies as a threat to its geopolitical interests and were determined to save Kashmir from the dangers of precisely the same kind of beliefs that Sampat had begun to nurture deep within his heart.[50]

Often Sampat would come back home late at night, his head full of ideas and the desire to think things through in the quiet of his room on the third floor. When he returned, he did not have to disturb the household because Prabhawati waited up to open the door and let him in.

SEASON OF BETRAYALS
(1953–67)

Sampat Prakash joined S.P. College (the oldest college in Kashmir, Sri Pratap College was established by Annie Besant in 1905) in 1953. It was the same year as Sheikh Abdullah was arrested. As the news spread across the Valley, people came out on the roads and expressed their outrage at the utter disregard for all democratic norms. It was a rage that Sampat shared with his fellow Kashmiris and he too joined the processions demanding the immediate release of the Lion of Kashmir.

The Sheikh and his wife[1] were fast asleep in Tourist Hut Number 57-A in Gulmarg, the famous tourist resort. He had gone there for a short break. On the night of 8 August 1953, he was woken up by the loud, incessant knocking on his door by his secretary, R.C. Raina, who told him that the Indian army had surrounded his hut and that the superintendent of J&K Police, Laxman Das Thakur, was waiting outside to arrest him.

Soon Thakur entered his room along with an official of the Sadr-e-Riyasat, Dr Karan Singh, who handed over the order dismissing the Sheikh's government. Then the official gave him another envelope. It contained a memorandum to the sadr-e-riyasat, signed by Bakshi Ghulam Muhammad, the deputy prime minister, and two ministers, Pandit Shyam Lal Saraf, a Kashmiri Pandit, and Girdhari Lal Dogra, a Hindu from Jammu, expressing 'no-confidence' in the Sheikh's government. Thakur showed the Sheikh his arrest warrant and told him: 'Sir, your government has been dismissed and I have orders to arrest you.'

It took some time for the Sheikh to regain his composure. He wanted to confirm all this, so he made everyone wait until he heard the news of his arrest at 8 a.m. on All India Radio. The Sheikh was then driven to Udhampur and imprisoned in the Tara Niwas Palace.[2]

Sheikh Abdullah was dismissed from office, held in jail along with twenty-two other members of his party who were charged with conspiracy and treason against the Indian State. This came to be known as the Kashmir conspiracy case.[3]

Bakshi Ghulam Mohammad, who was prime minister of Jammu and Kashmir, said in his radio broadcast: 'A fraud was being committed on the interests of the country. The slogan of independence was dangerous. Under the control of an imperialist power an independent Kashmir would have been a serious danger for the people of India and Pakistan...'

Sampat Prakash could not understand these conspiracy theories, but there were rumours that Nehru had ordered the arrest. And he, like hundreds of thousands of Kashmiris, had felt betrayed by Nehru. Sampat was only ten years old, but he remembered seeing the tumultuous welcome the Kashmiris had given the Indian prime minister in September 1949. Sampat and his father had stood on the banks of the Jhelum along with thousands of others to watch the spectacular boat procession in honour of Nehru. Nehru sat on a divan covered with gold embroidery in the middle of an open barrage. The barge was propelled by twenty red-turbaned paddlers. The people stood on both banks showering Nehru and the Sheikh with flower petals and their love.[4]

Sheikh Abdullah had welcomed Jawaharlal Nehru at Srinagar's Lal Chowk with the following Persian verse by Amir Khusro:

> Mun tu shudum tu mun shudi
> Mun tun shudam tu jan shudi,
> Ta kas na goyad baad azeen
> Mun deegram, tu deegray
> (I have become you, and you me;
> I am the body and you are the soul;

So that no one can say hereinafter that you are someone,
And I am someone else)

An emotional Nehru had embraced Sheikh Abdullah and pledged before a mammoth gathering of Kashmiris that they would be free to decide their future. At one time, the official website of the Jammu and Kashmir government carried the photographs of this gathering and reproduced Pandit Nehru's words, 'India will never let down Kashmir!'[5]

When the Kashmir question arose soon after the State's accession to India on 26 October 1947, Nehru had assured the prime minister of Pakistan, Liaquat Ali Khan, on 31 October that India's pledge to hold a plebiscite in Kashmir on whether it should accede to India or Pakistan 'is not merely a pledge to your government but also to the people of Kashmir and to the world'.[6]

On 2 November 1947, in a broadcast to the nation, Nehru said: 'We have declared that the fate of Kashmir ultimately has to be decided by the people. That pledge we have given, and the maharaja had supported it, not only to the people of Kashmir but to the world. We will not, and cannot, back out of it.'

The government of India's White Paper on Jammu and Kashmir, published early in 1948, is a good compilation of the pledges Nehru made on these lines.

Although Nehru had assured the Kashmiris that they would have the right to decide whether they wanted to join India or Pakistan, he knew that Sheikh Abdullah had opted to join India. It was this that perhaps gave Nehru the confidence to make such public statements.

In his historic address to the Constituent Assembly of Jammu and Kashmir on 31 October 1951, Sheikh Abdullah had said:

The most powerful argument which can be advanced in her favour is that Pakistan is a Muslim State, and a big majority of our people being Muslims the State must accede to Pakistan. This claim of being a Muslim State is only a camouflage. It is a screen to dupe the common man, so that he may not see clearly that Pakistan is a feudal state in which a clique is trying by these methods to maintain itself in power…Right-thinking men would point out that Pakistan is not an organic unity of all the Muslims in this subcontinent. It has, on the contrary, caused the dispersion of Indian Muslims for whom it was claimed to have been created.[7]

At the same time, the Sheikh was increasingly troubled by the growing tide of Hindu nationalism and the widening communal divide in India. A speech given on 31 October 1951 articulated his fears about the future:

Certain tendencies have been asserting themselves in India that may in the future convert it into a religious state wherein the interests of the Muslims will be jeopardized. This would happen if a communal organization had a dominant hand in the Government, and Congress ideals of the equality of all communities were made to give way to religious intolerance.[8]

In 1951, Syama Prasad Mukherjee had launched the Jana Sangh and in its very first manifesto, it announced its four priorities to help strengthen the unity of India: an educational system based on 'Bharatiya' culture; the use of Hindi in schools; the denial of any special privileges to minorities and the full integration of Jammu and Kashmir into the Indian Union.[9]

By December 1952, the Jana Sangh announced that it would contest elections on two issues: the amelioration of the condition of refugees from Pakistan and Article 370; the party also made alliances with the Akali Dal.

The Sheikh knew that there were people within the Congress Party who were sympathetic to these demands and that Nehru could do little to change these views. He began to think that perhaps it would be best if Jammu and Kashmir could become an independent country, free from India and Pakistan. The Sheikh knew that even if Kashmir joined India, there would be no peace.

In his autobiography, Sheikh Abdullah wrote:

I had my views. If we were to accede to India, Pakistan would never accept our choice, and we would become a battleground for the two nations. My colleagues felt differently. The Muslim League, they said, will always be dominated by feudal elements which are an anathema for enlightened and progressive views. The people's vision of a "New Kashmir" will never be accepted by the newly created Pakistan. Chains of slavery will keep us in their continuous stranglehold. But India was different. There were parties and individuals in India whose views were identical to ours. By acceding to India, then, wouldn't we move closer to our goal?

The other choice was an independent Kashmir! But to keep a small state independent while it was surrounded by big powers was impossible. If those powers guaranteed stability to an independent Kashmir, it was another matter. We spent hours agonizing over the three choices...[10]

The Cold War was by now at its height and Kashmir's geopolitical importance was such that it meant that Kashmir could become independent only if one of the superpowers backed its claim. It was Sheikh's intense feeling of Kashmiri nationalism that drove him to seek Western allies.

The intensity of this feeling of Kashmiri nationalism had been seen in the Constituent Assembly where Sheikh Mohammad Akbar, member from Tanmarg, recited at the request of Ghulam Mohammad Sadiq, the first elected president of the Assembly, a song whose opening lines were:

Lehra aye Kashmir key jhanday;
Hal walay dilgeer key jhanday,
Her dam lehra, her soo lehra,
Taba kayaamat paiham lehra
(Let this Flag of Kashmir be unfurled,
Whoever ploughs the land,
May it fly forever, in every nook and corner,
Till the Day of Judgment, may I behold thee)

When the poem was being recited, many members had tears flowing down their cheeks. The Assembly adopted it as the national song,[11] and every child attending government schools learnt it.

Sampat had, by this time, moved close to the Communist Party of India. He now felt a conflict between his loyalty to the party and his comrades and his Kashmiri nationalism. He could not understand why the Party did not support the Sheikh and the cause of Kashmiri nationalism. What disturbed him was the Communist allegation that Sheikh Abdullah was making Kashmir a colony of America and that he was an enemy of the people. He learnt that senior Communist leaders had been staying in a houseboat, plotting the arrest of the Kashmiri leader.

The Communist betrayal of Sheikh Abdullah was dictated by strategic reasons. They were worried by the growing influence of the Americans on the Sheikh, especially at a time when the US and Britain were backing Pakistan against India.

In fact, Britain and the US had already started to use Pakistan-administered Jammu and Kashmir as a military base and a centre for espionage, and by 1958, the US Air Force had two facilities to monitor communications in the Soviet Union and China.[12] The borders of Kashmir were as much contiguous with the Soviet Union and China as with India and Pakistan.

In December 1953, US vice president, Richard Nixon, declared that 'Pakistan is a country I would like to do everything for. The people have less complexes than the Indians.'[13] Two years later, in 1955, Pakistan joined the US administrator's new alliance systems—the Southeast Asian Treaty Organization (SEATO) and the Central Treaty Organization (CENTO). With its membership in these organizations, Pakistan officially became America's 'most allied ally' and its full partner in the global Cold War.[14] Not only America but Britain, too, was, from the onset of the first India-Pakistan war of 1947–1948, determined to assist Pakistan. The British foreign secretary, Ernest Bevin, warned his prime minister: 'With the Palestine position so critical, we simply could not afford to put Pakistan against us and so have the whole of Islam against us.' British diplomat, Philip Noel-Baker, went one step further, telling Sheikh Abdullah that 'he was satisfied that Pakistan had no hand at all in the invasion of Kashmir'.[15] Britain's geostrategic thinking had placed Pakistan, even before its realization as a state, at the centre of its vision for South Asia.[16]

In his memoirs, *While Memory Serves* (1950), Francis Tucker,[17] the last general officer commanding of the British Indian Eastern Command, says that the imperial military was 'for the introduction of a new Muslim power supported by the science of Britain'; imperial strategists deemed it 'very necessary to place Islam between Russian Communism and Hindustan'.[18]

Tucker went on to predict in 1950: 'Hindu India was entering its most difficult phase of its whole existence. Its religion, which is to a great extent superstition and formalism, is breaking down. If the precedents of history mean anything...then we may well expect, in the material world of today, that a material philosophy such as Communism will fill the void left by the Hindu religion'.[19]

After the first Indo-Pakistan war, Pakistan acquired supremacy over the strategically important areas of Gilgit and Baltistan. The US and Britain wanted control over the Northern Areas that were bordering the Central Asian Republics in the Soviet Union and the People's Republic of China. And the Communist Party of India knew that the only way the West could control these areas was by exploiting the religious sentiments of the people.[20]

This was also the time when the West was building an alliance with political Islam and this alliance would last till they had successfully managed the disintegration of the Soviet Union. The Canadian envoy to India, Escott Reid, during this period wrote in his book: 'The culture of Islam is much closer to that of the West than is the culture of Hinduism. Hinduism is indeed farther removed from the culture of the West than any other of the great contemporary cultures of mankind...India, on the other hand, has almost no common intellectual or religious roots in the West...'[21]

Even though all these facts were not then in the public domain, India had witnessed the British and American support for Pakistan in the United Nations. It had also been noted that while the Sheikh was in New York as a part of the Indian delegation to the United Nations, he had met Warren Austin, the US representative to UN. Later, in 1952, his meeting with Adlai Stevenson, high-profile candidate for US presidency, had created a storm in India, especially since it went against Nehru's policy of non-alignment.

Despite all the discussions with his senior comrades, Sampat Prakash could not rationalize the arrest of Sheikh Abdullah and looked upon him as an imperialist agent. But nor did he support the idea of Kashmir becoming a colony of either Britain or America.

Sampat still looked upon the Soviet Union as a friend of the Kashmiris. He had been told that the Communists always supported oppressed nationalities. But he was in for a rude shock when two senior leaders from the Soviet Union visited the Kashmir Valley a few months after the Sheikh's arrest.

In the winter of 1955, Srinagar was agog with the news that Nikita S. Khruschev, the first secretary of the Soviet Communist Party's Central Committee, and the Soviet premier, Nikolai Bulganin, were coming. Sampat remembers how warmly the National Conference welcomed the two Soviet leaders; there was a river procession with the people of Kashmir showering the Russians with flowers.

The famous Kashmiri opera, *Bombur ta Yambarzal* (The Bumble Bee and the Narcissus), was specially staged for the Soviet leaders. It was the first opera written in Kashmiri by a Communist poet and writer, Dina Nath Nadim, and based on the popular Chinese opera called *White Haired Girl*. Dina Nath had seen the original when he had visited China some years earlier. The play was a highly symbolic one, speaking of how Wav and Harud (Wind and Autumn), representing the imperialistic agencies, were dividing people.[22]

Sampat was excited by this visit, but his enthusiasm was dampened when he read that the Soviet Union had decided to support India's stand on the Kashmir dispute. Even as he related the events of those days, he asked me: 'Why did the Soviet Union not support the demand for an independent Kashmir? After all, Lenin supported the right to self-determination of nations.'

I asked him whether he had had an occasion to discuss the questions that troubled him with his leaders but he said he was too junior at that time, a mere student leader, so he did not have an opportunity to have any real conversations. He is, however, still troubled by the conflict between his deep sense of commitment to Communism and Kashmiri nationalism. Even today, at the age of seventy-six, he struggles with these questions.

At that time, what had troubled him the most was the way the Kashmiri Pandits behaved. He felt that they should have come out onto the streets to join the protests against the arrest of Sheikh Abdullah. Their silence was seen as acquiescence to the betrayal.

A Kashmiri historian, Mohammad Ishaq Khan (1942–2013), has described how the attitude of the Pandit neighbours had shocked his father:

> I was eight years old when my father swore to take revenge against his Kashmiri Hindu neighbours, the Thisoos, following their bizarre expression of glee by clapping and embracing one another at the news of Sheikh Mohammad Abdullah's arrest.
> See those ungrateful Pandits. They are celebrating the dismissal of their saviour. Didn't Sher-e-Kashmir protect them during the tribal invasion of 1947?[23]

On the other hand, the Indian home minister, Sardar Patel, expressed his anger with the Indian Muslims in a letter: 'To Indian Muslims, I have only one question. Why did you not open your mouths on the Kashmir issue? Why did you not condemn the action of Pakistan?'[24]

The Jammu-Kashmir issue had become an India-Pakistan issue and then a Hindu-Muslim one. In a memorandum submitted to the United Nations Commission for India and Pakistan (UNCIP), fourteen distinguished Muslims had written:

> Pakistan has made our position weaker by driving out Hindus from Western Pakistan in utter disregard of the consequences of such a policy to us and our welfare...Our misguided brothers in Pakistan do not realize that if Muslims in Pakistan can wage a war against Hindus in Kashmir why shouldn't Hindus, sooner or later, retaliate against Muslims in India?[25]

After the arrest of Sheikh Abdullah, his deputy, Bakshi Ghulam Mohammad, was immediately sworn in as the Prime Minister of Jammu and Kashmir. Born in 1907, Bakshi Ghulam Mohammad remained prime minister for eleven years between 1953 and 1964.

Bakshi Ghulam Mohammad studied at the C.E. Tyndale Biscoe School. He started his career as a schoolteacher and was posted to Skardu, in Baltistan, on the confluence of the Indus and Shigar rivers at an altitude of 8,200 feet. From there he was posted to Leh, the headquarters of Ladakh.

Bakshi and many of his Cabinet colleagues had been influenced by the ideas and ideals of the Communists. He organized students and workers during his youth, and from 1927 onwards he was with Sheikh Abdullah, all through the agitations against Dogra rule. He was imprisoned at the Reasi Jail for sixteen months. He was a founding member of the Muslim Conference, and was much admired within the National Conference for his exceptional ability to lead and to organize.

However, in the aftermath of the Sheikh's arrest, many Kashmiris viewed Bakshi Ghulam Mohammad as a traitor because he was party to the arrest. There were massive street demonstrations and protests; the protests became even more militant once Mirza Mohammad Afzal Beg was released from jail. Afzal Beg was one of the twenty-two who had been arrested with the Sheikh on the charges of espousing the cause of independent Kashmir.

Afzal Beg was released in 1955, and in August that year he established the Mahaz-e-Rai Shumari, or the All Jammu and Kashmir Plebiscite Front, with the approval of Sheikh Abdullah, who, however, did not ever formally join the Front. The Plebiscite Front had two demands: the release of Sheikh Abdullah and a plebiscite to decide whether the people of Jammu and Kashmir wanted to join India or Pakistan or become a sovereign state.

The Plebiscite Front had formed the principal opposition to the National Conference and its members faced repression and many served long jail sentences.[26] It was alleged that they had openly preached disaffection and sought to excite hatred against the governments of Kashmir and India. It was said that they inflamed communal feelings among Muslims, organized a volunteer force and supplied military information to Pakistan.[27]

The Plebiscite Front did not have members from the Kashmiri Pandit community. However, that did not stop Sampat Prakash from joining their rallies and demonstrations. Apart from joining their protests, he also joined the youth wing of the newly formed Democratic National Conference.

The Democratic National Conference had been formed by a group of nineteen members from the National Conference who had left the Party because of the rampant corruption and intimidation that had crept in by 1957. The money that the Central government had been pouring in, mostly in the form of loans, was one of the main causes for this corruption. Bakshi, whose family was known as the Bakshi Brothers Corporation, would even boast that if someone was unable to get rich during his time, they would never be able to do so.

Bakshi did not tolerate any dissent. He ruthlessly suppressed the Plebiscite Front activities and did not allow any criticism of the Delhi government. He created seventy-five peace brigades as instruments for his policy of repression and they became infamous for not only suppression of political dissent but criminal activities, including molestation of women.

The Democratic National Conference maintained headquarters at the Majesty Hotel in Srinagar. All the leaders were either Communists or Communist sympathizers. Those from Kashmir had come under the influence of Communists while studying in Lahore, Aligarh, Lucknow; while the members from Jammu had been nurtured by Comrade Dhanwantri.[28]

The president of the Democratic National Conference was Ghulam Mohammad Sadiq. The vice president was K.D. Sethi and the general secretary was Ram Piara Saraf. These were the Communist leaders who would inspire Sampat to devote his entire life to trade union politics.

Sampat was given the task of organizing the Democratic National Conference's students' unions in various colleges and he succeeded in inspiring the students of Amar Singh College, Gandhi College, Women's College and, of course, his own college, to form unions, and to participate in the protests against Bakshi's goonda raj.

He also took up the students' cause within S.P. College by asking awkward questions to distinguished speakers who came to address them. On one occasion, when a speaker praised Bakshi for being the architect of modern Kashmir, Sampat Prakash stood up and heckled him, asking whether he knew that Bakshi was known for his corruption.

Sampat's activities were a source of embarrassment to the college authorities. The principal of S.P. College, Jia Lal Koul, was the author of *A History of Kashmiri Pandits*. When Sheikh Abdullah had organized his Muslim Conference, the Kashmiri Pandits had organized a Pandit Conference. They invited the Sheikh to attend their meeting that was addressed by Jia Lal Koul. Koul addressed the gathering: 'Sheikh Abdullah was so impressed with the nationalist sentiments expressed therein, that he picked up a garland and jumped on the rostrum to garland the speaker'.[29] Jia Lal Koul had joined the Sheikh's party when it changed its name to National Conference, but had left it when he felt that the Sheikh was giving in excessively to Muslim religious sentiments.

The principal had been told that one of the students, Samvith Prakash, had organized a union in the college and had not only stopped attending classes, but was also responsible for the disruption of classes and growing indiscipline in the college. Samvith Prakash was summoned to appear before the principal.

The principal asked Samvith the meaning of his name and when he was told that it meant 'the First Ray of the Sun', he said that it was an unsuitable name for a troublemaker and a more appropriate name would be Mr Sampat. Jia Lal Koul must have seen the movie by that name in which Motilal, the famous actor, portrays a loveable conman by the name of Mr Sampat.

In the 1952 movie, Mr Sampat is a dazzler who cons his way out of difficult situations. He regales his listeners with stories and boastful accounts about his feats, thus winning friends and hearts. Although Jia Lal Koul was obviously not thinking about the positive aspects of Mr Sampat's character, the name appealed to the young student and he took it as his own and called himself Sampat Prakash; however, he continued to be a troublemaker.

Sampat still remembers another visitor to his college: Krishna Menon. He was the person who had given a marathon speech lasting nearly eight hours to the United Nations Security Council in January 1957. The Guinness Book of World Records confirms that it is the longest speech ever given at the UN. Krishna Menon visited Srinagar in September of the same year. Sampat, in his inimitable style, once recited lines from Menon's speech: 'We should enlarge the pool where everyone can take a bath; only by doing this we can swim with the democratic system'.

Sampat thought Menon would be heckled by the teachers sympathetic to the Plebiscite Front but no one asked him any questions. Menon's words 'either sink or swim with the democratic system' became embedded in Sampat's impressionable mind.

All of a sudden, on 10 January 1958, the news came that Sheikh

Abdullah was being released. A tumultuous joy swept into every home and it was as if the entire Valley was experiencing spring after a long, cold winter. There was joy in the heart of every Kashmiri nationalist. Everyone wanted to catch a glimpse of their beloved leader and they left for Srinagar in whatever mode of transport they could find—cycle, tonga, boat.

Sampat Prakash and his father, Neelkanth, were among the hundreds of thousands of people who lined up on both sides of the road to welcome him. Kud stood halfway between Jammu and Srinagar; the Sheikh had been released in the morning and the journey to Srinagar should have taken not more than six hours. They waited at the Polo View, but by afternoon there was still no sign of the Lion of Kashmir.

By the time Sheikh Abdullah arrived it was dark, but the enthusiasm of the crowds had not waned. It may have been just a glimpse of his hero, but Sampat was thrilled when he saw the Sheikh travelling in an open jeep as he inched his way towards his home in Soura.

A few weeks after his release, in February, Sheikh Abdullah tried to take over the office of the National Conference at Mujahid Manzil in downtown Srinagar. The office was under Bakshi Ghulam Mohammad's control. As a result, the Sheikh could not reach the building but he managed to get to the Hazratbal shrine on the left bank of the Dal Lake. This shrine is considered to be the holiest place of worship because it is here that the Moi-e-Muqaddas, or the Holy Relic, has been preserved for centuries.[30]

Sheikh Abdullah spoke in his powerful voice with an equally powerful message to the Indian state: 'Accession of Kashmir is not to be decided by guns and bullets, Kashmir does not belong to Krishna Menon, Nehru or Bakshi. The people alone can decide its future.'[31]

Sheikh Abdullah denounced the state government as traitors, accused them of oppression and tyranny, and described Bakshi Ghulam Mohammed as a 'sinful oppressor of Moslems and slave of infidel Bharat'.[32] Following this speech there was a riot and one person was killed and several injured.

A few months later, on 29 April, the Sheikh was re-arrested on charges of conspiracy to overthrow the government. There were massive protests against his arrest. Sampat organized protests in his college and took part in processions on the streets.

By the autumn of 1958, Sampat Prakash was to graduate. He had already taken his seat in the examination centre when a police inspector walked in and arrested him. He was conveyed to the Special Cell at Kothi Bagh near Regal Chowk, where he was abused, slapped a few times and, after being detained for three days, released. The police hoped this treatment would stop the young student from creating any more trouble. As a result of the detention, he had to stay in college for an extra year.

While he was locked up at the police station, he learnt that his friend Sadiq Ali[33] had also been picked up and detained. Sadiq was the son of a papier-mache artist and businessman and lived in the Hassanabad neighbourhood of Rainawari. He had studied in Islamia School and then joined S.P. College. Sadiq had known Sampat since childhood, and although the two were friends, Sadiq had not been drawn towards the Communists; he was an active member of the Plebiscite Front. Sadiq Ali had been caught taking photographs of the demonstrations and rallies when he was arrested and brought to the Special Cell. Here, he was tortured with a hot iron being pressed on his stomach and badly beaten for many days. The treatment given to members of the Plebiscite Front was much harsher, partly because they were the main opposition group and partly because a Kashmiri Pandit student was not seen as a threat to the system.

Sitting across from me, Sampat Prakash recalled the days after the Sheikh's arrest and the anger he had felt at the way he had been betrayed by India and Indians. It was true that Socialist leaders like Jayaprakash Narayan, Madhu Limaye and Piloo Modi had spoken out against the arrest, but that was not enough. If only there had been a debate in the Indian Parliament, challenging the government's decision to arrest the Kashmiri leader.

Sampat complained that no voices were raised in India against the rampant corruption during the Bakshi years. In the annals of official Indian history, Bakshi Ghulam Mohammad is portrayed as an able administrator who brought stability to Kashmir during his eleven-year rule.

I asked Sampat whether the allegations of Sheikh Abdullah's corruption and high-handed, undemocratic functioning had ever bothered him during those heady days. After all, the Sheikh had promised internal autonomy to both the people of Jammu and Ladakh but he had gone back on his promises. But Sampat said that at the time he, like most ordinary Kashmiris, was only involved in the events in the Valley.

—

Bakshi helped to integrate Kashmir with the Indian Union. In February 1954, the Jammu and Kashmir Constituent Assembly unanimously confirmed the state's accession to India. In April, the customs barriers between the state and India were removed; in the next month an order was passed extending the jurisdiction of the Centre to all subjects in the Union List; and in 1957, Jammu and Kashmir was brought at par with other states in financial matters, enabling the state to receive its share of Central funds. The next year, the jurisdiction of the Election Commission of India and the All India Services was extended to Jammu and Kashmir.

Bakshi's administrative drive and increase in Central funds led to rapid growth. The Jawahar Tunnel was constructed during his tenure and as a result there was an all-weather road which connected the Valley with the rest of the country, ensuring a dependable flow of supplies and good transport facilities.[34]

The budget allocation for capital expenditure in health increased by six times, and that for education increased by ten times. Education from kindergarten to the university standard was made free. The number of school-going children went up from 64,000 to 234,000. The number of primary and basic schools rose from 1,239 to 4,078, high schools from seventy-two to 246, arts and science colleges from seven to fourteen, of industrial training institutes from two to nine and professional colleges from one to eight. However, almost all these professional colleges and technical institutions such as the Sher-e-Kashmir Institute of Medical Sciences, were located in the Valley and as a result, Jammu felt left out.

Bakshi had established a new machinery to distribute concessions and had set up a highly subsidized economy to appease and placate the Kashmiris. For instance, rice was available at forty paise a kilo, while in Punjab, people had to spend five to seven rupees for the same amount.

But these sops did not win over the hearts and minds of the Kashmiris because of the rampant corruption and suppression of all dissent that accompanied them.[35] And they did nothing to assuage the feelings of resentment in Jammu and Leh. All the educational institutions and all the major industrial plants were located in the Valley, even though Bakshi had better representation from Jammu and Ladakh in his Cabinet.

Many years later, a Kashmiri assessed the years immediately after the arrest of the Sheikh in these words: 'After dethroning of Sheikh Abdullah, the money did not start flowing only from Delhi but also from Islamabad...these streams have made corruption seep into the blood stream of the Kashmiri who would need dialysis to purify his blood!'[36]

In 1962, the elections were so obviously rigged that when Bakshi won sixty-eight of the seventy-four seats, Nehru wrote to him on 4 March saying: 'In fact, it would strengthen your position much more if you lost a few seats to bonafide opponents.'[37] Bakshi had infamously said: 'Vote aap denge; ginenge hum' (You will cast your votes; but we will count them).[38]

Meanwhile, the Democratic National Conference was making a significant contribution towards the democratization and secularization of Kashmiri politics. Its emergence had raised hopes that Kashmir would finally have leaders whose integrity could not be questioned and that the vision of a Naya Kashmir would be implemented. However, there was growing criticism of the Party in the rest of the country on the grounds that it was seen to have caused disunity among the ranks of the pro-India Kashmiri nationalists.[39]

There were a series of splits within the Left movement. In 1960, the Democratic National Conference Party split; a section under Ghulam Mohammad Sadiq merged with the National Conference while another formed their own party called the Democratic Front with Ram Piara Saraf as its general secretary. The party was linked to the Communist Party of India (CPI) and Saraf became the first Kashmiri member of the Communist Party's National Council.

In 1967, the Sadiq faction of the National Conference merged itself with the Indian National Congress.[40] And in 1964, Saraf and Sethi joined the pro-Chinese CPI(M) when the Party split.

Sampat Prakash had worked wholeheartedly with the youth wing of the Democratic National Conference and when it split, he, too, followed Sethi and Saraf into the Communist Party of India (Marxist).

Ram Piara Saraf was born in 1924; he became active in politics soon after he finished his post graduation in history from the Punjab University at Lahore. In 1952 he was elected to the Jammu and Kashmir Constituent Assembly and served for ten years, representing the Samba-Bishnah constituency.

Krishan Dev Sethi was from Mirpur, now in Pakistan-administered Kashmir, which was one of the poorest areas of Jammu and Kashmir. Sethi was witness to the way peasants had been repressed by both the British and the Maharaja and, by the time he was fifteen years old, he was active in the National Conference under stalwarts such as Sardar Budh Singh. Budh Singh resigned from his post as deputy commissioner and launched a movement against forced labour. In 1934, he organized the Kisan Party. He had been in jail several times.

Budh Singh was elected president of the Dogra Sabha thrice, the only public organization permitted at that time, and the people of Kashmir elected him president of the National Conference twice.

Sheikh Abdullah called him his spiritual father. The Sikhs selected him to lay the foundation stone of the Panja Sahib, their most sacred shrine.[41]

Sethi himself had been active in the resistance against autocratic Dogra rule from his teens. Sampat had heard that when Sethi had been arrested the first time, he was still a boy and since the handcuffs had slipped off his slim wrists so they had to tie him up with a rope.

Sampat had been inspired by both these men, and when circumstances forced him to leave his beloved Kashmir Valley and move to Jammu, he was glad for it meant that he could work more closely with his senior comrades. Both Saraf and Sethi were based in Jammu.

It was in late 1958 that Sampat Prakash fell in love with a young woman. Their romance had all the poignancy of the love stories they loved to watch on screen. They also sat together and listened to songs from films such as *Deedar, Lola, Shabnam* and *Anarkali*. Both were from Kashmiri Pandit families and there was no reason why their love should not have blossomed into a lifelong companionship. But in those days, a woman was not supposed to choose her own husband. There was opposition to the marriage from her family and they did not have the will to defy society. Sampat was heartbroken. The pain was so deep that he became an atheist. How could he believe in a god who destroys such a pure relationship based on love and friendship?

Sampat could not bear to be in Srinagar any longer and he left for Jammu by the end of 1959. He had graduated and had got a job as a clerk in the Provincial Rehabilitation Department, which was concerned with rehabilitating the refugees who had come from Pakistan-administered Kashmir, as well as protecting the properties of the Muslims who had chosen to become citizens of Pakistan. One of the perks of the job was that he was assigned a large house to live in.

In 1962, Sampat received a telegram urging him to come home because his mother was seriously ill. He immediately took the bus to

Srinagar, but when he reached he discovered that his family had identified a woman whom they thought would make him a suitable wife.

So in October 1962, Sampat Prakash got married to Dura, a young Kashmiri Pandit woman who had passed Class XII. She was not a political person, neither did she understand her husband's turbulent nature but she had been brought up to be patient and dutiful, so she hoped that with time he would settle down. The young couple returned to Jammu.

In 1963, the couple was expecting their first child and Dura went to her parents for the delivery. The baby was to be born in the winter so Sampat went to Srinagar for the event. He was excited and had already decided he would name his son Lenin, after the legendary Russian revolutionary. It did not even occur to him to consult his wife; besides, he was sure the child would be a boy. When the child was born he did name him Lenin, but the baby died soon after birth. Sampat barely had time to grieve or comfort his wife. Kashmir was in the grip of another crisis—the Moi-e-Muqaddas or the Holy Relic, the hair of the Prophet Mohammad, was missing.

The Moi-e-Muqaddas (the Sacred Hair) is kept inside a glass tube, deep within the Hazratbal shrine on the banks of the Dal Lake. It is exhibited only on the first Friday following Eid Milad-un-Nabi and other special occasions. On 28 December 1963, the news that the Moi-e-Muqaddas had been stolen spread like a wildfire. People poured out onto the streets to express their disbelief and grief.

Sampat watched with dismay. He knew that this mobilization would only encourage Muslim organizations and it could lead to communal friction. However, the people stood in snow and bitter cold with just their little kangris to keep themselves warm. The Hindus and Sikhs organized snacks and food for the devotees going to the mosque; even Tika Lal Taploo, advocate and leader of the Jana Sangh, came out with his wife to distribute drinking water. He was seen weeping and embracing his Muslim friends.[42]

The tension was mounting. The Moi-e-Muqaddas was Kashmir's

greatest treasure; the people believed that it was Divine Will that had brought it to the Valley in 1700 and they had loved and revered it. There were rumours that Pakistan was behind the theft, while others held Bakshi responsible.

Nehru sent B.N. Mullick, the head of the Intelligence Bureau, to sort out the matter. Mullick flew to Srinagar and, with the help of Lakshman Das Thakur, the inspector general of police, found the Moi-e-Muqaddas on 6 January 1964. They had struck a deal with those responsible; it was never known who stole it and the secret has still not been revealed.

However, the people wanted to be assured that it was the genuine relic and that they were not being deceived. This assurance was provided by Maulana Mohammad Sayeed Masoodi, a religious leader who was known for the depth of his views and the sobriety of his judgements. When he stood to speak, the people listened for more than an hour, even as two inches of snow settled on his shoulders— he had refused to take the protection of an umbrella when the people were exposed to the cold. He convinced them that the Moi-e-Muqaddas that had been found was the genuine one and asked the people to return home.[43]

On 13 December 1990, Maulana Masoodi was gunned down by unknown assailants at the behest of Saif-ul-Islam, acting chief of the Hezb-e Ullah, which was a militant organization. He was accused of being a traitor to the Muslim community, and specifically of being responsible for the sabotage of the movement around the Holy Relic.[44]

Although the immediate crisis was over, Sampat had witnessed for himself how the incident had led to the mobilization of the religious Right in Kashmir's politics. The leaders of the Awami Action Committee[45] had been moderates and had not allowed the movement to become communalized, but in the thirty-seven days that the agitation lasted, many youth and students, too, had joined the Action Committee and they longed for militancy.

Mirza Mohammad Afzal Beg had already formed the Jammu and

Kashmir Student and Youth Front, but now the youth yearned for a more militant form of action. A section of them established an organization called Al Fateh and its cadres received military training in Pakistan. And in 1965, two Kashmiris—Maqbool Bhatt and Amanullah Khan—co-founded the Jammu and Kashmir National Liberation Front (JKNLF), the first armed group in support of an independent Jammu and Kashmir.

Events moved quickly. Nehru died on 27 May 1964 and Lal Bahadur Shastri became prime minister of India. Pakistan thought India would not survive the death of Nehru and that it would be easy to instigate a popular uprising and take over Kashmir. The Pakistanis knew that the Kashmiris were angry with Bakshi's corruption and the Sheikh's re-arrest. They knew that there had been massive demonstrations when he had been arrested and they had seen the mobilization of people during the crisis over the missing Moi-e-Muqaddas. Confident that Kashmir would be theirs, in May 1965, they launched Operation Gibraltar. During the Operation, several thousand trained guerrillas were sent into the Valley disguised as locals. The plan was to foment rebellion against India. However, the infiltrators were soon identified and their plans foiled. The infiltration led to the second Indo-Pak war which lasted twenty-two days and ended with the defeat of Pakistan. But to their shock, the people of Kashmir refused to play their game. The second war with Kashmir lasted for twenty-two days with the defeat of Pakistan.

Sampat celebrated the birth of his second son on 22 November 1964. He named him Lenin, and at home the little boy was called Marshall after Marshall Tito, the Yugoslavian leader of the Non-Aligned Movement. Even today he goes by these names.

In May 1967, Sampat's third son was born, and he had wanted to call him Stalin. However, it was in the same year that an incident happened that engulfed Jammu and Kashmir in the red hot flames of communalism. His wife took advantage of her husband's absence to register her third son's name as Ravinder. She did not know who Stalin was and wanted a name which she could identify with. This was her moment of triumph.

In July 1967, Parmeshwari Handoo, a young woman belonging to the Kashmiri Pandit community and living in Rainawari, fell in love. The young woman had a job in a department store and there she fell in love with the cashier, Ghulam Rasool. She converted to Islam and married him. This was certainly not the first such incident but this time the Kashmiri Hindus turned it into a political issue.[46]

The Kashmiri Pandits alleged that the police was prejudiced in favour of the Muslim boy and, in fact, the girl had been blackmailed and coerced into marriage. More than 8,000 Kashmiri Pandits gathered together at Lal Chowk and shouted slogans such as: 'Panch naara Panduan, chata naara Jai Hind!' The slogan made it clear that the Kashmiri Pandits looked upon themselves as a small minority like the five brothers in the Mahabharata who defeated the huge army of the Kauravas, and that their loyalty lay with India.

They damaged government property and injured four constables. Several houses in the old city were burnt; two persons were killed and about 300 injured. The city was clamped under curfew and scores of persons, mostly from the Plebiscite Front, were put behind bars.

Balraj Madhok of the Jana Sangh hurried to Srinagar and, in a highly provocative speech delivered at Shital Nath, advised Muslims to migrate to Pakistan. His speech brought Muslims out on to the streets. In Jammu, Hindus took out a long procession on 25 August and raided Muslim shops, burning some of them. The Farida, Chand, Taj and Paristan hotels were also looted. The government finally referred the matter to a court and that resolved the situation. Parmeshwari was from that time known as Parveen Akhtar and she faded from the pages of history.

Sampat Prakash knew that the Kashmiri Pandits did not really care about Parmeshwari. The real reason for their anger was that they felt threatened by the fact that the Kashmiri Muslims were now receiving education and training, and had become eligible for the jobs that the Pandits had monopolized so far. The immediate cause of their anger, however, was the job quotas introduced by the chief minister, Ghulam Mohammad Sadiq, to protect Muslims.[47]

Sadiq had also set up a Commission of Enquiry in November 1967 to look into the regional imbalances in development programmes and recruitment policies. The Commission had rejected a proposal put forward by Balraj Puri for granting autonomy to the Jammu region. Puri had, as early as 1948, suggested autonomy for Jammu and Ladakh within the J&K State to ensure equitable distribution of resources to all three regions—Jammu, Kashmir and Ladakh.

A movement for autonomy had already started in Ladakh under the leadership of Kushak Bakula. There had been incidents of violence which reflected tensions between the Buddhists and Muslims.[48] The Buddhist Ladakhis had for long resented Kashmiri domination. Shiekh Abdullah's decision to impose Urdu in Ladakhi schools and to discontinue scholarships for children from the backward areas had all added to the growing resentment. In addition, no allocation whatsoever had been made for Ladakh's development in the first budget. In fact, there was no separate plan for Ladakh till 1961.[49]

'In the final analysis it was all about getting jobs, wasn't it?' I asked Sampat Prakash. He did not answer but told me a story about Kashmiri Pandits and the desperate measures they had taken to keep their privileged positions in government service.

During the reign of Maharaja Ranbir Singh (1857–85), many Kashmiri Muslims had asked to be converted back to Hinduism because they had been forcibly converted to Islam.

Maharaja Ranbir Singh sought the guidance of Swami Dayanand Saraswati, the founder of the Arya Samaj. Swami Dayanand advised him that they could be taken back into the Hindu fold only after certain rites and rituals had been performed.

However, the Kashmiri Pandits tried to dissuade the Maharaja from taking such a step because they did not want any competition for jobs. But when they found that the Maharaja was determined to go ahead with the reconversion, they resorted to subterfuge. They filled a few boats with stones and brought them midstream before the Maharaja's palace on the Jhelum, and threatened to commit suicide by drowning along with the sinking boats as a protest against his decision. If the Maharaja allowed them to drown, he would be guilty of 'Brahm Hatya', the murder of Brahmins. The Maharaja naturally did not want to commit such a sin.[50]

The Kashmiri Pandits claim they opposed the reconversion because they were against proselytization; they have seen this story as a reflection of the tolerant creed of the Hindus, who have always been against the use of force for converting people of other faiths to their religion. They contribute to a pluralistic concept of religion and society allowing every individual to espouse his faith without any interference from any quarter.[51] Sampat Prakash and I laughed. I remarked that Kashmiri Pandits espoused Kashmiriyat only when it can be used to protect their interests. I told him that this was the conclusion of recent research.[52] Sampat mulled over this and nodded.

We were seated in a hotel room in Srinagar in February of 2010. I showed him a book I had bought on the recommendation of some young Kashmiri intellectuals who had come to see me. It was by Ashiq Hussain Bhat.[53] In a chapter on Kashmiriyat, he says:

> If Kashmiris were a separate quom, that would mean that others living in the rest of the State outside the Valley such as Mirpuris, Poonchies, Gilgits, Baltis, Ladakhis, Kashtwaris, Poglis, Baderwalis, Jamwal Dogras—the Dogras considered Jammu as their motherland and Kashmir Valley as a conquered territory to be ruled with the help of musket—had nothing to do with Kashmiris as a nationality was concerned.[54]

For Sampat, Kashmiriyat meant all these communities, not only the Hindus and Muslims living in the Valley. I asked him, 'Where have you seen Kashmiriyat work?' I was a little irritated with his stubborn belief in the old-fashioned idea of communal harmony, belief in the possibility that people of different religions and nationalities can live together in peace.

'In our trade union movement,' he answered without a moment's hesitation. Sampat said his experience within the trade union movement had convinced him that the people of Jammu and Kashmir, irrespective of their religious and regional identities, could live and work together.

RAGE AGAINST THE DYING
OF THE LIGHT
(1964–74)

Ghulam Qader Bhat was seventy-four years old when I met him in his daughter's home in Chadura town in Budgam district in 2009. He looked frail sitting on the carpet, leaning against bolster pillows, wrapped up in a large blanket. The moment we entered, his daughter welcomed us with warm blankets and kangris. It was January and I could feel the cold in my bones.

I asked Ghulam Qader about his memories of the early days of the trade union movement. His face lit up and although he spoke softly, there was passion in his measured words.

His village, Hafroo in Budgam, was a big one with 150 families. His family had a little land but not enough to make ends meet. Many families were given land during the Naya Kashmir programme but theirs did not get any direct benefits.[1] However, that did not deter the family from wholeheartedly supporting the programme.

Bhat studied in S.P. College; he had to walk more than 25 kilometres from his village to Srinagar because he could not afford to hire a tonga, the only means of public transport in those days.

In Srinagar, Ghulam Qader came across Communist literature. He named the magazines that he used to read with enthusiasm, such as *Soviet Desh*, the Urdu version of *Soviet Land*. He said he subscribed to it because all one had to do was to write to them and they would send their literature for free.

Ghulam Qader was transported back to the days of his youth when he first encountered an ideology which appealed to his sense of justice. He avidly read *Awami Daur,* edited by Sajjad Zahir, the veteran Communist from Lucknow; *Hamara Kashmir* which was a weekly and later a daily; and after he was appointed as a schoolteacher in 1954, he regularly read *Ustad,* the monthly magazine of the Teachers' Association edited by Dina Nath Nadim, the poet who was president of the Teachers' Association. He informed me with pride: 'I still have copies of *Ustad.*'

I asked him whether anyone objected to the Communist literature, or condemned it as being anti-religious. Ghulam Qader replied that there was no objection whatsoever because the Jamaat-e-Islami[2] had almost no influence in the Valley in those days. No other organization had any objection.[3]

Ghulam Qader attended the study circle run by Communists such as Agha Ashraf and Dina Nath Nadim. There he heard stories about revolutionaries such as Comrade Dhanwantri and M.N. Roy who visited Jammu.

Bhat also attended meetings of the Kisan Mazdoor Sabha[4] where he heard revolutionary songs—the words still stirred in him a longing for those days. He recited the lines of a song for me. I asked him to translate the words—the song promises the dawn of a new world.

Listening to the elderly Kashmiri, I was filled with nostalgia for the 1970s when activism had a different meaning altogether. It was based on the firm belief that commitment and sacrifice could change the world for the better.

During Sheikh Abdullah's time, two seats were reserved for school teachers in the Constituent Assembly. It is with pride that Bhat told me that the Muslim-majority Kashmir Valley nominated Dina Nath Nadim, a Kashmiri Pandit, while Hindu-majority Jammu nominated Ghulam Rasool Azad, a Muslim. Bhat said there was no feeling of communalism in those days, but I noticed that throughout the interview, he never used the word Kashmiriyat. Later, Bakshi Ghulam Mohammad arbitrarily abolished the nomination of teachers.

Ghulam Qader worked wholeheartedly for the Teachers' Association. He used to collect one rupee subscriptions from all the members and he still has the cashbooks and accounts which he had meticulously kept.

Bhat is a proud member of the CPI(M). He joined the party at the time it was formed in 1964—the year it split from the pro-Moscow Communist Party of India. The two most prominent Communist leaders in Jammu and Kashmir were Ram Piara Saraf and Kishen Dev Sethi. These two leaders joined the newly-formed CPI (M) and were arrested for their pro-Chinese stance in the aftermath of the Indo-China war in 1962.

For the first part of the interview, I had asked Sampat Prakash to let me talk to Ghulam Qader alone, mostly because Sampat would get so excited that he would not allow others to speak. Now Sampat and other comrades entered the room to join in the tea and snacks brought in by Ghulam Qader's daughter.

I asked Bhat where and when he first met Sampat. It was Sampat who answered.

After Saraf and Sethi were released from jail in 1966, they had decided that the Party needed to organize a trade union. Till then, the Communists had been active, largely in the Kisan Mazdoor Sabha. Sampat had already been in touch with Saraf and Sethi before their imprisonment, and when he moved to Jammu, he was a regular visitor to the Communist Party office in the Pucca Danga neighbourhood. He had seen them on stage when they had come to Srinagar to give speeches on the platform of the Democratic National Conference. Sampat had been inspired by these two leaders and had introduced himself to them. They combined within them all the qualities that he had grown to value—militant politics, astute analysis and personal integrity.

Now they contacted him to discuss the idea of starting a trade union. Communists and socialists had in the past organized trade unions such as the Government Sericulture and Silk Labour Union, the Turpentine Labour Union, the Telegraph Employees Union, and unions for carpet weavers, bus drivers and tongawallas. The labour force of 100,000 included Hindus, Muslims and Sikhs and their unions had 'a significant impact on the secularization of Kashmiri politics'.[5]

Saraf and Sethi felt that the time was ripe to organize a trade union of the government employees, especially since Ghulam Mohammad Sadiq had become the prime minister in 1964.[6] He was known for his personal integrity and his commitment to the basic tenets of good governance. Sadiq ensured that the labour laws were extended to his state and he established a trade union registered under the name of All Jammu and Kashmir Low Paid Government Servants Federation in 1964. The president of the union was Sadar Fakir Singh. But the union had no cadres and had been largely inactive. Saraf and Sethi thought it would be a good idea to breathe life into Sadiq's trade union and were hoping that Sampat Prakash would be able to do just that. They called all the leaders of the existing trade unions for a meeting.

Sampat described that first meeting in May 1966 at Sethi's home. The leaders of Teachers' Associations, Workers' Unions, and Government Employees' Associations were called to discuss how a trade union movement could be launched.[7] In that meeting, it was decided that a conference would be organized and Sadiq's union would be taken over. It was at this meeting that Ghulam Qader Bhat first met Sampat Prakash.

It was decided that the new organization would work under the same name as Sadiq's union but would also form associations in each department which would affiliate with the Federation. It was also decided that the president of the Federation would be Abdul Majid Khan and the general secretary, Sampat Prakash.[8]

Sampat had met Abdul Majid in the Communist Party office and had felt a deep respect for the man. Abdul Majid was from Ustad Mohallah in Jammu, and was a few years older than Sampat. He was an employee in the Public Health Engineering department and had gone on a hunger strike in support of the demands of his fellow employees, even before there was any trade union to back him. This was a courageous step at a time when the bureaucrats were very powerful and there was every danger of him losing his job. Later, he met the Communists and came under their influence.

At the beginning of 1967, the seventy to eighty committed cadres and members of the Communist Party were told to take a month off to prepare for a general strike in support of their demands for better working conditions. The strike was due to take place by the end of the year, but preparations for it started immediately. Sethi and Saraf held classes for the employees in the evenings and infused in them a spirit of defiance, even though it fell short of revolutionary ardour.

Sampat was totally unselfconscious when he informed me that he had never forgotten how Lenin had urged the Bolsheviks to remember that the three most important tasks before them were: change the traditional way of thinking of the people, instil in them a hatred of the ruling class and keep the Party prepared to seize the opportunity if time came to revolt.

When the leaders were due to visit a department, the visit would be announced by posters printed in the Government Press after office hours. The employees then learnt to make glue with flour which they would use to paste posters. It was a novel experience for the government employees to roam around Jammu at night, posters and glue in hand.

Working in Jammu was difficult for several reasons. Unlike the employees in Kashmir, the employees in Jammu were less attracted to radical activities. They were also under the influence of the Jana Sangh and were divided along caste lines. In order to generate a sense of unity among the employees, Sampat and the other leaders called meetings in which they would all sit together, discuss strategies and then eat together. In this way many caste rules were broken and a feeling of camaraderie developed.

The leaders would visit each government department at around four in the evening, just after office hours. There they would motivate the employees by first teaching them some militant slogans. I asked

Sampat if he remembered any of the slogans. And before my eyes I could see Sampat was transported back in time. He said he would begin by yelling: 'Afsaron ke khooni panje tor do, maror do!' (The bloody claws of the bureaucrats, break them, twist them!) And the employees learnt to respond: 'Afsarwadi nahi chalegi!' (Down with officialdom!) Shouting these slogans boosted the morale of the employees. Most of them were aimed against the bureaucrats and their oppression: 'Mantri pet bharte hain' (Ministers have their stomachs full) 'Santri bhooke rehte hain' (The employees die of hunger). The employees learned to call out slogans even against Indira Gandhi who was by then the prime minister: 'Chalis saal aazadi ke, bhook aur barbadi ke' (Forty years of independence, hunger and destruction). And then there were the slogans against the capitalists: 'Indira tere samajwad mai, bacche bhuke marte hai. Bacche bhooke marte hain, Tata-Birla palte hain' (Indira, under your socialism, children die of starvation. Children die of starvation, the Tatas-Birlas prosper).

Sampat continued to recount the slogans. He said it was very important that I wrote them all down because they were an important part of the struggle of the employees and inspired them with courage and dignity. Sampat, however, stressed that although the slogans were militant and sounded quite violent, the leaders always ensured that their rallies were very disciplined and there was almost never any incident of violence.

The shouting would end with classic Communist slogans like:

Trade Union ki kya buniyad?
Marxvaad, Leninvaad
(What is the basis of the Trade Union?
Marxism and Leninism)

And then a resounding: Red Flag up, up

By then the employees were ready to take to the streets, but first they had to learn to march in a disciplined manner.

Sampat and his comrades had come up with a novel idea to

prepare the employees for the strike, which was to begin in December. One of these was the 'Keep Right Movement', wherein the employees were told to break the usual traffic rule of walking on the left side of the road and instead to walk on the right side in protest.

For a month the employees gathered together outside their departments after office hours, formed neat rows of three and marched to the centre of the town during rush hour. The colourful processions of disciplined employees walking on the wrong side of the road, shouting slogans and waving their red flags attracted the attention of the public. This gave the local leaders the opportunity to address the meetings and gain experience and confidence in trade union mobilization.

By the time the Jammu employees had been given their first lesson in trade union work, the seeds had been sown in each department. So far, only a few people in each department had been involved; now these leaders would form full-fledged associations with their own charter of demands. However, for this strike, the Federation had only two demands: the regularization of their service and the payment of dearness allowance at par with Central government employees.

After touring the districts of Jammu and visiting every government department and setting up a district committee, Sampat and his comrades left for Kashmir. There the same pattern was repeated and district committees were formed. As in Jammu, the employees in Kashmir were chosen as the executives and given an opportunity to address meetings, but first, senior comrades helped them articulate their grievances and then heard them as they practised their speeches.

Then, on 4 December 1967, the strike started in right earnest. The government employees, teachers, workers in government factories and drivers started their agitation. The workers did not stay at home; they went to their offices, factories and schools but did not work.

I asked Sampat why they did not strike work and stay away from their workplaces. He said that by going to their departments, the employees and workers had to face their bosses and learn how to directly confront bureaucrats.

The party leaders, Saraf and Sethi, went underground and tried to guide the trade union leaders from behind the scenes. The police had started looking for the other leaders and this forced Sampat Prakash to go underground as well, and thereby escape immediate arrest. However, he would disguise himself and appear at trade union meetings and address the workers before disappearing again.

The twenty-eight-year-old Sampat had to be careful that he was not arrested and so he spent nights at the homes of different people. His wife, Dura, had to manage their two sons alone. It must have been a terrifying situation for her and when she heard that the other leaders had been arrested on 8 or 9 December, she knew that her husband, too, would be taken into custody; it was only a matter of time.

On 9 December, after addressing a meeting of workers, Sampat quickly slipped away, and as he was getting into a taxi, he saw that some policemen in plain clothes were following him. He was passing by a canal and just at its edge, he told the taxi driver to stop. He jumped into the icy waters and swam across the river. The strict lessons in swimming at Tyndale Biscoe School had obviously come in handy. Sampat had a reputation of being a bit of a swashbuckler and I could see he enjoyed telling his stories of adventure and heroism.

The agitation had been going well, but then Saraf took a decision which led to it fizzling out. He told Sampat to call for a full-fledged strike. A poster was brought out to inform the government employees to stop attending their offices. This was exactly the opportunity the chief minister, Ghulam Mohammad Sadiq, was looking for to break the strike, and he instructed policemen to wear civilian clothes and man all the departments. The press reported that the employees had started returning and this demoralized the striking employees and the strike petered out by the end of December. The employees were back in their offices, but they had lost their wages for the days that they had not shown up. And the leaders were still in jail. Ghulam Qader managed to stay underground and escape arrest. But he did not take refuge in a safe home. He was worried about the fate of the families of the comrades who were arrested. It was severe winter and they would not have food or fuel. Ghulam Qader carried bags of charcoal on his shoulders from his village to Srinagar and distributed it among the families of the arrested comrades, so that they would be able to light up their kangris. He also managed to send them rice, rajma beans and dried vegetables to keep them from starving.

Ghulam Qader did not tell me this story; he is incapable of boasting or self-aggrandizement. I heard this story only because his comrades phoned me in Goa from Srinagar to tell me that I must include a description of Ghulam Qader's contribution in this book.

Sampat knew he would have to mobilize support for the thirty-seven arrested workers in Jammu and seven in Kashmir. He decided to contact the Indian trade union leaders. He informed Saraf that he was going to Delhi to approach the central trade unions. In Delhi, he met the representatives of the Central Government Employees Confederation, the All India State Government Employees Federation and the All India Trade Union Congress affiliated to the Communist Party of India.[9]

The Indian trade union leaders sent a team of trade unionists to Jammu where they sat on a 48-hour solidarity hunger strike in support of the demands of the Low Paid Government Servants Federation. This was the first time that Indian trade union leaders had shown such solidarity with the employees of Jammu and Kashmir. And when it was announced that the Indian trade unions would call for a Bharat Bandh, the chief minister had to sit up and take notice.

The Indian trade union leaders met with Ghulam Mohammad Sadiq and he assured them that he would release the arrested leaders, and that he would also concede to their demands. Sadiq was from a Communist background and his natural sympathy lay with the employees. However, he had one condition. He told the Indian leaders to make Sampat Prakash see sense and stop his Naxalite activities.

Sadiq informed the leaders that he wanted to support the trade union because it was a vital force against both the followers of the saffron flag (the Hindu nationalists) in Jammu and the followers of the green flag (the Islamists) in Kashmir. But if he was to back the union, it would have to sever its link with the Naxalites.

He had received reports from the intelligence agencies that Sampat Prakash had been distributing Mao badges to the employees and raising Naxalite slogans such as 'Chairman Mao is our Chairman'. He said that the Central Home Ministry had instructed him to arrest Sampat Prakash.

I asked Sampat Prakash whether it was true that he had distributed badges with pictures of Mao Tse-tung. He looked a little sheepish and confessed that he had brought two bags of these badges that R.K. Watal, who worked at the Chinese embassy, had given him. He told me that, looking back, he thought that Saraf's call for an absolute strike and his refusal to negotiate was just an example of Left adventurism. Could he not be accused of the same, I asked. He laughed with a twinkle in his eyes.

In February 1968, Sampat Prakash travelled all over India addressing meetings in which he vividly described the miserable condition of the Kashmiri employees. He told his trade union colleagues and comrades that the employees were treated like serfs who could be ordered around by the bureaucrats, who shouted at them and often humiliated them. On top of that, the employees were paid a pittance. Their salaries lasted for just two weeks, even though they spent it only on basic necessities. For instance, 70 per cent of the Class IV staff was on duty for twenty-four hours; there were no shifts. Their children could not even afford to go for picnics and excursions. The senior officers, on the other hand, lived the lives of feudal lords.

Sampat received good response from his Indian comrades. For most of them, it was their first glimpse into the condition of the people in Kashmir. In the course of this tour, Sampat Prakash was chosen as the Secretary (North Zone) of the All India State Government Employees Federation.

—

I had heard about the working conditions of the government employees from the trade union leaders I had interviewed. They spoke of how their dignity was undermined every day because they did not have even the bare necessities of life. The testimony of seventy-three-year-old Abdul Rashid Khan moved me deeply. Abdul Rashid worked in the sheep and animal husbandry department where the shepherds had to take the sheep herd belonging to the department[10] to graze in the mountain pastures for three months in a year. They had to keep an eye on them for twenty-four hours because sheep have a tendency to wander. The shepherds had no place to sleep, not even a flimsy tent to protect them from rain or snow. There was a time when a bureaucrat came up with the idea that the sheep should be made to wear socks to keep them warm, and the shepherds were given an additional task of putting socks on the four hooves of each sheep!

Abdul Rashid said that employees were often dismissed from the department arbitrarily. The bureaucrats looked upon the shepherds like they looked upon the sheep, as animals. On one occasion he saw an employee being led away by the police; he had gone mad because he had not been paid for four years. It was because of his association with the union that Abdul Rashid found the courage to get the man released. He said that after joining the union he was able to look the bureaucrat in the eye and make his demands in a firm voice. He even went on a hunger strike in support of the demands of his fellow employees, and soon after, he himself was dismissed.

When I met him, he was on the way to his medical shop; he said he still had debts to pay. That was why he was working at this age. The struggles did improve the condition of the shepherds but there was a great deal more that needed to be done for them.

———

Sampat knew that his wife would be having a tough time because his elder son, Lenin, was just a toddler and the younger son still a baby. He knew that the crime branch would be keeping a watch on his home but he still managed to enter unseen. Now, he could hold his baby, and his wife could assure herself that her husband was safe.

Little Lenin was thrilled to see his father and in his excitement he wandered out of the house to share the good news with the uncles who had been kind to him and had been asking after his father. He had no idea that the uncles were waiting to arrest his father.

Sampat Prakash was arrested on 18 March 1968. He was kept at the interrogation centre in Jammu for a week. The interrogation was intense but he was not tortured. The detectives wanted to know the addresses of the people in whose homes he had spent his nights, where the posters and pamphlets were printed and how they were distributed. Sampat Prakash refused to answer. He felt that as a leader he had the responsibility of not betraying the trust of his comrades.

Finally, he was sent to the Jammu Central Jail and put in a solitary cell meant for condemned prisoners. Sampat was furious. Why was he being treated like a criminal when not a single violent incident had occurred during the entire agitation? The employees had merely demanded their rights under the labour laws and were fighting for their legitimate demands.

The superintendent of the jail, Jaswant Singh, was notorious for his ill-treatment of the prisoners; Sampat made up his mind to teach him a lesson. The next day when the jailor opened the door of his cell, Sampat Prakash gave him a resounding slap. The other prisoners watched, astounded by his audacity. The jailor conceded to Sampat's demand and put him with other political prisoners.

Among the prisoners were members of the Plebiscite Front, including its general secretary, Ghulam Mohammad Bhaderwahi, who was one of the stalwarts of the National Conference from the Jammu region and a close aide of Sheikh Muhammad Abdullah. Bhaderwahi was nearly twenty years older than Sampat. He had been active in politics since 1937 and had been arrested twice before.

He later joined the Police Telecommunication Wing but was discharged on the allegation that he had contacted someone in

Pakistan over the official wireless set. Amnesty International declared him a 'Prisoner of Conscience' for spending twelve years in prison. Later, in 1977, Bhaderwahi contested elections against the Janata Dal candidate.[11]

The leaders of the Plebiscite Front told Sampat Prakash that prisoners were often deprived of their rations and were not even given drinking water. They had been agitating over these issues, but now, together, they organized a strike inside the jail.

Sampat Prakash was in jail for four months. It was during this period that he learnt a lot more about the history of Kashmir. The Plebiscite Front leaders had many books, including Stein's translation of *Rajtarangani*, the 'River of Kings' or the story of Kashmir's rulers from ancient times. He also read the writings of Maulana Masoodi and learnt about the long history of oppression of the Kashmiri people from the time Ashoka invaded the Valley. Later, after the insurgency began, the militants would try and disown the Valley's history of Hinduism and Buddhism.

Although she was often angered by her husband's rather flamboyant style of politics, Dura did recognize that Sampat was a caring husband and a loving father. She would visit him regularly, along with the two boys. One day Sampat was told that his wife had come to meet him, but when he went into the superintendent's room, where they usually met, she was not there. Instead, he was told that they had orders to transfer him to Reasi Jail, some three hours away from Jammu. He and Sheikh Bhaderwahi were packed into a police jeep and taken to Reasi.

The conditions in the jail were dreadful. The cell was filthy and, at night, mosquitoes made it impossible for the two to sleep. There was no electricity, only a lantern, which cast more shadows than light, and which was left outside their cell. They were given two convicts to help them cook the rations they bought at an allowance of thirty-seven rupees a day.

The superintendent treated them very badly and they did not have access to basic amenities. Sampat wanted to take revenge so he asked one of the convicts who had been assigned to help them to come to his cell one night. With a pair of scissors, he cut up his blanket which he had been allowed to keep as a political prisoner, and then helped the convict, a lifer by the name of Naba, to lower himself down the improvised rope and escape to freedom. When I asked whether the convict was caught, Sampat laughed and said of course not, but the superintendent was suspended for the convict's escape.

The jailor, however, treated Sampat with respect because he was the general secretary of the government employees union which stood for the rights of people like him. He even brought him a copy of the preventive detention law under which Sampat had been detained.

Reading the Act, Sampat realized that the preventive detention law was against the Constitution of Jammu and Kashmir, so he decided to challenge it. He asked Bhaderwahi whether he would like to be a co-petitioner, but the latter did not have much faith in Indian laws and declined.

Under the Indian preventive detention law, the person detained has a right to know the grounds of his detention and have his case heard by an Advisory Board. However, the Kashmir law did not require any reference to an Advisory Board which meant that the person could be kept in detention indefinitely.

Sampat, with some help from the jailor, wrote to the chief justice of India explaining the circumstances under which he had been detained. He described the activities of the trade union as well, and attached press cuttings which carried photos of the rallies.

Sampat had the petition ready by the time Dura came for her monthly visit. He instructed her to address the letter to the chief justice and post it in Pathankot because he knew that any letter posted within Jammu and Kashmir would be intercepted by the intelligence agencies. The Supreme Court received the petition in the first week of May.

A few days later, senior police officers came to visit Sampat

Prakash at the Reasi Jail and asked him whether he had sent a petition to the Supreme Court. When he denied it, they told him they had seen the petition and recognized his handwriting. The Supreme Court had directed that Sampat Prakash be produced before the court so they drove him to Delhi. When they reached Delhi, Sampat Prakash found himself lodged in Tihar Jail.

Tihar was the biggest jail Sampat had seen. The jail authorities had been told he was a dangerous Naxalite who had tried to set up a base in Doda. Sampat found himself locked in a cell with a man many years his senior, who called himself Natwarlal. Natwarlal's real name was Mithilesh Kumar Srivastava and he was India's most famous con man who had, among other spectacular con jobs, sold the Taj Mahal to gullible foreigners not once, but three times. He had used more than fifty aliases. Bollywood had made several films based on his life.[12] Natwarlal was really surprised that the Kashmiri trade union leader had never heard of him.

Natwarlal told Sampat that at one time, he had even offered to help the law enforcement agencies but they never took him up on his offer. Later, when he was a much older man in a wheelchair, he disappeared on the way to court, and to this day no one knows what happened to him.

Natwarlal had formal legal training but more than that, he had vast first-hand experience of the working of the legal system since he had been charged in at least a hundred cases.

Natwarlal seemed to have been impressed with Sampat Prakash—perhaps the con man found in him a kindred spirit in so far as temperament went because he offered him legal advice which proved very valuable. Natwarlal explained how Sampat could avail himself of legal aid from the best lawyers in the Supreme Court through the legal aid scheme. He drafted a petition stating that Sampat Prakash was a dismissed employee who was in jail; he had no means of engaging a lawyer and, thus, needed legal aid.

Sampat had confessed to Natwarlal that he was a Communist and the con man informed him that the best criminal lawyers in the

Supreme Court were Communists—surely they would help their comrade? Natwarlal's list of top criminal lawyers included M.K. Ramamurthi and R.K. Garg, both of whom were members or sympathizers of the Communist Party.

A few days later when he was being taken from the Supreme Court to the jail van, he asked the police to let him visit the lawyers' chambers and managed to find Ramamurthi's chambers. There he introduced himself as a comrade and was warmly welcomed. Ramamurthi said he would send his junior to the jail to get all the facts and he kept his promise.

Sampat Prakash was furious when he read the reply filed by the chief secretary of Jammu and Kashmir, P.K. Dave, to his petition. He had accused Sampat of being a violent man who had instigated the employees to armed revolt to overthrow the legal government, and of going underground in Doda.

In the court things had gone very well, but Ramamurthi felt that there was a need to challenge provisions of the statute itself, apart from challenging the detention order under which Sampat had been imprisoned. That is how Sampat Prakash's petition landed before the Constitution Bench of the Supreme Court of India.[13] Sampat not only won his case but many other political prisoners in Jammu and Kashmir were also released. I asked him whether he knew that his case had set out important principles of federalism and was being taught by international jurists. Sampat, of course, knew its importance but was pleased to hear that it had come to the attention of jurists.

In Tihar Jail, Sampat met many kinds of people, including revolutionaries associated with armed struggles in Telegana and Tripura. These older comrades gave him lessons in organizing underground movements which would help him in his later years. Because of this, his time in jail was well spent. It was in the winter of 1969 that Sampat found himself back in Kashmir, ready to strengthen the trade union.

A few months after being released, Saraf invited Sampat to Samba where Sampat and a few other comrades met Charu Mazumdar, the legendary Naxalite leader from West Bengal. Sampat said he 'became a fan' of Mazumdar because he supported the Kashmiri struggle for self-determination. Meanwhile, Saraf and Sethi had developed sharp differences and they too split; each joined different factions of the Naxalite movement. Sampat went with Sethi.

During this period, there was no political party to guide or control the government employees' trade union and Sampat and his comrades were distressed by the fissures in the Communist movement.[14] Now there was an even greater need to strengthen the trade union movement and Sampat began working to create independent associations within each department. Till then, each department had representatives who came for the Federation meetings.

––––

May Day in Jammu Province was celebrated either on 26 or 27 April before the Darbar[15] shifted to Srinagar, the summer capital. Sampat Prakash decided that May Day in 1970 would be a grand affair. The government employees working at the block level were asked to mobilize a busload of people from each department.

When the day arrived, hundreds of government employees from all corners of Jammu travelled through thick forests and over steep, narrow roads, shouting slogans which resounded in the mountains. Each block was to make their own red flags and banners, and so on May Day, more than a hundred vehicles gathered in Jammu. It was a show of strength in an area which had seen the saffron flags of the Hindu party and organizations more often. There was a sea of red flags at the Parade Ground and the trade union leaders gave fiery speeches to inspire the employees and instil in them a unity for future struggles.

Sampat recited paragraphs from his speech—full of quotes, poems and rhetoric. It was the intensity of his beliefs that shone through and I am sure he was right when he claimed that he was considered one of the best orators. 'On that day, I was man of the match,' he told me. I believed him.

––––

In 1971 came the national liberation movement for the creation of Bangladesh. Sampat Prakash's natural sympathies lay with Bangladesh. He longed to organize rallies in support of a movement that he saw as a liberation movement, akin to the Vietnam struggle or even the Kashmiri nationalist movement. But in Kashmir, the mood was very different.

Sampat realized that an anti-India sentiment was growing among the bureaucracy, businessmen and the youth. They saw the Bangladesh War as Indian expansionism—an attempt to break a Muslim state. They felt it was a conspiracy between the Indian intelligence organization, RAW, and the Soviet intelligence agency, KGB, to break up an Islamic state.

Despite this mood, even the Plebiscite Front did not take out any anti-India rallies or support Pakistan openly. Neither was there was any pressure from his cadres to organize anti-Indian rallies.

Sampat knew that even if he had mobilized some members of his union and taken out pro-Bangladesh demonstrations, he could not undermine the feeling of religious solidarity with Pakistan. He was beginning to see how religion took precedence over nationality in the minds of the Kashmiris, with the Muslims supporting Pakistan and the Kashmiri Pandits supporting 'Hindu' India. After all, Kashmir's national poet had said many years ago: 'Though I would like to sacrifice my life and body for India, yet my heart is in Pakistan.'[16]

The war ended with a decisive victory for India and the creation of the Republic of Bangladesh. In Kashmir, Chief Minister Ghulam Mohammad Sadiq died. A few months before his death, Sadiq had released all the trade union leaders who had been imprisoned and had given them their back wages. However, he did not reinstate them. In other words, Sampat Prakash and his comrades, the leaders of the union were free, but without their jobs.

The new chief minister was Syed Mir Qasim (1971–75). Mir Qasim had also studied in S.P. College and later went to Aligarh Muslim University where he came in contact with Marxist historian Irfan Habib and other Communists. He had taken part in the Quit

Kashmir Movement and had been involved in implementing the land reform agenda of the Naya Kashmir programme. He was close to Sheikh Abdullah, but later joined the Democratic National Conference. Finally, he established the Congress Party in Kashmir.

Sampat and his comrades decided to make the new chief minister aware of the strength and vitality of the government employees trade union. On the day he took oath in Jammu, he was greeted by a vociferous group of government employees, along with the blue-collar workers of the Chenab Textile Mills, established by the Birlas at Kathua in 1962. The leader of the mill workers union was Babu Singh, a committed Naxalite.

While there were a few hundred people at the swearing-in ceremony, the workers had more than two thousand people with their charter of demands.

When Mir Qasim reached Srinagar, he was again greeted by the government employees demanding the establishment of a Pay Commission. And in February 1972, Sampat Prakash called for a two-day strike in support of the demands. It was, as usual, a pen-down, chalk-down, tool-down style of strike.

Since Mir Qasim and his Congress Party had no base in the Valley, he thought that having the employees on his side would be to his advantage. Besides, there was a danger that they might heed a call for boycotting the elections which were to take place the following year, in 1972, and the government employees were needed to man the polling booths. He called the leaders of the union for negotiations. This was the first time that the Low Paid Government Servants Federation entered into formal negotiations with the government of Jammu and Kashmir.

For the first time the political climate was favourable for the trade union to function. The new generation of bureaucrats were not like the feudal lords of the past. They were more professional. The trade union leaders now toured the towns and villages of Jammu and Kashmir, in effect, pursuing the Workers' Charter of the Naya Kashmir programme. However, the Communists could not use the name, Naya Kashmir, because their betrayal of Sheikh Abdullah had discredited the programme itself.

In 1973, Sampat had an idea. He thought about organizing private school teachers who had no pension or gratuity. He decided to start with his old school, Tyndale Biscoe. The main branch was in Lal Chowk, right across from the trade union office.

Sampat strode into the staff room and told the teachers that he would help them organize themselves into a union. The headmaster, Satpal Razdan, and the teachers had heard of the trade union leader and were happy to accept his offer. The teachers made a charter of demands which included the right to pension, gratuity and the framing of proper service rules. The demands were submitted to the principal of the school, John Mead Ray, an Englishman. The principal refused to listen to their demands and the teachers started their strike. When the students arrived with their parents, they were sent home. John Ray closed the school down and refused to negotiate with the teachers. Sampat and his comrades surrounded the school building as well as John Ray's residence.

Then the union leaders held a press conference in which they announced that they would begin classes in the open and appealed to the parents to bring their children back to school.

John Ray thought he could mobilize the bureaucrats because twenty-five heads of department were all former students of Tyndale Biscoe School. But the parents supported the strike and the teachers began to conduct classes in the open.

When the police officers arrived, Sampat threatened to intensify the agitation. The Motor Garage Union brought two buses and they were parked close together so that their roofs could serve as a platform on which Sampat could stand and address the growing number of supporters.

I asked Sampat why the police did not stop the agitation. He said that a senior officer's father had been an approver in Bhagat Singh's trial and Sampat had threatened to expose his background. Also, the bureaucrats were sympathetic because they resented the Englishman's arrogance.

Sheikh Abdullah's wife, Akbar Jehan, was asked to intervene and finally John Ray had to agree to negotiate. However, he refused to do so with the trade union but consented to talk to the bureaucrats. The demands were accepted and the teachers went back to work happily.

The other private schools could not concede to the demands, however, mainly because they did not have access to the kind of funds Tyndale Biscoe had.

Sampat confessed that a section of the Muslim intelligentsia, who had resented the Christian missionaries' presence in the Valley, had supported the agitation. And it was this communal feeling that was, in a large measure, responsible for the success of the strike. The nine-day agitation had brought this latent feeling to the fore.

Sampat and his comrades knew that to counter the communal feeling and replace it with secular politics, they would have to strengthen their organization by ensuring it had roots going deep into even the remotest of the villages. If there was anything Sampat wanted passionately, it was to build an organization which could withstand communal politics and religious fundamentalism.

Sampat Prakash said the Hindu Right consistently carried out a propaganda accusing the union members of being Chinese agents, or Chini Nawaz. The RSS had tried to infiltrate into the Federation which is why they had to be on their guard against the saffron flag in Jammu.

And in the Valley, the threat of the green flag was ever present. The Jamaat-e-Islami had been working hard to spread their base in Kashmir.[17] They tried to cash in on the anger against the arrest of Sheikh Abdullah. During Bakshi's time they had opened madrassas and schools. Sampat remembered that they had stuck small posters with just one statement: 'Tajub hai ki aap ko namaaz ke liye wakht nahin' (It is surprising that you don't have time for namaaz).

The Jamaat-e-Islami cadres were present in the government departments, especially education, revenue, and public works. They used the mosques to spread their influence in remote villages and by the time Mir Qasim became chief minister, the Jamaat-e-Islami had a significant vote bank.

Mir Qasim admits in his autobiography, *My Life and Times*, that he had enlisted the services of the Jamaat-e-Islami to prevent Sheikh Abdullah's supporters from undermining the Congress. He even recognized the Jamaat-e-Islami as a legitimate political party in 1970–71 and they won five seats in the Legislative Assembly, while the Jana Sangh won three.

From that time onwards their presence could not be wished away. The Low Paid Government Servants Federation had to be constantly on their guard against infiltration by the Jamaat-e-Islami cadres.

It was not an easy task to build up the trade union because by now there were thirty-four government departments and each had its own unique problems. Besides, some problems were specific to geographical areas such as Doda,[18] Rajouri and Poonch, where the employees' physical hardships were much greater because of the mountainous terrain. The union managed to get them a special high altitude allowance.

I asked Sampat to describe some of the strikes that were organized in the 1970s. He said one of the most memorable was the strike of the safai karamcharis (cleaning staff) working in the municipalities of Srinagar and Jammu in September 1973. In Jammu, the cleaning staff was referred to as sweepers, considered as untouchables by Hindu society, and in Kashmir they were stigmatized by the Muslims and lived in a colony at the bottom of Hari Parbat. Sampat visited the homes of the sweepers, listened to their stories and studied their living conditions and motivated them to organize themselves into a union.

At the time the president of the municipality ministerial staff was Hriday Nath Wanchoo, and Ami Sheikh was the president of the municipality. Wanchoo was approximately ten years older than Sampat and had been working in the municipality for several years. He had founded a consumer society on a no-profit-no-loss basis and opened a school for the children of the poor. He was murdered by militants in December 1992.[19]

Sampat had watched the sweepers clean the toilets and sewage drains and that gave him the idea of demanding a special risk allowance for them. He organized them into an association and called for a strike. Even those sweepers who had permanent jobs were told to go on strike in solidarity and so were the members of the other associations.

In those days, many officers did not have flush toilets and depended on the safai karamcharis to clean them. The bureaucrats and police officers were personally affected and they threatened to crush the trade union. The majority of the safai karamcharis were women and many had babies. Sampat led the women and their children upstairs, directly into the august presence of the chief secretary, Sushital Banerjee. To the utter horror of the bureaucrat, the women deposited their babies and toddlers in his room and left.

Outside, black clouds had started gathering as if to help the striking employees. Sampat told them to block all the sewers so that they would overflow in the rain. The government dared not resort to a lathi charge or beat the women; their verbal threats to Sampat were of no avail. The sewers overflowed and the employees continued their strike.

The strike lasted nine days and ended in success with the cleaning staff receiving better pay and permanent jobs. Even more importantly, the women started to get maternity leave. The strike resulted in the safai karamcharis being committed supporters of the union.

The Department of Gardens and Parks had a big staff, mostly gardeners, whom Sampat described as 'the guardians of Kashmir's famed beauty'. They were responsible for planting seeds and growing the flowers in the nurseries before transplanting them into hundreds of gardens, big and small, all over the state. In autumn, when the leaves of the chinar trees turned from green to copper-red and fell on the ground, the gardeners swept them and heaped them in neat piles.

They worked for long hours, often in the rain or snow, without any shelter. The gardeners did not have any uniforms or regular working hours, and officers would frequently make them look after their private kitchen gardens, for which they were not paid.

The union helped the gardeners to organize themselves and formed a charter of demands for them. The gardeners marched with black flags from their gardens to Lal Chowk in support of their demands. The other associations also sent their members in solidarity. When they were threatened, Sampat used violent language. He told the officers that if they made any gardener work in his house he, Sampat, would cut off his limbs and throw them into the Dal Lake. Sampat said that such language worked every time because the bureaucrats behaved like feudal lords and had to be taught to respect the employees.

The gardeners' demands were fulfilled; they worked in shifts with an hour off for lunch, they were given uniforms and overtime, and most important of all, they were regularized. This association became the backbone of the Federation and the gardeners came whenever the movement needed their support.

Sampat goes on to tell the story of the Road Guards Association. It consisted of daily-wage earners who were called lal-topi coolies at the time.

These workers were treated very badly by the engineers and even junior engineers would use them as their personal servants, ordering them to buy vegetables from the market as well as do other household chores. For their labour, they were paid fifty paise a day, and their working and living conditions all over the state was appalling. They had heard of the government employees federation and it was they who made the first move. When they were told to meet at the Exhibition Ground, the trade union leaders were surprised to see that 200 'road coolies' had turned up, obviously sacrificing their wages for the day.

Sampat went to meet these men in their homes and was deeply moved by their stories. He met one of their leaders, Ghulam Ahmad Magray, whose father wept when he met Sampat. The father told Sampat that his daughter had finished her BA and was engaged to an engineer, but the marriage had been called off when the groom's family discovered that the father of the bride was a road coolie who was obliged to wear a red cap. Sampat Prakash declared that from then onwards the 'red topiwalas' would be called road guards; he threatened that if he heard anyone call them coolies he would cut their throats.

When I looked a little alarmed, Sampat Prakash reassured me once again that though he always used violent language, no violent incident was allowed to take place; he and the other leaders were very meticulous about instilling strict discipline in the members of the union.

The road guards' strike lasted for a week in October 1973 but they continued to agitate for their demands. In consequence, by 1978, they were regularized, declared to be Class IV employees and entitled to gratuity, pension and, if the employee died while in service, his son was given his job.

The trade union had to organize strikes just to get the government to issue uniforms, raincoats, umbrellas and gumboots to the poorest staff. They also tried to get the government employees classified according to the nature of their work and not be divided into gazetted and non-gazetted or Class I to Class IV which smacked of feudalism.

In the summer of 1973, Sampat Prakash was in Pahalgam for a break. There he noticed the ponywallas standing in the rain, waiting for people to hire them. He talked to them and discovered that most of them came to Pahalgam from distant villages during the tourist season; they took tourists for rides and pilgrims to holy places such as the Amarnath cave in Kashmir or Vaishno Devi in Jammu. But while they waited, they had no shelter and their wages were not fixed.

Sampat gathered the ponywallas and took them straight into the deputy commissioner's office where the ponies and their owners sat around till the officer agreed to fix their wages. The association of the ponywallas included members from all the tourist places—Gulmarg, Sonamarg and Anantnag.

The achievements of the trade union inspired every section of the government employees. Many participated in their marches, rallies and attended their meetings. For instance, there was an employee by the name of Syed Nassarullah who had joined the High Court as a stenographer. He came from a large family of seven brothers and two sisters, and their father was a teacher in the Islamia School.

Nassarullah had got the job of a stenographer but there were no grades and no chance for any promotion. He would retire as a stenographer. The young employee had attended the union meetings and by 1977 he had the confidence to form an association called the Jammu and Kashmir Judicial Employees Welfare Association. The association was not affiliated to the Low Paid Government Servants Federation, however its leaders had helped him form his association.

It was during this time that the report of the Third Pay Commission came out, but it did not have anything to offer the employees of the judicial services. Nassarullah is now sixty years old, but when he describes the events of those days he begins to look like a young activist. He said that his friends and he had organized a one-day strike which covered all the ninety-two courts across Jammu, Kashmir and Ladakh. Then they had a three-day strike and later a week-long agitation.

Nassarullah gave me a blow-by-blow account of their agitation, aware that he was talking to a lawyer. He said they won a big victory when Farooq Abdullah created 154 posts and provided avenues for promotion. Nassarullah continued to tell me details of other struggles in which the association had successfully exposed corruption in the judiciary; filed a writ petition and in 1996, when the Central government set up the first National Judicial Pay Commission, Nassarullah and his friends made sure that the concerns of the subordinate judiciary and the staff were also addressed.

'I retired as an administrative officer of gazzetted rank in 2007.' He looked at me, brimming with pride. He said that not a single member of their association, except for one, joined the militancy. He added in a sombre tone, 'The employees would vote for staying with India but till the day we Kashmiris can decide for ourselves, we consider Kashmir a disputed territory.'

I asked Nassarullah the one question that I have asked everyone I interviewed: 'What has been the biggest achievement of the trade union movement?'

He said there were two achievements. The first was that the living and working conditions of more than four million government employees, including teachers, clerks and workers in public sector units, improved substantially.

The second was that the employees had learnt to live with dignity. Within a decade of their work they had enough political clout that even if a judge mistreated any employee, the association could get him dismissed from service. When Mohammad Iqbal, a munsif (judge) at Kulgam, kicked an employee in July 1974, the union took up the issue. They called a strike. The chief justice of the Jammu and Kashmir High Court came to meet them at Kulgam and had to concede to the demand that the munsif be dismissed.

A decade earlier, the employees had feared to speak out in front of the bureaucrats, but now they challenged every act of humiliation and indignity.

I asked them whether the government employees in Ladakh were also involved in the agitations. Sampat replied, of course they were. But you have not told me about them, I complained. He picked up his diary and read out the names of the comrades who were sent by the party to organize the strikes in Ladakh. The most senior person in the group was Pushkar Nath Peer, who worked as an accountant in the finance department.

The first strike in Ladakh lasted for two days in February 1972. Two years later, the Ladakhi employees had chosen leaders from their own midst because they did not want to be dominated by the Kashmiris. Attaullah, a Ladakhi Muslim and the flock master in the animal husbandry department, and Sonam Norbu, a Ladakhi Buddhist working in the medical department, became the leaders.[20] Sampat reeled off more names and I told him that I was not writing a party pamphlet where I could annex all these names and dates of strikes. I needed stories. 'But you must mention M.D. Khan and

Syeda Banood from Kargil district,' Sampat persisted. He was again making sure that all communities were represented in my book. It was his way of underlining the contribution of the trade union to Kashmiriyat.

Before leaving, I asked Ghulam Qader Bhat what he thought was the most important contribution of the trade union movement. He said it resulted in substantially improving the conditions of the employees. He showed me photographs of himself addressing a meeting. The black-and-white photograph captured the atmosphere of the times when people believed that they could change the world through acts of self-sacrifice and dedication.

Ghualm Qader turned to me and said: 'In those days trade union work was ibadat (worship). Now the employees have been corrupted and think of their rights but not their responsibilities.'

Sampat intervened: 'In those days they got a salary of just Rs 25, now they get Rs 14,000 and have become middle-class with aspirations of that class.' The two leaders agreed that the period between 1964 and 1974 was the golden era of the trade union movement.

DARK SIDE OF THE MOON
(1974–84)

On New Year day of 2009, I was driving towards Shopian to interview Gulam Mohiudin Punoo, another veteran of the Jammu and Kashmir Low Paid Government Servants Federation. On the way we passed the remains of what once must have been mansions, surrounded by gardens. Now all that remained was the charred and burnt remnants which looked incongruous in the midst of all the natural beauty. Sampat, who was sitting in the car billowing smoke from his cigarette, informed me that these were the homes of Kashmiri Pandits.

The houses were in village Hali, once the homes of the educated and influential Kashmiri Pandits. They belonged to judges of the Jammu and Kashmir High Court, doctors and surgeons. Sampat said the owners had intentionally kept them in this state as a reminder of the injustice done to their community. Every year, the owners returned to perform special prayers at this site.

Punoo greeted us with enthusiasm. He was excited that a book was being written on the history of the trade union. He was the only one who could match exact dates to the agitations and strikes in the various departments. He gave me a copy of an article he had written, entitled 'The State Employees' Movement in Jammu and Kashmir' published in the *Employees' Forum*'s Special Issue in 1989. In the article, he has given a brief description of the thirty-six government departments and corporations affiliated with the Low Paid Government Servants Federation.

Punoo brought out dozens of files filled with the Federation's correspondence, petitions and pamphlets. Sampat looked at them and exclaimed: 'Oh so that is where all our files disappeared!'

Punoo had kept them safely during the days when the other leaders were all in jail during the Emergency in 1975. During those days the police had raided the homes of all the leaders and it was almost a miracle that Punoo had saved this historical evidence of the years of struggles. But he was reluctant to part with his treasure even for a few days. He insisted that I tell him what I want.

I could see Punoo had a wily intelligence which must have served him well during the Emergency. Sampat was obviously angry that Punoo had not informed him that he had the files, but then knowing Sampat's lifestyle, I am sure they would not have been preserved this well. I ignored the tension between the two men and asked Punoo about his involvement in the trade union movement.

Punoo was born in 1942 in Hergam Village. After graduation, he joined the Horticulture Department in 1964. He had been motivated by P.N. Kaul, a senior Communist leader, to join the union. Kaul was a stenographer in the Secretariat and the secretary of the Civil Secretariat Non-Gazetted Employees Union and in charge of the Kashmiri province. Punoo said that his mentor was the first man to get arrested during the strike in December 1967. Punoo remembered with pride that he had been beaten up during that strike and also remembered the name of the police officer who beat him—Inspector General of Police, D.N. Kaul.

A woman entered the room with tea. Punoo introduced me to his wife, Rahat Bano. She did not have the usual Kashmiri warmth; she appeared angry and as she sat down to pour the tea, she looked at me and said: 'You should take my interview. You should know how much I have suffered because of this man.' Her face was contorted with years of pain and hurt. Rahat Bano was a retired government school teacher.

I pushed the tape recorder towards her and asked her to tell me her story. Rahat Bano was married when she was barely nineteen years old and from then onwards she taught in single-teacher schools where there were no facilities, except one mat on the floor for the children to sit on. There was no transport either and she would have to walk to the school and back, reaching home in the evening, after which she would have to cook for her children. She also looked after the family orchard and suffered criticism from her in-laws who even tried to make Punoo divorce her.

'He never gave me one paisa; I brought up our children by myself. I had to cook for them, help them with their homework and provide for them.'

The only time her voice softened a little was when she proudly told me that her daughter, Shireen, was a government teacher, her son, Hilal, a PhD in dairy technology, and the other son, Abdul Rauf, an employee in the horticulture department.

Rahat Bano bitterly complained that her husband spent all his wages on the union, but she did not even know what a trade union was since he never took her to Srinagar. Sampat intervened to ask her: 'But your salary did go up, didn't it? When you started you got Rs 250 and when you retired your salary was Rs 13,000. Is that not an achievement?'

But Rahat Bano refused to concede that the trade union had done her any good; all she knew was that it had ruined her family life and put an almost unbearable burden on her young shoulders for which she could never forgive her husband.

I noticed that Punoo had remained silent all along. He looked at me and without emotion admitted that all his wife's charges against him were correct. He did spend all his money on trade union activities and never gave any to his family, and many times when he had to live underground, he could not even visit them. It was also true that his parents harassed her.

Sampat interjected to say that he used to take his wife and children for holidays, but Punoo cut him short with a curt: 'Your wife did not have to face the kind of problems that my wife had to face. There is no comparison.' Sampat had earlier told me that he had beaten Punoo when he said he was going to divorce his wife. Punoo obviously bore a grudge, or unpleasant memories had come in the way of the excitement of writing the history of the trade union.

Rahat Bano picked up the cups. As she took away the tray, I promised that I would include her story in my book. She did not bother to respond.

When I asked Punoo to tell me about his most memorable days while working for the trade union, he immediately replied: 'During the Emergency.'

Punoo was referring to the national Emergency imposed by the Indian prime minister Indira Gandhi in 1975.[1] I knew of the human rights violations that took place in the country during those days; the arbitrary arrests, censorship and even torture of student leaders. But I had no idea what had happened in Kashmir at that time. Sampat and Punoo narrated the story.

———

Soon after the elections in 1972, Mir Qasim contacted Sheikh Abdullah who was still in jail. Mir Qasim asked whether he was willing to begin talks with the Indian government. The Sheikh was angry at first, but he must have felt demoralized after the resounding defeat of Pakistan and the creation of Bangladesh. India and Pakistan had signed the Simla Agreement[2] in which they agreed to treat the conflict in Kashmir as a bilateral matter. The Agreement took Kashmir away from the international gaze. Sheikh Abdullah realized that the demand for a plebiscite would not be conceded and there was no hope of successfully challenging the Accession to India. Therefore, it would be best to negotiate for autonomy.

On 12 June 1972, Sheikh Abdullah met Indira Gandhi; thereafter, she appointed G. Parthasarthy, who was then the vice chancellor of Jawaharlal Nehru University, to negotiate with the Sheikh.

On 13 November 1974, the Kashmir Accord was signed between Mohammad Afzal Beg, representing Sheikh Abdullah, and G. Parthasarthy, on behalf of the government of India. According to this Agreement, popularly called the Indira-Sheikh Accord, Kashmir was recognized as a constituent unit of the Union of India; the Plebiscite Front was dissolved. Mir Qasim stepped down from the post of chief minister and Sheikh Abdullah was sworn in as the chief minister on 25 February 1975, but with the rest of the Congress government in place. The Sheikh was not even allowed ministers of his choice.

In Pakistan, Bhutto denounced the Accord as a sell out and called Sheikh Abdullah a traitor. Bhutto called for a strike on 28 February 1975, to protest against the Accord. On 12 March 1975, China denounced the Accord as a violation of the resolutions by the UN General Assembly. In Kashmir, Maulvi Farouq decried the Accord, and in Jammu, Hindu nationalists condemned it because it still recognized the validity of Article 370 (even though in a diluted form).[3]

Punoo, like the other members of the trade union and thousands of Kashmiri nationalists, were angry with Sheikh Abdullah, the man they had called Sher-e-Kashmir, the Lion of Kashmir. It was a betrayal of the dreams of all those Kashmiris who had suffered imprisonment and sacrificed their lives in the hope of seeing Kashmir as an independent country.

People felt that the Sheikh had surrendered the plebiscite slogan for the sake of power; that he had signed the Accord under tremendous pressure from his family to pave the way for family rule in Kashmir.

Some people even felt it would have been better if the Sheikh had died in jail, without betraying his people's dream of Kashmir's independence. If that had been so, his tomb would have been a ziyarat or a place of pilgrimage in the Sufi tradition. Now he would go down in history as a traitor. His tomb, to this day, is guarded by the Indian Army.

May Day of 1975 was especially significant in the history of the trade union. This time the union did not focus on its usual issues of dearness allowance or wages or the service conditions of the government employees. Instead, they organized rallies to condemn the Accord by which Sheikh Abdullah had been released from jail and had been sworn in as the chief minister of the state of Jammu and Kashmir.

The May Day rally was successful. Sampat Prakash recited the speech he had made on that occasion. It was a long speech in which he said that the Accord was not signed by the man who was worshipped as Sher-e-Kashmir, but by a Paper Tiger, and he then went on to analyze the Accord and expose the fact that it was indeed a betrayal of the Kashmiri people's aspirations for independence. His political analysis was full of historical references and buttressed by quotes from poems.

Even as I heard Sampat, sitting in my drawing room in Delhi, I felt the depth of emotion and the clear political analysis come through, despite the innumerable quotes, hyperbole and rhetoric.

Sheikh Abdullah had received reports of the rally and how Sampat Prakash had criticized him in public. He did not take kindly to such criticism. He did not tolerate dissent. Therefore, when Prime Minister Indira Gandhi imposed the Emergency on 25 June 1975, Sheikh Abdullah extended it to his state. He then had warrants issued against the trade union leaders. The Sheikh also targeted leaders of the Jamaat-e-Islami and the Jana Sangh who were arrested and detained in jails in Jammu and Kashmir.

Punoo and the other trade union leaders went underground, but continued their activities by organizing smaller meetings and distributing pamphlets. But, on 26 March 1976, Punoo and more than twenty other leaders were arrested under the infamous Defence of India Rules.[4] Eventually, the number of arrested trade union leaders went up to 103. The leaders had been singled out not only for their opposition to the Accord but also because their leader, Sampat Prakash, was still associated with the Naxalites.

Finally, Punoo and the other union leaders were released after four months because of the efforts of their lawyer, Tika Lal Taploo. Taploo was shot dead by militants in September 1989.

On the day the Emergency was announced, Sampat Prakash was not at home; he had slept at the house of a comrade in the downtown area of Srinagar. He had a cup of noon chai, salted tea, and left for a meeting at his Federation office at Lal Chowk. He had not read the newspapers or heard the news of the Emergency on the radio.

At Lal Chowk, he saw the deputy superintendent of police, Ratinder Koul. The man had studied in Allahabad and had become a Communist there. On his return to Kashmir, he had joined the Democratic National Conference and Sampat knew him from those days. The policeman greeted Sampat and extended his hand in a handshake. Koul's was a firm handshake, maybe a little too firm. When the police officer did not let go of his hand, Sampat's sixth sense was alerted.

Without letting the policeman know that he suspected anything was amiss, Sampat asked him whether he would like a paan. The policeman knew that Sampat bought a paan from Chaurasia Paanwala every day and had no reason to believe that this was a ruse. Sampat crossed the road and went to the paan shop and under the very eyes of the policeman, escaped through a narrow by-lane he knew well.

The policeman gave chase but luckily a bus came between them and Sampat managed to lose him. Sampat ran along the embankment of the Jhelum River and reached Zero Bridge, where he jumped into a taxi. Sampat asked the taxi driver whether the vehicle had enough petrol for a long journey. When the driver said there was, Sampat told him to drive to Jammu.

Just before the Banihal Tunnel, the driver insisted on taking a break to have a quick lunch. Sampat asked him to hurry and while the driver was eating, he bought newspapers. From them he learnt that more than a hundred of the union leaders had been arrested. In those days there were no mobiles and it was not easy to find a public phone booth.

At Udhampur, Sampat went to the house of his trusted friend, a doctor. The friend immediately exclaimed: 'You were not arrested?'

From the doctor's house, Sampat contacted his wife, Dura, and told her to deposit some money with a businessman in Jammu. From Dura he learnt that the police had raided their home, thrown out all their belongings and locked up the house. This procedure is called khurki zabti, or seizure of goods by the police to pressurize the person into surrendering to save his family. But Sampat was not going to give himself up and his wife was keenly aware of this. She took their two young sons and shifted to her sister's place. This was just an illustration of how authoritarian and revengeful Sheikh Abdullah could be.

When Afzal Beg learnt about the plight of Sampat's family he was angry with the Sheikh for being so vindictive. He told Sheikh Abdullah that even if he had wanted to arrest the trade union leader, he should have at least allowed Sampat's family to return to their home. He reminded the Sheikh that Sampat, too, had been imprisoned for the cause of Kashmir. Later, when Dura told him she was back home with the children, Sampat was relieved that his family was safe.

Sampat continued his journey in the taxi till he crossed the border into Punjab, stopping only at Jammu to collect the money his wife had left at the businessman's shop. Sampat noticed that the businessman had added to the amount.

Even at the railway station at Pathankot, Sampat knew that it would not be safe to buy a ticket in his name so he travelled without reservation and reached New Delhi. From the station he went straight to the Vithalbhai Patel House where the political leaders had their homes. Sampat was glad to find that the trade union leaders of the All India Trade Union Congress (AITUC), affiliated to the Communist Party of India, and the trade union leaders of the Centre of Indian Trade Unions (CITU), affiliated to the CPI(M), had not been arrested. In any case, the CPI was supporting the Congress and had no objection to the proclamation of the Emergency.

Sampat was not safe in Delhi, so he travelled under an alias to Madras,[5] where the Emergency didn't apply. He knew that the Emergency was not going to be lifted any time soon and, therefore, decided to depend upon his comrades to look after him while he made plans for the future.

From the information he was able to gather, he found that eighty of his trade union comrades had been arrested and were still in jail. This meant that the associations and unions were now bereft of leaders, and the families of the arrested would be without any means of survival.

Sampat needed to think, and work out a strategy on how the union was to function in this new situation. Sitting in Madras he made meticulous plans. He remembered Dasarath Deb from Tripura who had been in jail with him in 1968. He had told Sampat that all the activities could continue even while one was underground, and Sampat intended to do just that, in addition to preparing the members to face the difficult days ahead.

Before going back to the Valley, he stopped over in Delhi and met his old comrades, including Sethi, who was underground as well. Sampat shared his ideas and plans with them. He also met another comrade, Abdul Majid Khan, who said that he would look after three districts in Jammu.

Sampat returned to Jammu and met Tilak Raj, the president of the Jammu province of the State Motor Garage Association. It was one of the oldest unions and had been set up before Sampat joined the movement. The Motor Garage Association supplied cars to all the ministers and senior government officers, and Sampat felt that travelling by government cars would offer protection. The president of the association was in jail, so he contacted the other members without revealing his plan; they could be trusted but were not disciplined enough to not talk loosely.

Sampat insisted on travelling in the car usually used by the superintendent of police or the deputy commissioner. The driver, Munawar Khan, took the day off on the excuse that the car had developed some trouble and another car and driver were sent to the superintendent of police that day. The car was released the moment Sampat reached the State Motor Garage Department in Srinagar.

In Srinagar, Sampat contacted his old friend Jawaharlal Dhar in Rainawari. Dhar was the general manager of the Travel Corporation of India, and in that capacity had contacts with the owners of houseboats and carpet magnets. From them he raised money for the trade union leader and also arranged for his stay in houseboats so that he would be safe from the police.

Another comrade, Ghulam Mohammad, president of the Shikarawalas' Union, organized the transport while Sampat was in his hideout. In any case the owner of the houseboat was Mohammad Yusuf Chapri,[6] his friend from college days. Yusuf used to entertain Sampat and his comrades; although he himself never drank, Yusuf would provide his friends with expensive alcohol, mostly bottles left behind by visiting tourists.

Yusuf regaled us with stories of those days when I went to interview him. However, he said that his own story was more interesting than Sampat's. He suggested that I write a book on him instead, and in return, he would let me stay in one of his houseboats.

I urged him to tell me his story which did turn out to be quite remarkable. Yusuf Chapri's father and grandfather were boatmen and guides for foreign adventurers such as Francis Younghusband and Aurel Stein, the man who translated the *Rajatarangini*, and other explorers who came to study the birds, butterflies and flowers of Kashmir. Yusuf insisted that since the Englishmen were not allowed to buy land in Kashmir, they, with the help of his family, came up with the idea of houseboats.[7]

Yusuf said that his father and brothers supported Sheikh Abdullah till the time he turned the Muslim Conference into the National Conference. His elder mother,[8] who was a very religious person, used to deliver speeches in Persian alongside the Sheikh. Yusuf claims that his father introduced Akbar Jehan to Sheikh Abdullah, and that is how they got married.

Yusuf apologized for not serving us a wazwan[9] but I told him that I could not do justice to the feast because I could no longer eat like I used to. Over a sumptuous meal, he told me that his best houseboat is called Neil Armstrong, after the first man who landed on the moon. He had written a letter to Neil Armstong, sent presents to the astronaut and invited him to Kashmir. Then one day, on 20 July 1989, the US issued a stamp in honour of the twentieth anniversary of the lunar landing.

Chapri's prized possession is a letter he received from the postmaster general of the US, Anthony M. Frank: 'Dear Mr Chapri. Today I had the unusual opportunity to dedicate a stamp in honour of the 20th anniversary of the Lunar Landing. During that ceremony, at which President Bush spoke, I had the opportunity to get the autograph of all the three astronauts, including Neil Armstrong. While Mr Armstrong does not give autographs, I told him the story of your houseboat, and he broke his rule in order to sign the enclosed program.'[10]

'It was a proud moment not only for me but for every Kashmiri,' Chapri said and claimed to be the first Kashmiri to have booked land on the moon for a sum of Rs 140,000. But since he found out that there was no water on the moon, he had lost some of his enthusiasm because as a Muslim he needed water for wuzu (ablutions before offering namaaz).

We had a good laugh. Then Chapri became serious and reeled off the names of the Kashmiri Pandits who have inspired him, such as Nandlal Bakaya who taught him mountaineering when he was in Tyndale Biscoe School, and Gunjoo, who later worked with the *National Geographical Magazine*. I could not help but wonder whether he genuinely held his Kashmiri Pandit teachers in real respect or if there was a political subtext to convey his 'secular' credentials to me.

I realized that Chapri's friendship with Sampat Prakash was not based on shared ideas or ideologies; he was not inspired by the Soviet Union or Communism. Chapri's father remained a staunch supporter of the Muslim Conference and was jailed several times. Yusuf said his father and brother were the unsung heroes of Kashmir. Yusuf described himself as a Sufi.

Yusuf Chapri described his friend Sampat Prakash as 'a good

Pandit'. Chapri said there have been Kashmiri Pandits who really loved Kashmir and worked for its independence such as Raghunath Vaishnavi, who spent seventeen years in jail for supporting the cause of Kashmir. He did not want Kashmir to join either India or Pakistan. He was a follower of M.N. Roy and supported the Dixon Plan.[11] For Chapri, an independent Kashmir would include Jammu and Ladakh, and he told me that he did not hate India because 'there are many Muslims there'.

Yusuf presented Sampat with a large bottle of Kashmiri masala which his wife had prepared especially for him. He apologized for her not joining us. I asked him why he had affection for Sampat Prakash and his Communist comrades. His reply was straight from his heart: 'They are good people, they help people so I help them. Sampat has done a lot for the people. Now he is in with the Hurriyat.'

I asked Yusuf whom he supported. He has dedicated his life to saving the environment. He asked, if the Dal Lake dried up and the mountains vanished, what was the point of fighting for the independence of Kashmir?

Yusuf asked permission to recite Iqbal and settled down to sing the poem which has two lines that are haunting:

Aisa sukun dhundta hoon
Jis per takdeer bhi fida ho jayay
(I am looking for such a peace
That even fate would be enamoured with)

When we returned from Chapri's home to my hotel room, we met Ashwini Dhar, Jawaharlal Dhar's son. He had come with Sampat and was keen to know who I had interviewed. But when I mentioned Chapri, he remained silent. Sampat told me how Chapri had betrayed Jawaharlal Dhar and even now there was a dispute over the land that was pending in court and Ashwini had to pursue it. Sampat changed the subject and continued his story...

After a while Sampat got tired of living in houseboats and shifted to a beautiful guest house where Nehru had once stayed in Chashmashahi, one of the fabled Mughal gardens. Sampat was well looked after by both the members of tourism association and the gardeners whom he had unionized.

Sampat did not want his address known and continued to meet the union members in a shikara rowed by one of Yusuf's nephews. One of his trusted lieutenants would contact the heads in each department and take them to meet their leader who would be waiting in the shikara drifting on the waters of the Dal Lake. In this way, Sampat kept the location of his residence a secret. He said he was not afraid of informers amongst his trade union members, but it was possible that the excitement of seeing their leader would lead them to talk, alerting the ever-vigilant CID.

Sampat spoke to union members of the associations in each department and discussed the problem of raising money for the families of his jailed comrades. He had contacted twenty to twenty-five members of different associations and they quickly started collecting enough money to ensure that the families received half the wages every month. Apart from organizing financial support, Sampat and the other union leaders also continued the opposition against the many measures that Sheikh Abdullah had taken.

The Sheikh had wanted to ensure that his state was not over-dependent on the Centre, thus, he opposed the continued subsidy on rations that had been introduced by Bakshi Ghulam Mohammad as a part of his strategy to integrate Kashmir and make people more reliant on India. The Sheikh, on the other hand, wanted to introduce the concept of landed cost of ration instead of subsidized rations to reduce dependency on India. However, the removal of the subsidy would have meant a burden on the poor and Sampat decided to start an agitation against the move. The trade union leaders were able to print their pamphlets and posters in the Government Press where the union was strong and looked after by Nisar Ali Mir.

When the posters and pamphlets came to the notice of the

Sheikh, he was very angry. He had never taken kindly to dissent and criticism. Now he was furious that the trade union leader had managed to evade the police for so many months. But for the moment, Sampat continued with his activities; it would be several more weeks before he would be caught.

Sampat wrote letters to the individual families of his union leaders who were still languishing in jail, asking them to be strong and thanking them for their support. Each letter was delivered by union members and in this way Sampat made personal contact without actually meeting the families.

The next step was to launch a movement for the release of the jailed leaders. He organized meetings in every district as well as a day-long hunger strike, even in Srinagar. The wives and children of the jailed comrades came and shouted slogans. The press covered these events. By now the newspapers had started speculating that Sampat Prakash had returned and was hiding in Srinagar; thus, it was time for him to move to Anantnag. There he stayed at the guest house run by the power department union which allowed him to continue organizing the union.

By this time winter was setting in. In November, the Secretariat shifted to Jammu,[12] and with it went the ministers, bureaucrats and other state employees. During this period, their official residences were looked after by their staff, who were all government servants and members of the Low Paid Government Servants Federation.

As a result, Sampat could now live in the vacant, spacious mansions of ministers and bureaucrats, such as Devi Das Thakur, the deputy chief minister; Sonam Norbu, the works minister from Ladakh; and Mirza Mohammad Afzal Beg, the revenue minister. Sampat chuckled with glee as he remembered the luxury of living in the official residences of top bureaucrats.

Meanwhile, Sampat had started collecting Sheikh Abdullah's speeches. He wanted to make a comparison between what he was saying now and what he had promised only a decade ago. He was preparing for a big meeting in which he would expose the Sheikh's doublespeak. But before that could happen, he went to every district to talk to the employees.

On 25 December 1976, Comrade Punoo, along with Comrade Ghulam Rasool Mir, had organized a meeting for their leader at Visu village in Anantnag.

Punoo had been having a very difficult time since he had been released from jail. He had continued with trade union activites, even though he knew that the police were looking for him. He could not sleep in his home and had to move around continuously from village to village.

Punoo was present when Sampat addressed the meeting that night. After the speech, they made a collection for the families of their arrested comrades. Sampat, Punoo and Ghulam Rasool slept in the village while it snowed all night. The next morning, the three of them walked across the snow-covered fields to the next village, Qazigund. Sampat kept slipping in the snow so they decided that it would be better if he took a bus. Punoo put his two comrades on the bus while he walked to another village.

As was usual during their underground days, the two trade union leaders did not sit together. Sampat sat in front while Ghulam Rasool sat at the back because he was carrying the documents. This was a necessary precaution; in case the leader was arrested, the incriminating documents would not be found on him.

Sampat had grown a long beard. He wore a suit, a Karakul hat and a shawl folded neatly over his shoulder, and spectacles—he looked every bit like a Muslim businessman. On the front seat, next to the window, there was another man who was dressed in a similar fashion. At the next stop, the man got down from the bus, carrying a large leather bag. Assuming the man had disembarked, Sampat occupied his window seat. But the man had got down to urinate and when he returned, he did not ask Sampat to vacate his seat. Sampat found this odd but did not give it another thought. A few minutes later, when Sampat saw a police car following their bus, he realized that the businessman, too, had seen the police.

Soon after, the police boarded the bus and told Sampat to disembark. They were chasing a charas smuggler and had mistaken Sampat for the businessman who was still on the bus. The police officer looked at Sampat and recognized the trade union leader by his piercing eyes. He exclaimed with delight, 'Sampat, it is you! I will get a promotion and you will get some rest from your activities.'

The police officer was none other than Ali Mohammad Watali,[13] and he knew that Communist leaders never travelled alone so he asked where his companion was. Sampat did some quick thinking and pulled up a passenger with a dirty bag, telling the befuddled man: 'Don't worry, don't get scared.'

The police put both the men into the car and drove off. On the way, Sampat told them that the other man was just an innocent passenger and that he should be allowed to go. The police stopped the car and virtually threw the man out. Ghulam Rasool Mir was thus able to get away safely with the diaries with valuable addresses and other documents.

Sampat was taken to the interrogation centre Number 16 at Gupkar in Srinagar. The chief interrogator there was a Kashmiri Pandit. Sampat asked Watali to get him a box of Gold Flake cigarettes and took the money out his pocket. Watali laughed. He said the police had been told to look out for anyone buying several boxes of Gold Flakes.

On the first day, Sampat was made to take off his warm clothes and shoes but was allowed to wear his pants and shirt. He was kept like that in the bitter cold and then they handcuffed him for the night. A young boy, Jumma, was put in charge. The boy was a member of Sampat's union and offered to buy him a cigarette and also brought a cup of hot tea for the trade union leader. Late at night, when it was safe, the boy took off the handcuffs and allowed Sampat to sleep and to raise his feet. But before dawn broke, Sampat was in handcuffs again.

In the morning, the officer was polite and allowed Sampat to wear his coat. The prisoner and the officer sat across a table. The interrogator wanted Sampat to tell him the names of the people he had stayed with during the months when he was underground, and what transport he had used. Sampat said he would embrace death rather than reveal the names of those who had protected him. As for the transport, if he revealed the facts, then officers would be implicated since he had been using their cars. He had used the car of the chief secretary six times, besides the official cars of senior police officers. Sampat said he had stayed at the homes of officers and ministers. However, he did not disclose the names of the bureaucrats or his own trade union members. Following this, he was also interrogated by officers from central intelligence agencies.

There was pride in Sampat's voice when he said he gave no names and no information despite the intense interrogation. Then he paused and he looked at me. 'But if I had been tortured, I do not know how far I would have held out,' he said. In hindsight, Sampat felt that the Kashmiri police were sympathetic with him and that saved him from torture.

After he had been at the interrogation centre for a few days, a police officer told him that Maqbool Butt, the legendary Kashmiri nationalist, was also detained there. The officer asked Sampat whether he would like to meet Maqbool Butt.

Sampat was very excited at the prospect of meeting Maqbool Butt. While narrating the story about their meeting, he said that Butt was at least ten years older than him. In fact, Maqbool, who was born on 18 February 1938, was just a year older. But in Sampat's eyes, his hero seemed much more politically mature and his knowledge of Kashmir was much deeper, which was why he assumed that he must be older. It was Maqbool Butt's sharp intelligence that impressed Sampat the most.

—

Maqbool Butt was born into a peasant family in Trehgam village in Kupwara district. His father was called Ghulam Qadar Butt; Maqbool's mother died when he was an eleven-year-old schoolboy.

Not much is known about his early life except that his political ideas were shaped by his experience of living in a village where the peasants were treated like slaves. Maqbool Butt described the terrible conditions he witnessed around 1945 when he was a child, in a letter to Azra, the daughter of a friend, Ghulam Mohammad Mir, who was in Lahore jail with him.

The letter was written on 12 April 1972:

> This jagirdari system existed in our country during the Dogra rule too. The poor peasants had to do all the hard work but the landowner would take all the produce. The landowner in our area was called Divan, whom we had seldom seen. There were his agents called kardaar, whose job it was to collect grain and fruits, etc. once produced by the farmers. The year I am talking about had poor crops due to bad weather. This left the farming families with very little to give to the Divan. Having given away all the produce it did not mount up to the usual season's quantity, which brought the whole area under the wrath of his agents. They started a series of crackdowns on the houses and stores of the poor peasants and many were whipped. When it did not produce results, the Divan himself came to our village in a motorcade. This was the first time ever a motorcade came to our village. We were all amazed to see it. All the farmers in our village got together and pleaded before him for concession. They told him in detail the reasons for the low harvest but he did not believe them. He insisted upon having his usual share of the crops even if it meant that the children of the peasants had to starve to death. He also expressed his anger towards his agents and strictly instructed them to extract the full share. These agents knew very well that the peasants were left with nothing to be given to the Divan. But had no courage to argue with their master. As the jagirdar went to his car after giving instructions all the children of the village were told to lie down on the road in front of the car by their elders. The kardaar was also part of this plan. Hundreds of village children lay down in front of the jagirdar's car and pleaded for concession and to

write off the extra share or drive over them. I was one of those children and remember to this day the fear and chaos that ruled us. Everyone, young and old, was in tears. They knew that if jagirdar left without giving concessions their lives would be made hell. Eventually, the jagirdar agreed to some amendments to his final decision.[14]

At school in Maqbool's time it was usual for rich parents and their children to sit separately from their not so well off counterparts. Maqbool Butt, who had done very well academically, challenged this practice and insisted that all the children and parents should sit together without distinction.[15]

Sampat Prakash did not know these aspects of Maqbool's life, but he had heard about the daring escape Butt and his comrades had made from Srinagar jail after being sentenced to death in August 1968. In his defence, Maqbool Butt denied all charges; he told the court that he had indeed crossed the Ceasefire Line but then he had merely entered his own country and surely it was not necessary to obtain a permit for moving around in one's own country.

The court found him guilty and passed the death sentence. On hearing the sentence he told the judge, Neelkanth Ganjoo:[16]

'Judge Saab abhi wo rasee nahee bani jo Maqbool Butt ko phansi de sakey' (the rope has not yet been made that can hang Maqbool Butt). If the Indian authorities of occupation think that by hanging me they can crush the Kashmir struggle they are mistaken. The struggle actually will start after my hanging.

A few months after being sentenced to death, Maqbool Butt and his comrades dug a tunnel and made their escape from Srinagar prison in December 1968. They walked back to Pakistan-administered Kashmir, but once they crossed into Pakistan, they were detained and interrogated for three months in Muzaffarabad.

According to Sampat, such an escape would not have been possible without the help of the jail authorities who must have had been sympathetic to the cause of the Kashmiri revolutionaries.

Maqbool Butt was arrested several times, both in India and in Pakistan. He was accused of being an agent of India and of Pakistan. On one occasion, Maqbool Butt wanted to highlight the Kashmir issue internationally and masterminded the idea of hijacking an Indian Airlines plane on 30 January 1971, en route from Srinagar to Jammu and brought the plane to Lahore, Pakistan. At first the hijackers were treated as heroes, but later Butt and the others were arrested and put in jail on suspicion that they had carried out the hijacking on the instigation of Indian intelligence agencies.[17]

Those Kashmiri nationalists who did not want Kashmir to be a part of either India or Pakistan often found themselves in this position. In a letter written to Azra, he explained the difference between India and Pakistan and their attitudes towards the Kashmiri cause:

> You have also written that Kashmiris have sacrificed their lives for Pakistan but Pakistan brands them as 'agents'. Here, your views are slightly misplaced. It is not Pakistan that accuses Kashmiris of spying but the ruling traitors of this country. It is the same bunch of rulers who has denied the peoples of this country freedom and democracy and eventually disintegrated it. Indeed, the role these bunch of traitors have played has been far worse than spies. That is why they brand all patriotic (Kashmiris) and friends of (our) people as foreign agents or spies. These rulers who committed crimes against their own people and called authentic leaders as 'agents', accuse us (Kashmiris) of spying but we should not get angry. As for the actual Pakistan, the people of this country are concerned they will accept the truth when it is brought before them. The sentence given to us is not the (work of) real Pakistanis. The cruel (men) of ruling (class) who open fire on their own people are responsible for our sentence. Obviously the rulers who declared war against their own peoples cannot offer anything to anyone else but injustice. Pakistani ruling class never ever supported Kashmiris in their fight for freedom, as they should

have done. Indeed this class has no interest in the freedom of Kashmir.'

I asked Sampat Prakash whether he thought Maqbool Butt had streak of communalism, but Sampat was emphatic that Maqbool was all for an independent Jammu and Kashmir, which would include people from all ethnic groups and people from all religious persuasions.

Sampat added that Maqbool Butt was a member of the Kashmir Independence Committee formed by Amanullah Khan[18] in 1963. The Committee consisted of middle-class Kashmiri activists, including journalists, students, businessmen and lawyers. They vehemently opposed the idea, being put forward by Pakistani and Indian foreign ministers, of dividing Kashmir on communal lines.

Amanullah Khan thought it was necessary to have an armed wing of the Plebiscite Front. That was how it was decided that the Jammu and Kashmir National Liberation Front (JKNLF) would be formed on 13 August 1965 with the aim of engaging in: 'All forms of struggle including armed struggle to enable the people of Jammu Kashmir State to determine the future of the State as the sole owners of their motherland'.[19]

Maqbool Butt told Sampat Prakash that he and Amanullah Khan were keen to unite the Plebiscite Fronts in India and Pakistan. However, these efforts were meaningless after Sheikh Abdullah's pact with Indira Gandhi in 1974.

According to Sampat, during their conversations at the detention centre, Maqbool Butt encouraged him to take the initiative of organizing Kashmiri Pandits to support the cause of an independent Kashmir. Maqbool expressed his frustration that the Kashmiri Pandits had decided to accept the Accession and not join the Kashmiri Muslims in fighting for Kashmir's independence.

Maqbool and Sampat enjoyed each other's company. They shared a commitment to Kashmiri nationalism. Both knew that they would not be together for very long, and thought that they should do one act in solidarity with the other Kashmiris who were also under detention. The two Kashmiri nationalists had seen the records of the detainees in files kept inside a wooden cupboard. They decided to destroy these records so that the prosecution could never prove any case.

Sampat feigned illness and when the doctor arrived he told him that he was finding it difficult to sleep and got him to prescribe some Calmpose tablets. That night, Sampat made tea and dissolved some of the sleeping pills in it and offered it to the CRPF guards. Once the guards were asleep, the two leaders used the burning coals from their kangris to set fire to the cupboard.

The detention of the two leaders at the interrogation centre had, in fact, been illegal. Now the authorities had to 'show' their arrest and send them to judicial custody. Sampat Prakash was sent to Jammu Central Jail in February 1976; Maqbool Butt was transferred to Tihar Jail a few months later in July 1976.

———

The Emergency lasted twenty-one months and ended with Indira Gandhi calling for elections, and a thumping majority for the newly-founded Janata Party[20] that came to power in March 1977. Most of the political prisoners, including the other trade union leaders, had been released. Sampat Prakash, however, continued to languish in Jammu jail.

In Jammu jail, Sampat met Shabir Shah, a much younger man of whom Sampat had heard. He was one of the founding members of the People's League, which had been set up in the aftermath of the creation of Bangladesh and the Simla Agreement. However, it never became as prestigious or popular as the Jammu and Kashmir Liberation Front (JKLF).

Shabir was soft-spoken and neatly dressed. He had been in and out of jail since 1969 for advocating the right of the Kashmiris to decide their own future. He told Sampat that Maqbool was his leader and that he revered him. Sampat had hoped to have some meaningful discussion with Shabir on the political situation in Kashmir, but to his disappointment, he found the man had not read any political literature. Realizing that Shabir had no ideas or any vision, Sampat got some books on Mao and Che for him.

Apart from Shabir Shah, there were two other leaders at Jammu jail at the same time. They were Chaman Lal Gupta, a Member of the Legislative Assembly and staunch member of the Jana Sangh, and Syed Ali Shah Geelani, a member of the Jamaat-e-Islami. Geelani supported the right to self-determination of the Kashmiris but he advocated that Kashmir should join Pakistan. These leaders, too, were released, but Sampat and Shabir continued to be detained. As a gesture of solidarity, Geelani and Chaman Lal brought fruits and almonds for them in jail.

On 26 March 1977, President's Rule was imposed in Kashmir because the Sheikh Abdullah-led National Conference had been reduced to a minority following the withdrawal of support by the Congress Party. The Janata Party was ruling at the Centre and Sampat's old friend, George Fernandes,[21] was in government. Sampat had been introduced to George Fernandes in 1968 when he was underground and had gone to Delhi to contact the trade union leaders. Joseph, the president of the All India Audit Employees Association, had introduced the two. George had just been elected as an MP and was in Delhi. Over the years, their acquaintance developed into mutual respect and friendship. Now that the Sheikh was not in power and President's Rule had been imposed, George ensured that Sampat was released in June 1977.

A few weeks later, Comrade Jyoti Basu[22] came to Srinagar with his family and stayed with Sheikh Abdullah. It was a family holiday but the veteran Communist agreed to meet Sampat Prakash and his comrades at the Circuit House. The trade union leaders wanted Jyoti Basu to use his influence with the Sheikh to get their dismissal orders revoked. The Sheikh, however, refused to reinstate the 2,400 dismissed workers, leaving them in a very difficult financial situation.

For some time, Sampat had been facing some serious problems in his political life. So far, he had been a member of the Communist

Party of India (Marxist-Leninist) or the CPI-ML. In other words, he was a Naxalite. The Party had expected him to follow their orders and to control the trade union's activities. But the CPI-ML operated in secrecy and did not have the experience of working openly in a democratic fashion. As far as Sampat was concerned, the trade union was a broad-based organization which had to accommodate different political viewpoints and function through democratic elections.

Within the top leadership of the CPI-ML in Jammu and Kashmir, there had been a split as well. Saraf was still holding on to his Naxalite ideology, while Kishen Dev Sethi and Abdul Majid had moved closer to the Congress Party. Many Communists had joined the Congress Party and had supported the Emergency.

However, Sampat knew that he could not continue with Saraf's CPI-ML if he wanted to carry on with trade union activities. Neither could he join the Congress Party because it had betrayed the Kashmiris by arresting the Sheikh and then, by forcing the Accord, had taken away all hope of freedom. Sethi and Abdul Majid Khan were not ethnic Kashmiris; they were from Jammu and did not have any feelings for Kashmiri nationalism. So for them, there had been no such dilemma.

But Abdul Majid Khan had a strong support base in the trade union, and Sampat knew that if he left, the union would split right down the middle. Finally in 1979, the trade union did split and Abdul Majid Khan and Sampat Prakash went their separate ways. The two leaders would never work together in one organization again. Punoo went with Abdul Majid and was elected general secretary of the union, which also went by the same name: the Low Paid Government Servants Federation.

Sampat felt that some of the employees who went over to Majid Khan did so because he was a very honest and inspiring leader with a long track record of selfless service to the workers, but a part of the reason, perhaps, was that they felt a certain loyalty to a fellow Muslim. I asked Sampat whether it could have been because he was a little anarchical in his functioning and, perhaps, authoritarian too.

He looked pensive and said yes, that was also true. Some of the leaders tried to form their own union, the Employees and Workers Federation, but they could not sustain it.

In 1979, Sampat decided to join the CPI(M). I asked him how he decided to join a party which had never supported the right of Kashmiris to self-determination. He said that he felt the most important thing was to save the trade union and it needed the support of a disciplined party.

Sampat motivated many of the Naxalite sympathizers to join the CPI(M), and in March 1980, they formally announced the formation of the unit of the Party in Jammu and Kashmir with Mohammad Yusuf Tarigami[23] as the party secretary. The CPI(M) leaders advised that Sampat and his comrades should continue to use the old name, Jammu and Kashmir Low Paid Government Servants Federation, and so they continued to do so.

——

During this period, several international events had an impact on Kashmir's political scenario. There was a military coup in Pakistan and Zulfiqar Ali Bhutto, the prime minister, was jailed and then hanged in April 1979. There was anger and distress in Kashmir because Bhutto was a hero for the Kashmiris. He had once proclaimed that Pakistan would continue to fight India for a thousand years till Kashmir was liberated. The hanging of Bhutto by General Zia-ul-Haq, a pro-Jamaat-e-Islami man, turned the Kashmiri anger against the organization's members in Kashmir.

Over the years, the Jamaat-e-Islami had made steady progress. The chief of the organization, Syed Ali Shah Geelani, had admitted that in the 1970s, children of the members had been inducted into 200 to 250 madrassas. By 1975, the organization had distributed its literature widely and ran a daily newspaper. It also had access to petro-dollars.[24]

The timing of the rise of the Jamaat reflected the coming of age of a generation of Kashmiri Muslims who had been educated and whose political thinking was shaped by developments in the Islamic world.

Although the Sheikh had been steadfast in his commitment to fighting the Jamaat-e-Islami, he too used Islamic symbols to mobilize people. Moreover, the Congress Party had been appealing to the majority community in communal terms, in order to win back those who had shifted their allegiances to the Jana Sangh. While they instigated the autonomy movements in Jammu and Ladakh, the Sheikh turned to the people of the Muslim-dominated districts of Jammu on the basis of their religious affinity.

Sheikh Abdullah had banned the Jamaat-e-Islami in Kashmir and had come down heavily on them during the Emergency. When Bhutto was executed, the National Conference cadres used the occasion to attack members of the Jamaat-e-Islami and destroy their properties. According to the party, the Tehreek-e-Hurriyat-e-Islami,[25] 1,245 houses, 513 foodgrain godowns, 338 cowsheds, sixty-five Jamaat libraries, twenty-four Jamaat offices, and twenty-two factories had been burnt down.[26]

Around 125 Jamaat-run schools with 550 teachers and 25,000 students were banned. So were another 1,000 evening schools run by their organization which reached out to an estimated 50,000 girls and boys.[27] However, most of these teachers were absorbed into government schools or the Jamaat schools, that renamed themselves and continued functioning.

Sheikh Abdullah's antagonism with the Jamaat-e-Islam went back to the early days when he had received the support of the Ahmadiyyas. The Ahmadiyya movement was an Islamic reform movement established in 1889 in Qadian, a small town in Punjab, by Mirza Ghulam Ahmad (1855–1908), who claimed to be the metaphorical second coming of Christ.

It has been claimed that the Reading Room was the brainchild of the Ahmadiyya maulvis and the first meetings even before Sheikh Abdullah joined were held in the house of Khwaja Dadr-ud-Din, secretary of the Anjuman-i-Ahmadiyas.[28] The Ahmadiyyas funded educational work in Kashmir and in Punjab.[29]

For the Ahmadiyyas, Kashmir is a special place because they believed that the Messiah Christ was buried at Srinagar's Roza Bal. It is also interesting that many Ahmadiyyas wrote in the Kashmiri language, thus emphasizing the regional identity of the Kashmiri Muslim.[30] In the early 1950s, Mirza Tahir Ahmad, the fourth caliph of the community, wrote *Murder in the Name of Allah*, a searing critique of Maududi's concept of jihad.[31]

Maulana Maududi founded the Jamaat-e-Islami on 26 August 1941. After the Partition of British India into two sovereign states, Maududi migrated to Pakistan and declared that the organization should be split into two and work in accordance with the political structure of each country. Therefore, in April 1948, the Jamaat-e-Islami members who had opted to stay in India, met in Allahabad and declared that Jamaat-i-Islam Hind would be a separate organization from the original Pakistani one. And in the same year, the Jamaat-e-Islami Kashmir declared itself to be independent of both and framed its own Constitution in 1953.[32]

Maududi was the first person in the subcontinent to say that Islam is not concerned merely with the spiritual salvation of mankind; its intent and purpose is to establish God's sovereignty on earth, in other words, establish Islamic states. He tried to establish his Islamic credentials in a country whose creation he had opposed by taking up two interrelated issues: dispute with India over Kashmir and the status of the Ahmadiyya community in Islam.

Maududi's agitation to exclude the Ahmadiyyas from the Muslim community in 1953 was linked to his concept of jihad in Kashmir. He wanted them declared as apostates, but there were no takers for his extreme views and Maududi was arrested and charged with sedition and sentenced to death for his stance on the Ahmadiyya question.[33]

Ever since the Partition of India, the Ahmadiyyas in Pakistan were subject to both repression and discrimination. Their mosques were burnt down, they were persecuted and finally, under pressure from Jamaat-e-Islami elements, Bhutto passed the Second Amendment to the Pakistan Constitution and declared them to be kafirs, non-Muslims.

By aligning himself with the Ahmadiyyas, Sheikh Abdullah all his life had tried to curb the influence of the Jamaat-e-Islami's version of Islam. He had even banned the World Islamic Youth Council, planned by the youth wing in 1980. As a result, during his time, the electoral base of the organization had become narrower.

But then world events took over. Although Maududi died in 1979, that year saw an unprecedented rise in the influence of his ideology. His death coincided with the Iranian Revolution which became an inspiration to the Muslim youth all over the world and, charged by its success, they were ready to help the Taliban in their fight against the Soviet invasion of Afghanistan.

In addition, there was the American (and British) dependence on militant Islamists to achieve their foreign policy objectives which had been continuing since the early years of the Cold War. This was soon to lead to the end of the Cold War and the beginning of the War on Terror.

The US saw the Soviet invasion of Afghanistan as a threat to the capitalist world order. In early 1980, a high-level US delegation with Secretary of State, Warren Christopher, arrived in Islamabad and offered $400 million in military aid to fight the Soviet Union which they declared was 'a threat to the peace and security of Pakistan, the region and the world'.[34]

In July 1979, US President Jimmy Carter secretly sanctioned the fostering of the expansion of Islam in Central Asia to spread a 'fundamentalist' version of the religion. Charlie Wilson, a Texan Congressman, is said to have converted an ordinary CIA assignment into the largest covert operation in American history.[35] The US alliance with Islamist radicalism was greatly strengthened during the two terms of Ronald Reagan's presidency. And the Afghan war was expanded into the CIA's greatest ever operation, with some $5 billion of direct US aid, matched dollar for dollar by Saudi Arabia, and the level of arms and equipment shipments peaking at 60,000 tonnes per year by the late 1980s.[36]

These events had a direct bearing on the course that militancy would take in the Kashmir Valley. In less than seven years after Russia withdrew from Afghanistan, the victorious Islamic freedom fighters, the mujahideen, found a new cause—the liberation of Kashmir.

———

When Sheikh Abdullah died in 1982, people poured onto the streets for his funeral. Even if they could not condone the Accord he had signed with Delhi, they knew the man had fought hard and with single-minded devotion for the cause of Kashmir for decades. And this was the time to put aside their grievances and show their love and respect for the Lion of Kashmir. Sampat was just one of the many thousands who felt a sense of loss and grief on his passing.

With Sheikh Abdullah's passing, a major obstacle in the way of the spread of Jamaat-e-Islami's ideology had been removed. The tide of political Islam would now rise to engulf the Valley, but not without a fight from the Kashmiri nationalists.

———

Having joined the CPI(M), Sampat and his comrades began to prepare for the state elections in 1983. For the elections, the CPI(M) had decided to field Yusuf Tarigami as its candidate from the Kulgam constituency. The CPI(M) had neither money nor a jeep to travel around for the campaigning. They made a request to Mir Qasim who obliged by giving them a jeep and a truck.

Yusuf Tarigami was up against was Abdul Raza Mir, a staunch Jamaat-e-Islami member who had won in 1972. During the campaign, the Jamaat-e-Islami cadres attacked the CPI(M) and Sampat Prakash had to be hospitalized for the injuries he sustained. Yusuf lost the elections and his deposit was forfeit.[37]

Events moved quickly thereafter. In the election of 1983, Farooq Abdullah, the son of Sheikh Abdullah, won. On 3 February 1984, some members close to the JKLF kidnapped Ravinder Mhatre, the

Indian deputy high commissioner posted in Britain, while he was on a visit to Birmingham. The militants demanded the immediate release of Maqbool Butt, who was still languishing in Tihar Jail, in exchange for the Indian diplomat. The Indian government, however, was firm about not negotiating, and two days later, the diplomat was found dead.

On 11 February 1984, Maqbool Butt was hanged in Tihar Jail. Sampat felt a sense of personal loss, so did thousands of Kashmiris.

Hearing Sampat's account, I felt a pang of guilt. I confessed to him that I had read the news of Maqbool Butt's hanging and had not felt any anger or sadness. Although I was already active in the human rights movement, we did not hold any meeting condemning the hanging.

I looked at Sampat and said: 'It took me more than a decade to understand the political significance of Maqbool Butt's hanging.' Sampat asked how the change had come about and I told him it was because of my involvement with the Northeast. In fact, by the time Maqbool was hanged, I had already filed the first cases against the Indian Army for committing human rights violations during counterinsurgency operations in the Naga-inhabited areas of Manipur.

As I spoke, I realized there are many significant similarities between the Naga national movement and the Kashmir movement: Angami Zapu Phizo, the Naga leader, and the Sheikh were both born in 1905; both wanted to preserve the cultural identity of their ethnic groups; both were promised a real autonomy in the shape of Article 370 for Kashmir and Article 371-A for the Nagas, but the provisions were watered down. Also, while the Sheikh was in jail, Phizo went into exile. Both the Nagas and the Kashmiris signed accords in 1974–75, which were viewed as betrayals. And now, both the Kashmiri and Naga national movements had moved closer to religious nationalism.

Sampat asked: 'Nagas are also becoming fundamentalists?' And I told him about the role of the Baptist fundamentalists and the clashes with Catholics in Naga villages. Sampat fell silent. Then he continued the story of Kashmir...

———

A few months after Maqbool Butt was hanged, Sampat Prakash decided he needed some rest and time to think things over, so he went to a hotel owned by a friend in Pahalgam. It was up in the mountains, and Sampat had hoped that the silence would have a healing touch. But to his utter surprise, he heard a lot of noise in the rooms; many people were discussing something in animated voices. He went out to request them to lower their voices but when he saw the faces of the people, he was shocked. He saw eight or nine members of the Legislative Assembly from the National Conference, plotting the downfall of Farooq Abdullah.[38]

Although he did not particularly respect Farooq, who had attended S.P. College at the same time as he, he did not like the undermining of the electoral processes either. Sampat made some excuse, got a taxi and left early in the morning and arrived at Farooq's house. Sampat had no problem getting through the security since the guards recognized him. He went inside to find the chief minister having coffee. Sampat told him what he had seen. Farooq was incredulous, so he phoned his police officer who told him not to listen to Sampat, the troublemaker. The next day, on 2 July 1984, Farooq Abdullah's ministry was summarily dismissed and Ghulam Mohammad Shah, the husband of his sister Khalida, was installed as chief minister.

Sampat advised Farooq to sit on dharna. He sat for just one day and soon after, G.M. Shah imposed curfew. The Indian opposition parties did not protest against the unfair and arbitrary dismissal of Farooq Abdullah as they had done when Rama Rao was dismissed in Andhra Pradesh.[39]

From the time Ghulam Mohammad Shah (1920–2009) became chief minister, communal tensions ran so high that of the first ninety days of his rule, seventy-two days were under curfew, earning him the title Gul-e-Curfew or the Curfew Flower. It was during his time, in February 1986, that an attack was mounted on Kashmiri Pandit families living in Anantnag district. This was the first such attack and sent a shock wave through the entire community.

But matters were far more sinister than what they appeared to be. Balraj Puri, a Jammu-based journalist, had reported that he had found no evidence of any involvement of the Jamaat-e-Islami in the communal violence. He discovered that this was the result of some grisly calculations by secular parties. In fact, the Muslims had responded to Balraj Puri and his team and raised money to rebuild the temples, and the Kashmiri Pandits decided not to leave their villages.[40] Although Balraj Puri's intervention showed that people in the villages still did not harbour feelings of communalism, the overall situation was deteriorating. Governor Jagmohan was against Article 370; the share of Muslims in government services fell and the ban on sale of meat on Janamashtami invited defiance by Qazi Nissar, the mirwaiz of south Kashmir, who slaughtered sheep in the open. Jagmohan looked on Kashmiri identity as a threat to Indian identity; he could not distinguish between the Kashmiri Muslim identity and the Islamic identity which was being encouraged by the US and Pakistan.

The pro-Pakistan sentiment was growing in Kashmir. It manifested itself during an international cricket match played between the West Indies and India at the Amar Singh Stadium in Srinagar in October 1983. Pro-Pakistan slogans were raised, Pakistani flags waved and the Indian team was booed; when the Indian team lost the match, there was delirious celebration.

These developments, however, did not have an impact on the government employees and their trade union movement. By 1984, Gulam Mohiudin Punoo, along with the comrades who had gone over to Abdul Majid Khan, had returned to the Low Paid Government Servants Federation led by Sampat Prakash. They recognized his dynamism, even though they did not always agree with his unorthodox methods.

In the course of his trade union work, Punoo had visited almost every corner of Jammu and Kashmir. I asked whether he ever went to Ladakh. He sat up and said: 'I organized the strikes all over Ladakh.' In September 1987, he wandered around Numa, Khalsi, Kargil, Drass and Zanskar and organized strikes in all these places around the demand for implementation of the Fourth Pay Commission. In this way the government employees kept alive the idea of unity of the three regions within the state.

We had been sitting in Punoo's home for several hours and it was time to go. But he had not finished. He said I must write that the most important contribution the Federation had made was that the employees continued to work all through the months and years of insurgency and saved the Kashmir economy from complete ruin. 'And our horticulture department had a big role in that. It is the most important source of livelihood for the people.'

As we left, I asked him to tell me one memorable incident from his life. Without hesitation he said it was the trip he made with other comrades to the big government nursery at Pallanwala village in Akhnoor district, right on the border with Pakistan. They had heard that the condition of the employees there was miserable. At the nursery, they met Jaichand, the gardener. Jaichand told them that he, along with the nursery, had been under Pakistan occupation several times during the wars; he had seen the Indo-Pak wars from close quarters. The trade union leaders asked whether he preferred to be under India or Pakistan. Without any hesitation he replied, 'I love this garden, I don't care whether it is under India or Pakistan, as long as it blooms.'

Punoo retired in 2000 and now spends time organizing the small orchard owners who face innumerable problems in packaging and preserving their fruits.

GATHERING OF THE STORM
(1982–90)

In 1982 Sampat's elder son, Lenin, joined the Regional Engineering College.[1] He had grown up in a political environment with trade union comrades coming to their home at all times of the day and night. He loved to hear his father's passionate speeches at meetings and one of his dearest memories was of the time his father had taken him to a rally in Delhi where he remembered holding a small red flag and shouting slogans while being carried on the back of a cycle.

When, as a child, people would ask him about his unusual name, he would reply saying that the original Lenin had changed Russia and he would do the same in Kashmir. But he also remembered the hard times the family had to endure when his father was in jail; the way his mother had to struggle and how alone she had felt. Lenin concentrated on his studies through the weeks and months from 1982 to 1986. He did not involve himself in politics and to Sampat's disappointment, he still does not.

The other students studying with Lenin, especially the Muslim boys, seemed to be more politically conscious. They were inspired by stories of the struggles of the people in Iraq, Iran, Palestine and Afghanistan. Students from all these countries were studying in Kashmir, particularly in the Regional Engineering College. But when I asked Lenin whether he remembered if the atmosphere in college was politically charged, he replied that he did not attend any of those meetings.

Lenin was focused on his studies, he wanted to lead a normal life; to become an engineer and have a family. Mohammad Afzal Guru, who was barely three years younger than Sampat's eldest son, also had a similar dream, of becoming a doctor, having a family and leading a normal life.

Mohammad Afzal Guru was born on 13 June 1967. He was the third son of a Kashmiri businessman from Seer Jagir village, a few kilometres from Sopore town which is just about thirty-five kilometres from Srinagar. Afzal's father, Habibullah Guru, was by no means poor; he had made his money in the timber and transport business. In the 1970s, the family had a colour television and the neighbours would gather together to watch Bollywood classics over the weekends. Afzal's father owned an Ambassador car and, some say, he lived like a king. Habibullah Guru's dream was that his son should become a doctor when he grew up. But he died when Afzal was only eleven years old and the burden of looking after the family fell on Aijaz, Afzal's elder brother.

Afzal and his three brothers, Aijaz, Riyaz and Hilal, lived in their two-storey brick house with their mother Ayesha Begum. Both his elder brother and mother were keen that Afzal fulfill his father's dream and study to become a doctor. And Afzal made this his dream as well.

The four brothers completed their elementary schooling at Doabgow High School. Afzal used to walk through fields and apple orchards and cross the rivulet Puhuru to reach his school. Sometimes he would sit on a tyre and float down the Jhelum River, which flowed through their village. Afzal loved to swim in the cold waters of the Jhelum.

Before he left for school, Afzal would fetch water from the river for his mother, and when he returned he would help her wash the clothes and utensils.

In school, he was considered to be good at sports, theatre and other cultural activities. On many an occasion he would be chosen to lead the Indian Independence Day parade held in his school. His teachers were both Muslims and Kashmiri Pandits and he seemed to have won their hearts with his humour and diligence.[2]

Senior journalist Muzamil Jaleel, who was Afzal's batchmate in school, wrote in the *Indian Express*: 'For me, Afzal was a friendly schoolmate who loved poetry and talked of books during those festive lunch breaks...we became good friends. I always knew Afzal as the best student of our class, who would surprise the teachers with his wit and intelligence.'[3]

While Afzal was still in school, a film called the *Lion of the Desert* was released in Kashmir in 1985. This film fired the imagination of the Kashmiri youth. I never asked Afzal how many times he watched the film, but I do know that the young men of his generation saw the video many times, especially after the film was banned in Kashmir.

The *Lion of the Desert* is a Libyan film financed by Muammar Gaddafi's government.[4] It is based on the life of Omar Mukhtar, a Bedouin leader who fought against Italian colonialism that the Italian army, led by General Graziani, was seeking to impose in Africa. Omar Mukhtar, a teacher by profession, takes on the fascist forces knowing that the war will not be won in his lifetime. The Italians commit many barbaric acts such as killing prisoners of war, destroying crops and grouping villagers during their counterinsurgency operations.

There is a scene where Mukhtar refuses to kill a defenceless young officer, insisting that Islam forbids him to kill captured soldiers. He proclaims that he is only fighting for his homeland, and that Muslims hate the notion of war itself. In the end, Mukhtar is captured and tried as a rebel. His lawyer states that since Mukhtar had never accepted Italian rule, he cannot be tried as a rebel, and instead must be treated as a prisoner of war (which would save him from being hanged). The judge rejects this, and the film ends with Mukthar being executed.

Like most Kashmiris, Afzal was a deeply emotional man and the film made a lasting impression on him.

From Doabgow High School, Afzal Guru went to the Higher Secondary School at Sopore and, in 1988, he joined the Jhelum Valley College of Medical Sciences. The students who studied with him at the medical college remember that he was popular with the women students because he could sing ghazals beautifully and loved to listen to music. He had a big portrait of Iqbal in his hostel room, and he also loved the poet, Ghalib. There was always a quiet philosophical side to Afzal. When he felt troubled or alone, he would visit the shrine of Baba Shakur-ud Din on a hillock, on the banks of the Wular Lake, and enjoy its silence and beauty.

One of the founders of the medical college was Afzal's uncle, Dr Abdul Ahad Guru, a famous cardiologist who had graduated from the prestigious All India Institute of Medical Sciences in Delhi. He had specialized in cardiovascular and thoracic surgery under the renowned Professor Gopinath, who had performed the first open heart surgery in India. The first open heart surgery in Kashmir was performed by Dr Guru; he was also on the board of the state's premier medical institute, the Sher-i-Kashmir Institute of Medical Sciences.[5]

Afzal considered Dr Guru as his mentor not only in academics but also in politics. Dr Guru, who was born in April 1940, was of the same generation as Maqbool Butt. He had seen the condition of the people under Dogra Raj and the grinding poverty of the Muslim peasants. His generation had been influenced by ideas of socialism and their nationalism was linked to the idea of economic justice.

The doctor was known to be a passionate Kashmiri nationalist and a member of the Supreme Revolutionary Command Council of the JKLF.[6] In 1989, Dr Guru had helped in negotiations when the JKLF kidnapped Rubaiya Sayeed, the daughter of the then home minister, Mufti Mohammed Sayeed, who was viewed as a collaborator of the Indian state.[7]

Afzal was deeply influenced by both Maqbool Butt and Dr Guru's ideas and ideals. Although Maqbool Butt had organized secret cells and arranged for military training for Kashmiris, Afzal was not so keen on armed resistance; he was more concerned about helping the poor. Maqbool wanted an independent Kashmir; it was not just political freedom that he dreamt about but also social and economic justice.

Maqbool Butt once said: 'For us, Azadi means not just getting rid of foreign occupation of our beloved motherland but also to remove hunger, poverty, ignorance and disease and to overcome economic and social deprivation. One day we shall achieve that Azadi.'[8]

Perhaps the Kashmir of their dreams would be a Muslim Kashmir, but it certainly would have place for people of other communities.

———

However, as events unfolded, the dream of an inclusive vision of Jammu and Kashmir was erased. And soon, even the memory of this vision began to fade.

Towards the end of his life, Sheikh Mohammad Abdullah tried to reinvent the National Conference as a party for Muslims. He introduced the Jammu & Kashmir Grant of Permit for Resettlement (or Permanent Return to) in the State Bill in the Jammu and Kashmir Legislative Assembly. The Bill was passed but the governor refused to give assent to it. The Act allowed the refugees created by Partition to return to Jammu and Kashmir and reclaim their properties. The CPI(M) leaders such as B.T. Ranadive and Jyoti Basu argued that the Act was part of an imperialist project to fuel secessionist groupings in Jammu and Kashmir.

Sheikh Abdullah died soon after and his son Farooq Abdullah became chief minister. One of the first things he did was to pass the Act again. The furore compelled the President of India to refer the issue to the Supreme Court. The Supreme Court upheld the validity of the Act in 2001. The controversy over the law led to the polarization of the two communities within the state—the Hindus and the Muslims.

This polarization became even sharper during the elections in

June 1983 which were fought between the National Conference, seen as a party representing the Muslims, and the Congress, projecting itself as an organization representing the Hindu-majority areas of Jammu. The Indian prime minister, Indira Gandhi, was explicit in her campaign in Jammu that Jammu was a part of Hindu India, and which had been neglected by Muslim Kashmir.[9]

The Congress Party also alleged that Farooq Abdullah was giving shelter to the Sikh militants and allowing them to run training camps in Jammu. Farooq denied the allegation. There were other serious allegations that the Khalistan movement was being encouraged by the CIA and the Pakistani intelligence agencies.[10]

Farooq Abdullah won the elections in 1983. The National Conference won forty-six seats, sweeping through the Valley and the Muslim majority areas of Jammu. The Congress Party refused to accept defeat and engineered a split in the National Conference. Farooq's sister's husband, G.M. Shah, along with eighteen cabinet colleagues formed the National Conference (Khalida), and in July 1984 Farooq Abdullah was dismissed and Shah was sworn in as chief minister.[11]

G.M. Shah's rule was marked by nepotism and corruption, and he was forced to impose curfew for most of the months that he was chief minister. Then in January 1986, the Indian prime minister, Rajiv Gandhi, allowed the doors of the disputed Babri Masjid to be opened, giving the impression he was favouring Hindus. This led to unprecedented communal disturbances in Jammu and Kashmir in February. In March 1986, Governor's Rule was imposed in the state and was followed by President's Rule in August.

However, even though Farooq Abdullah had been treated poorly by the Congress Party, he signed an accord with Rajiv Gandhi and agreed to an electoral alliance with the Congress.

Initially, Farooq had tried to project the National Conference as a Kashmiri party which was resisting Indian domination, and the Congress Party was looked upon as an usurper. But once the National Conference joined the Congress, it was seen as a party which had surrendered to India. In fact, even Indira Gandhi had failed to realize that making the National Conference subservient to the Congress would serve neither the interests of the Kashmiris nor of India.

After the Accord, Kashmiri nationalists identified the National Conference with the government of India and Farooq Abdullah was called a 'tilak dhari pujari of Vaishno Devi' (a priest of the Hindu shrine with a Hindu mark on his forehead).[12]

Balraj Puri explained the situation: 'There are indeed striking parallels between the way New Delhi ruled over the state and the way Kashmiri leaders ruled over Jammu. New Delhi failed to realize that Kashmiri identity is a source of strength for the national identity, nor did the Kashmiri leaders realize that a composite and harmonized identity built on the basis of regional characteristics was the surest guarantee of the overall Kashmiri identity. Just as discontent against the central government in Kashmir often becomes anti-Indian, similarly discontent against the state government in Jammu often tends to become anti-Kashmiri and at times anti-Muslim, both in Jammu and in Ladakh.'[13]

The Congress was confident that the alliance with Farooq Abdullah would help them win the next elections in Jammu and Kashmir that were due to be held in March 1987. But what no one realized was that a storm was about to rise which would engulf the state and change the course of its history forever.

———

In Kashmir, the alienation of Muslims had resulted in the union of several Muslim organizations and, on 2 September 1986, these organizations[14] announced the formation of the Muslim Mutthahida Mahaz, or the Muslim United Front (MUF). Its class base comprised mainly wealthy sections of society, orchard owners, businessmen and rich peasants. Its constitution specified that the MUF would 'not involve itself in any non-Muslim political activity'.[15]

The objectives of the MUF were: Promotion of solidarity among Muslims; Preaching adherence to the fundamental principles of

Islam; Preservation of Islamic culture, heritage and traditions; and Promotion of cooperation among Muslims

The MUF recruited Muslims from Ladakh and Jammu and soon the whole state resounded with their slogans; they attacked bars and directed girls to cover their heads.[16] In Doda, posters appeared directing girls to cover their heads when going to school; shopkeepers were told to close their shops for two hours on Fridays and offer prayers. On 4 March 1987, the MUF leaders appeared in the white robes of pious Muslims and declared that Islam could not survive under the authority of a secular state and that Farooq Abdullah was an agent of Hindu imperialism.[17]

The MUF announced that it would contest the 1987 elections. They said it was a part of their religious crusade and their declaration mobilized a large voter turnout. One of the candidates put up by the MUF was a young man called Maulvi Mohammad Yusuf Shah. Sampat had seen him at the Exhibition Grounds in Srinagar, leading the prayers in a mosque located in the grounds where the trade union leaders often held their meetings. The two men had had brief discussions and Yusuf Shah had appreciated Sampat's stand against Sheikh Abdullah on his taking over as chief minister.

Mohammad Yusuf Shah was a member of the Jamaat-e-Islami and had been a polling agent for Syed Ali Shah Geelani in the 1983 elections. Yusuf Shah and his companions had inspired the youth with slogans such as: 'Aawa Aawa Aawa Aawa Aawa Inquilab' (The Revolution has come); 'Rehbaro-Rehnuma Mustafa, Mustafa' (The Prophet is our Guide) 'Muslim Mutahidda Mahaz ka matlab kya? La ilaha illallah' (MUF means Islam); 'Assembly mein kya chalega? Nizame-Mustafa' (There will be Islamic rule in the Assembly).

Elections were held on 23 March 1987. The people in the Kashmir Valley expected the MUF to win with an overwhelming majority. Instead, Farooq Abdullah, with the backing of the Congress, won by a thumping majority. The people believed that the elections had been rigged and that sparked off agitations right across the Valley.[18]

Even though the MUF leaders had been imprisoned, the agitation against the rigged elections gathered intensity. There were meetings, bandhs and long processions. On 20 August 1987, a slogan was raised that announced the coming of the storm: 'Jabri nata tode do; Kashmir hamara chhordo' (Sever the forced union; leave Kashmir)[19]. The slogan for independent Kashmir had been raised and it had an instant appeal.

Alarmed by the growing popularity of the MUF, the Congress-National Front had rigged the elections and had resorted to strong-arm tactics by arresting the MUF candidates and beating up their polling agents. Many people in Kashmir say that if the elections of 1987 had been fair, the MUF would have won and come to power and then there would have been no insurgency. However, other experts have calculated that even if there had been no rigging, the MUF would have won only ten to twenty seats.[20]

Kashmiris usually trace the roots of the insurgency to the rigging of the 1987 elections, the arrest and torture of the MUF leaders and the denial of the democratic aspirations of the youth. They point out that the MUF candidates who had been imprisoned came out and joined the armed insurgency. For instance, Maulvi Mohammad Yusuf Shah became the commander of the Hizbul Mujahideen under the name of Syed Salahuddin, a Kurdish warrior who had fought in the Crusades.

However, Salahuddin has denied that he is a product of the rigged elections of 1987. In an interview to the journalist Hilal Ahmad of *Greater Kashmir*, he claimed that the insurgency would have taken place whether the MUF had won or not. He told the journalist:

> It is absolutely wrong that I picked up arms because the elections were rigged. Muftis are giving the election results a wrong twist. I was a freedom fighter long before I fought elections. I have inherited this from my forebears. My brother, Sayed Ghulam Muhammad, was the district president of Plebiscite Front in Budgam. My grandfather, Haji Ghulam Mohiuddin, was

tortured by a very infamous police officer; his mouth stuffed with hot potatoes, kicked and beaten, because he used to observe Indian Independence Day as a 'black day'. We fought elections so that we could pass resolution in the assembly for freedom of Kashmir. India knew that. That is why they rigged the elections. People remember that when I was campaigning for the elections, I used to begin my speech with *ay mard-e-mujahid jaag zara*.[21] Fighting elections were a means to educate masses about the freedom struggle. We wanted endorsement of public sentiment in the assembly. Otherwise who would have voted for my person, I was nobody. But people voted for the sentiment. Even the relatives of my opponent Ghulam Mohiuddin Shah voted for me. And those who were campaigning for elections became top resistance leaders. We were ideologically driven by the struggle for freedom.

There was a case against me in which the then SSP had said that I was not campaigning for elections but for freedom.

If the Muslim United Front (MUF) had won the elections, we would have tabled a resolution for right of self-determination. India would have dissolved the assembly and that would have triggered the freedom struggle. Majority of the MUF members were in favour of such a resolution. The MUF was anti-India by its very nature and essence. We were going to use elections to get to the goal, but that didn't mature.[22]

I read out the letter to Sampat Prakash and asked him whether he, too, thought that the insurgency would have happened even if the 1987 elections had been fair or not. He said, yes, the Islamists were getting ready. Some had even gone across the border for training. The Kashmiri militants had established contacts with Pakistan, more specifically with its intelligence agency, the ISI, since the early 1980s.

Sampat said that he knew that the JKLF had found a novel way of recruiting boys for training without alerting the police. He said that when he had made enquiries, he found out that they were organizing cricket matches in every neighbourhood to enlist cadres.

The year 1989 saw the end of the Soviet occupation of Afghanistan and the release of a great deal of militant energies and weapons. With the help of the CIA and the ISI, an estimated 35,000 Muslim radicals from forty Islamic countries had joined Afghanistan's fight between 1982 and 1992. Now the forty or so training camps were used to train the Kashmiri freedom fighters.[23]

It was two years earlier, however, in 1987, that both the JKLF and Jamaat-e-Islami had received authorization for an offensive with the full support of Pakistan.[24] One of the first JKLF cadres to go across the border was Abdul Hameed Sheikh.[25] Hameed Sheikh was born in 1967 in Srinagar, and because of his parents' economic condition, he could not finish his studies. During his stint across the border, he was trained to use assault rifles and grenades at an ISI-run camp.

He then organized the nucleus of the JKLF armed group. From 1989 onwards, this group exploded bombs and carried out assassinations. On 13 July 1989, the militants attacked a bus carrying CRPF jawans, killing two and injuring ten soldiers; then there was a bomb blast in Khyam Cinema, and in August they killed Yusuf Halwai, an active member of the National Conference. They attacked activists of the National Conference, as well as Communists and Kashmiri Pandits they thought had betrayed the cause of Kashmir's independence. And, in November 1989, they called for a boycott of the Parliamentary elections.

In January 1990, Jammu and Kashmir came under the Governor's Rule once again. The Assembly was placed under suspended animation and, subsequently, dissolved on 19 February 1990. The state remained under President's Rule between July 1990 and 1996.

The Indian armed forces had by now been moved into the state in an attempt to curb the insurgency and Kashmir soon became one of the most militarized territories in the world. It was a war; and to many young Kashmiris it seemed that the dream of the liberation of Kashmir was coming close to realization. They left their jobs, their studies and their homes and joined the other recruits crossing the border to receive training in armaments.

Sopore and its adjoining areas, including Seer Jagir, became a strong base for militants. Foreign militants, called guest freedom fighters, especially from Pakistan, Afghanistan and Sudan, had a free run. The area had turned into a 'liberated' zone, with militants proudly displaying the weapons they had seized in encounters with the Kashmiri police.

Sampat Prakash, like other Kashmiris, was watching the scene. When he was asked how they could estimate the number of young men who had crossed over, he said that the best way was to go the shoe shops and check how many Action shoes had been bought each day. At bus stops, conductors could be heard inviting the men: 'Sopore, Kapore, Upore.' Among the young men boarding the buses were many lumpen elements as well, such as charas smugglers and gamblers; there were also men who earned a living by selling cinema tickets in the black market as well as daily-wage earners.

Sampat said that no one has explained how these young men could go across the border so openly. Why was there no attempt to stop this exodus? A part of the reason was that the government machinery had all but collapsed, but even so, the Indian armed forces never checked the buses ferrying the men.

—

The highly charged atmosphere and the momentous events could hardly have left Afzal Guru, the medical student, untouched. He was an idealist as well as a committed Kashmiri nationalist, who firmly believed that Pakistan would help the Kashmiris fulfil their dream. It was a belief that was shared by so many young men of his generation. Afzal had managed to pass the first year of his MBBS course, but he knew he would never forgive himself if he did not sacrifice his personal dream of becoming a doctor for the cause of his beloved Kashmir.

We do not know the exact date on which he left. It was probably 1989 because he did not write the examinations for the second year, much to the disappointment of his family, especially his older brother

Aijaz, who had worked hard to support his brother so that their father's dream could come true.

Afzal's training lasted three months. Sometimes, in the quiet moments, he found time to read. One of the militants who was with him in Pak-administered Kashmir remarked that on one occasion he saw Afzal reading an Urdu novel by Ismat Chughtai.[26] Afzal, like other members of the JKLF, was a Kashmiri nationalist and sincerely committed to fighting for an independent Kashmir—a Kashmir which included all communities. Whether their vision of Kashmir can be called secular could be a matter of debate, but their agenda was emphatically not to Islamize Kashmir; what they wanted was to be free from both Indian and Pakistani occupation. At that point of time, Afzal's dream was of a free and independent Kashmir and not to establish an Islamic state or the Islamization of Kashmiri society. The JKLF had the absolute support of Pakistan, or so people like Afzal Guru thought.

But when he was in Pakistan, Afzal saw that the country was not interested in supporting the cause of Kashmiris; instead, they were using the Kashmiris for their own political reasons. Perhaps he also saw the larger game being played by the Americans.

It was in August 1988, a month after the JKLF had launched its national liberation movement, that the ISI Directorate convened a meeting with the head of the Jamaat-e-Islami of Pak-administered Kashmir, Abdul Rashid Turabi, and the head of the pro-Pakistan Tehreek-e-Jehad-e-Islami to discuss how they could Islamize the movement and thus promote the idea of a merger with Pakistan.[27]

Afzal had seen the flow of funds to the pro-Pakistani groups supported by the ISI. More importantly he had understood how India and Pakistan had together killed the JKLF. Their intelligence agencies had smashed the JKLF to smithereens and from the splinters had emerged twenty different organizations. In fact, both countries were equally opposed to the creation of an independent Jammu and Kashmir; India wanted Kashmir to be a part of Indian territory; Pakistan wanted Kashmiris to accept Pakistani sovereignty.

After his return to Kashmir, Afzal Guru found that he was not fighting the Indian state; instead, he found himself trying to stop the in-fighting between the JKLF cadres and Hizbul Mujahideen cadres who were supposed to be struggling for the liberation of Kashmir.

The Hizbul Mujahideen had entered Kashmir in September 1989; it was the militant wing of the Jamaat-e-Islami. Its objective was to integrate Kashmir with Pakistan and ensure the Islamization of Kashmir. It was headed by Syed Salahuddin who was known as Yusuf Shah, the man who had stood as a candidate in the 1987 elections in Kashmir.

The Hizbul Mujahideen in India-administered Kashmir shared intelligence with the Indian army to help them locate JKLF militants. As a result, 500 of cadres of the JKLF were killed mainly by the Hizbul Mujahideen militants.[28]

The 'freedom fighters' or mujahideen were a law unto themselves; they went around Pakistan-administered Kashmir flaunting their weapons and extorting money from shopkeepers. In fact, they had become so fearless that members of one of the Kashmiri organizations went to a billiard parlours and used intact grenades as billiard balls.[29]

Afzal Guru could not find any organization to which he could offer his wholehearted allegiance. The JKLF had been decimated and he did not agree with the objectives of the Hizbul Mujahideen. Temperamentally, he could not work with any group to whom he did not feel absolute loyalty. It was also said that when Afzal was ordered to extort money from Sopore businessmen, he refused. It was then that he decided to leave the life of a militant and return to his studies.[30]

Afzal longed to become a doctor but he could not afford to go to medical college. There was no one to support him; Aijaz was angry with him for giving up his studies and going across the border. In any case, Aijaz was now married with a family of his own and could not afford to support his younger brother.

The Indian army had moved into Sopore in 1993 and had carried out intensive counterinsurgency operations, including setting an entire bazaar on fire and destroying the economy. In the same year, on 31 March, Afzal's uncle, Dr Abdul Ahad Guru, was shot dead while he was on his way back home from the hospital. The controversies around the question of who was responsible for his assassination reflect the complexities of the Kashmiri movement for self-determination.

An international human rights organization investigated into the reasons behind the assassination of this famous cardiothoracic surgeon.[31] The Report stated:

> Dr. Abdul Ahad Guru, a renowned Kashmiri cardiothoracic surgeon, was assassinated by unidentified gunmen in Srinagar on March 31, 1993. Dr. Guru was a member of the governing council of the Jammu and Kashmir Liberation Front (JKLF), and his political position made him a target for rival militant groups as well as elements within his own organization. He was also an outspoken critic of human rights abuses by Indian security forces in Kashmir, and met frequently with the international press and international human rights groups. While it is not possible to say for certain who was responsible for Dr. Guru's murder, there is substantial circumstantial evidence implicating militant groups. At the same time, serious questions remain about the government's actions before and after the murder.

However, the Report recorded that:

> Government sources have claimed that Dr. Guru was targeted because he was involved in negotiations with Minister of State for Internal Security Rajesh Pilot and others about a political settlement to the conflict. However, in a letter dated April 7, 1993, to Dr. Guru's son expressing condolences on the death of his father, Minister Pilot stated that he never met Dr. Guru.

Dr Guru's body was found about a kilometre from the nearest security post. This would indicate that the Indian state had been involved in his murder; the militants would not have carried out the assassination near an Indian army post.

A senior bureaucrat posted in Kashmir at that time, Wajahat Habibullah, wrote that Dr Guru was killed by a militant of the Hizbul Mujahideen by the name Zulkarnain who was in the custody of the police. The militant was offered his freedom in exchange for the assassination of the doctor, but the director general of police, B.S. Bedi, made sure that Zulkarnain was killed soon after.[32]

This revelation exposed how the state forces used the inter-group rivalries for their own insidious purposes. They made it look as if Dr Guru's killing was the work of the Hizbul Mujahideen, a pro-Pakistani fundamentalist group which had a running battle with the JKLF to which Dr Guru was aligned. But those who were close to him knew that Guru was on good terms with the Hizbul Mujahideen.

The state had targeted Dr Guru and his family many times before. They had tried to frame him in false cases, and even arrested him and his family members. At the same time, they had also used his services when they needed someone to negotiate with the militants for hostages. It was Dr Guru who had successfully brokered the release of Rubaiya, the daughter of the then home minister.

Sampat Prakash said that he had made his own investigations into the killing of Dr Guru. He said George Fernandes had come to Srinagar in 1990 when he was minister-in-charge of Kashmir Affairs. He had met the heads of the various intelligence agencies and they had all thought that it would be best to replace the National Conference with the JKLF and make Dr Guru the chief minister. The mirwaiz had agreed to be a part of the coalition. It was further agreed that the 1953 position would be restored and the Delhi Agreement would be fully implemented.[33] George had had a dialogue with the JKLF as well and then returned to Delhi.

According to Sampat, the former prime ministers, V.P. Singh, Rajiv Gandhi, and Atal Bihari Vajpayee, and the CPI(M) leader, Harkrishan Singh Surjeet, were privy to the discussion. George was so excited about the agreement that in his enthusiasm, he picked up the phone and told the mirwaiz, Maulvi Farooq, about it. The conversation was overheard by the Jamaat-e-Islami members at the telephone exchange and they informed the ISI. That is why both Dr Guru and the mirwaiz were killed by pro-Pakistan militants.[34]

I asked Sampat how he knew this story. He said George Fernandes had himself told it to him. But he had also confirmed it by asking the security guards, who were members of his union, who had been present during the negotiations. A comrade in the Post and Telegraph Union, who had made enquiries at the telephone exchange, also confirmed the story.

But then what about Wajahat Habibullah's version? Sampat said it could be that Pakistan had sympathizers within the Kashmiri bureaucracy, or it could be that someone in the Indian intelligence agencies did not want the talks to be successful. In Kashmir, politics has always been complicated.

—

Sampat and his comrades in the Low Paid Government Servants Federation had been watching the events unfold with growing unease, particularly the large protests organized by the Muslim United Front. The MUF had even tried to set up a trade union called the Muslim Employees Federation with Abdul Ghani Bhat as its president. Professor Bhatt used to teach Persian in Sopore College till he was dismissed. However, when the Muslim Employees Federation called for the employees to assemble, there was almost no response. The employees already had an organization which had served them well; they were not going to sacrifice it at the altar of Islamic militancy.

In any case, the Low Paid Government Servants Federation had been mobilizing the employees for strikes in support of their demand for the implementation of the Fourth Pay Commission. Sampat thought that it would be important to continue with this movement as it would unite all the employees and also counter the growing popularity of the MUF without actually confronting it.

From August 1987, MUF supporters had started taking out processions in the afternoon after the Friday prayers. Right across the Valley, men would pour out of every mosque shouting slogans:

'Yahan kya chalega? Nizam-e-Mustafa'; 'Musalmaan ke teen nishan, Allah, Mohammad aur Quran'; 'Azadi ka matlab kya? La Illahi il-Allah' and 'Jabri nata tode do, Kashmir hamara chhor do'.

The Low Paid Government Servants Federation timed their processions to coincide with the ones organized by the MUF. For a month, on every Friday at two in the afternoon, after the namaaz, the union took out processions demanding the implementation of the Fourth Pay Commission. These processions took place at all district headquarters and even at the tehsil level. In Srinagar, employees from the hundreds of government offices streamed out of their departments and marched to a central place, usually the Sher-e-Kashmir Park.

The union members were extremely disciplined: marching three men in a row, they would carry their red flags and shout their slogans with gusto: 'Red flag up, up Capitalism down, down; Implement Fourth Pay Commission Now'.

Often, the trade union's slogans were louder and more dramatic and their flags were held higher. After a month of agitation, the Federation called for a three-day strike, from 22 to 24 September 1987. The government wanted to negotiate, and among those who went for the talks were Rashid Khan, the man who had fought so valiantly for the rights of the shepherds, Punoo from the horticulture department, a younger comrade, Nisar Ali Mir, who worked in the Government Press, and another executive member called Ishtiaq Qadri, a medical worker. The union members were successful in their negotiations with Farooq Abdullah and 80 per cent of the demands were met.

The union continued its activities in Jammu and Kashmir. In November 1989 came the Parliament elections and the JKLF called for a boycott. In the first week of December, Sampat's union leaders saw an advertisement in the local newspapers. It was a statement from Javed Ahmad Mir of the JKLF warning Sampat Prakash and his comrades to leave the Valley within twenty-four hours.

The trade union leaders informed Sampat Prakash about this warning and asked what they should do. They all agreed that he should not return to the Kashmir Valley for some time and that the other members should also lie low for a while.

That is the reason why Sampat Prakash had to leave his beloved Valley from 1990 to 1994. However, Sampat was not the kind of person who felt paralyzed in the worst of times. He was aware of the widespread human rights violations being committed by the Indian security forces and decided to show his solidarity for the Kashmiri movement by broadcasting these atrocities all over India.

The Party to which he belonged, the CPI(M), thought it was ill-advised to focus on human rights violations because it would add grist to the mill of the pro-Pakistani Islamic militants financed by the Pakistani intelligence services. Sampat did not disagree with their analysis, but he knew that the outrages being committed every day would only further alienate the Kashmiris from the Indians. He suggested that the Party organize a big conference on Kashmir where they would take up the human rights issue, as well as the dubious role of the ISI in Kashmir. But the Party bosses did not agree.

Since the party refused to give him even tacit permission to take up the issues he thought were important both for Kashmir and for his own political survival, he decided to leave the CPI(M) and in 1990 he joined the Hind Mazdoor Kisan Parishad (HMKP), headed by George Fernandes.

George gave him the space to campaign about the plight of the Kashmiris, and so between 1990 and 1994, Sampat travelled all over India talking about and publicizing the human rights violations being committed on the people of the Valley by the Indian security forces. His comrades in the trade union kept him informed of the events and sent him local newspaper cuttings and photographs of the atrocities, which he exhibited at various meetings.

At about this time, another Kashmiri Pandit, Hriday Nath Wanchoo, now retired from trade union activities, was documenting the violations perpetrated by the Indian security forces. P.M. Varadarajan, a lecturer of Law at Oxford, who was writing a report on human rights violations in Kashmir on behalf of the Paris-based

La Fédération internationale desligues des droits de l'Homme, met Wanchoo. The trade union leader told him that he had estimated that approximately 15,000 persons had been shot dead by the security forces between January 1990 and 1992 and over 300 killed during interrogation, further there were at least sixty documented cases of rape during the same period.[35]

In early 1994, Sampat received a message that one of his comrades, Gul Mohammad Gania, was dying. He had cancer and it would be just a matter of a few days before he passed. Sampat Prakash took a taxi from Jammu and went straight to Anantnag, to his comrade's home. He spent a whole day with him, holding his hand and chatting about the good old days. Then he left by taxi, back to Jammu.

I asked Sampat why he had taken such a risk. He looked at me and said: 'There is such a thing as humanism.' Then he told me how Gul Mohammad and his wife Sara had come down for the weddings of both of his sons—Lenin's in 1991 and Ravinder's in 1992. Sara was the president of the Hospital Nurses Association and her husband had been in charge of Anantnag district. Sara had played the tumbaknari on both occasions and the couple had danced. They, too, had taken a grave risk because a JKLF militant called Manzoor Darzi lived near their home and was known to have killed many Pandits; he certainly would not have approved of this friendship.

Later the same year, in the summer of 1994, Sampat had another opportunity to go back to the Valley. At that time, he was in Dhanbad, Bihar, attending a HMKP conference. He had gone there with eight other members of his union and they had spoken about the situation in Kashmir.

The newspapers had reported that Yasin Malik had been released from a sub-jail in Mehrauli. He had been arrested on 6 August 1990 but had not been produced before a court of law till May 1993. He had suffered a stroke while in jail. Yasin had also written to the then prime minister, Narasimha Rao, about the reign of terror let loose in Kashmir by the Indian security forces.[36]

A day after his release, on 18 May, Yasin returned to Srinagar and was given a hero's welcome. He was showered with flower petals and dates, and as an Indian journalist, Harjinder Baweja, noted, 'his welcome was similar to the response Sheikh Abdullah used to receive during his heydays'.[37] George Fernandes wanted to send a confidential letter to the Kashmiri leader, and he chose Sampat as his emissary.

Although George was no longer in government, he had maintained close links with the militants and had hoped to be able to play a role in brokering peace.[38] George, like many other Indian leaders felt that Yasin Malik would be the best person with whom the Indian government could negotiate and resolve the Kashmir conflict.

In fact, the Americans and the British had already helped to broker a peace deal with Yasin Malik.[39] Yasin Malik had said that from the 1980s, the Western states, including the European Union, had tried to persuade him to abandon armed struggle and start a non-violent movement. They promised him their support if he would alter the focus of his movement.

Members of the Indian civil society had facilitated the negotiations, and while Yasin was in jail, several Indian intellectuals visited him. Among them were Kuldip Nayyar, a senior journalist; V.M. Tarkunde, former judge; Tapan Bose, a filmmaker; and Nalini Singh, a journalist.[40] George Fernandes knew of these events and had been informed by his sources that Yasin was willing to give up armed resistance and negotiate with the government of India.

Yasin's credentials as a Kashmiri nationalist could not be questioned. He enjoyed a credibility which no other leader enjoyed at the time. He was one of the four members of the legendary HAJY (for Hameed, Ashfaq, Javed and Yasin) group—the first to return to Kashmir after training in armed resistance from Pakistan. The other three members were: Sheikh Abdul Hameed (killed in 1992), Ashfaq Majid (killed in 1990) and Javed Mir.[41] In July 1988, the HAJY group had planted two bombs, one at the Golf Course and the other at the Telegraph Office in Srinagar; this was the beginning of the Kashmir uprising.

Besides, Yasin had always said that he wanted the Kashmiri Pandits to return to the Valley and that he was committed to facilitating the process. He had respect for Kashmiri Sufi traditions, unlike the pro-Pakistani Kashmiri leaders who repudiated them and were more inclined towards the Salafi interpretation of purist Islam. More importantly, he had never supported the idea of Kashmir merging with Pakistan.

Sampat willingly agreed to go to Srinagar to deliver the letter because he saw it as an opportunity to return to the Valley and resume his political work. He was aware that the situation in the Valley had changed. There was a growing disillusionment with the militancy, especially the role of foreign militants. There had been a public protest against the murder of a Pandit family in April 1992 in which 5,000 Kashmiri Muslim women had taken part. People had also protested against the kidnapping of Nahida Imtiaz, the daughter of Saifuddin Soz, a National Conference leader. There had been protests over attacks on Hindu shopkeepers, and in some places the people were raising another kind of slogan: 'Jo mangega Pakistan, Usko milega kabristan' (Whoever asks for Pakistan will receive a grave). Sampat had never met Yasin Malik and was looking forward to their meeting.

Sampat Prakash went to Yasin's home in Maisuma with Ghulam Mohammad, secretary of the Road Transport Corporation Employees Union. Ghulam Mohammad knew Yasin's father, who was a government bus driver and a member of the union.

Yasin's sisters took Sampat to meet their brother in SMH Hospital. He was warmly welcomed by Yasin and the two men established cordial relations. Yasin even invited Sampat to stay with him while he addressed a press conference from his hospital bed. The next day the union members were shocked to see Sampat Prakash's photograph in the newspapers along with Yasin Malik.

Sampat had one more task before leaving Srinagar. He wanted to see his old home in Rainawari. Accompanied by his comrade, Nisar Ali Mir, he went there.

Sampat Prakash knew that there would be no relatives to welcome him in Rainawari. His parents and extended family had shifted to Jammu in 1990; he still remembered when his home in Jammu became a refugee camp when all his uncles, cousins, sisters and even the sisters-in-law with their families came down from the Valley. Sampat's uncle, Balajee Kundu's liquor shops had been destroyed by the women activists of the Dukhtaran-e-Millat, or the Daughters of the Faith,[42] and the family had paid a hefty ransom to free him. But the others were safe and living in Jammu. There were fifteen to sixteen people living in Sampat's home and then Dura's family, too, joined them.

The house at Rainawari was empty, as he knew it would be, but he had thought that it would still be a home and perhaps he could carry back a few things for his mother, some memories. Nothing, however, had prepared him for the shock of what he saw. The house was truly empty: the doors swung on their hinges, all the utensils, mattresses and pillows, and electrical fittings and fixtures had been removed. There was not even a carpet on the floor, and neither was there any furniture. Sampat noted with dismay that his prized records had been taken. He went to each of the four houses, walking through the rooms in a daze. Each one had been stripped bare, everything looted—the sanctity of his home had been violated.

Sampat Prakash felt a deep surge of anger. His neighbours, the Baqaals, appeared after they saw him come out of his empty home. They embraced and invited him to their house. They served him tea and tried to tell him that the looting had been done by the CRPF that had set up a post near the house. But Sampat made his own enquiries and discovered that one of the Baqaals had instigated the vandalizing of his home. He even found out that Rasheed Baqaal, who had joined the JKLF, had invited his friends and taken part in the desecration.

From his home, he walked down to the home of his friend, Jawaharlal Dhar. That house, too, had been ransacked and looked like a haunted place. Nisar made enquiries about who was responsible and found out that it was the milkman who had supplied milk to the Dhars.

Sampat was angered not so much by the loss of his property but by the fact that the empty houses had made a mockery of his cherished ideal of Kashmiriyat. The bitter truth had dawned on him that the looting and robbing of the homes and shops of the Kashmiri Pandits was largely committed by the local people, while foreign militants were responsible for the rapes and the murders.

—

Yasin Malik announced a unilateral ceasefire and said that he would no longer use arms to achieve his goal of liberating Kashmir from Indian occupation. He added that he would continue his resistance through democratic means. In June 1994, he went on an indefinite hunger strike to protest against the entry of criminal elements into the JKLF and other organizations; his strike was condemned as 'un-Islamic' by Islamic militants.

In the winter months, Sampat read that Yasin Malik was in Jammu. Soon after, he found Javed Mir, an activist of the JKLF, on his doorstep with a message from Yasin to meet him at Samrat Hotel. Sampat was excited at the prospect of meeting Yasin again. Yasin greeted him with the same warmth he had shown at the hospital. He invited Sampat back to Srinagar and said that since he had no home, he would arrange accommodation for him and his family. Yasin encouraged Sampat to revive his trade union activities and the two leaders agreed to meet the next day to finalize the programme for Sampat's return. Yasin arranged for a car to drop him back.

However, the next day, when Sampat arrived, Yasin was not very warm. He also noticed that Ishtiaq Qadri was present. Qadri had been a member of the Low Paid Government Servants Federation. He was an ambitious man and, in 1990, had instigated some people in the JKLF to threaten Sampat and his colleagues so that they would leave the Valley and he could take over the union leadership.

There was something ominous about his presence. Sampat knew

that Qadri would not like the idea of him returning to the Valley. He must have poisoned Yasin's mind and that accounted for the cold reception Sampat had received from the Kashmiri leader.[43] There was no further conversation on the future of the trade union that day. It would be several years before Sampat could finally return to the Valley and resume his political work.

—

Mohammad Afzal Guru, too, was living in exile during those years. The assassination of his mentor, Dr Guru, the counterinsurgency operations in Sopore and the lack of discipline in the movement had compelled him to give in to his family's pressure and to surrender to the Border Security Force. He officially became a surrendered militant. However, the Border Security Force would not give him the certificate until he had motivated two other Kashmiri militants to surrender as well. Afzal managed to fulfil this condition and was issued the certificate that should have been his passport to a peaceful life. But that was not to be. The intelligence agencies wanted him to give them more information on other militants and Afzal was not willing to do that.

Then it occurred to him that he could go to Delhi where his cousin Shaukat Hussain Guru was living. Shaukat was studying at the Delhi University; perhaps Afzal could also get admission and continue his studies in some field other than medicine.

Shaukat was temperamentally very different from Afzal. He was tall, flashy and had a way with women. He was married to a Sikh girl, Navjot, who had converted to Islam, and went by the name of Afsan Guru.

Navjot was one of the four arrested and charged with conspiring to attack the Indian Parliament. I still remember when I first set my eyes on the sad, distraught figure of the young woman, heavily pregnant, sitting in the courtroom, crying quietly. The only person who had a hand on her shoulder to give her comfort was a uniformed policewoman.

Navjot must have once been a spunky Punjabi woman who defied her family and married the tall, handsome Kashmiri Muslim. Everyone in her family had opposed the marriage, including her mother. The only person who stood by her was her father, a quiet Sikh man with enormous fortitude and dignity. On one of our meetings, he said he believed Sikhism had much in common with Islam.

However, the rest of Navjot's family and relatives did not approve of alliances with Muslims. A part of the hostility could be explained by their experiences during Partition which had left wounds that had never healed. Bismillah Geelani told me that it was very rare to find Sikhs and Muslims as friends. I asked him how was it that Kashmiri militants had an alliance with the Khalistanis? 'Those are political alliances,' he replied.

But Navjot and Shaukat were not political people and their marriage was not a political alliance; it was a love affair and neither expected to have their first child in Tihar Jail. In fact, Shaukat was hoping that he and his wife could join her brother in Australia. They could have a good life there.

In the meantime, Navjot's father encouraged his son-in-law to start a fruit-selling business so that he could earn a decent living. He had even presented him with a truck to help him out. The old man never thought that this truck would become an exhibit in a criminal case in a designated court under the new anti-terrorist law.

When Afzal arrived in Delhi, Shaukat and Navjot were still not married, but he was a witness to their romance as well as their marriage. Shaukat introduced Afzal to another Kashmiri, Syed Abdul Rehman Geelani, a student in the Linguistics Department of Delhi University, who helped him get admission into a distance education course at the university. All through this period, the three Kashmiri men—Geelani, Afzal and Shaukat—had different dreams and ambitions, and they did not meet very often. They could never have imagined that one day they would be accused of planning to attack the Indian Parliament.

Between 1990 and 1996, Mohammad Afzal Guru stayed in Delhi. He earned a little by giving tuitions, and even managed to graduate from Delhi University. Unlike his other two fellow Kashmiris, Afzal never took to life in Delhi. He missed the beauty and quiet of the nights in his village and, above all, he missed his mother, Ayesha Begum. It was Afzal who used to help her with household chores and even washed her clothes. Now only his youngest brother, Hilal, was with her, but he was working as a construction labourer. His other brother, Riyaz, had also shifted to Delhi and had set up a shop selling handicrafts.

In 1996, both Mohammad Afzal Guru and Sampat Prakash finally returned to their beloved Kashmir Valley. And it would be six years after that, in 2002, that their paths would cross—not in Kashmir, but in a trial court in Delhi. By that time, both India and Pakistan would have become nuclear powers.

IN THE EYE OF THE STORM
(1990s)

I could see the trade union leaders waiting for me at the bus stop. The moment I stepped out of the bus, they took my suitcase and we deposited it in a shop near the Government Press. Nisar Ali Mir said, 'That has been our unofficial office.'

Nisar Ali told me that one of his first jobs in the trade union movement was to secretly publish the pamphlets and posters in the press, and then paste them all over the town at night—in those days there was no other means of communication. It was at the Government Press that he met the senior trade union leaders like Shishupal[1] and Abdul Majid Khan. He specially remembered Abdul Majid's beautiful handwriting. Nisar Ali Mir's face wore a sad expression when he turned to me to say: 'After the leaders were dismissed from service, they had to face terrible hardships and poverty. But none of their difficulties ever lessened their passion for justice, and they are loved and remembered by the employees even now.'

I asked Nisar Ali what it was like in the days when the insurgency began in the late 1980s and 90s. Anyone who witnessed the number of people who took to the streets in those early days would have recognized that it reflected the outpouring of the anger, pain and resentment against Indian state policies. Some of the biggest rallies were held in the first few months of 1990.

Nisar Ali's face lit up and without hesitation he said the most memorable moment in his political life was when he met the leader of the JKLF, Ashfaq Majid Wani. The leader had called Nisar Ali and Sampat Prakash to a hotel to discuss the Federation's role in the uprising with them. The trade union leaders told Ashfaq that since they were government employees, they could not openly support armed resistance. They had, however, called for the speedy implementation of the recommendations of the Fourth Pay Commission, but if the recommendations were not enforced, the Federation intended to call for a boycott of the elections. By the time the Parliamentary elections of 1989 were announced, the Federation had declared that the government employees would not go on election duty since their demands had not been met entirely. Farooq Abdullah had conceded only 80 per cent of their demands.

Nisar Ali was one of the many thousands of people who poured onto the streets of Srinagar on 30 March 1990 for the funeral of Ashfaq Majid Wani, who had been killed in an encounter. He was just twenty-three years old. Ashfaq had studied at the Tyndale Biscoe School and later at the S.P. College and was known to be good at sports, including football, table tennis and athletics.

Sampat said that Ashfaq's funeral was even attended by senior bureaucrats. The sentiment at the time was strongly in favour of independent Kashmir, but it was neither pro-Pakistani nor was it for jihad. The members of the JKLF were basically children of the National Conference, and represented Kashmiri nationalism.

However, this seemed to me to be a simplistic way of looking at the ideology of the JKLF. Unlike the National Conference leaders of the past, many of whom had been influenced by the Russian and Chinese revolutions, Ashfaq's sources of inspiration were very different. In a rare interview with Ashfaq's father, Abdul Majid Wani, we get a glimpse of the events that shaped his ideals and ideas.[2]

———

On 8 September 1982, Abdul Majid Wani was one of the million people who had gathered for the funeral of Sheikh Mohammad Abdullah. An avid supporter of the National Conference, Wani, along with many family members, had assembled at the Polo Ground in Srinagar to catch a last glimpse of the mortal remains of the Sheikh.

His son, Ashfaq, however, had refused to accompany the family. At the time, the father thought that the refusal was just part of a teenager's rebellion. Later he realized that it reflected his son's pain and disillusionment that had congealed in his heart into hatred against the government.[3] He had become disillusioned with the prevailing political scenario, which favoured Indian suzerainty. He viewed the Indian occupation as 'a yoke of slavery'.[4]

Ashfaq's father said that Iran's Islamic Revolution of February 1979[5] had left an indelible mark on his son and he had studied the history of the events leading to the uprising. While he was a student at Tyndale Biscoe, Ashfaq had suggested to the principal that they should hang a picture of Ayatollah Khomeini instead of Jesus Christ. He had also insisted that students be allowed to attend Friday prayers at the mosque.

Ashfaq was sixteen years old when Maqbool Butt was hanged on 11 February 1984. The news had deeply disturbed the teenager and he tried unsuccessfully to garner support for a day commemorating Maqbool Butt the following year. His failure, however, did not dispirit him. In 1986, instead of asking people to support him, he marched alone through Hari Singh High Street with a green flag, shouting anti-India slogans and extolling Butt as a national hero. In this way he managed to attract two hundred boys who were standing on the street, and the city square resonated with slogans for freedom.

A year earlier, in 1985, Ashfaq and four other students formed the Islamic Students League, which rejected the un-Islamic and man-made concepts of Socialism and secularism. The other members of the core group were—Hameed Sheikh, Javed Ahmad Mir and Mohammad Yasin Malik, the future HAJY group.[6]

Ashfaq used to listen to the speeches of the moulvi who was then officiating at the Gowkadal Mosque, a stone's throw from S.P. College. An exceptional orator, his efficacious rhetoric fanned the passions of the throngs of people that gathered there on Fridays.

Ashfaq, a regular at the mosque, was not an exception. The sermons were around the theme of imperialist Soviet Union and its invasion of Afghanistan. The maulvi would compare the Indian occupation of Kashmir with the Soviet occupation of Afghanistan.

For the Islamists, the Taliban had succeeded in disintegrating the mighty, godless Soviet Union. This victory of the Taliban filled hope in the hearts of many Kashmiris because they believed that they, too, could liberate Kashmir from Indian occupation with the help of their Muslim brothers from all over the world.

I understood how Iran's Islamic Revolution could have inspired the Kashmiri Muslim youth, but I did not understand how they could have been so ignorant of the fact that the fall of the Soviet Union had been engineered by the US. Without the massive funding and arms, the Taliban could never have succeeded. That is why the Kashmiri insurgents looked to the West for help; that is why through the years of insurgency, despite the anti-American rhetoric, the youth in Kashmir never brought out demonstrations against the US and its outrages in West Asia. According to Sampat Prakash, this was because the Kashmiri movement itself had received so much support from the West—the media, the international human rights organizations and funding through NGOs.

Moreover, there were other, more immediate sources of inspiration for the Kashmiri youth. In 1985 Ashfaq went to see the *Lion of the Desert*, which, according to his father, stoked the fire raging in his son's heart. The film was a cathartic experience for Ashfaq, who, his father said, watched the movie with 'a heavy heart and at the climax, with his incandescent rage mingling with disillusionment, he buried his eyes in a handkerchief and wept'.

Hundreds of youth watched the film, and even after it had been banned by the government, the video continued to be circulated. As a friend of Ashfaq's recounted, 'The movie had worked its magic. It had evoked the demons of India's failed legacy in Kashmir.'

In 1987, Ashfaq was arrested for his involvement in demonstrations organized by the MUF to protest against the rigging of the election.

He was lodged at the Central Jail, Srinagar. After nine months, he was released on parole to attend his uncle's wedding. While serving food to the guests at the reception, he overheard Mohiuddin Shah, a veteran National Conference politician, say that agitations against the government were futile, whereupon Ashfaq retorted, 'The government made two grave mistakes as far as Kashmir is concerned. First, they acceded to India and second, they let me out on parole.' The next day he left with Yasin Malik for Pak-administered Kashmir.

———

Nisar Ali, like his trade union comrades, had a burning desire to see Kashmir independent. They had the same aspirations as hundreds of thousands of Kashmiris, which is why he could not understand why the newspapers had printed a threatening notice against him and other trade union leaders, ordering them to leave the Valley. He and most of the members, including Sampat Prakash, had always supported the cause of Kashmiri nationalism. Then why the threat? And that too from the JKLF; why did the JKLF want them to quit Kashmir?

Nisar Ali said the threats were real and had been published in the local papers. His family members had read them and feared the worst. Many Communists and members of the National Conference had to leave the Valley and take refuge in Jammu, but there was no arrangement for the Kashmiri Muslims who had to leave their homes. At least Sampat had a home in Jammu, unlike the other comrades who had nowhere to go.

Nisar and the other union leaders decided to contact Abdul Qadir Wani, the publicity secretary of the JKLF, and ask for a meeting with the organization. The militants sent a Gypsy to fetch Nisar and Abdul Rashid. Nisar still does not know where they were taken because they were told to keep their heads down, but the meeting did take place.

Nisar Ali gathered the courage to ask the militants why they had threatened the trade union leaders. After all, it was only their

Federation which had dared challenge Sheikh Abdullah. They had fought the injustices of both the Central and the state governments. How could they be labelled as traitors? They did not get an explanation but the militants told them to use their wide network of contacts to collect funds for them. Nisar Ali said that they would discuss the matter and it was only then that they were allowed to return safely. However, this was not to be his last encounter with the militants.

———

In the first week of June 1990, I found myself touring the villages of Kashmir as part of a four-member fact-finding team sent by the Committee for the Initiative on Kashmir. I had just returned to Delhi from the Northeast, where I was fighting a case against the Indian armed forces for having inflicted horrific atrocities on the Nagas living in the Senapati district of Manipur during Operation Bluebird, one of the largest counterinsurgency operations carried out by the army.[7]

After the tour of the villages, the other three members—Saqina Hasan, Premila Lewis and Suhasini Mulay—left, handing me their notes and giving me the responsibility of drafting our report. I stayed in the official residence of Ashok Jaitley, the then additional chief secretary of Jammu and Kashmir.

Normally, I would not have stayed in the home of a bureaucrat while on a fact-finding mission which involved documenting human rights violations by the government, but the situation in Kashmir then was quite extraordinary. Even senior bureaucrats were targets of state repression.

Jaitley gave me a letter signed by senior officers of the Indian Administrative Service to the governor of Jammu and Kashmir to protest against the 'indiscriminate killings of large numbers of peaceful processionists by nervous and trigger happy security forces'.[8] It especially mentioned the firing on the funeral procession of Mirwaiz Maulvi Farooq who was assassinated in 1990. On 21 May, when the funeral procession was passing near Islamia College, the procession was fired upon; sixty people died and the coffin itself was riddled with bullets.

There was also another letter to the Citizens of the World, addressed to the United Nations, initially signed by 137 officers of the government of Jammu and Kashmir. But that number increased to more than a thousand. It cited examples of firing on unarmed Kashmiris on different occasions when they were peacefully protesting against the repression by Indian security forces. They mentioned the firings in Zakura and Tangpora when the people were marching towards the office of the UNMOGIP to hand over a Memorandum demanding a referendum in accordance with the UN Resolutions. The Memorandum had stated that the killings and human rights violations 'brought shame to Indian democracy and left a scar on the psyche of Kashmir which would never be removed'.[9]

In their letter, the officers said that 'hundreds of civil servants have lost their jobs without undergoing the formality of even an enquiry. Many of them are imprisoned. Doctors have even been pushed into a strike at a time when they are needed most by the society. Their persecution continues while they are deliberately prevented from treating the sick and the injured'.[10]

The letter addressed to the United Nations was written mostly by Kashmiri officers who wanted the UN to intervene and solve the crisis. They were sympathetic to the militants and according to Sampat Prakash, some had even crossed over to Pakistan for training.

However, the letter addressed to the governor by bureaucrats such as Ashok Jaitley had been written with the hope of finding a remedy for the destructive policy conceived and conducted by Governor Jagmohan without consultation with seasoned and senior bureaucrats.[11]

The Central government did not differentiate between the two and as a result both the IAS officers and the officers of the state service were treated as anti-national and many were suspended. This problem came up in the Indian Parliament.

On 16 May 1990, the home minister, Mufti Mohammad Sayeed,

told the Rajya Sabha that 106 officers of the state had been sacked for being 'sympathetic to the cause of the separatist movement'. When the member of Parliament from Kashmir, N. Salaria, asked whether the officers had been asked for an explanation before they were dismissed, the home minister replied that there was 'no question of seeking any explanation when people had been found crossing the border to get training in subversive activities'.[12]

A few months after I left Kashmir, the government employees went on a seventy-two day strike between August and November 1990, in support of the demand for the reinstatement of the bureaucrats. I asked Nisar Ali whether their Federation had organized the strike.

The strike had been controlled by the bureaucrats and was under the banner of the Rabta Committee, and not the Low Paid Government Servants Federation. Nisar Ali's voice had an angry edge, which I had not heard before, when he recalled how the bureaucrats had used the employees for their own ends and had broken up their Federation.

Nisar Ali said that the employees were very disciplined throughout. The ones who suffered the most were the Class IV employees who had no money and so the trade union leaders collected funds for them. At the end of the seventy-two days, the bureaucrats got back their jobs and were subsequently promoted with good salaries. The employees, on the other hand, were not given wages for the duration of the strike. They were told that the seventy-two days would be converted into leave. This meant that the younger employees could, over time, convert their leave into cash but the older ones who were due to retire, lost amounts ranging from Rs 50,000-Rs 100,000 of their salaries.

Nisar Ali said that the strike was called off by Ghulam Hasan Aasmi, a union leader of the civil secretariat who was favoured by the bureaucrats. He said that someone must have made him withdraw the strike without negotiating for the rights of the employees who had formed the backbone of the strike.

The other leader who emerged during the strike was Ishtiaq Qadri who had been active during an agitation in the Medical Workers Association. Although he had played an important role during the seventy-two-day strike, he was not allowed to speak by Abdul Majid Mattoo, a civil engineer and one of the dismissed government servants. Ishtiaq and other trade union leaders, who were associated with the Low Paid Government Servants Federation, were known to be Communists and were thus not welcome; this ideology had slowly become an anathema.

Soon after the strike, Qadri announced that he was going to form another union, the Government Employees Conference, and invited Nisar Ali Mir to be its general secretary. The union was affiliated to the All Parties Hurriyat Conference (APHC) which was formed in March 1993; hurriyat in Arabic, Persian and Urdu means 'liberty'. The Hurriyat Conference was originally an alliance of twenty-six organizations committed to espousing the cause of Kashmiri independence. Since the international community disapproves of violence by non-state actors, the Hurriyat projected itself as a legitimate platform, pursuing its goal through peaceful means. It had the support of Pakistan, and there were even reports saying that it had the backing of the US. It was said that the Hurriyat was a creation of American interests in Kashmir and had been formed through the efforts of a Washington-based think-tank, the US Institute of Peace (USIP), under the presidentship of Robert Oakley, a former US ambassador to Pakistan.[13]

Although the Cold War was officially over after the disintegration of the Soviet Union, the Western policy of support for radical Islamists continued as long as the latter served their foreign policy interests.

Since the Low Paid Government Servants Federation had been identified as a Communist or anti-religious organization, it could no longer work under this name in Kashmir. However, it continued to operate under the name in Jammu and in Ladakh.

In Jammu, the Federation had to fight the Hindutva forces that were gaining ground. By 1990, the Bhartiya Mazdoor Sangh, affiliated to the RSS, had become the biggest trade union in the country. It had made significant inroads into the government employees unions and some associations that were affiliated to Sampat's Federation switched loyalties.

It was in same year that the BJP president, L.K. Advani, started his infamous chariot journey through the country, and by 1991 the Party had won more than 20 per cent of the votes in the country.

Nisar Ali said that although the union was affiliated to the Hurriyat, it was able to maintain a degree of autonomy by not becoming a front for any of the armed groups. At the same time, Nisar Ali and other Kashmiri employees felt a deep sense of oneness with the cause of Kashmiri freedom.

In April 1993, Nisar Ali Mir read in the newspapers that a police constable by the name of Riaz Ahmad had been killed while in custody of the security forces. The police were very angry but, since they had no association, they did not know how to react. Nisar Ali took the initiative and simply walked into the Police Control Room and spontaneously gave a speech to the policemen telling them that they had a constitutional right to protest. Nisar remembers this speech as the best one he has ever given.

The armed police were then given their first lesson in trade union organization. Nisar told them to raise their right arm and shout: 'Balwinder Singh Bedi murdabad'—(Bedi was the police chief). The police obeyed Nisar. Nisar would shout: 'Balwinder Singh Bedi' and the police would respond with a full-throated: 'Murdabad'.

Next, he asked them to call a meeting of the entire police force, which was not a difficult task since there was a telecommunication system that connected all of them. Soon, each police station had been alerted about the meeting.

Once the policemen had assembled, Nisar realized that he needed a mike, so he went to the nearby Batmaloo mosque and asked permission to borrow theirs. And then Nisar Ali inspired the police to form an association and invited them to affiliate themselves to his union. Nisar led the police in demonstrations and conducted meetings with a great deal of discipline. The strike was never allowed to become violent or unruly.

In retaliation, the government dismissed 109 policemen and the Garhwal Regiment was called in to restore order. The organization did not last. Nevertheless, the policemen got their first taste of trade unionism, and the dismissed policemen were finally reinstated after six years.

I asked Nisar Ali why I could not find any references to a police strike on the Internet. I had also searched the newspapers but had found nothing. He replied that the strike was famous all over the country as a police mutiny. 'But it was not a mutiny, it was a strike; we were merely asserting the rights we have under the Constitution.'

There was quiet pride in Nisar's tone when he described the police strike. He said that it was the last one till 2000. In that year, when the militancy had begun to die down, the government employees came out once again in their numbers and went on a forty-two-day strike in support of their demands for the regularization of services of daily-wage earners, the enhancement of the retirement age from fifty-eight to sixty and removal of pay anomalies.

Sampat and his family had been living with Nisar Ali ever since they sold their home in Rainawari. A room had been kept aside for them. Sampat said he even offered to sell his home in Rainawari to Nisar, but Nisar had refused to buy it. According to Nisar, his community, the Shias of Kashmir, had decided not to be a party to distress sales.[14] This was according to a directive issued by Aga Syed Yusuf Al-Moosavi Al-Safavi, a Kashmiri religious scholar and leader of Shia Muslims, who had forbidden them from buying land that had been confiscated during the 'Land to the Tillers' movement at the time when Sheikh Abdullah was implementing agrarian reform under the Naya Kashmir programme.[15]

According to Nisar Ali, the Hurriyat should have made a trust of the properties belonging to the Kashmiri Pandits and safeguarded it till the time they could return. But that was an ideal solution which only an idealist could dream about. By 1996, the situation in the Valley had become a little less volatile after the elections. However, it was also clear that the Kashmiri Pandits would not be returning to the Valley in the near future. It was at this time that the Kashmiri Muslims initiated the process of buying properties which had formerly belonged to Pandits. Brokers started contacting the Pandits living in refugee camps and those living in Jammu and Delhi. Sampat reluctantly admits that some of the government employees, too, were involved in the excerise.

Sampat's mother, Prabhawati, who had been contacted by a broker, also decided to sell their home in Rainawari. The three-storey house was in her name and after consulting her sons, she sold it for a paltry sum of Rs 300,000.

When Prabhawati related the painful details of how she decided to sell the property, one of her sons' wife intervened, saying bitterly, 'If Article 370 had not been there, the Pandits would have got a better price for their properties because non-Kashmiris could have bought the land, homes and orchards. More than 400 homes of Kashmiri Pandits in Rainawari were sold to Kashmiri Muslims. Now the Pandits have nowhere to go back to.'

Sampat countered her by saying that Kashmiri Muslims had suffered as much as the Kashmiri Pandits. A stony silence greeted his remark. He looked at one of his sisters-in-law and said: 'Didn't Abdul Ghani Parray buy a fridge for you when he came to see you in the camp?'

Sampat's young nephew intervened: 'Yes, I remember. He came to see us when we were living in one small room and when he asked for water we gave him a glass of warm water because we did not have a fridge. He did buy a fridge for us but we paid him for it.' The nephew added that he had to study in the camp and face discrimination from people in Jammu as well. Sampat persisted: 'I told your mother to at least write a letter of condolence to Abdul Ghani Parray when his son-in-law was killed in the Gawkadal massacre and his son disappeared.'[16]

I later met Abdul Ghani Parray in Natipora. He was an old man with a neat white beard, a book in hand and eyes that were full of kindness. He was sitting in a warm room with a huge window through which light was pouring in. I could not see any heater but the room was warm enough for us to take off our woollens. He explained that the room was warm throughout the day because firewood was kept burning in the hearth under the room, which kept the stone floor warm. The stones were special because they did not get too hot. And the smoke was brought in through pipes so that there was warm water in the bathroom. Parray said that this was also how the mosques in Kashmir were kept warm during the winter months. This unique way of heating was introduced by Mirza Haider Dughlat, a Kazakhistani who invaded Kashmir in 1540. His grave lies in Srinagar, a reminder of the links between Kashmir and Central Asia.[17]

Parray had retired as a government schoolteacher. He had known Sampat since they were both young boys. The two were temperamentally very different—Parray was quiet and dignified, never raising his voice, while Sampat had a volatile temper and was quick to show his anger.

Although Abdul Ghani Parray did not join the Communist Party, he did help the union leaders. He told me that he had seen the terrible condition Sampat and his comrades were in after they were dismissed. 'Sampat did not have money to buy cigarettes, but he would never ask for money.'

The man was so calm and dignified; his words measured, without a trace of anger. He spoke of his friendship with Sarvanand, Sampat's uncle, with warmth and respect. Abdul Ghani described how the Muslims and Hindus had lived together in harmony. But then why had the Kashmiri Pandit neighbours not felt grief when his son had disappeared and son-in-law killed? Sampat said: 'I don't understand.' His anger with his own relatives was apparent. Parray soothed him by turning the conversation to other topics.

—

The anger of the Kashmiri Pandits was directed mostly against the JKLF, an organization that Sampat nonetheless believed to be secular and genuinely committed to Kashmiri nationalism.

I asked Sampat Prakash why he had supported the JKLF even though they were responsible for the killings of so many Kashmiri Pandits? He said that in the early days, the JKLF could justify the murders by saying that the person assassinated was working against the movement, or was an informer. For instance, the JKLF justified the execution of Judge Neelkanth Ganjoo in November 1989 on the grounds that he had passed the death sentence on Maqbool Butt.

Then there was the assassination of Lassa Koul on 13 February 1990. He was the director of the Doordarshan TV station and his murder was explained on the grounds that he was calling the militants 'terrorists'. But would a warning not have sufficed?

I asked Sampat Prakash how the JKLF could have justified the murder of Sarla Bhat, a Kashmiri Pandit nurse working at the Sher-i-Kashmir Institute of Medical Sciences. He said that they had claimed that it was because she was providing information to the intelligence agencies on the militants admitted into the hospital. When Sarla's body was found on 14 April 1990, it showed that she had been raped before being murdered; this was something which could not be justified even by sympathizers of the JKLF.

Sampat Prakash did not justify these murders but he insisted that the JKLF was not a communal organization and that they killed both Hindus and Muslims. Apart from Lassa Koul, they had also killed ten Muslim journalists. It was a bizarre way of defining secularism, but the brutal reality was that the brunt of the civilian casualties was borne by the people belonging to the majority community—the

Kashmiri Muslims. For instance, in the first three months of 1990, the number of Hindus killed was twenty-three, the Muslims twenty-five. In the next four months, between April and June, the number of Hindus killed was sixty-seven, Muslims ninety-four; and between July and August the number of Hindus killed was thirty-two, Muslims forty-nine.[18]

The militants had targeted both the National Conference members and the Communists. Many of the Communists left the Valley and took shelter in refugee camps in Jammu. In June 1990, when I had gone to Kashmir on a fact-finding tour, we had stopped at Jammu to interview the Kashmiri Pandits who had taken refuge there. What had shocked me was that most of the refugees were Communists. However, the Hindu Communists and Muslim Communists did not stay together. The fact that they were divided along communal lines disturbed me more than anything I saw.

Sampat had been a witness to this divide and had spent many hours in heated discussions with his comrades who had now started advocating a separate homeland for Kashmiri Pandits, which they called Panun Kashmir (our own Kashmir).[19] Many of these discussions took place in the Kashmir Coffee House, near the Tawi bridge in Jammu.

One day, in 1992, Sampat Prakash walked into the coffee house hoping to have a political discussion with some of the intellectuals on the situation in the Valley. On entering the café, he found a group of Kashmiri Pandit intellectuals. Among them was Dr Mohan Krishan Teng. He had a PhD from Lucknow University and was teaching at S.P. College; later he taught at the Kashmir University. He was a respected teacher and a member of the Communist Party of India. He had joined the CPI (M) when the Party split in 1964 and subscribed to People's Democracy. He had now become an advocate for a homeland for Kashmiri Pandits. In December 1991, Teng and his supporters had organized a convention in Jammu called

'Margdarshan'. The delegates had adopted a resolution stating that the 700,000 Kashmiri Hindus, including those driven out of Kashmir in the past, yearned to return to their 'homeland' and that the organization would fight for 'the establishment of a Homeland for the Kashmiri Hindus in the Valley of Kashmir comprising the regions of the Valley to the East and North of the river Jhelum'.[20] Sampat was dead against this demand and the politics which had given birth to it; he felt that even the articulation of such a demand was like sounding the death knell for Kashmiriyat.

In the past, Sampat and Teng had had many a heated argument. But that day when he entered the café, he was taken aback when Teng stood up to greet him. Sampat ignored the gesture and fired the first volley in an attempt to provoke the Kashmiri Pandit.

Then, someone said to him: 'Congratulations, you and Dr Teng are about to become relatives.' Sampat was stunned when he was told that his son, Ravinder, had agreed to marry Teng's daughter. He hadn't heard the news because he had just arrived from Kashmir and had come directly to the café without going home.

At first Sampat thought that the young people were having a love affair, but he was even more upset to learn that his sister's mother-in-law and his wife had conspired to make this happen. The two women had even got the horoscopes of the two matched, and the astrologer had ratified it. Sampat's parents, too, had approved and his mother had gone to the temple to seek god's blessings. Now they were all was waiting for Sampat's approval.

Sampat went home, called his son and asked him whether he had thought through his decision to marry the daughter of a man his father violently opposed. Teng and he would always stand on opposite sides and this clash of political ideology could very well come in the way of family relations, i.e. between father and son.

Ravinder reassured his father by saying that he would never publicly oppose his political stand. But what about Teng's daughter? How would she cope with the political clashes between her father and would-be father-in-law? Ravinder said that Teng had told his daughter that she would have to learn never to contradict her father-in-law, never to oppose him politically or to argue with him.

Having no choice in the matter, Sampat had insisted on a simple wedding with no exchange of expensive gifts. After the wedding, Sampat took his new daughter-in-law to meet the Hurriyat leaders and when he invited some of them to his home, Teng's daughter found herself serving tea to the members of the JKLF.

Sampat had taken me to meet Teng in Faridabad several years ago and I heard the raging debates between the two men. Sampat was emotional and passionate; Teng countered with reasoned arguments. Sampat accused the Kashmiri Pandit intellectuals of not showing any empathy with the Kashmiri Muslims who had been victims of horrendous crimes committed by Indian security forces against unarmed Kashmiris, such as the killings at Gawkadal. Teng responded by pointing out that no Muslim organization had ever condemned the killing of the Kashmiri Pandits and had actually driven them out. Teng called it ethnic genocide. Listening to the two of them, I began to see how both the Panun Kashmirwalas and the militants had made it impossible for ordinary Kashmiris of both communities to express their feelings in an open manner. Later, I also read the story of Manohar Lal, a government servant and a Kashmiri Pandit who was witness to the Gawkadal massacre.

Manohar Lal lived near Gawkadal and he told a journalist, Umar Manzoor Shah, that the day of the massacre was the 'most dreadful day of my life'. Lal, who along with his family still resided in the locality, said he was in his home when he heard bullets slamming all around. 'Then there were screams and cries. I peeped through my window and what I saw at that time still traumatizes me. I still have sleepless nights when I recall that incident,' he said.

Lal and his family had stayed on in Kashmir even though all his relatives, like other Kashmiri Pandits, had fled the Valley soon after the militancy started. 'I have witnessed all the gory scenes here. I stand witness to the events and how innocents were killed and tortured every day during that period.'

During those days, he and his family stayed at home and his Muslim neighbours provided them with essentials. A month after the massacre, his wife, Rachna, went to the market and was told by many people to leave the Valley, but Manohar felt that this was their home, the place of 'our ancestors'. 'We should be together in harsh and good times.'

Every year, on 22 January, Manohar Lal participates in a protest demonstration against the massacre. 'I participate in the demonstration to register my silent protest against the incident that took place before my eyes. While participating, I keep my identity a secret. I do not tell other protesters that I am a Pandit,' he said.[21]

Sampat Prakash insisted that if the Kashmiri Pandits had decided to stay on, the situation would never have come to such a pass. After all, so many Kashmiri Muslims had continued to stay in the Valley even though they were threatened by both the militants and the Indian security forces. But Dr Teng argued that if the Pandits had stayed on they would all have been massacred.

While Teng asserted the right of Kashmiri Pandits to be acknowledged as the true bearers of Kashmiri culture and civilization, Sampat Prakash said that the Kashmiri Pandits had not adequately acknowledged the role of Kashmiri Muslims in building that culture. Sampat said that the Kashmiri Pandit had forgotten the many ways in which the Kashmiri Muslim had served him over the years: the Kashmiri Muslim made the bricks to build his home, cut the stones for his temples; the Kashmiri Muslim carpenter made the beams and doors for the temples; the Kashmiri Muslim mason mixed the cement and the sand, and even made the idols. The stone flooring of Kheer Bhawani had been laid by the Muslims. What did the Kashmiri Pandit do? He installed the idol, purified the temple with holy water and milk, and did not allow the Kashmiri Muslim to enter it.

Sampat continued his impassioned speech—the Kashmiri Muslim made the quilts, the mattresses and pillows used by the Kashmiri

Pandits; he embroidered the cloth worn by the Kashmiri Pandits; he carved the wood and even caught the fish and butchered the goat for the Kashmiri Pandit.

Sampat had asserted many times that the Kashmiri Pandits should have looked for jobs other than government jobs; their obsession with government jobs prevented them from taking advantage of other opportunities in the private sector.[22] The Kashmiri Pandits were just clerks and pushed the pen and little else.

Teng listened patiently but his heart was not ignited by the fire of Sampat's passion. Teng was polite but firm and he insisted that the secular forces in India had been guilty of patronizing Muslim-identity politics. He called the movement for Azadi a terrorist movement; the militants were not insurgents but mere terrorists.

Dr Teng claimed that thousands of Kashmiri Pandits had been murdered by the Kashmiri militants.[23] According to him, the human rights organizations had always focused only on the number of Muslims killed by security forces and not the Pandits killed by the militants.

The fact is that international human rights organizations such as Amnesty International and Human Rights Watch serve the foreign policy interests of Britain and the US. Human Rights Watch's institutional culture is shaped by its leadership's intimate links to various sections of the US government. The policies of these organizations coincide with the US foreign policy as it certainly did all through the period of insurgency in Kashmir.

However, by summarily dismissing the human rights violations documented meticulously by these organizations, the Indian government only added to the alienation of the Kashmiris from Delhi. The Left parties condemned the human rights organizations as agents of imperialism, but did little to address the very real grievances of the Kashmiris.

The problem is of estimating the extent of the human rights violations committed in Kashmir. This is because of the propensity of Kashmiris, both Hindus and Muslims, to exaggerate the figures of the people arrested, tortured or killed. A survey of the number of Kashmiri Hindus killed between 1990 and 2000 puts the figure at 650, of which 399 were killed in 1990 alone.[24] Sampat Prakash said that he had made a list of 544. On the other hand, Dr Teng claimed that more than a thousand Kashmiri Pandits were killed, but would not acknowledge that the bulk of the civilian casualties were Muslims. The militants had targeted members of the National Conference, the Congress Party and the Communists without discrimination.

Dr Teng and his organization insisted that the Pandits were terrorized by the militants and that is why they left their homes and came down to Jammu. They called it an exodus. However, there are no reliable figures which can indicate the number of Kashmiri Pandits who actually left the Valley.

Some say it was 700,000, others say it was 100,000. One of the main reasons for this ambiguity is because the numbers of Pandits in the Valley in 1989 can only be adduced from the census of 1941, the last time the Pandits had been counted and listed as distinct from the category of Kashmiri Hindus. And in that census, fewer than 79,000 Pandits were listed in the Valley.[25]

It's from this baseline that demographers have sought to work out the number of Kashmiri Pandits in the Valley in 1990. Using the rough measure of the average decennial growth rate in the state as a whole, available through the censuses up to 1941 and then the 2001 census, they arrive at the number of Pandits living in the Valley before 1990 to be about 160,000 to 170,000.

According to the political scientist Alexander Evans, 95 per cent of the Kashmiri Pandits left the Valley in 1990, i.e. any number between 150,000 and 160,000. However, a 2010 report of the Internal Displacement Monitoring Centre of the Norwegian Refugee Council suggests that 250,000 Pandits have been displaced since 1990. Whereas a CIA report suggests a figure of 300,000.[26]

Sampat Prakash claimed that Governor Jagmohan definitely had a hand in the migration of the Kashmiri Pandits. He said that the governor had made several announcements over the radio, telling the

Pandits that refugee camps had been set up in Jammu to receive them. He had also assured the government servants that they would continue to draw their salaries. However, he warned them that he could not guarantee their safety if they decided to stay on.

But that is not the whole truth. There was a section of the militants who were keen to push the Kashmiri Pandits out of the Valley, even those who were sympathetic to their cause. Some people believe that a part of the reason why Hriday Nath Wanchoo was targeted and why Sampat was threatened was because the militants did not want any Kashmiri Pandit speaking on behalf of the Kashmiri people. It was for that very reason that an ordinary person like Manohar Lal could not show his solidarity openly.

Sampat was angry that many of the Kashmiri Pandits continued to draw salaries but had taken up other jobs; for instance, government doctors would take their salaries but had started their own private practice in Jammu and even in Delhi. He felt that this was not only dishonest but also showed how little they cared for Kashmir.

According to Sampat, the Kashmiri language unites both Kashmiri Hindus and Kashmiri Muslims; but Kashmiri Pandits project themselves as the sole protectors of this ancient language.

What I found really strange was that the Kashmiri Pandits who took so much pride in Kashmiri culture and language could forget their language so easily; even their children do not speak Kashmiri these days. I put this question to Dr Ajay Chrungoo, another active member of the Panun Kashmir movement, and whose father had been a member of the Communist Party of India. He had asserted that the Kashmiri Pandit community was the link with Kashmir's past, its culture and rich heritage. Chrungoo confessed that even his children did not speak Kashmiri.

However, the language in which the Kashmiri militants communicated was not Kashmiri but Urdu. Later when Afzal was in jail, I discovered that he wrote letters in English even to his Kashmiri friends, with a few lines of poetry in Urdu thrown in. But never in Kashmiri.

I asked Dr Teng why he was really pursuing the demand for a homeland for the Kashmiri Pandits when he knew no one would go back. Most Pandits had already sold off their homes and had settled in the plains. His response was that they were fighting for survival; they know that the community is going to be wiped out of the pages of history. He said this calmly, without passion, but with absolute conviction.

Unfortunately, what gets lost amidst this kind of political discussion is the very real humanitarian problem faced by the Kashmiri Pandits still living in the refugee camps. In 1990, Sampat saw that the Kashmiri Pandits living in the camps did not have even basic amenities. He said that it was the RSS workers who provided comfort and succour to the families. There were no toilets and many had to use the open fields. There was no water and the heat of Jammu was unbearable; many fell sick. The feeling of injustice and loss was real and painful then and continues to be so.[27]

When Sampat Prakash took me to meet his mother and other family members living in the Najafgarh area of Delhi, I understood a little of the deep loss they felt; their inability to reconcile to the situation they found themselves in. The family lived in a small house but there was a vacant plot in front of the house. The family had chosen not to build on it. It was a small plot surrounded by brick walls, and when they opened the wooden gate, I saw a garden—a desperate attempt to recreate the beauty of the landscape they had left behind. They said they had planted flowers but none had bloomed so far. Yet, Sampat and his mother sat on two plastic chairs and asked to be photographed in the garden.

I noticed that the young children in their family did not really understand the significance of the little garden. They would never know what it was like to breathe fresh air or enjoy a picnic under almond blossoms.

Each of the 75,343 families that had to leave the Valley because of fear, threats, intimidation or government encouragement had to face its own tragedy; each had to struggle to survive. They had to ensure their children were educated and found jobs.

Whenever I talked to the Kashmiri Pandits, they spoke of the cool fresh air, the smell of flowers and the taste of the haak or colander greens. The Kashmiri Pandits never talked about the sufferings of the Kashmiri Muslims who had been left behind in the Valley. No one ever mentioned their Muslim neighbours, their friends or colleagues. They missed the landscape of the Valley; for them India was their political home because they looked upon Kashmir as an integral part of India.

———

When Sampat insisted that I see his Rainawari home, I was given a taste of the hostility a Kashmiri Pandit feels when he or she goes back to the Valley. It was a bitterly cold afternoon in January 2009 and I stood in front of the building that had once been his home. Sampat wanted to visit his room so he got permission and went upstairs while I waited on the street.

Four or five young Kashmiri men in white kurta-pyjamas and skull caps watched me from a distance. I heard one of them say loud enough for me to hear: 'Must be Kashmiri Pandits come to see their old homes.' There was utter contempt and hatred in the tone; and they looked on with unsmiling faces. My blood ran cold.

Sampat returned. I looked on with respect at the man who continued to believe in the possibility of the two communities living together. Sampat insisted that I interview Ali Mohammad Bhatt, the President of the Shikara Owners Association. He lived in a 200-year-old house on an island in the Dal Lake. The office of the association was in Nehru Park, on the edge of the lake. It was a small wooden building with a corrugated tin roof painted green.

These boatmen have been in Kashmir since AD 112-72 when Pravasena Kashmiri was the king and he brought them from Sangaldeep (Sri Lanka) to facilitate riverine traffic. But the community claims that they have learnt the art of boat building from Noah himself and missionaries have even observed that the boats do resemble the traditional Noah's ark.[28]

The shikara is the logo of the Kashmir Tourism Department and Ali Mohammad knew that no visitor in Srinagar, whether a local or the prime minister, could leave the Valley without a ride in the little boat called the shikara. But few visitors to Kashmir give thought to how the shikarawala survived during the insurgency when there were no tourists and very few visitors.

Wearing a grey woolen pheran, sitting on the floor, the fifty-year-old shikarawala told me about his family. He had four brothers and two sisters; all four brothers, too, were shikarawalas. Ali Mohammad's parents looked down at us from their framed photograph hanging on the wall. His father was the president of the union from 1951. He was a well-respected man who had settled family disputes and kept the community together through difficult times when they earned very little. It was only after their association had become a member of the Low Paid Government Servants Federation that the shikarawalas learnt the art of agitation.

Ali Mohammad recalled the first strike organized by the shikarawalas. It was in 1983. He described how they did not ply their boats for fifteen days and demanded a raise in the rates for rides set by the Tourism Department. The strike was successful and from Rs 50 per ride they got Rs 100. The current rate is Rs 200. They even managed to get a grant for building new shikaras. A shikara survives only for ten to twelve years after which a new one is required. However, since many could not afford a new one, they would keep repairing their old boats. There were ten workshops in which the boats were made.

There was no pride in his voice as Ali Mohammad recalled these achievements. He said that the gains of those struggles had been wiped out during the insurgency. Ali Mohammad's eyes were expressionless when he spoke about the hardships during the days and nights of curfews. The neighbours shared their food with each other; the vegetable growers contributed from their produce, but that was still not enough.

The shikarawalas sold whatever they had; some sold the gold they had bought for their daughters' wedding, while others sold their radios, television sets, and anything else that could fetch them some money. They were forced to sell these items cheaply, but despite this, they could afford just one meal a day, and there were days when they had nothing to eat at all. Ali Mohammad said that many of the shikarawalas had to send their children to work as daily wagers so that they could earn a little cash. He knew some shikarawalas who were so desperate that they wanted to sell their boats, but there was no one to buy them. 'It was the shikarawala who suffered the most during the militancy. We suffered even more than the shopkeepers,' he said.

The only time Ali Mohammad's eyes lit up was when he remembered the shooting of films on the lake. He reeled off their names with much more enthusiasm than he had for the names of politicians. Did he see any of the films? He said the only film he saw was *Jab Jab Phool Khile*, which was based on the love between Raja, a simple shikarawala, and Rita, a rich tourist woman, recently returned from abroad.

His eyes shone when I asked whether he remembered the last scene when the poor Kashmiri shikarawala pulls the rich Hindu girl into the train at Bombay Central Station and takes her to Kashmir. The film was a blockbuster but no one had noticed that the rich Hindu girl had run off with a Muslim shikarawala.[29] How come no one objected to such a story? Ali Mohammad had a simple explanation: everyone enjoys a good love story.

Did any of the shikarawalas or their children join the militancy? He insisted they did not, in fact they did not even accept the food the militants offered to them. He said there were several crackdowns where they lived. The army beat up many shikarawalas but they never caught a single militant from their community.

Now the shikarawalas are struggling against eviction from their homes because they are being blamed for the silting and for the growing pollution in the Dal Lake. At one time there were 1,700 registered shikarawalas, now there are 4,500. The number of houseboats have increased to 1,200, and the sewage comes from them, but they blame the shikarawalas for the pollution. He said he has a septic tank in his home and it is the houseboats that have dirtied the Dal Lake.

Ali Mohammad looked at me and said: 'Give us rehabilitation; give our children jobs and we will leave the Dal Lake. But the government should remember that people come to Kashmir to ride in the shikara. It is a highlight of their visit.'

I told him that all I can do is write his story.

A FOREST OF DEAD LEAVES

(1996–2001)

Because of the continued threats to his life from the militants, Sampat Prakash had not been able to enter the Kashmir Valley for almost seven years except for two brief visits in 1994. He was keenly watching the situation, waiting for an opportunity to return home and revive his trade union activities. He finally got the opportunity in 1996, when elections were announced in the Valley. It would be the first since 1987. The general elections to the Indian Parliament had already taken place in May 1996; the elections to the Assembly would be held in September 1996.

George Fernandes had informed Sampat that the National Conference had decided to stand for elections, and he thought it would be a good idea for Sampat to canvass for the party. It was a challenge for Sampat because he well knew that he was putting his life at grave risk, especially since the Hurriyat had called for a boycott of the polls. But he felt that the elections could open some democratic space in the bleak political landscape of Kashmir. Sampat did not want a seat in the Legislative Assembly or in the Indian Parliament, he just wanted to use the National Conference network to reach out to people and tell them to vote.

Sampat contacted his trusted comrade, Nisar Ali Mir, and asked what he thought of the idea of his return. Nisar had been working with the Hurriyat all these years, and many in the Hurriyat had also expressed their feeling that it would be good if Sampat Prakash returned to the Valley so that at least one token Kashmiri Pandit could be seen working there.

The National Conference arranged for a personal security officer (PSO) and a bulletproof car for Sampat Prakash. He knew that it would not be safe for him to stay in a hotel or with Nisar Ali Mir, thus the National Conference allotted him the official residence of Bakshi Ghulam Mohammad since the occupants had left Kashmir.

Sampat had decided that he would use the opportunity to create a movement against the renegades. The renegades were former militants who had either surrendered or been captured and had then either opted for or been coerced into working with the police and the Indian Army. One of the most dreaded renegades was Mohammad Yousuf Parray, popularly known as Kuka Parray, and his organization, Ikhwan-ul-Muslimeen.

Mohammad Yousuf Parray was born in 1958 in Village Hajan of Baramulla district. He had little formal education but was a popular folk singer and dancer; he also wrote poetry in Kashmiri. He joined the JKLF in 1989 and went across the border to Pakistan for arms training. He had returned a disappointed man as he felt that Pakistan was not helping Kashmir but destroying its ethos.

Parray, under the code name of Jamshed Shirazi, had started the Ikhwan-ul-Muslimeen with the objective of fighting the Jamaat-e-Islami ideology and in particular the Hizbul Mujahideen. In one raid on a Jamaati leader, he recovered 1,000 gold biscuits, Rs 2,000,000 and 600 packets of brown sugar. Parray said that the man was actively working for Pakistan-based Lashkar-e-Taiba.

In March 1996, he asked for a government enquiry into how terrorism had become such a profitable industry in Kashmir, and it is said that it was he who persuaded Farooq Abdullah to stand for elections. Parray himself floated a political party called Awami League and announced that he would be standing for elections.[1]

Indian intelligence agencies acknowledge that it was largely because of Parray's efforts that the level of militancy came down significantly and elections could be held.

However, the use of former militants for counterinsurgency led to a proliferation of pro-India militant groups[2] who not only worked with Indian security forces but were also responsible for large-scale human rights violations. Parray was himself involved in illegal timber smuggling, threatening journalists, and in the elimination of militants.

Apart from these militias, the Special Operations Group (SOG) of the Jammu and Kashmir police was also used for counterinsurgency. It had many non-Kashmiri members, as well as victims of the militancy, who carried out personal vendettas by torturing people suspected of being militants.

Sampat had written a leaflet and made some posters condemning the Special Task Force (STF), formerly the SOG.[3] Successive governments had promised to disband their illegal detention centres where people had been picked up on mere suspicion and detained for weeks, even months, and tortured without being formally arrested or given access to any rights under the criminal law.

Sampat's trade union colleagues rallied around and helped him distribute the posters but he insisted that they did not accompany him or work openly with him. They had no protection and they could become targets of both the militants and the renegades. At that time the trade union leaders did not come out openly against the renegades; however, they later took out rallies and processions demanding that the task force be dismantled. They attacked the government of Farooq Abdullah for giving the renegades unlimited power which allowed them to rob, kidnap, and even rape.

Nisar Ali Mir had become a target of both the militants and the renegades during the early years of the insurgency, between 1990 and 1994. On one occasion, during the time when Jagmohan was governor, Javed Shah,[4] the notorious renegade, had kidnapped Nisar Ali and Ishtiaq Qadri from Lal Chowk and taken them to their headquarters which was in a deserted home of a Kashmiri Pandit family in Shivpura. The empty houses of Kashmiri Pandits were being used as interrogation centres, and people reported hearing screams of terror and pain from the homes that had once been filled with the laughter of children.

At the house, Nisar reported having seen a ferocious dog of enormous size. It was claimed that many had died just upon encountering that dog. Nisar saw other renegades sitting around; most of them seemed to have been indulging in body-building exercises and looked strong and formidable. Among them, Nisar recognized Ghulam Mohammad Lone, who was popularly known as Papa Kishtwari.[5] He had once worked as a watchman in a factory in Pampore but now worked for the STF. Nisar Ali said that at the time, the director general of police, Gurbachan Jagan, had estimated there were 5,000 such renegades working for them. The renegades told Nisar and Ishtiaq to stop calling for strikes and to discontinue their trade union work. It was Papa Kishtwari who ordered that the two leaders be taken back. They felt relieved because many others in similar situations had been killed by these men.

The same year, Nisar Ali and Ishtiaq Qadri were both picked up by militants and taken to a large vegetable field in Bemina. The militants also warned them to stop their trade union activities. While the renegades had not explained why they wanted the trade union activities to stop, the militants had made it very clear that they did not like the secular nature of their politics.

I was seated in the double-storeyed home of Nisar Ali Mir. It was located in a quiet locality of Harwan. There was a deep blue carpet spread on the floor. The room was warm and I noticed the heater was run on cooking-gas cylinders. Nisar said it was a design copied from Turkey.

Nisar Ali's daughter, Hasina, had been sitting in the room listening intently. She was just eighteen but had lived through dark and terror-filled days. There were days when she and her sister had been alone in their home with their little brother because her father was underground and her mother was in hospital with a heart ailment. She said the Indian security forces had even tried to scare people by launching Operation Bhoot[6]. The security forces would knock on doors dressed as ghosts and make terrible noises; and there was an Operation Snake when they slide a black snake into people's homes, including, once, in Nisar Ali's home. Hasina said she and her sister were so frightened after that incident that they stayed away from their home for more than a month. And if the security forces did not come, the militants would arrive, demanding food and shelter. Hasina said that Kashmiri people are known for being soft-hearted, kind and compassionate, as a result of which the security forces took advantage of their nature. 'They played with our fears and no one in India protested; not even a candlelight vigil was organized for us.'

Listening to her talk about Operation Bhoot, I was reminded of Ishamuddin, a magician I had met during the trial of the men accused of attacking the Indian Parliament in 2001. The magician performed at kids' parties and I was told that he had a trick I might be interested in: he could get people out of jail. On an impulse I had called him and he said he could take a person out from a locked cage. I had laughed and said it would be far easier to take people out of jail by magic than by lengthy court procedures.

Ishamuddin said he had travelled all over India and once he had found himself in Kashmir. In Baramullah, while he was performing his most popular trick of cutting a beautiful woman in two, he noticed that a belligerent-looking man with a beard had joined the group. He was fully armed with bullets strapped across his chest and an AK-47 in hand. Ishamuddin felt a bit uneasy with the militant staring at him, and concentrated on slicing the woman as she lay between two wooden boxes. As he sliced her, the ferocious-looking militant fainted.

I would not have believed the story but Geelani's younger brother, Bismillah, was with me when Ishammudin was telling his story. He said Kashmiris were faint-hearted. 'You have made us tough,' he said. By 'you', he meant us Indians. Bismillah said before the insurgency Kashmiris used to faint at the sight of blood and would cry even if they saw an injured bird. When I introduced Bismillah to Ishamuddin as Geelani's brother, the magician's face turned pale and he left quickly.

I thought of telling these stories to Hasina, but realized she needed to talk, not listen. She looked at me and said: 'Ever since I was born, I feel I have been living in fear. If we go for a wedding, we are not sure whether we will return safely. Almost every night I dream I am running away.'

There was silence as her words hung in the air, but she was not done. She looked a little uncertain before she told me about the latest attack on their family. She said that just four months ago, at the end of 2008, Sampat Prakash (she called him 'Our Big Daddy') and his wife had come to stay in their home. That day there had been many people in the house, because her sister was to get married soon. It was late when they got up the next morning. Something, however, seemed amiss. As they all lay unconscious, they realized that they had been gassed and robbed. Hasina said her mother had secretly saved money from her husband's wages and bought gold for her three daughters' weddings. All of it was taken, she added quietly.

Nisar Ali added that he went to the police station to file a case but the SHO refused to register a First Information Report. Despite all the pressure the trade union leader could bring to bear, there was no report, no investigation. The militants had committed the robbery to teach the man a lesson for harbouring a Kashmiri Pandit in his home.

———

Sampat took me to meet a comrade, Badruddin Khan, who told me with some pride that he had been on the hit list of the Hizbul Mujahideen. Badruddin, a seventy-five-year-old veteran trade union leader, impressed me with the clarity of his thoughts and analysis. He said in order to understand why the militants perceived him to be a threat, I must listen to his story.

He said he was a Kashmiri nationalist and did not use the 'Khan' after his name which referred to the fact that his ancestors were originally from Afghanistan. Badruddin had four brothers and two sisters; none of whom went to school because his father could not afford to send them.

Badruddin was the youngest and he was not even six years old when he was sent to work in a workshop where the colourful gabba—the traditional Kashmiri floor covering used by those who cannot afford expensive carpets—were made. The little boy was given the task of filling coal in the chillums of the hookahs. On one occasion he picked up the colourful wool and got it all entangled so the foreman beat him with a cane and made him lie down on a particular kind of grass which caused his body to break out in rashes.

Then his father sent him to another workshop where they did weaving. There a man tried to teach him the Quran but when he could not pronounce an Arabic word he was beaten up. This time the child refused to go to work and asked to be sent to school. He was sent to a jabri—compulsory—school. They were called jabri schools because the Maharaja had made education free, but mandatory.

In school he had a teacher; a Kashmiri Pandit who instilled in him a love of science. The man was the editor of the weekly *Martand*, and was a well-dressed and enlightened man. There was another teacher, Saifuddin Qarri, who introduced Badruddin to books by Maulana Maududi. Qarri was a member of the Jamaat-e-Islami and was against armed resistance.

Later, Badruddin met another Pandit who engaged him in debates. The Pandit claimed that Communism was the final solution; Badruddin argued that Islam was. The Kashmiri Pandit, whose name he could not remember, gave him a pamphlet on Islam and Private Property. In that pamphlet it said that if a man owned 100,000 acres of land and another had nothing, Islam did not give him permission to take the land forcefully from its owner.

He met another prominent Communist who lived in the same neighbourhood, Bahauddin Zahid. He owned a small shop and sold cigarettes from a bicycle even as he distributed Communist literature. Zahid organized the poorest people and Badruddin was deeply influenced by him and followed in his footsteps.

In 1953, after Sheikh Abdullah was arrested, Badruddin became involved in the movement demanding his release. He distributed posters and had close encounters with the police. Soon after, Badruddin got a job in the Accountant General's office and from the start he led the struggles against the arrogance of the bureaucracy and finally, successfully united the employees under an association. In Kashmir he faced opposition from the Jamaat-e-Islami and in Jammu from the RSS.

However, it was not his trade union activities which attracted the attention of the future militants, but his weekly columns in an Urdu weekly called *Chattan* (Rock) that caused consternation among many. Between 1985 and 1988 he attacked religious fundamentalism and the Jamaat-e-Islami's ideology. He gave examples from history on how it was their ideological beliefs that had always made them the allies of the imperialist agents to defeat nationalists such as Bhutto in Pakistan and Nasser in Egypt. He said the Islamists collaborated with US imperialism throughout the Cold War and this collaboration continued with the support for the mujahideen fighting the Soviet Union in Afghanistan. Badruddin said that once the Americans had emerged victorious in the Cold War, they needed another enemy to justify their continued quest for world domination. As a result, they invented the radical Muslim as their new enemy who had to be fought in a never-ending war against terrorism.

Badruddin's articles did not endear him to the Jamaat-e-Islami and that is why in 1990, he found himself on the hit list of the Hizbul Mujahideen. In fact, the commander-in-chief of the organization, Salahuddin, accused him of being responsible for his ouster from the Exhibition Grounds where he had been preaching at the local mosque. After he received the threat, Badruddin had to live in hiding for more than a year before a friend within the Jamaat-e-Islami intervened and ensured his safety.

Baddruddin smiled and said: 'I was close to the Communists but I was never a member of any Party.' He explained the reason for this was that except for the Naxalites, the others had betrayed Kashmiri nationalism. Besides, most of the Communist leaders, such as Sadiq and Durga Prasad Dhar, were very elitist and their lifestyles did not allow them to identify themselves with the poor.

I remember when as a teenager I had visited Kashmir for the very first time in 1967, my father's friend, Durga Prasad Dhar,[7] or Uncle DP as I called him, had insisted on bringing me to Srinagar to see the land of my ancestors. He was a man of immense charm and warmth. I still remember how suffocated I felt in the large bustling household, even though everyone was so warm and hospitable and I was almost force-fed a bewildering number of rich and spicy meat dishes. There was nothing Communist in the practice; it was feudal and oppressive. A year later, I visited Kashmir with my parents and was upset by the fawning and flattery of the officials of the hospitality department.

But, going back in 1990, the people seemed to have changed. They had suddenly found self-respect and stopped being servile. The insurgency was responsible for giving back people their dignity. I asked Badruddin and Sampat whether they agreed with my observation. They said it was true, especially in the beginning when the insurgency was led by the Kashmiri nationalists.

Badruddin said that after the Taliban's victory in Afghanistan, when the foreign militants came into Kashmir, the insurgency lost its appeal. He said that there were an estimated 3,000 foreign militants operating in the Kashmir Valley in 1994,[8] and they were responsible for the violence and even the rapes of Kashmiri women. His conscience did not allow him to support the insurgency even though he continued to have deep empathy for Kashmiri nationalism. Now Badruddin spends his days running an organization called Care and Concern Forum. He helps people write petitions, and takes up cudgels on behalf of women. His regret is that he could not continue his research on the alliance of Jamaat-e-Islami with imperialism.

The other senior trade union leader on top of the militants' hit list was Ghulam Qader Bhat. Bhat told me he was tenth on the Hizbul Mujahideen hit list. The school where he was headmaster at the time was in a village under the influence of the Jamaat-e-Islami. People would ask whether he was a Communist and he would reply that he believed in social and economic justice. His colleagues would say that the headmaster was an angel. There were two teachers who were from the Kashmiri Pandit community and he told them not to attend school because of the danger to their lives. He still remembered their names: Sushma and Makhan Lal.

The frail man described the plight of his fellow teachers who resisted the demands of the militants or even dared to criticize their actions. For instance, when the vice chancellor of Kashmir University, Professor Mushirul Haq, was assassinated, one teacher from Ganderbal said it was wrong to have killed the vice chancellor. The militants heard what he had said and shot the teacher dead, calling him an Indian agent. His body lay in the drain and no one had the guts to give him a decent burial. Finally, he was buried in his own garden.

There was a time when the militants invited themselves into his home and he had to feed them for a month. The militants were there to discuss whether foreign tourists should be allowed to visit Kashmir, and Ghulam Qader Bhat said he told them that there was no need for a discussion since they took their orders from across the border.

Bhat's most painful experience occured when a militant fell in love with his daughter, who was then studying medicine in Russia. The daughter agreed to marry him to save her father from a possible assassination but her husband became a drug addict and life became unbearable for her. Finally the headmaster rescued his daughter from the clutches of the forced marriage. At the time when I was speaking to Bhat, his son-in-law was in jail. The headmaster's daughter said that the militants did not think of the future of their own children. They destroyed the education system.

The headmaster said the insurgency was revenge for the breaking up of Pakistan, and the creation of Bangladesh. But if the Communists had understood the sentiment in Kashmir they could have intervened more effectively, but the Communist Party of India went with the Congress, which had no support in the Valley. The CPI (M) also did not understand the Kashmiri ethos. He said the Communists did not understand the sentiment for Azadi. He said everyone in his family supports the ideas of Socialism. Then, without warning, there were tears running down his cheeks. 'I miss my Kashmiri Pandit friends and comrades. I believe they will return one day,' he said.

I asked him what he thought of the demand for Panun Kashmir and he answered promptly: 'Panun Kashmir is the other side of the Pakistan coin.'

I asked Sampat whether the neighbours in Rainawari or even his comrades in the union had ever asked him to return to the Valley. He said he had always lived in the homes of his comrades and had always been warmly welcomed. Many times he would visit them with his wife and even with his children. Every time, without exception, they were made comfortable but Sampat noticed that no one invited him to come back, and no one had asked whether he would like to come back to live like he had done before.

I told him that there were various surveys which showed that the people in the Valley wanted the Pandits to return. One of them, conducted by the Ministry of Home Affairs in 2002, said that 67 per cent of people in the Valley supported Kashmiriyat and wanted the Kashmiri Pandits to return.[9] For Sampat, the surveys reflected the government's wishful thinking rather than the people's wishes.

Sampat refused to dwell on this question which obviously disturbed him. I remembered Sampat's old friend, Yusuf Chapri, telling me that 'everyone wants the Kashmiri Pandits back. In their hearts they want it'.

Chapri told me that the Dhars never ran away from the Valley and asked me to buy a book by a Kashmiri Pandit who was kidnapped and who lived in captivity for eighty-three days. He said it shows the real relationship between the two communities. Later, I bought the book, *Eighty-three Days: The Story of a Frozen River*.[10] Dr S.N. Dhar was taken hostage in March 1992. He described the acts of solidarity he encountered during his captivity; on two occasions Kashmiri Muslims tried to help him escape. He described his captors as young gunmen who were innocent and caring and some of them held the Kashmiri Pandits in high esteem. When he was finally released, the Kashmiri neighbours came out to celebrate his safe return, showering him with almonds and shireen.[11]

Dr Dhar noticed that even those who talked of Azadi, called

freedom jihad. The doctor said that after his experience he 'could now see more clearly some of the reasons that had led to the present situation. For example, the apprehension amongst the Muslims of Kashmir of the dilution of Muslim identity in the Valley by remaining with secular India with its Hindu majority.'

———

In 1997, Sampat Prakash was to retire. But before he could do so, the BJP filed a case against him before the Election Commission, charging him with violating government rules which did not allow him to take part in politics. They were referring to his campaign against the renegades. If the charge was proved, Sampat would lose his post-retirement pension. It would be disastrous for his family. Sampat was furious that the government servants who were campaigning for Panun Kashmir could do so with impunity, whereas he was being singled out because he was campaigning against the STF camps.

However, the bureaucrats and the police officers stood by him. The file did not move; it was locked up in the drawer of a senior bureaucrat, who assured Sampat that he would keep the filed locked till after the day of his retirement. Then even if he was convicted, he could not be deprived of his pension. Sampat recognized, in this act of solidarity, the vestiges of what he still called Kashmiriyat.

It is interesting that none of the trade union leaders I interviewed mentioned the word Kashmiriyat. It was not a word that resonated with their feelings. It was too much a part of the official Indian propaganda. However, almost everyone pointed out that they were proud that they had a Kashmiri Pandit as their leader.

They were also proud of the fact that most of them had remained true Kashmiri nationalists and yet had not joined the ranks of the insurgents. I asked Sampat whether he had exact data on the government employees who did join the insurgents but that has never been his strength. Like a good cook, he goes by estimates and educated guesses!

Sampat admitted that there were some like the schoolteacher,

Shafi Rangrez of Doda, and Majid from Rajouri who did join the militants and they took all the office bearers with them. Shafi joined Shabir Shah and became an important leader and somewhat of a local hero.

Individual members did join the insurgency. However, it was equally true that there were many employees who were killed by the militants. What was most interesting was that despite the extreme situation, the trade union leaders did not disown their commitment to democratic secular politics.

In the post-elections scenario, Sampat Prakash, his comrades and colleagues decided to begin their trade union activities; they renamed their organization the Trade Union Centre. Sampat was chosen president and Nisar Ali general secretary. Their union was affiliated to George Fernandes's Hind Mazdoor Kisan Parisahd (HMKP).

Nisar Ali Mir and other comrades insisted that Sampat Prakash should formally call on the Hurriyat and inform them that the trade union would work as an independent entity.

In his inimitable style, Sampat barged into their office while they were in the midst of their executive meeting. The Hurriyat leaders accused him of electioneering in defiance of their call for boycott; he answered that he was not an Indian agent and he had been campaigning against the renegades. They accused him of supporting the National Conference and he replied he had no love lost for Farooq Abdullah who had betrayed the cause of Kashmiri independence. Sampat told them that he and the members of his union had not supported any of the political parties; all they had done was expose the barbaric acts of the STF camps.

He told the Hurriyat leaders that the fight for the independence of Kashmir could not be allowed to be led by foreign militants who knew nothing of Kashmiri culture and had no respect for Kashmiri traditions.

Sampat had his grievances and questions. He accused them of

being involved in the murder of Kashmiri leaders such as Mirwaiz Farooq. The mirwaiz was the hereditary religious and political leader who had refused to take any public stand on the demands made by Hizbul Mujahideen, such as Kashmir's merger with Pakistan or the Islamization of Kashmir. The mirwaiz could have become the head of the Hurriyat, a move that Pakistan would not have liked. Although the Hurriyat at the time claimed the mirwaiz had been killed by Indian intelligence agencies, it was known to people such as Sampat Prakash that the person behind the assassination was Mohammad Abdullah Bangroo.[12] Bangroo had fought in Afghanistan alongside the Taliban.

Sampat asked the Hurriyat leaders how they could treat both the mirwaiz and Bangroo as freedom fighters? There were so many such examples in the Martyrs Graveyard in Srinagar where both the assassin and those assassinated were buried and treated as freedom fighters. Can a killer be portrayed as a messiah and a Kashmiri patriot as a traitor? How can you justify such bankruptcy of politics in the name of freedom?

Sampat was not quite done. He was angry and he asked the Hurriyat leaders, sitting in front of him, quite bluntly why they had not stopped the burning of Kashmiri Pandit homes. Even if they could not have prevented the burning and looting, at least they could have condemned the acts of vandalism, couldn't they?

After both sides had had their say and the air had been cleared of suspicions, accusations and counter-accusations, Sampat brought up the topic of the future of trade union activities. Sampat said he and his comrades wanted to build an independent trade union and on that he would take no orders from anyone.

Recounting this episode, Sampat looked at me directly and declared: 'As long as I am alive, I will not allow Kashmir to become an Islamic state.'

Many Hurriyat leaders invited Sampat for a meal at their home. One of the first to extend an invitation was Abdul Ghani Lone. During the meal, Sampat told Lone that he wanted to return to work in Kashmir and Lone, his senior by nearly fifteen years, had said with a smile:

> Zamana bade showk se tujhe sun raha tha
> Tu hi so gaya dastan kehte kehte
> (The entire world was listening intently
> But you fell asleep telling your tale)

Professor Abdul Ghani Bhat, the chairman of the Hurriyat, also invited Sampat Prakash and his comrades for a wazwan, a Kashmiri feast. Bhatt had studied in S.P. College and later at Aligarh Muslim University. He was a staunch believer that Kashmir should merge with Pakistan.

Sampat was quite surprised to find Comrade Ram Piara Saraf at the Hurriyat leader's home. Saraf looked much older and the two met warmly after two decades; they agreed to meet the next day for a longer time. Saraf wanted the trade union to fight for the division of Jammu and Kashmir into seven ethnic areas.[13] This plan took into account the fact that the state of Jammu and Kashmir was one of the most culturally and linguistically diverse states within India. Sampat Prakash did not like the proposal; it meant a division of Kashmir along communal lines and that was something he could never accept.

————

Sampat and his comrades began their trade union activities in the Kashmir Valley once again, but the political situation had changed a lot in the seven years that Sampat had been in exile. There was no family which had not suffered a personal loss, or witnessed the death of a loved one. Women were called half-widows because they did not know whether their husbands were alive in the custody of the armed forces or dead; and there were the children who had watched their fathers being dragged away by the security forces, never to return. And there were those whose family members had been killed by militants or renegades.[14]

In this background, the old trade union slogans did not seem appropriate. The trade unionists decided on one slogan in the form of a demand: 'Katl-e-aam band karo; Kashmir masla hal karo' (Stop the mass murders; resolve the Kashmir conflict).

Sampat had retired from service and needed to rest after the hectic and intense campaigning. He decided to go with his wife to Leh where his younger son, Ravinder, was posted. This was his first visit to Ladakh and he contacted the local leaders of the Low Paid Government Servants Federation. He trekked to the remote areas and studied the conditions under which the government employees had to work.

Sampat had not realized how much the Buddhist Ladakhis resented the dominance of the Kashmiris over their affairs. The Ladakhis had been agitating for autonomy since 1967 and had launched a full-fledged agitation in January 1981 that had led to the setting up of Ladakh Autonomous Hill Development Council in 1995. Kargil, which had been a part of Baltistan, had a Shia majority and wanted a separate autonomous council.

Sampat had sympathies for the Ladakhi movement for autonomy, but most of the Kashmiri members of his union did not. They had not directly participated in the campaign for autonomy even though the representatives from Ladakh, such as Dr Sonam Dawa, had spearheaded the movement.[15]

However, they did help their Ladakhi comrades fulfil their special demands: exemption from paying income tax (along the lines of the exemption given to tribals in the Northeast); a 'hard duty' allowance because of the severe winter conditions in which government employees had to work; and preference for local candidates in government service over outsiders, which included Kashmiris.

———

Around the time Sampat Prakash was in Ladakh, Mohammad Afzal Guru returned to Kashmir Valley. He returned in 1997 after completing his graduation in Delhi through distance education. Afzal longed to be with his mother and he thought that after the elections things would settle down and he could return home. He got a job as a commission agent for a pharmaceutical company and sold medicines and surgical equipment and managed to earn a few thousand rupees every month. It was good to be back with his family.

Afzal's mother then decided to get him married. His wife, Tabassum, and he were cousins, children of two sisters. Tabassum is one of the five children of Ghulam Mohammad Buhroo, a well-known businessman in Baramulla, and a trustee of a local school. On 1 November 1998, Afzal married Tabassum, a vivacious young woman. When he had gone to ask for her hand, Tabassum was playing hopscotch in her courtyard. She was just eighteen years old, ten years younger than Afzal. The video of their marriage shows Afzal dancing and singing on his wedding.[16] Afzal called her Pyaari, the lovable.

Afzal and Tabassum dared to hope and dream of living a normal family life, having babies, watching them grow and filling their home with the laughter of children. They soon had a son and Afzal felt an indescribable joy. Afzal wanted to name him Shams Tabrizi, after the twelfth-century poet and philosopher and spiritual instructor of Rumi, the Sufi poet. Tabassum, however, raised a genuine concern. She said that the Kashmiris would, as usual, shorten Shams Tabrizi to Tabrii, which means axe, and her son's name would become a butt of ridicule. Afzal recognized this and, in the presence of his father-in-law and other family members, scanned the bookshelf, his gaze fixing on a volume titled *Divan-e–Ghalib*. Before further ado, Afzal announced: 'What about Ghalib?' and his father-in-law approved with 'Marhaba!'[17]

For Afzal, the most precious moments of his life were those that he spent with his beloved Tabassum and their son Ghalib. Many times, he would return home from work late to find his wife fast asleep and he would carry her to bed as gently as he would his baby son. He cooked meals and felt tenderness for his wife as deeply as he felt for his son. Afzal was not as carefree as he was in college, but he still enjoyed listening to Michael Jackson, going for treks and picnics and visiting friends and family.

The parents enjoyed sharing the delights of their baby seeing the snowflakes of his first winter and the magic of the world turning white; then the beauty of spring and the joy of seeing the colours of the flowers and the red apples growing in the famous Sopore orchards; and then again the autumn colours when the chinar leaves turned from green to copper-red and then gold before falling off, and once again the snow. They watched Ghalib take his first tiny steps and laughed with delight when he spoke his first words. And they even dared to talk about his future.

At the same time, Tabassum realized that she would always live with a dark shadow that could come and wipe out the sunshine from their lives at any time. Two days after their wedding, in November 1998, Afzal was called to the Indian army camp in the village by one Major Thapa of the Rashtriya Rifles. The Rashtriya Rifles was an elite regiment raised in 1993 as a counterinsurgency force in Kashmir. It worked with the Special Operations Group. The major threatened Afzal with dire consequences if he refused to give information about the militants present in Sopore. From then onwards Afzal lived two lives. The life spent with his wife and son and life in detention with the Indian Army.

Every Sunday, Afzal had to present himself to the major and often, even twice a week. He, along with other surrendered militants, was abused; often the violence of the verbal abuses was worse than the physical beatings. He and the others were made to clean the barracks and the toilets and only then allowed to go.

Later that year Afzal moved to Baramulla, where he set up a shop selling surgical equipment. He had learnt to keep this dual life in separate compartments. But even that was not always possible and the sanctity of his home was constantly violated by Indian Army officers who would come knocking on his door. Tabassum and Afzal's mother knew that the shadow could resurface any day and he could disappear forever.

Between 1998 and 2000 Afzal managed to work hard and do well in his business, but he had to pay Rs 300 to 500 a month to the

Special Police Officer (SPO) in charge of his neighbourhood.[18] Despite these expenses he managed to save enough money to buy himself a two-wheeler in 2000. The vehicle helped him in his business and he could also take his wife and son on rides to the bazaar or to visit family and friends. Just two months after he bought the scooter, his life took another turn and became a living hell.

Afzal was in his shop when the Kashmir police came and dragged him out on the basis of information given to them by a renegade by the name of Irshid Masood, the SPO of New Colony.[19] The renegade had reported to the police that Afzal had contacts with the militants. Afzal was taken to the Palhallan camp of the STF. There he was greeted by DSP Vinay Kumar who kicked him so hard that he fell. After five hours of beating, the police realized that they had picked up the wrong Afzal. But, instead of releasing him, they took him to the Special Task Force camp at Humhama, near Srinagar.

There he was greeted by another police officer, DSP Davinder Singh. The policeman ordered him to confess to being in touch with militants and possessing weapons. When Afzal told him that he did not possess any weapons he was stripped naked and put in freezing water and given electric shocks. Afzal was forcibly made to drink water and given electric shocks for three hours by an inspector called Shanti Singh, while the officer watched. Petrol was poured into his anus and chillies stuffed into it and he was kept in that state the whole day.[20] Afzal fell unconscious and when he regained consciousness he found himself in a small dark cell. He heard two people whispering to each other and asked who they were. He stretched his hands out to find that they were also in the same cell. They, too, were victims like him.

One of these men was from a locality in Srinagar. He paid Rs 25,000 to the DSP and was released. The other man introduced himself as Tariq from Tral. He had also been tortured. Afzal spent twenty-five days with him. He advised Afzal to co-operate with the STF otherwise he would not be allowed to live a normal life.

Tariq was later named in the chargesheet as one of the three men who masterminded the conspiracy to attack the Indian Parliament. The other two, Ghazi Baba and Masood Azhar, were well-known militants, but we never learnt anything about this mysterious man, Tariq, either from the media or during the trial.

Afzal was never given an opportunity to tell the court about the circumstances in which he met Tariq or how Tariq had lured him into committing the act of terrorism. Of course, even if Afzal had the opportunity, I wonder whether the judge would have listened. After all, in order to understand Afzal's story, one would have to practically know the history of insurgency and counterinsurgency in Kashmir. And history cannot be presented as evidence in a court of law. Afzal was a victim of history.

Afzal found himself unexpectedly released. Ever since he had been picked up and the extortion demand been made, his family had been busy raising money to get him out of the hellhole. They had found out where he was being held and the DSP had demanded a sum of Rs 100,000 for his release.

Tabassum sold the little gold jewellery she had been given at the time of her marriage, but the amount they could raise was only Rs 80,000. The family had no choice but to sell the scooter Afzal had bought for Rs 24,000, and with the money in hand they rushed to rescue Afzal. He had been in illegal custody for twenty-five days since middle of July 2000 and, on his release, the STF gave him a certificate appointing him a Special Police Officer for six months.'[21] Afzal admitted that when he came out of the STF camp he was a 'broken man'. Since then he lived in a world where few men have been, and from where very few can return to the normal world. It is a murky world of informers, intelligence agents and militants. It is a world where no journalist has penetrated; where the meaning of words such as truth, freedom, honesty and bravery take on entirely different meanings.

Afzal decided to leave his village home and rent a room in Srinagar and carry on his business from there. He thought he would be relatively safer in the town rather than in his village. Besides, he also needed medical treatment after the severe torture.

From the time he shifted to Srinagar, Tariq had begun to keep in touch with him. Davinder Singh did not contact Afzal directly. He would make contact through Altaf Hussain, who was the brother-in-law of a senior police officer at Budgaam. Altaf Hussain had asked Afzal to coach his two sons, one was in class ten and the other in his final year of schooling. The father had been threatened by militants and did not dare send his children for coaching after school hours because he feared that either he or his sons would be kidnapped.[22]

I asked Afzal the names of other people whose children he had taught. I thought it would be an important aspect of his life that needed to be focused on. But Afzal said that if he made those names public, the students would face stigma and he did not want to harm them. He gave the same answer to Senior Counsel Indira Jaising who filed the Curative Petition on his behalf in the Supreme Court. She was deeply impressed by how honourable Afzal was. Afzal was not the kind of human being who would sacrifice principles for the sake of expediency.

Then, one day, in the first week of November 2001, Altaf took Afzal to meet Davinder Singh. The police officer told Afzal that he had a job to do—he was to take a man to Delhi and help him find accommodation. The policeman told him that it was a minor task which should not be too difficult since Afzal had lived in Delhi. Afzal was told that the man's name was Mohammad; he had assumed that the man was a fellow Kashmiri but he soon discovered that Mohammad could not speak Kashmiri.

Afzal said Mohammad arranged for his own accommodation, but he helped Mohammad buy a second-hand car from a garage in Karol Bagh. Afzal had no idea that the car, a white Ambassador, would be used by five militants to barge into the Indian Parliament in a suicide attack.[23] After that, Mohammad told Afzal that he could go back to Kashmir.

Afzal decided that it would be safer to live in Delhi, away from the clutches of the STF. Perhaps he could have a good life after all. He saw a flicker of hope. He found a room in Indira Vihar and paid an advance rent of Rs 7,000. He left the keys with the landlady before leaving for Srinagar on 14 December 2001, telling her that he would return with his family after Eid which was a few days away. Afzal left for Kashmir, but he would never reach his home and family in time for Eid that year or ever again.

Afzal took a bus to Srinagar. When he reached, he received a call from Tariq asking him when he had come back from Delhi. The next morning, on 15 December 2001, while he was waiting for a bus to Sopore, the police caught him and took him to the Parimpora police station where Tariq was waiting for him. Tariq beat Afzal up and took away the Rs 35,000 that Mohammad had given him. He was blindfolded and taken to the headquarters of the STF and from there to Delhi. Later, the prosecution would claim that Afzal had been arrested along with his cousin Shaukat in Srinagar where they had driven up in Shaukat's truck. I do not know Shaukat's story but Afzal said neither of them knew how to drive and he had no driving licence.[24]

In Delhi, Afzal Guru was taken to the police station of the Special Cell at Lodi Road, where he learnt that he had been accused of conspiring to attack the Indian Parliament. He was beaten, tortured and humiliated. It was the holy month of Ramzan and the policemen urinated into his mouth, telling him he could break his fast with their urine. He was also forced to have anal sex with his cousin Shaukat.

A few days later, on 17 December, Afzal was produced before the national media. Sitting in handcuffs (never seen on television) at the Lodi Road police station, Afzal was made to confess before a stunned nation that he was a part of the conspiracy to attack the Indian Parliament.

Afzal had, overnight, become the most hated man in India—the face of terrorism. No one wanted to hear Afzal's story. Later when I asked him why he had made that confession, he told me that the Special Cell had arrested his younger brother, Hilal Ahmad Guru, and had kept him hostage at a STF camp. He was willing to confess to anything to save his brother from the fate he had suffered. However, even in those dire circumstances, though Afzal incriminated himself, he refused to falsely incriminate a fellow Kashmir, Syed Abdul Rehman Geelani, a lecturer in Zakir Hussain College under the Delhi University. Geelani had also been picked up and charged with being part of the conspiracy to attack the Indian Parliament.

By the end of the month, Afzal Guru was sent to Tihar Jail along with his cousin Shaukat Guru, his wife—who was pregnant—and S.A.R. Geelani. While the other three were released, Afzal Guru never left Tihar Jail. And, in February 2013, he was hanged inside the jail.

The media flashed the photographs of the three men. That was when Sampat Prakash got his first glimpse of the tall, flamboyant Shaukat Guru. The man with a beard and a sardonic smile playing on his lips was Abdul Rehman Geelani and the shortest of the three, bespectacled, sporting a big moustache and a mass of black hair was Mohammad Afzal Guru. Even in the photographs, Afzal's eyes held one's attention with their burning intensity. The woman remained invisible, as did her sufferings.[25]

AMONG A CARAVAN OF BELIEVERS
(2001–07)

On the morning of 13 December 2001, Sampat Prakash was in Srinagar, staying as usual in Nisar Ali Mir's home. It was there that he saw a live telecast of the attack on the Indian Parliament. By then he had retired and had taken the year off to construct his house in Jammu, but had come to Srinagar to enjoy the winter.

Since he had returned to the Valley in 1997, he had been visiting the Hurriyat office along with his comrades in the trade union movement. He would be invited by the Hurriyat leaders to address some meetings; perhaps they wanted the presence of a token Kashmiri Pandit. One such occasion was a meeting on 21 May 2002 to commemorate the twelfth death anniversary of Mirwaiz Maulvi Farooq.

The event began with a rally from Razaykadal, the headquarters of the Mirwaiz's Awami Action Committee, after the midday prayers. Sampat Prakash went straight to the Idgah grounds where a crowd of more than 15,000 people had gathered. He noticed that Syed Ali Shah Geelani was not present. It seemed odd since he was a senior Hurriyat leader.

The Hurriyat leaders began addressing the rally but the crowds started shouting slogans like 'saudabazi nahin chalegi' (we won't allow a sell-out). The slogans were aimed at those members of the Hurriyat who were in favour of a negotiated resolution to the conflict. Sampat also spoke, but at the back of his mind he wondered what had happened to Abdul Ghani Lone who was also supposed to speak.

189

Abdul Ghani Lone was approximately ten years older than Sampat. He had graduated from Aligarh Mulsim University in 1957 and had stood for the Assembly elections as a Congress candidate in 1967. He had formed the Jammu and Kashmir People's Conference in 1978. Lone had initially supported the militancy in the early 1990s, but he had begun to speak out against the guest militants, and there had been attempts to eliminate him, including a car bomb attack. Lone, who had been imprisoned many times, was not only against India's rule but also against Pakistan's. His objective was to establish a united but independent Kashmir.

Sampat had always liked Lone Saheb, especially because the man did not like flattery and appreciated constructive criticism. He wondered why Lone was late for the meeting. He got down from the stage to have a quick smoke when he heard the shots. Two men dressed as policemen had shot Abdul Ghani Lone as he was walking towards the stage.

Lone's son, Sajjad Lone, blamed Pakistan, the ISI and the hardline Hurriyat for his father's murder. However, in Pakistan, the United Jihad Council alleged that Indian agencies were behind Lone's death.[1]

When Syed Ali Shah Geelani turned up to condone the death, he was shouted at by Lone's angry supporters and forced to leave. It was leaders like Syed Ali Shah Geelani who made Sampat uncomfortable about working with the Hurriyat. Geelani was ten years older than Sampat. He had been a teacher in a government school and was a scholar in Urdu and Arabic. In 1950, he joined the Jamaat-e-Islami and edited their magazine, *Azan*.

Geelani had consistently stood for the complete merger of Kashmir with Pakistan. He did not mince words and he firmly believed that:

> The Muslims are a complete separate nation on the basis of their religion, culture, civilisation, customs and practices, and thought. Their nationalism and the foundation of their unity cannot be based on their homeland, race, language, colour or economic system. Rather, the basis of their unity is Islam and Islam alone, and their belief that there is no God but Allah and

that Muhammad is Allah's prophet...Hence, Hindus and Muslims [are] two different nations.[2]

The assassination of Lone had left Sampat Prakash wondering how he could continue to work with the Hurriyat. He could never support their pro-Pakistan sentiments. Yet, there were few political alternatives to choose from.

He liked Shabir Shah but the man did not have a mass base, and that left Yasin Malik's JKLF. Sampat still looked upon the JKLF as a secular organization. He had met Yasin in 1994, but since then the JKLF leader had not contacted him and no opportunity had presented itself to enable them to work together. Therefore, Sampat Prakash decided to concentrate on building his house, although he still kept up with the Kashmiri leaders.

———

Sampat heard the news of the attack on the Indian Parliament and wondered when India and Pakistan would go to war.

The government, a coalition led by the BJP, immediately blamed Pakistan. The then home minister, L.K. Advani, announced that 'the five looked like Pakistanis'. The next day the government declared that the technical evidence pointed to the fact that the attack was carried out by the Lashkar-e-Taiba (LeT).

The Lashkar-e-Taiba was established in 1987 as an Ahl-e-Hadith organization of Wahabi orientation.[3] This was the organization that introduced the notion of individual Muslims fighting a jihad without state sanction or the consensus of the religious scholars—a notion that is without parallel in the Islamic tradition. The Lashkar-e-Taiba is credited with having initiated the strategy of fidayeen (suicide squad) attacks in Jammu and Kashmir. It has formed two sub-groups called 'Jaan-e-Fidai' and 'Ibn-e-Tayamiah'. While the first group consists of highly motivated militants, the second comprises terrorists suffering from incurable diseases.

The use of suicide bombers to carry out attacks has been a recent phenomenon in Kashmir. The first suicide attack took place in

August 1999, soon after Pakistan's humiliating pull back from Kargil, when Lashkar-e-Taiba fighters blew themselves up while storming a Border Security Force post in Kupwara district.

Since then there have been forty-five suicide attacks—twenty-nine in 2001 alone. Delhi, the national capital, has been struck in two of its most symbolic locations—the Red Fort on 22 December 2000, and then the Parliament complex on 13 December 2013.

Unlike their counterparts in the Sri Lankan Tamil rebel group, the LTTE, who used suicide squads as 'guided missiles' to target individuals, the militant groups operating in Kashmir have used suicide bombers to gain entry or to blast their way into high-security government installations as they did in the case of the attack on the Indian Parliament

Interestingly, 98 per cent of the fidayeen attacks in Kashmir have been conducted by foreigners—Pakistanis and Afghans—and only in two cases have local Kashmiris been known to have become offerings to martyrdom. The first Kashmiri suicide bomber was Afaq Ahmed Shah, a young boy who dropped out of Class XII. Afaq's father, Yusuf Shah, was a schoolteacher and his son dreamt of becoming a doctor. He had himself photographed in a doctor's white coat and the framed photo hung on the wall of his room.[4] None of his family members, including his three brothers, thought it odd that Afaq had started visiting the local mosque and coming back and reading the Quran out loud and crying in his room. But on 19 April 2000, the family was shocked to learn that the seventeen-year-old had driven a stolen red Maruti car, laden with explosives, through Srinagar's 15 Corps Headquarters in Badami Bagh and blown himself apart. Afaq was known to be a shy boy, hardly an angry young man out to fight the system. But he was deeply depressed at having failed to clear his examinations twice.

The second suicide bomber from Jammu and Kashmir was Mohammad Aslam who was a SPO who had blown himself along with Pakistani suicide bombers in an attack on the SOG Complex in Srinagar on 7 December 2000.

There is some controversy about the first Kashmiri woman suicide bomber, Yasmeena Akhtar, who died in an explosion in October 2005. Although Jaish-e-Mohammad claimed she was a suicide bomber, independent observers have said that she was blown up while carrying explosives.

It is interesting to note that Asiya Andrabi of the Dukhtaran-e-Millat is opposed to the use of women as suicide bombers. She argues that Islam did not allow women to be combatants, especially suicide bombers. 'It is against the dignity of a Muslim woman that the parts of her body be strewn in a public place. If a combatant or a suicide bomber is a woman, her dead body is bound to fall or be scattered in a place full of men.'[5] However, she does not disapprove of suicide missions committed by men and she does not think of such missions as un-Islamic.

Hafiz Saeed, the head of the Lashkar-e-Taiba, justifies suicide missions on the ground that: 'The powerful Western world is terrorizing the Muslims. We are being invaded, humiliated, manipulated and looted. How else can we respond but through jihad? We must fight against the evil trio, America, Israel and India. Suicide missions are in accordance with Islam. In fact, a suicide attack is the best form of jihad.'[6]

Given this history of fidayeen attacks, the government claim that the attack on the Indian Parliament was engineered by the Lashkar-e-Taiba could have been correct. The attack also fits into the overall objective of the organization.

The organization's aim is not to merely challenge India's sovereignty over the state of Jammu and Kashmir. Their agenda, as outlined in a pamphlet titled 'Why Are We Waging Jihad?', includes the restoration of Islamic rule over all parts of India. They further seek to bring about a union of all Muslim majority regions in countries that surround Pakistan. Towards that end, the Lashkar is active in J&K, Chechnya and parts of Central Asia.

The LeT has consistently advocated the use of force and vowed that it will plant the 'flag of Islam' in Washington, Tel Aviv and New Delhi.

Hafiz Saeed advocates that the liberation of Kashmir from India will result in the success of all other Muslim struggles.[7] In fact, it was the LeT that was responsible for radicalizing the Kashmiri Muslim youth by introducing the Ahl-e-Hadith doctrines into the Kashmir struggle.

Hafiz Mohammad Saeed was born in May 1950. His family lived in Simla and at the time of the Partition of India, when they were going to Pakistan, thirty-six members of his family were killed in communal violence. Some people believe that this explains his visceral hatred for India.[8] Hafiz Saeed graduated from the University of Engineering and Technology at Lahore. In 1987, he, along with Osama bin Laden's key lieutenant, Abdullah Azam, and Zafar Iqbal founded the Lashkar-e-Taiba or the Army of the Righteous in the Kunar province of Afghanistan.[9] It was the armed wing of the Markaz Dawat ul-Irshad or the Centre for Proselytization and Preaching. The Centre, which Hafiz Saeed had set up with the Abdullah Azam and General Zia-ul-Haq, is situated in Muridke, approximately forty kilometres from Lahore.

The headquarters houses a madrassa, a hospital, a market, a large residential area for scholars and faculty members, a fish farm, agricultural tracts, a mosque and a swimming pool. The LeT also reportedly operates sixteen Islamic institutions, 135 secondary schools, an ambulance service, mobile clinics, blood banks and several seminaries across Pakistan.[10]

The organization publishes its views and opinions through its website, an Urdu monthly journal, *Al-Dawa*, which has a circulation of 80,000, and an Urdu weekly, *Gazwa*. It also publishes *Voice of Islam*, an English monthly, *Al-Rabat*, a monthly in Arabic, *Mujala-e-Tulba*, an Urdu monthly for students, and *Jehad Times*, an Urdu weekly.[11]

Hafiz Saeed has openly admitted that he does not think democracy and Islam can coexist and his slogan has made this clear: 'Jamhooriyat ka jawaab, grenade aur blast.'[12]

Experts have pointed out that the Lashkar-e-Taiba was the Inter-

Services Intelligence or ISI's preferred instrument for war against India and that it had no record of any attacks inside Pakistan.[13] In this background, the Indian government's claim that the Lakshar-e-Taiba was behind the attack on the Indian Parliament was not surprising.[14]

However, the Lashkar denied that it was involved in the attack on the Indian Parliament, and the former ISI chief, General Javed Ashraf Qazi, admitted that the attack was carried out by the Jaish-e-Mohammad. His statement was broadcast on Indian television on 6 March 2004.[15]

—

The Jaish-e-Mohammed (JeM) was a relatively new militant organization launched in Karachi on 31 January 2000 by Maulana Masood Azhar. Azhar's evolution from clergyman and teacher in a Karachi madrassa to an international jihadi leader, began in Bahawalpur where he was born on 10 July 1968. His father, Allah Bakhsh Shabir, was a headmaster in the government school. Azhar lived with his ten siblings and helped in the family dairy and poultry farm.

In his book, *The Virtues of Jihad*, Azhar reveals that his father had Deobandi[16] leanings and was extremely religious. Azhar's first contact with the jihadi movement was when he joined the Binori madrassa.[17] There were more than 36,000 students or Taliban who studied in more than 3,000 madrassas and these students went across to Afghanistan to fight the Soviet troops.

In many of these madrassas, the boys were trained from the time they read the Urdu primer which taught the alphabet glorifying jihad: Jeem for jihad; Tay for tope (cannon); Kaaf for Kalashnikov and Khay for khoon (blood).

Azhar went to fight in Afghanistan and was considered one of Pakistan's most valuable international jihadists who set up Harkat-ul-Ansar[18] affiliates in Chechnya, Somalia and Central Asia. In 1993, he was credited with teaching Somalian militants how to trim the fins of their rocket-propelled grenades so that they would explode in mid-air and bring down US helicopters.[19] The short, heavily built man with a booming voice is reported to have gone from mosque to mosque with ISI officers by his side giving rousing speeches: 'Marry for jihad, give birth for jihad and earn money only for jihad till the cruelty of America and India ends.'[20]

In February 1994, he was arrested in Jammu while travelling on a false Portuguese passport, and imprisoned. In 1999, however, Azhar's release was organized by none other than Al Qaeda chief, Osama bin Laden, who urgently needed his help. On 24 December 1999, an Indian Airlines flight, IC 814, from Kathmandu was hijacked by Pakistani hijackers and the plane landed in Kandahar which was under the control of the Taliban. After negotiations, India agreed on 1 January 2000, to release three Pakistani militants held in Indian jails—Mustaq Ahmed Zargar, Ahmed Omar Saeed Sheikh and Maulana Masood Azhar—in exchange for more than a hundred passengers. The three militants and the five hijackers were escorted across the border to Pakistan. Bin Laden threw a lavish party for Azhar on his release.[21]

Just a month after his release, Maulana Masood Azhar established the Jaish-e-Mohammad with the blessing of the religious leaders of Deoband. The Jaish-e-Mohammad's primary objective is to 'liberate' Kashmir from Indian control and integrate the state within Pakistan. The group aims to achieve this by engaging the Indian security forces in a holy war. Consequently, they are critical of the more moderate organizations in the Valley, such as the JKLF. The JeM openly acknowledges the existence of its schools across Pakistan which train and prepare young men about the importance of engaging in a jihad against Indian rule.[22]

On 13 December 2001, the Jaish-e-Mohammad attacked the Indian Parliament in broad daylight. The investigation by the Special Cell of the Delhi Police revealed that Maulana Masood Azhar was involved along with his commander, Ghazi Baba, and one Tariq Ahmad.

Ghazi Baba was believed to be the commander-in-chief of the Jaish-e-Mohammad. There is very little information about him, and it is still not clear whether his real name was Shah Nawaz Khan or Shahbaz Khan. He had several aliases, including Sajjid Jihadi. This is the reason why when the Border Security Force claimed to have killed him in August 2003, a journalist remembered the words of the Corps Commander, General Nirbhay Sharma: 'So many Gazi Babas have been killed by so many agencies since December 2001.'[23] As for Tariq Ahmad, there was no information about him; which made Afzal's claim that he was a renegade seem important enough to merit investigation.

In any case, all these three masterminds, Maulana Masood Azhar, Ghazi Baba and Tariq Ahmad were declared absconders and they were neither caught nor were they tried in a court of law. Even less is known about the five suicide bombers who actually attacked the Parliament except that they were all men and their names were Mohammad, Raja, Hamza, Rana and Haider.

Afzal admitted that he had escorted a man called Mohammad from Srinagar to Delhi and helped him buy a car which was used for the attack. This, Afzal voluntarily told the court. But he added that he did not know the other four men; the Special Cell coerced him to say he knew their names.

However, there was no attempt made by the government to explain who these men were and what had motivated them to carry out such a terrorist act. No one came forward to claim their bodies. As a result, we do not actually know anything about the five since they were all killed by the Indian security forces on 13 December 2001.

Many questions still remain unanswered about the attack on the Indian Parliament. The people in India were naturally shocked and angry, and this anger was directed at the four people—the three Kashmiri men and a Sikh woman—who had been arrested and put on trial. They became the faces of Islamic terror.

The attack on the Indian Parliament forced the US to acknowledge that India was a victim of cross-border terrorism and India soon became a staunch ally of the US in the War on Terror which had been officially launched just two months previously when the Twin Towers in New York were attacked on 11 September 2001. In their hurry to join the War on Terror, the prosecution did not bother to conduct a thorough investigation of the case and relied on the media and public sentiment for convictions. They succeeded at the trial court stage when the three men were given death sentences.

———

When I was contacted by Abdul Rehman Geelani, through a friend, to take up his case, I was in Goa recovering from a long illness. It was only when I went to Delhi that I realized the importance of the case for the future of Indian democracy. The trial of three Kashmiri Muslims would be taking place at a time when the US had launched a war against terrorism which was targeting Muslims, and in India we had a government which was promoting Hindu majoritarianism. I decided to take up the campaign to prove Geelani's innocence and, with that in mind, I set up an all-India committee for his defence.

Ultimately, the success of our campaign and efforts in the court led to the acquittal of Navjot Singh or Afsan Guru, the wife of Shaukat Guru, Afzal's first cousin, and the lecturer in Delhi University's Zakir Husain College, Syed Abdul Rehman Geelani. The punishment for Shaukat was reduced from death penalty to ten years' imprisonment and he walked out of jail in January 2011.[24]

The acquittals angered the intelligence agencies and the Special Cell; more importantly, it outraged the Hindutva forces who then focused all their wrath on Afzal Guru. How could Pakistan get away with an attack on our Parliament without anyone being punished? The Hindu Right wing demanded that Afzal be hanged. He was being called the mastermind when, in fact, he was a mere pawn in the game. The fact that he was denied a lawyer, the fact that he was not involved in the planning of the attack, that he was not involved in the killing of anyone and, most importantly, that he had been acquitted of the charge of belonging to any terrorist organization had become irrelevant details. It was a Kashmiri who had again become the victim of the competing nationalisms of India and Pakistan, and he was the victim of the war against terror.

The mastermind, Maulana Masood Azhar, still remains free and continues to pour venom on India.

———

In Kashmir, Afzal Guru did not become an issue till much later. After all, he was a surrendered militant. Sampat was totally unaware of the campaign I had started for Geelani; most of the media had refused to give it any importance.

Therefore, Sampat Prakash was really taken aback when he got a call from his old friend, Jammu-based journalist, Balraj Puri, sometime in mid-July 2002 with an unexpected request.

Puri had phoned to ask Sampat if he would appear as a defence witness for S.A.R. Geelani, one of the accused in the case. Puri told Sampat that he had received a call from Nandita Haksar, who was Parmeshwar Narain Haksar's daughter.[25] Puri said that Nandita was a human rights lawyer and was representing Abdul Rehman Geelani.

Sampat expressed surprise because he knew Haksar to be a bureaucrat who, at one time, had been secretary to Prime Minister Indira Gandhi. Haksar had secular credentials and had been close to Kashmiri Communists such as D.P. Dhar and G.M. Sadiq, but had never supported the cause of Kashmiri independence. Sampat had never heard of Haksar's daughter.

Balraj Puri assured him that her father's integrity and it was important to help her with the case. Besides, the accused was a young Kashmiri lecturer in a Delhi college and there was no evidence against him except a two-and-a-half minute telephone conversation he had had with his brother a day after the attack on Parliament.

Sampat Prakash's curiosity was roused and he asked what was required of him. Puri told him that Nandita wanted an expert witness to translate the two-and-a-half minute conversation for the court. Puri said that Nandita was insisting that a Kashmiri Pandit should be a witness, and so he had called Sampat.

Sampat immediately realized that this was a political opportunity for him to demonstrate the values of Kashmiriyat. For him, the word Kashmiriyat described a culture and politics which emphasized Hindu-Muslim solidarity. Although he had already made up his mind to go to Delhi, he thought it would be good idea to first consult Abdul Ghani Bhat, who was at the time the chairman of the Hurriyat, before he took his decision. Professor Abdul Ghani Bhat's Jammu and Kashmir Muslim Conference was staunchly pro-Pakistan and supported Kashmir's accession to Pakistan.

Despite his pro-Pakistan stance, Sampat was attracted to Abdul Ghani Bhat because he had the demeanour of a teacher rather than a political leader. It was a reflection of the fact that the man had taught Persian for twenty-two years before he was dismissed in 1986 on charges of anti-India activities. He once said that he had landed in politics as a dreamer and he still had the air of a professor rather than a seasoned politician.

Bhat mulled over the problem and told Sampat that it would be good if a Kashmiri Pandit stood for the young Kashmiri accused of conspiring to attack the Parliament. However, once he was acquitted, Sampat should ensure that young Geelani did not become a hero, 'Tell him to go back to teaching and not try and become a leader.' Sampat was not quite sure what the professor was warning him against.

I asked Sampat whether he had ever bothered to find out what Geelani's political antecedents were and he said no, he had not. It was only much later that he discovered that Geelani's father had been a close associate of Anwar Shah Kashmiri, a prominent Islamic scholar from Deoband. His father had tried to reform the way the Kashmiris practised Islam but had faced stiff opposition from the local Ulema. His father had died in 1979. The family believed that he was poisoned.

Sampat asked me whether I knew these facts, and I said, like him,

I discovered all this only much later. I had been introduced to Geelani by his friend who told me he was close to the Maoists and that he was a Leftist. It was only later that I learnt that the family was staunchly Jamaati, they looked upon music, photography and Western culture as anti-Islamic. Geelani himself was ambiguous about his beliefs.

Sampat heard the tape and satisfied himself that the conversation did not link Geelani with the conspiracy to attack the Parliament. He decided to testify in the court as a defence witness. However, he thought it would be best to take his comrades in the trade union into confidence and ask their opinion on whether he should do so. They advised him against it, especially since the BJP was in power at the Centre. He would be endangering his life, they said. Moreover, the Parliament had been attacked by Ghazi Baba and Maulana Masood Azhar of the Jaish-e-Mohammad, so how could he support such people?

Sampat did not support the Jaish-e-Mohammad, but he believed, as I did, that Geelani was innocent of the charge of conspiring to attack the Indian Parliament.

Sampat was excited about the prospect of appearing as a defence witness. He felt that if he and I, another Kashmiri Pandit, were seen to be showing solidarity with Kashmiri Muslims, it could pave the way for another kind of politics.

I still remember the first day Sampat Prakash walked into my apartment, or rather burst in to it. His piercing eyes set deep in his weathered face missed nothing and he was disappointed with what he saw. And he told me so. He did not like my name, my cooking, and the fact that I did not wear dejhors dangling down from my ears as a married Kashmiri Panditani should. He said he did not understand why my parents had not given me a Kashmiri name, taught me how to cook the Kashmiri way and, worst of all, why I had not even pierced the cartilage of my ears.

I was so taken aback by his observations that I did not express my feminist indignation. Instead, I told him my parents had brought me up as an Indian, not a Kashmiri. I was named after Tagore's granddaughter and at home we prided ourselves in eating Bengali-style fish and, on occasion, dosas. I had been taught to identify with all things Indian, not Kashmiri.

Later, I showed Sampat the speech my father gave in 1972, when he was invited to address the Kashmir University: 'Religion goads man to attain something larger than himself, surrender to it or to merge with it. But supposing one's god is called Bharat or India or Hind or Hindustan. Then what happens?' My father would lustily sing Iqbal's famous song written in celebration of India, 'Saare Jahan Se Achcha', a song embodying yearning and attachment to the land of Hindustan. In 1905, the twenty-seven-year-old Iqbal had viewed the future society of the subcontinent as both a pluralistic and composite Hindu-Muslim culture.

My father frequently quoted from the famous lines:

> Mazhab nahin sikhata aapas mein bair rakhna
> Hindi hain ham, watan hai Hindustan hamara
> (Religion does not teach us to bear ill-will among ourselves,
> We are of Hind, our homeland is Hindustan)

But my father never told me that Iqbal had changed the words to fit his new thinking just five years later. In 1910, he wrote:

> Chin o Arab hamaraa hindostan hamaara
> Muslim hain hum; watan hai saara jahaan hamaara
> (Central Asia [although in modern Urdu, Chin means China,
> Chin referred to Central Asia in Iqbal's time] is ours, Arabia is
> ours, India is ours; we are Muslims and the whole world is ours)

I found out about Iqbal's change of heart and his new song only during my campaign for the release of Geelani.

In our home the only god we worshipped was India. It was because of that upbringing that I was prompted to take up Geelani's case and work for four years till he was acquitted. It was a gesture of solidarity from an Indian to a Kashmiri, who I believed was a victim of the war on terrorism, a war in which a Kashmiri Muslim could easily be framed.

But Sampath could never understand our version of secularism or nationalism because it meant giving up our culture, language, poetry and, above all, our nationality. Sampath defined himself as a Kashmiri first and other identities refined that definition. Looking back, I think his disappointment was more political than cultural. If I had been a proper Kashmiri Pandit I could have been an example of Kashmiriyat—a Kashmiri Hindu woman lawyer defending a Kashmiri man framed as a terrorist.

I felt it would have been false to claim to be Kashmiri when I had no roots in Kashmir, physical or emotional. My ancestors had come away from the Valley in 1804 and by the 1820s were well-established in the bylanes of Shahjahanabad. They had lost all touch with Kashmir, its people, culture and history, and mostly importantly, its language.

But then I did not have roots in any place in India either. My roots were in a notion of India which existed only in my imagination.

Although I did not claim to be from Kashmir, I did support the cause of Kashmiri nationalism. And strange as it may sound, I had understood Kashmir only after working in the Northeast, especially with Naga nationalists. When I introduced Sampat to my Naga husband, he shook hands warmly in political solidarity, even though he could never understand a person from a non-verbal culture.

Being a man who never gives up, he continued his efforts to make the campaign for Geelani's acquittal into a battle for Kashmiriyat. Sampat insisted on presenting me to the Delhi Hurriyat office in Lajpat Nagar to meet Professor Abdul Ghani Bhat. He said it was absolutely necessary in political terms.

The entrance to the office was through a crowded, noisy road but inside there was a quiet; the green carpet spread on the floor gave the room a Kashmiri feel.

I noticed that Sampat was very respectful towards the professor, almost reverent. I could not help wonder if this was a reflection of his genuine respect for the man or a reflection of the political equation between the Kashmiri Muslim leader and the Kashmiri Pandit in the Kashmir of today.

The professor graciously welcomed me. I was not surprised by his dignity and grace, but what was entirely unexpected was the warmth of his welcome and his kindness. He told me a story of a boy who had given him tea while he was in jail, an act of kindness which took on an immense significance in the circumstances. It was a quiet way of expressing his appreciation for my act of solidarity in taking up Geelani's case pro bono. I was surprised by the subtlety of his expression which was in marked contrast to the unabashed flattery I had often experienced in Kashmir.

I was a little taken aback when I realized he knew that I had taken cases on behalf of the Nagas against the Indian security forces; he also knew that I had been to Kashmir on a fact-finding mission in 1990. Our conversation was brief and I made it clear that we would not accept funds from Kashmiri organizations for our campaign or court proceedings—I told him I would raise the money in India.

I was deeply moved by the fact that after all those years of fighting the Indian state, the years of imprisonment and the accumulated anger against India and Indians he must have harboured, he could still appreciate my gesture.

Nearly ten years after I met him, I read that Professor Abdul Gani Bhat was the first Hurriyat leader to have the courage to admit that 'Lone Sahib, Mirwaiz [Mohammad] Farooq, and Professor Wani were not killed by the army or the police. They were targeted by our own people. The story is a long one, but we have to tell the truth'. He was speaking at a seminar organized by the JKLF in Srinagar. He also admitted that the United Nations resolutions have outlived their relevance in Kashmir, and there was a need to take on board the new realities. He also said that the Taliban would not liberate Kashmir; Kashmiris must liberate themselves.[26]

Sampat Prakash was pleased with the way our meeting with Professor Bhat had gone. And he was also happy to learn that I had persuaded another Kashmiri Pandit, Sanjay Kak, to testify in court as a defence witness. Sampat informed me that Sanjay was a nephew of Jia Lal Koul, his principal at S.P. College.

It was largely because of the testimonies of Sampat Prakash and Sanjay Kak that Geelani was finally acquitted of charges of conspiring to attack the Indian Parliament. Both the witnesses independently translated the conversation and testified that the conversation could not link Geelani to the attack on Parliament. The Sessions Court had sentenced him to death in 2002, but on 29 October 2003, the High Court acquitted him. And the Supreme Court confirmed the acquittal in August 2005.[27]

There was jubilation in many parts of India when the news of Geelani's acquittal became known. I got calls from all kinds of people who took a great deal of trouble to find my phone number to congratulate me. I was a little confused by this reaction; the calls were not from friends congratulating me for my achievement. It was as if all these people had suddenly felt a relief from the suffocation of living in fear, of the helplessness of watching India slide towards fascism. The acquittal was a victory for those who believed in Indian democracy. In Kashmir, the news of the acquittal also gave rise to a flicker of hope that perhaps Kashmiris could get justice in India.

Sampat Prakash and his trade union comrades were equally jubilant when they heard the news. They were there at the airport to welcome the young lecturer and take him in a victory procession all the way from the airport in Srinagar to his home in Baramulla. Sampat Prakash felt a joy he had not felt for a long time; for him, Kahsmiriyat had received a fresh lease of life.

However, Sampat's elation was short-lived. When the procession reached Baramulla, he was not given the reception he had hoped for. Geelani's family was neither committed to the idea of Kashmiriyat, nor did anyone want to acknowledge the role the trade union leader had played in Geelani's acquittal. For them, it was divine intervention that had rescued their kin from the jaws of death, not a Kashmiri

Pandit. Sampat did not even get an invitation to stay overnight in the Geelani home. He accepted the invitation of Ghulam Qader Rather, the district president of his Trade Union Centre and a retired schoolteacher, to spend the night in his home. Ghulam Qader's younger brother was a lawyer and president of the Jihad Council. Rather and other union leaders gathered together and asked Sampat Prakash why he had gone to court on behalf of a Jamaati.

Sampat Prakash was shocked to learn that Abdul Rehman Geelani's family were staunch supporters of Jamaat-e-Islami. In fact, they had been responsible for bringing the organization into Kashmir. The local trade union leaders expressed their reservations about the possible role Geelani could play in the future to create space for secular or democratic politics.

Sampat and his comrades were a little disturbed when, on his second visit to Kashmir after his acquittal, Abdul Rehman Geelani requested Sampat Prakash to facilitate his meeting with Dr Mohammad Qasim Faqtoo, who had been convicted of the murder of Wanchoo, the trade union leader. Sampat was appalled by the idea.

Mohammad Qasim Faqtoo was the chief of intelligence of the Jamiat-ul-Mujahideen which had been founded in 1991. The organization's publicity chief, Abdul Manan, had issued a statement clarifying the ideology of the organization: 'The demand for self-determination is distorting the image of the ongoing movement. It is a struggle for the establishment of Caliphate.'[28]

Faqtoo's wife, Asiya Andrabi, was the founder of Dukhtaran-e-Millat (Daughters of the Nation). She was responsible for enforcing the dress code on women in accordance with the Jamaat's interpretation of what to wear. She herself was a science graduate but she could not continue her studies because of her brother's opposition.

Faqtoo had been arrested from Srinagar airport when he was returning from Delhi on 5 February 1993, and he had been in jail ever since.

At first Sampat refused to help Geelani meet Faqtoo. But the other trade union leaders prevailed upon him to help the young man whom they had helped rescue from the jaws of death. Besides, Faqtoo was the new leader many looked up to.

Faqtoo had acquired a doctorate in Islamic studies while in prison, founding his religious beliefs on the teachings of the neo-fundamentalist Jamiat Ahle Hadith—not Geelani's Jamaat-e-Islami. He had been brought into the movement by Mohammad Abdullah Bangroo who, many years later, presided over the assassination of Mirwaiz Mohammad Farooq—the father of the current chairperson of the All Party Hurriyat Conference (APHC), Mirwaiz Umar Farooq.[29]

Sampat Prakash had not learnt to distinguish between the old Jamaat-e-Islami leaders like Syed Ali Shah Geelani, and the new generation of Islamists like Faqtoo. Geelani had stood for elections and served in the assembly in 1972, 1977 and 1987—more terms than any chief minister of the state. In 1997, the then Jamaat chief, G.M. Bhat, called for an end to the 'gun culture'. Three years later, dissident Hizbul Mujahideen commander, Abdul Majid Dar, declared a unilateral ceasefire, even though the ceasefire did not last long. In January 2004, the Jamaat's Majlis-e-Shoora, or central consultative council, went public with a commitment to a 'democratic and constitutional struggle'.[30]

These changes were not welcomed by the Kashmiri Muslims of Abdul Rehman Geelani's generation. They were critical of the Jamaat-e-Islami's lack of radical thought. In India, the Jamaat-e-Islami Hind was criticized by youth who broke away and formed the Students Islamic Movement of India (SIMI). SIMI calls for jihad and works towards establishing a Caliphate.[31]

In May 2003, Jamaat moderates led by Bhat's successor, Syed Nasir Ahmad Kashani, retired Syed Ali Shah Geelani as their political representative. Now, younger Jamaat leaders spearheaded the new Islamist tendencies that manifested themselves in Kashmir. These younger members were deeply influenced by the events unfolding in the wider world. In 2006, commentator Sheikh Showkat Hussain wrote: 'The fate of Islamic movements cannot be divorced from the fate of the Muslim ummah and its various segments, be they in Palestine, Lebanon, Chechnya or Kashmir.'[32] The Jamaat, he argued, could not keep aloof from these issues.

The mass support for these radical Islamists came, for the most part, from poor neighbourhoods like Batpora—insurgents released from prisons, without hope of a job or marriage; school dropouts; daily-wage labourers. New Islamists were now the driving force behind street protests, struggles against prostitution and alcohol use, campaigns for the enforcement of social morality targeting Western cultural practices, and human rights abuses by Indian security forces.

According to the police, Faqtoo mentored a new generation of jihadists from jail. It is no wonder, then, that for Abdul Rehman Geelani, Faqtoo was a hero; for Sampat he was a terrorist without an ideology or vision for the future.

———

Nearly two generations of Kashmiri militants had grown up after the exodus of the Kashmiri Pandits; they had neither any memories of a happy and harmonious past nor did they have any commitment to a pluralistic society in the future. For them, the words secularism, Socialism and pluralism were a part of the armoury of the Indian state, and possibly of the West, to dominate the Islamic world, which included Kashmir.

Bismillah, Geelani's younger brother, was a product of those trends. In my long talks with him, Bismillah said that he had never had occasion to interact with Hindus or people from different political backgrounds, not even Kashmiri Pandits. He was witness to the return of two Pandit families to Baramulla. There was tension when they appeared in the town which had been their home. Bismillah said that the guest militants were against their return but the Hizbul Mujahideen said they should be welcomed back. Bismillah heard the angry exchange between the Kashmiris and the foreign militants. The Kashmiris pointed out that Kashmir was their homeland; the foreign militants reminded them of their contribution in their struggle. Bismillah felt sorry for the Kashmiri Pandits and even went to speak to them, but in the end they had to leave. In the early days of the militancy, people did come out to protest against atrocities committed against the Pandits. For instance, there was a time when 5,000 women came out in the streets of Srinagar to protest against the slaughter of a Pandit family in April 1992.[33]

Bismillah would often ask me whether I thought it was communalism if Muslims wanted to live apart from Hindus so that they could practice their religion without hindrance. It was because of my conversations with him that I began to realize that the dichotomy between religion and secularism is not tenable.[34]

Bismillah had many questions that were troubling him and he wanted to have a discussion with Sampat Prakash, but he did not feel confident enough to ask. He had never had an open and frank discussion with a Kashmiri Pandit. Finally, Sampat Prakash did have long conversations with him which went on for weeks. Bismillah transcribed it, and the transcript ran to more than eighty typed pages. Unfortunately, I do not have the whole typescript, but a part of that conversation was published and it makes for interesting reading, even though it is a much abbreviated version.[35] It is an important conversation between a Kashmiri Pandit and a Kashmiri Muslim.

———

Sampat Prakash and the trade union leaders with whom he had worked with since 1967 had retired and the union work was now being carried on by a younger generation of fighters who would often seek counsel from the veterans. But Sampat longed to be involved in the political scene in Kashmir. He was uncomfortable working with the pro-Pakistan Hurriyat which was also committed to the promotion of an Islamic State. He had been mulling over the idea of formally joining the JKLF, which still had a huge base among the Kashmiri people. Moreover, the JKLF had stood by the commitment it had made in 1994 after Yasin was released from jail: it would not use arms to fight for its demand for an independent Kashmir. It was not a part of the pro-Pakistan Hurriyat.

Many of the union leaders opposed Sampat's decision, partly because they thought that the trade union should function independent of all political organizations, and partly because many of them supported the Hurriyat's pro-Pakistan stand which seemed more practical.

For Sampat it was not going to be easy to justify joining the JKLF to his family and the Kashmiri Pandit community since the organization had been responsible for the killing of many Pandits. As it is, the community felt that Sampat had betrayed them by testifying on behalf of a Kashmiri accused of attacking the Indian Parliament. But Sampat had noticed that Yasin Malik had always distanced himself from these killings and had consistently called for the Kashmiri Pandits to return to the Valley.

In June 2003, Yasin Malik had carried out a massive signature campaign in the villages of Kashmir on the issue of an independent Kashmir, and he had collected more than 800,000 signatures within the first month. He had not only given up armed struggle, but had more than adequately proved his democratic credentials. A few months later, Yasin reiterated his commitment to secular values in an interview. He said: 'People say we cannot be a viable state. We are a region that is rich in culture, in natural beauty. Why do we need a military? We want no quarrel with our neighbours. The goal of our struggle is an independent, secular, democratic country, which is the only viable, honorable solution. We want to assure the people of India and Pakistan, who I know are sentimentally and romantically involved with Kashmir, that they will be able to see an independent Kashmir as their own home.'[36]

Looking at all these developments, Sampat Prakash persuaded several senior leaders of the executive of the Trade Union Centre to seriously think about joining the JKLF. He arranged a meeting of his comrades with Yasin Malik and, after that meeting, in April 2007, he and some of his colleagues formally joined the JKLF. In his usual colourful language, Sampat called his alliance with Yasin a nikah, a bond of marriage, which would last forever.

Yasin must have been observing the activities of the trade union and, therefore, would have known that Sampat had testified in court as a defence witness in the Parliament attack case. These were the events which prompted him to invite Sampat Prakash to accompany him on a Journey of Freedom (Safar-e-Azadi) that he was planning to undertake. This was an offer which Sampat Prakash could not refuse. He was excited with the idea of the Journey of Freedom. He felt it would be a journey which epitomized his idea of Kashmiriyat; a Kashmiri Pandit and a Kashmiri Muslim travelling through the 8,600 villages of Kashmir and then going on to Jammu.

Sampat knew that it would be a gruelling experience to travel by truck across the Kashmir Valley, addressing meetings and sleeping in tents. He consulted his family and his wife said it would kill him. But the thought that he, a Kashmiri Pandit, and Yasin, a Kashmiri Muslim, would travel together to fight for the independence of Kashmir was something that made him almost delirious with anticipation. It was an opportunity to revive the spirit of Kashmiriyat; he hoped to make an impact on the younger generation which had grown up not having met a single Kashmiri Pandit in their lives.

———

Sampat was in Delhi at the time. Yasin had already camped in Zalangam village in Kokernag tehsil on 4 May 2007; his Safar-e-Azadi was to begin in two days' time. This was the village where Yasin's father, Ghulam Qadir Malik, had been born. Even before the journey could start, Yasin and his comrades were arrested and locked up for a few days. As a result, the Safar-e-Azadi was temporarily disrupted.

It occurred to Sampat that Yasin had not done his homework; lack of planning could be critical in such situations. After all, if the procession was to visit the villages it would have to pass 209 army camps and some 800 bunkers; without explicit permission for the Journey of Freedom there was no way they could just drive into these villages.

Yasin came out of jail and went on an indefinite hunger strike. In Delhi, several people intervened, including members of Parliament such as Nirmala Deshpande, a Gandhian, and the former prime minister, A.B. Vajpayee. Yasin's supporters petitioned the European Union office. With all these interventions asking why a Kashmiri could not take out a peaceful procession, the government in Srinagar acquiesced and the Safar-e-Azadi began the same month. It was on 20 May 2007 that the journey began in the small village of Matigavaran, near Daksum in the Kokernag tehsil of Anantnag district, now renamed Islamabad. In his first speech, Yasin said that the JKLF was against the trifurcation of the state on religious lines. He said they would not allow the partition of Jammu, Kashmir and Ladakh on religious or ethnic lines; he said the people should sit together and decide their future and their destiny.

Sampat Prakash proudly sat next to Yasin Malik on one plank of wood in a truck which had been decorated with all the symbols of Hindu-Muslim unity which Sampat still called Kashmiriyat, alongside scenes of torture and violence inflicted by the Indian state. Yasin explained to the thousands of people who had gathered to welcome the Kashmiri leader that the basic purpose of the journey was to make India and Pakistan aware of the fact that the inclusion of Kashmiris is necessary to arrive at a solution to the Kashmir dispute.

The moment the caravan of vehicles arrived at the base camp, the JKLF activists would get busy pitching fifteen tents. Some tents were for individual leaders while others served as dormitories for activists; one of them housed the media equipment and CDs were made of the day's journey and sent to the media every day. A large tent served as a kitchen. The man in charge of the kitchen was none other than the famous militant, Muhammad Zaman Mir. The meals were usually simple—vegetables and rice or roti. But, even then, more than 200 people had to be fed.

At dusk, the JKLF leaders would light up the torches (mashaals). The job of preparing these torches was given to Meharjudin, who had been a JKLF activist since the time he had witnessed the massacre of innocent Kashmiris at Gawkadal. During the three-month Safar-e-Azadi, Meharjudin made more than 150 mashaals every day. From the base camp, the activists would walk with the lighted torches to the villages in the vicinity, holding public meetings and talking to people. Yasin told the people that for mystics, the lighting of torches symbolized the highest spiritual protest; sending a message to both India and Pakistan that a new movement had started in Kashmir that would force both the countries to solve the Kashmir issue immediately.

The villages reverberated with pro-Azadi slogans shouted as vociferously by the women and children as by the JKLF activists and the youth. The women also burst into songs and sang traditional Kashmiri ballads to welcome the caravan. The children danced with joy while the youth were thrilled to get an opportunity to shake hands with the chairman of the JKLF, Yasin Malik.

Sampat felt a thrill he had not experienced for a long time. The welcome by the people was truly overwhelming. None of the political parties who came out to canvass for votes ever received this kind of response, and they always came with the security forces. The leaders of the APHC preferred to meet people in their heavily guarded headquarters or in mosques. Here was Yasin Malik going around without an escort, moving freely amongst his people, and what a response he was receiving.

In the mornings, while they waited for their lunch to be cooked, Yasin and Sampat talked to the villagers, visited the homes of those whose sons had been killed by the security forces. The people wanted to share their experiences of living in the dark days filled with terror when the Indian security forces barged into their homes. The horror of the rape, the torture and murders were still fresh in their minds and the wounds in their hearts had not stopped bleeding yet.

Sampat was especially thrilled to see the women get onto their truck and shout slogans and sing songs; to him it was a revival of the

Kashmiri spirit. The fact that so many women were coming out to welcome Yasin and singing their hearts out would not be encouraged by the Islamist organizations; it would be un-Islamic according their interpretation of their religion.

In reality, however, the JKLF, like the other Kashmiri militant organizations, never had its own women's wing. For that matter, neither had Sampat produced any women leaders in the trade union movement so that I could include their stories in this book. When I accused him of being as patriarchal and feudal like other Kashmiri men he became really angry. Later, however, he said that I was the first woman who had ever challenged him.

The activists had to work hard all day. They performed all the menial tasks such as washing their dishes, cleaning the tents, washing and chopping vegetables and also washing their own clothes. Yasin was frail after all the years he spent in jail and his health was not good; Sampat was nearly seventy years old. But both leaders felt energized by the warmth of people's response.

The activists had committed themselves to being on the journey from the start to finish even though sometimes there were urgent family calls. A shining example of this commitment was Sukhwant Singh alias Santy, a JKLF activist who was driving the truck in which Yasin and Sampat travelled. The Sikh did not think twice about not being able to go home to Qazigund when his sister returned after many years of living in New Delhi. On some days, he even found the energy to dance along with the people.

But there were memories which people did not want to resurrect, not because they were painful but because the memories made them very uncomfortable. Those were the suppressed memories which Sampat could not allow to be forgotten. In Soaf Shali village lay one such memory and Sampat, never lacking courage, gave it a voice.

It was in this village that on 29 April 1990, three armed men had entered the house of Sarwanand Kaul Premi. Sarwanand had started his political life working in the All India Spinners Association and was a committed Gandhian. He was a scholar and had translated the

Bhagwad Gita and Tagore's *Geetanjali* into the Kashmiri language. He had felt so sure that he was safe in the village where he had lived all his life. He and his family had continued to live here even though theirs was the sole Kashmiri Pandit family in the village. He must have felt a deep sense of betrayal the day the militants entered his home, ransacked it and took away valuables and dragged him out. Unable to watch his sixty-three-year-old father being dragged out, his twenty-seven-year-old son had insisted on going with him. The two of them were tortured before being murdered.

Sarwanand's daughter, Jyoti, was married to Chaplin,[37] Sampat Prakash's cousin's son. Sampat knew Sarwanand personally and he was angry that the JKLF had never apologized for the murder. And even when they had come to the village, Yasin did not mention the old scholar.

Yasin's caravan passed many villages in which there were Kashmiri Pandit families who had chosen to remain throughout the years of insurgency. They would come out and listen to the speeches but would not join the processions. Sampat knew that the JKLF activists had noticed that the Kashmiri Pandits and Sikhs had not joined the processions in their villages; they had listened to the speeches from the edge of the crowds and then disappeared back into the safety of their homes. Sampat would go to their homes, sit and talk to them and listen to their experiences.

Towards the last week of June, the Safar-e-Azadi reached the village of Aishmuqam, some twenty kilometres from Pahalgam. The village is known in every corner of Kashmir on account of the historical shrine of Sheikh Zain-ud-din who had lived in the fifteenth century AD. He was one of the principal disciples of Sheikh Nur-ud-din, the leading Rishi of Kashmir. The shrine of Baba Zain-ud-din Rishi is perched at the top a hillock, approximately hundred metres above the road level and is clearly visible in all its majesty from the Anantnag-Pahalgam road.

This was a scene of a clash between the Islamist militants and the villagers. The militants had tried to stop the people from celebrating the Urs (death anniversary) of Baba Zain-ud-din Rishi and the villagers had resisted.

The caravan continued further. By 23 July, they had reached central Kashmir. Yasin and Sampat were thrilled to see the response at Rebban Shopian and Kanelwan Bijbehara where more than 300 women were waiting with sacks of rice and fresh vegetables for them. Older women pushed their way to the front so they could take Yasin's face in their hands and kiss his forehead. The women sat around Yasin singing folk songs while Zaman cooked extra meals for their guests. Sampat noticed how the eyes of the most hardened militants became moist on hearing the soulful songs filled with longing for freedom.

At night, the villagers joined the JKLF activists in taking out a torchlight procession from the shrine of the Sufi saint, Sheikh Nur-ud-din. The villagers expressed their happiness because this was the first time they had been able to come out at night since the insurgency began in 1990.

Throughout the journey no one shouted pro-Pakistan slogans such as 'Jio Jio Pakistan' except when they passed through the Jamaat-e-Islami bases. There the JKLF's goal of 'Kashmir banega Khudmukhtar' (Kashmir will be independent) was countered by the Hizbul Mujahideen slogan: 'Kashmir banega Pakistan' (Kashmir will become Pakistan). But the Jamaat-e-Islami could not derail the caravan-on-wheels even when it passed Soibugh village, the stronghold of the Jamaat and home of Syed Muhammad Yusuf Shah or Syed Salahuddin, the commander-in-chief of the Hizbul Mujahideen. Despite the Hizbul Mujahideen's formidable organization, backed by Pakistan's arms, training and ideology, it had never been able to gain popular appeal. People supported their fight against India but rejected their attempts to stop people from offering prayers at Sufi shrines.

In his speech at Soibugh village, Sampat Prakash recalled how the Kashmiris had welcomed the mujahideen from Pakistan and from other parts of the world. Kashmiris had spread out their carpets and welcomed them into their homes, shared meals with them, and when the security forces came, had even hidden them in their daughters' beds. But very often these guest militants had turned out to be renegades and had not respected the local culture and even violated the hospitality of the Kashmiris.

I asked Sampat what the percentage of foreign militants was compared to the local Kashmiris. He said that no estimate was possible. Abdul Ghani Lone had claimed that the percentage was not more than 20 per cent although, at the time, India claimed that the number was 80 per cent. Lone, on the other hand, claimed that the casualty figures showed that the 80 per cent who die are Kashmiris.[38] The police recently claimed that 45 per cent of the militants were foreigners.[39]

The Safar-e-Azadi caravan went into villages which the Indian army had not dared enter for years because of the presence of militants. But Yasin's caravan was warmly welcomed by people even in places that pro-Pakistan organizations had bases in. At one point, the security forces warned Sampat Prakash not to go to the homes of employees to sleep, as he would often do; they told him he would be safer sleeping in the tent even though the JKLF was not armed. But none of these warnings and caution was taken into account as the Safar-e-Azadi moved through north Kashmir.

So far, the journey had been without incident. But as they approached Chowkibal the brakes of their truck failed. Yasin and Sampat could have been thrown down the mountain but Sukhwant Singh, their Sikh driver, saved them and the journey continued to Uri, the Line of Control and finally, on 6 September 2007, they triumphantly entered Srinagar city after a three-month tour.

As dusk fell, the JKLF activists lit the mashaals and carried forward the procession which marched through the narrow lanes of Danderkhah, Magarmalbagh, Maharaj Bazar, Lal Chowk, Maisuma, Habba Kadal, Nawab Bazar and other areas of the old city. The Safar-e-Azadi caravan stopped at the Batmaloo Sahib shrine and from there toured every part of the city for three days till 11 September.

People opened their windows and showered flower petals on the activists, almonds and sweets were also thrown and the leaders were garlanded with flowers.

By this time, Yasin Malik and Sampat Prakash had addressed more than 600 meetings through the length and breadth of the Kashmir Valley. Although they were both tired, they looked forward to their next leg of the journey through Jammu. But that would be after the month of Ramzan. Yasin Malik decided to meditate and pray for a month.

Sampat returned to Jammu for a well-earned rest and some home-cooked food. As he recouped, he thought through his experience. He realized that the JKLF had very committed members, people who had remained honest and were ready to sacrifice everything for the cause of Kashmir. But there was no organization. It was all controlled by one man, Yasin Malik.

In the trade union movement, local leaders were always given importance so that the organization had strong roots. But Yasin did not give any importance to the local leaders by inviting them to address the meetings. Many dedicated leaders were left standing on the sidelines listening to Yasin. Sampat had also found it strange that the media from outside Kashmir largely ignored the Safar-e-Azadi. The only time the media expressed interest was when the caravan camped in militants' strongholds or when they passed through the constituencies of important leaders. Some leaders of the Hurriyat, too, had provided food and support, but they wanted to remain anonymous, not wanting to openly support the JKLF initiative.

Sampat had also noticed that some people associated with non-government organizations (NGOs) had joined the Safar-e-Azadi. They were close to Yasin and they had tried to tell Sampat to tone down his speeches.[40] It was difficult to know on whose behalf these NGOs worked. Some had been started by former militants, such as Baba Badr, while others were floated by various political parties in the Valley. And then there were many others floated by the intelligence agencies—Indian, Pakistani and the CIA.[41] Sampat dismissed the influence of the NGOs on the course of the Kashmir struggle. I disagreed. In my mind the Western states and interests worked through these NGOs and the agenda was hidden and insidious.

By November 2007 Sampat was bracing himself for the second leg of the Safar-e-Azadi which would be going through Doda, Poonch and Rajouri, the Muslim-dominated areas in Jammu. Sampat mobilized employees in these areas. They had put up the posters he had given them and had received permission from the administration to set up camp on the Idgah grounds in Doda.

Sampat was waiting for Yasin to arrive. All the JKLF leaders came to Doda, including Zaman who would once again manage the kitchen. But a day before the journey was to begin, the police arrested all of them despite their protests that they had the requisite permission.

The Safar-e-Azadi did not manage to reach Jammu. It was then that Sampat realized that the government and intelligence agencies had allowed Yasin Malik to make his journey towards freedom as a way to gauge the mood of the people. They had learnt two important facts. First, that the threat perception was false: the militants, though present, exerted little force or influence. Obviously, there were certain vested interests who wanted to build up this threat so as not to allow demilitarization. Secondly, their journey had exposed the massive support for the JKLF as opposed to the pro-Pakistan militant organizations or the political parties which stood for elections. The intelligence agencies had used Yasin Malik and now there was no reason to allow him to continue to build his base.

I met Sampat Prakash in Delhi when he was in the city to organize an exhibition around the Safar-e-Azadi. He was excited and gave me a CD of the journey. He said that we should have an entire chapter on the journey in the book. I watched the CD and noticed that Sampat was virtually invisible. It seemed very odd, especially since Yasin wanted to project himself as a secular leader who wanted to include all communities of Jammu, Kashmir and Ladakh in his vision of independent Kashmir.

Sampat admitted that he was very disappointed that the JKLF CD had not shown him and Yasin together addressing the meetings; such a picture would have become a powerful symbol of Kashmiriyat. Even the newspapers did not carry photographs of the two leaders together, though they did occasionally mention Sampat's presence or quote a line from his speech.

I asked Sampat why the JKLF had blanked him out. Was it done consciously or was there some other possible explanation? Could it be because Sampat Prakash did not represent the Kashmiri Pandits and the Pandits did not see him as their leader? Perhaps, if he had an organizational backing from a section of the Kashmiri Pandits, the JKLF may have been forced to acknowledge Sampat's presence. For the time being, however, Sampat was just a token Kashmiri Pandit— a token is quite different from a symbol.

Yasin was not acceptable to the Kashmiri Pandits. Although he had invited them back to the Valley, he never asked them to join the JKLF. He had never apologized for the killing of the Pandits by his organization. Besides, in the context of the Kashmir Valley, he was under political pressure to assert his identity as a Kashmiri Muslim.

A few years after the Safar-e-Azadi, Syed Ali Shah Geelani, an unrepentant follower of the Jamaat-e-Islami, published the second part of his autobiography, *Wular kay Kinare*. Geelani described the JKLF as a 'non-religious party'. The JKLF strongly condemned the criticisms Geelani had made about their organization. The JKLF published a pamphlet to counter Geelani's assertions in which they said: 'JKLF is a caravan of firm believers in Allah and lovers of Prophet Muhammad (SAW)[42] so many people at times have tried to malign JKLF and its leaders by false propaganda and bundles of lies.

'JKLF and its members love and respect every deed of our beloved Prophet but we don't believe in putting ourselves as good Muslims and terming others as bad ones as it is the discretion of Allah almighty only to decide so'.

Then the JKLF went on to assert that the party considers the issue of Jammu and Kashmir as a political issue 'and our struggle is for every citizen of the state as we do not believe in discriminating people on the basis of their caste, religion, creed or colour'.[43]

I wondered how far could Sampat Prakash, a Kashmiri Pandit who still considered himself to be a 'humble student of Marxism and Leninism', feel at home in a caravan of firm believers?

KASHMIR AND THE WAR
ON TERROR

In January 2009, I was sitting with a group of young professionals; journalists and lawyers in Srinagar. They had just learnt that the Lashkar-e-Taiba had issued a statement declaring that it was ready for talks. I was about to say that this was good news when one of the young men said, 'They too have betrayed us.'

They had come late in the morning and sat with me till late evening. I listened, they talked. But there was no analysis or debate about the future of Kashmir, no vision for its future. It was purely an outpouring of anger, resentment and bitterness about the injustices the Kashmiris had suffered at the hands of India, especially the Indian security forces.

However, their anger was also against America and its war against terror. The young men sitting opposite me saw themselves as a part of the wider Muslim community and their grievances merged seamlessly into the grievances of all Muslims without national, political or historical contexts. They were conscious of being a part of the population of more than one-and-a-half billion Muslims spread across more than fifty countries. Their anger over the human rights violations by the Indian security forces merged with their outrage against the horrors perpetuated by the CIA while interrogating prisoners in Abu Ghraib, Guantanamo and Bagram. The American interventions in Afghanistan, Iraq, Horn of Africa, the Sahara region and the Caspian region to the drone attacks in Pakistan had made them feel a part of the collective rage across the Muslim world.

These young men could hardly be expected to feel sympathetic about the Indians killed in the attack by the Lashakar-e-Taiba in Mumbai in November 2006 in which 166 people had died. After all, Indians had not expressed the same grief when thousands of Kashmiris were killed by militants and Indian security forces operating in the state.

Besides, David Headley, one of the main people involved in planning the Mumbai attack, had said in an e-mail: 'Our opinion here is that the casualties in Mumbai are should (sic) really be taken as Collateral Damage from the Daisy cutters (bombs) that have been falling in Afghanistan as well as the over 70000 dead in Kashmir over the last 20 years at the hands of the Terrorist Indian Army. As you can see that more than 500 commandos had a hard time containing 10 kids. These pieces of shit have no stomach for a fight. All their valor is reserved for the girls in Kashmir'.[1] Kashmir newspapers did focus on Headley's statement on Kashmir. There was less focus on the view expressed by many experts that Headley was a double agent and was working for the Pakistani intelligence agencies and, perhaps, also for the CIA.

I understood the anger and even some of the pain being voiced by the Kashmiri men sitting with me. But I did not understand their request to help them find a way to go to America. They were angry with America for the war against terrorism in which Muslims had become targets but they themselves longed to escape to the US, the land of opportunities. And the Americans welcomed them by offering scholarships and plum jobs. But only a miniscule number of Kashmiri Muslim youth could ever hope to go to America. Those who stayed behind were getting attracted to puritanical Islam.

The base of Ahl-e-Hadith followers was increasing significantly and the attacks on Sufi shrines was just a small indication of its growing attraction. This increase has also been greatly facilitated by the funds which have been made available by the Pakistani intelligence agency and Saudi funders.

The Jammu and Kashmir police and Central Intelligence officers say that Ahl-e-Hadith's funding comes primarily from Saudi Arabia. Based on US intelligence, they believe that the House of Saud, rulers of Saudi Arabia, had approved a $35-billion plan to build mosques and madrassas in South Asia in 2005.[2]

It is estimated that 1,500,000 members, over 16 per cent of Jammu and Kashmir's Muslims, now follow the Salafi school.[3] Besides the 700 mosques and madrassas it has built, the Ahl-e-Hadith is believed to have funded 150 schools, several colleges, orphanages, clinics and medical diagnostic centres. It has also proposed a Rs 2 billion Islamic university, Transworld Muslim University (TWMU), in Hyderpora, Srinagar, affiliated to leading Saudi institutions.[4]

Sampat had also noticed that the Ahl-e-Hadith, whom he calls Allahwale, had been actively organizing meetings all over Kashmir. He had even attended some of their meetings and had found bureaucrats and government servants openly attending them. The speakers discussed various aspects of Islam but there was no mention of Kashmir or the movement for self-determination. At the end of each meeting, collections were made for the construction of mosques; these mosques were being built in the Saudi architectural style. Gone were the colourful Kashmiri mosques which resembled pagodas.

⎯

The tension between nationalism and religion had become more acute, but it had always existed in Kashmir, as it had in other parts of the world. When Kashmiris speak to the outside world, it is in the language of nationalism—about the injustice done to Kashmiris by Indians or Pakistanis.

It was for this reason that the trade union movement could bring together, within its organization, members who were pro-Pakistan, pro-India, as well as those who wanted an independent Kashmir.

I still remember the day sometime in April 2015, when Sampat brought around fourteen members of the union to my home in Delhi. The trade union leaders were feeling really good after returning from a meeting in Ahmedabad, organized by the Hind Mazdoor Kisan Panchayat (HMPK) and inaugurated by the union agricultural minister, Sharad Pawar.

Sampat proudly told me that he had told the HMKP leaders that the Trade Union Centre would attend only if a resolution, declaring that Kashmir was a disputed territory, and acknowledging the right of the Kashmiri people to be a party to any negotiations between India and Pakistan on the Kashmir conflict was passed.

Mohammad Raja Amin described how they had made a dramatic entry into the auditorium at the start of the meeting, shouting slogans; Sampat said their throats were like megaphones and the hall reverberated with:

> Jis Kashmir ko khoon se seecha
> Woh Kashmir hamara hai,
> Zalimon, katilon katl-e-aam band karo
> Masl-e-Kashmir hal karo
> (The Kashmir we've irrigated with our blood
> Is our Kashmir,
> Oppressors, murderers, stop the killings
> Resolve the Kashmir issue)

The 3,000 delegates sat in their chairs transfixed. The Kashmiris went right around the hall and when they finally sat down, they were greeted with a thunderous applause in solidarity.

I made cups of tea and snacks. As always, I was conscious that I could not compete with Kashmiri hospitality, so I offered to take them out for dinner. There was hesitation. Then Raja Amin looked at me with a bright smile and said, 'Then we will have vegetarian food. We like vegetarian food.' For a minute I wondered what had prompted him to say that and then I realized they were worried that the meat the restaurant served might not be halal. I smiled and told them I would be taking them to Karim's in Jama Masjid.

Mohammad Raja Amin was younger than Sampat Prakash. He had joined the government employees union after the first strike organized in 1967. He vividly remembered the time in 1969, when 200 of his colleagues at the Government Press had come together and shouted slogans. He too had joined them and felt empowered. He said he still had a photograph of the time he addressed a meeting. It had been held in Tagore Hall and the hall had resounded with slogans.

Raja Amin was very proud of the strikes he had organized, especially the strike while he was in jail during the Emergency. He had been dismissed from his job and, when he came out, he had no money. Since he did not wish to be a burden on his family, he and another colleague, Syed Hussein, went to Nepal and started a clothes business there. They had opened several showrooms but were cheated by a Pakistani businessman and lost everything and returned home empty-handed—except for the Nepali wife Raja brought back to India. En route to Karim's, Raja Amin offered to give me a meal of noodles when I came to his home in Kashmir.

The mood at Karim's was upbeat. I enjoyed the company and heard stories from the men's past—about strikes and demonstrations, struggles and protests. They had gone along with many political parties, from the Naxalites to the CPI(M) and now they had affiliated with the socialist HMKP.

Raja Amin opposed Yasin Malik's JKLF, which stood for an independent Kashmir. He said that it was an impossible dream; neither India nor Pakistan—or for that matter the Western powers—would allow Kashmir to be independent.

But was it only because he thought it was impossible or was it because he felt Kashmir should logically be a part of Pakistan? I think Raja felt awkward admitting his affiliation to an Islamist ideology, perhaps out of political expediency or because he thought it may hurt my feelings.

Later, in a formal interview, Raja Amin filled me in on his background. His father had owned a godown which was used for storing items like tea, spices and other such goods. His mother came from a family that was involved in the trade of pashmina shawls, though she herself was a housewife. Raja had Kashmiri Pandit neighbours and the grandfather of one of his friends had been born in jail. He had Kashmiri Pandit boys in his class but he admits that his close friends were Muslims. I wondered if he mentioned his Kashmiri Pandit neighbours just to please me.

Raja was around seven years old when the Sheikh was arrested. He remembers seeing supporters of the Jamaat-e-Islami being beaten up during Bakshi's rule for demanding the Sheikh's release. Raja Amin's father had opposed the conversion of the Muslim Conference to National Conference and he was also beaten up by Bakshi's men several times. As a child, Raja remembered writing 'Pakistan Zindabad' on a blackboard and shouting the slogans of the Plebiscite Front.

Over a hearty meal of kebabs, korma and rotis, the trade union leaders and I discussed how we could carry forward the campaign to save Mohammad Afzal Guru from the death penalty. We all shared the hope that we could save him from hanging. The campaign for Geelani had created a democratic space for the campaign for Afzal, and for talking about Kashmir.

—

Although Afzal had lived in the closed and claustrophobic cells of Tihar Jail, his mind was open, and he continued to read extensively. Tabassum said that after Ghalib was born, Afzal would complain, 'Waai Pyaari mye mileha kanh goaph' (O Pyaari, I wish I could find a cave to read in). After his imprisonment, Tabassum would tease him: 'Goaph mileye?' (Have you found the cave now)? to which Afzal would smilingly retort, 'Zabardast goaph!' (Incredible cave!).

Afzal wrote long letters to friends. Sometimes he made copies and would give me one or send it to me through his channels. Most of these letters were in English. In the letters, he discussed his ideas about religion and nationalism. Often, we would follow up what he had written with animated conversations inside the jail.

Like many other Kashmiri Muslims, Afzal too had become disillusioned by the idea of nationalism and had taken refuge in

Islamist ideologies. For Afzal, both India and Pakistan had betrayed the Kashmiris. He was worried about the radicalism of the new generation. He called it indoctrination and expressed his concern in a letter written from Jail No 2, in Tihar Jail, to a fellow Kashmiri:

> Our home is in a state of ANARCHY. (Morally-politically, socially etc) sandwiched between two antagonistic Forces. One country is simmering other on indoctrinating the highly volatile kids mobilizing the noble feelings of these uneducated and unaware youth for their own existence and survival. They want to engage the huge Army stricture with huge budget by handful highly motivated people. The other side the Army want to rest and to have highly luxurious life. It is this hypocrisy that made few people to change the state of simmering of pot into boiling state. It got boiled but unfortunately these two countries do not learn rather they do not want make people live in peace. They are living on the threshold of the same boiling stage. I was not alone nor am I. I don't belong to any org. I belong to feelings and ideas (felt globally) by those who are being humiliated tortured and silenced unwilling.

Afzal was wrestling with ideas of religion and nationalism. In a long letter written to me on 8 January 2008 (Appendix 2) he asked:

> Respected Nandita, When Naga conflict is not Christian why conflict in Kashmir is branded as Islamic.[5] Fundamentally it is political, social and historical in nature. Robert A Pape's[6] book, *Dying to Win*, has given a sophisticated analysis of 300 suicide attacks (from 1980–2003) out of which 76 were executed by LTTE. The common cause he says is political and social injustice, oppression and brutal policies of political establishment or occupational powers.

The same point had been made by Graham E. Fuller, a senior member of the American Intelligence Service, when he wrote:

> Indeed viewing Islam as an explanation obfuscates a clear vision of the issues. Islam, particularly in its more extreme ideological

form, can complicate, even exacerbate, but not create such problems. The issues and problems, instead spring from quite specific, concrete regional political, economic and social challenges—including inadequate education—that transcend religion, however wrapped in Islamic (cultural) rhetoric they may be.[7]

Afzal's letter reflected his anger against the Indian state for its 'senseless policies' which were responsible for radicalizing the youth. Sitting in solitary confinement, his thoughts were with the Kashmiri youth facing the Indian 'state's senseless policies'. He wrote:

> The constant humiliation and trauma will enhance and ignite the heat of conflict. These policies will cultivate the militant and radical culture towards irreversible end. Police stations have become terror and slaughter houses. Families of killed person do not go to police station because it is police station which is spreading the sense of terror into the hearts and minds of people. You may be feeling this exaggeration of state terror but this is a bitter fact of constitutional colony that is Kashmir.

Afzal could see that Kashmir was making a shift towards a more radical Islam and he knew the role of Pakistan and its intelligence agency in this development. But he thought India could not stem the tide by offering economic development alone. He wrote to me:

> Jesus the son of Marry (Maryam) (Peace be up them) says Man does not live by bread alone. Economic packages can not bring peace in Kashmir. The people who are constantly living in the flux of humiliation and fear does not need bread for which Allah has given every person for a single mouth. What people need is a political framework in which they don't feel themselves vunerable, humiliated or terrorized. The people of Kashmir want a honourable space to live on this planet. They are not demanding stars.

Afzal goes on to say: 'I am myself the living epitome of this terror.' The solution, according to Afzal, lies in greater democracy:

The closure of all democratic means and vents will naturally push the educated youth towards radical wall. Noam Chomsky says if we do not believe in Freedom of expression for the people we despise we don't believe in it at all. RSS's philosophy and its political, social and militant offshoots and offsprings are communalising and polarising whole of political and social fabric and this culture of hatred is penetrating the other local institutions as well and don't exclude Tihar jail. There is no doubt ISI is also playing its role in this process through its own devices of hatred. In fact ISI is nurturing on anti-Indian rhetoric.

Afzal went on to share his reactions to my book on the Parliament attack case. I had discussed my views on religion and nationalism, secularism and democracy. Afzal was excited when I first presented him with a copy of my book, *Framing Geelani, Hanging Afzal: Patriotism in the Time of Terror*, which was released in March 2007. When he met me in jail, he had expressed his enthusiasm and said I had understood the Kashmiris. 'After all, you are a Kashmiri,' he had teased.

Afzal disapproved of my views on religion: 'There is no doubt that the majority of the prisoners who read your book were moved by your untiring efforts for SARG's[8] acquittal and your concerns for human rights violations but I have reservations regarding your analysis and understanding religions and their institutions, even when you speak through Amina Wadud or Turkish poet.'[9]

Afzal admitted that he did not know the background of many of the things I had written about, but added that religion could not be understood solely by intellectual activity. He quoted Iqbal: 'Wholly overshadowed by his intellectual activity the modern man has ceased to live soulfully i.e. from within.'

After Afzal was hanged, I read out his letter to a group of friends in Goa. They listened to the ten-page letter in deep silence. Then one of them, John Fernandez, said: 'I agree with everything Afzal says, except for his views on women.'

Afzal had written:

The banner of woman's liberty is dewomanizing the womanhood. Naturally and religiously she is known as mother, sister, and wife. Now she is known as girlfriend, prostitute, or receptionist. Giving unwillingly her privacy and smile to unwanted and unknown men. She is sales promotor from shoes to tyres from water to washing machines. This woman (who is called mother and sister) is undressed through electronic and mass media just to sell these products. Sheer demonization by west.

I am not sure whether I would completely disagree with the references to the objectification of women through over-sexualized images.

Like John, I did not agree with most of Afzal's views on women, but then I did not agree with those of Sampat Prakash and his comrades' either. Sampat Prakash and his trade union leaders were patriarchy personified. I was appalled by Sampat's feudal and authoritarian attitude towards his family and by the lack of women leaders in the union. I had repeatedly asked to interview women and they kept promising to introduce me to them, but it never happened. Perhaps what had brought us together was our common commitment to an inclusive nationalism or patriotism.

Afzal wrote: 'Your book reflects one thing very clear you are very much patriot than anyone like modi. Since modi's nationalism is devastating but your patriotism is logical. I am not against your patriotic feelings...'[10]

———

My book, *Patriotism in the Time of Terror*, helped in the Save Afzal campaign not only in India, but also in Britain. I was excited to learn that the South Asia Solidarity Group, an organization of Leftist-minded South Asians, had decided to ask Moazzam Begg to release my book on 14 April 2007 at a function in London.

At the time, all I knew about Moazzam Begg was that he was a British citizen who had been arrested in January 2002 by the Pakistani police and then handed over to the Americans who took him first to their detention facility in Bagram in Afghanistan and transferred him to the infamous Guantanamo Bay. After a campaign for his release and the intervention of the UK government, he had been released in 2005 without being formally charged. Since his release, he had established an organization called Cageprisoners (now called simply CAGE) whose mission was to highlight and campaign against the state policies which had been developed as part of the War on Terror.

CAGE describes itself as 'an independent advocacy organisation working to empower communities impacted by the War on Terror. The organisation highlights and campaigns against state policies, striving for a world free from oppression and injustice (and) working with survivors of abuse and mistreatment across the globe'. I thought it was entirely appropriate that a former prisoner and a victim of the War on Terror released my book on Kashmiri prisoners, who were also victims of the War on Terror.

A few years later, sometime in 2010, Amrit Wilson[11] of the South Asia Solidarity Group wrote an e-mail asking me to defend the decision to have my book released by Moazzam Begg. She wanted me to intervene in the controversy raised by Gita Sahgal, the head of the Gender Unit of Amnesty International and the daughter of Nayantara Sahgal (Nehru's neice), who had resigned from Amnesty International because she felt that the international human rights organization had compromised its integrity by working with what she called 'Britain's most famous supporter of the Taliban'. She was referring to Moazzam Begg.

Gita wrote that Amnesty had lost its moral bearing and risked alienating liberal sympathizers by working with CAGE. Gita made a distinction between taking up the rights of prisoners and working as equal partners with people who subscribed to the Talibani ideology.

There are many important dimensions of this debate, including the conflict between women's rights and human rights. I have personally experienced this conflict in my own work and have written about it.[12] Victoria Brittain, a British journalist who helped pen Moazzam Begg's story,[13] pointed out that Gita had attacked Moazzam on three counts: his attitude to women, his support for the Taliban and the support for 'violent jihad'. A petition supporting Gita states: 'We believe that Gita Sehgal has raised a fundamental point of principle which is about the importance of the human rights movement maintaining an objective distance from groups and ideas that are committed to systematic discrimination'.

Brittain pointed out that the petition was in tune with the new US Supreme Court ruling that prevents humanitarian groups from speaking to groups considered by the US to be terrorists, even for legal advice or peacemaking.[14]

Some feminists had criticized Gita on the grounds that the language and logic Gita and her supporters had used to articulate their critiques, seemed to be very similar to what the Americans and their allies used, and at the same time Muslim identities and ideologies were being criminalized. The critique of the Talibani ideology should not have been made in a way to render invisible the state-sponsored violence suffered by Muslim men and women.

A section of the feminists has allowed themselves to be co-opted into the West's War against Terror. At a time when Muslim communities were being targeted across the world and a religion was being equated with a threat, defending Moazzam Begg became a part of the fight to expose the hypocrisy of the West and the so-called War on Terror.

The counter-terror measures adopted by the US, Britain and France were eroding the very democratic principles considered the pillars of a 'free' society and this was the danger we were facing in India. The War on Terror was turning inward into a culture of fear at home. For me, defending Moazzam Begg was very much like defending Afzal Guru.

Moazzem Begg was arrested again in February 2014 and detained at the Belmarsh Prison in London. For the second time in his life, Begg was imprisoned for months without being tried. On 1 October, less than a week before his court date, all seven charges against him—including that he had attended a terrorist training camp in Syria and funded terrorism—were dropped. The question that automatically arises is: Was it a rebel camp funded and supported by the West?

Begg told the BBC why he had gone to Syria: 'I was in Syria before ISIS and before [Al Qaeda's] al-Nusra Front was proscribed. I was involved in interventions when they had taken hostages. I had got other groups to pressurise them and got [people] released'.[15]

Begg's arrest and subsequent release exposed the links that the US and Britain had with a section of the Islamic militants, such as the al-Nusra Front, which was first financed by the West and then subsequently banned by them.

Begg, like Afzal, was not innocent of the involvement in the resistance to the War on Terror. Begg first came under the suspicion of the British intelligence agencies in the late 1990s, when he opened the Maktabah al-Ansar, a bookshop in Birmingham, which developed a reputation for stocking jihadist literature. One of the books he commissioned was called *The Army of Madinah in Kashmir* by Dhiren Barot.[16] The book recorded the experiences that Barot had when he travelled to Pakistan in 1995 and took part in militant campaigns against Indian forces in Kashmir, using the pseudonym Esa Al Hindi.

Begg had become a person of interest for the British security services and the intelligence services. Moazzam Begg and Afzal Guru both confessed to having visited training camps for militants, to having sympathy for the resistance to the War on Terror, which they perceived as a war against Muslims.

I had never met Moazzam Begg, but a few months after he released my book, I had an opportunity to visit Birmingham, where he was born and grew up. Amrit Wilson invited me to speak on our campaign to save Afzal Guru at an event the Solidarity Group was organizing to celebrate 150 years of South Asian resistance (1857-2007). The meeting was held in the School of Oriental and African Studies at the London School of Economics.

Amrit told me that they had initiated an Early Day Motion and twenty-two Members of the British Parliament had already signed.

An EDM is a way MPs can demonstrate their support for a cause and it helps the campaign, although it rarely results in a debate in the Parliament. The EDM had been initiated by a Left-wing MP, John McDonnel.

Amrit also told me that Sajjad Haider Karim, a member of the European Parliament from England, who was originally from Pakistan-administered Kashmir, had taken up Afzal's case at the sub-committee on human rights of the European Parliament.

While I was glad that Afzal's case had received so much support, I was intrigued by the fact that so many British Members of Parliament were taking interest in a Kashmiri prisoner sentenced to death for conspiring to attack the Indian Parliament.

I found some answers when I went to Birmingham on the invitation of the British Mirpuri Kashmiris. Naeem Malik drove me to Birmingham. Naeem, a member of the South Asia Solidarity Group, was originally from Pakistan and had been active in the campaign for the release of prisoners from Guantanamo. In his review of my book he had written: 'For somebody living in the West, originating from the sub-continent from a different side of the dividing line, Nandita Haksar's book comes as an inspiration and a ray of hope in the otherwise gloomy and oppressive world we find ourselves in today.'

Naeem told me a little of the background of the community we were about to meet. The community speaks the Mirpuri/Pothohari language. The first-generation migrant Mirpuris were not educated and they had little or no experience of urban living in Pakistan. Migration from Mirpur and its adjacent areas started soon after the Second World War as the majority of the male population of this area and the Pothohar region had worked in the British armed forces. However, the mass migration phenomenon took place after the Mangla Dam project, which was built in the 1960s, and eventually flooded the surrounding farmland. Mirpuris in Britain are still in touch with their families back home in Pak-administered Kashmir as remittances are sent to them to help fund farming enterprises and family businesses. Maqbool Butt had begun his political career by taking part in the agitation against the dam in the 1960s.

Naeem said that when the Mirpuris had come to the UK, they had been active in the trade union politics because at the time many had worked in factories. Since then they had become well off and had become more involved in the movement for self-determination for Kashmir. The time coincided with the time that Maqbool Butt was hanged in Tihar Jail.

There are 747,000 Mirpuris in the United Kingdom, forming about 70 per cent of the British-Pakistani community. The Kashmiris had formed an organization, the Kashmir National Identity Campaign, to get recognition as British-Kashmiri rather than British-Pakistani. Now they form an important constituency. I learnt that since 1990, the number of Kashmiri councillors across Britain had significantly increased, so has their importance within the political parties. The appointment of two Lords of Kashmiri origin and scores of British-Kashmiris getting party nominations, and some in very safe seats, shows that their significance has been increasing.

Later, after Afzal was hanged, the British-Kashmiris were able to persuade sixty British and European Union Parliamentarians to sign a petition asking the Indian President, Pranab Mukherjee, to hand over the mortal remains of Muhammad Maqbool Butt and Mohammad Afzal Guru to their relatives for proper burial. The petition was handed over to the officials of the High Commission by Professor Azamat Khan, Professor Zafar Khan, Showkat Maqbool Butt (son of Shaheed Maqbool Butt), Sadiq Subhani and Najib Afsar.

The chairman of the All Party Parliamentary Group on Kashmir, Andrew Griffiths, MP; vice chair, Debbie Abrahams, MP; Raja Najabat Hussain, chairman of Jammu Kashmir Self-Determination Movement (Europe); and Professor Azmat Khan, JKLF president in Britain, also presented a copy of the petition to the British prime minister, David Cameron, asking him to intervene in the return of the mortal remains of the two Kashmiris. I was told that Hussain promised 'to help elect at least 100 "Friends of Kashmir" to the Parliament'. So while I was glad for the support for Afzal, it did appear as if these British Members of Parliament were addressing not their constituents in Bradford or Birmingham, but their constituencies based 5,383 miles away in Mirpur in Pakistan-administered Kashmir.

There was always going to be an international dimension to the Kashmir question; the difference was that this time the Kashmiris themselves were party to the political complexities.

After the London bombings carried out by British-born Muslims, in which fifty-two people were killed and 700 were injured, the British government had to rethink its policies both at home and abroad. In 2004, the Home and Foreign Offices issued a joint resport, 'Young Muslims and Extremism', in which they admitted:

> A particularly strong cause of disillusionment amongst Muslims…is a perceived 'double standard' in the foreign policy of Western governments (and often those of Muslim governments), in particular Britain and the US…This perception seems to have become more acute post 9/11. The perception is that passive 'oppression', as demonstrated in British policy, e.g. non-action on Kashmir and Chechenya, has given way to 'active oppression'—the War on Terror, and in Iraq and Afghanistan are all seen by a section of British Muslims as having been acts against Islam.[17]

While in Birmingham, Naeem took me to meet various leaders. The signboards were in Urdu and the bank announced that it was run on Islamic principles. Inside the homes I felt I had been transported back to the 1960s, the furniture was large and heavy, the buttery cakes looked and tasted as if they had been freshly made in some Srinagar bakery.

A journalist gave me copies of a local Urdu paper which had published two parts of his long review of my book; the third part, he said, had not come out because there were objections from the ISI. When I asked him why the ISI would object to my book, he replied:

'Read the review and you will understand.' I never did read the review because I misplaced the paper.

The ISI had a tight control over the political movement in Pak-administered Kashmir. A report by the Human Rights Watch[18] documented the state of freedom of expression in Pak-administered Kashmir in a report: 'The Pakistani government has long limited dissemination of news in Azad Kashmir. There is no locally-based news agency. Azad Kashmir only has one daily newspaper and so people largely rely on local editions of Pakistani newspapers for news and information.'

Among the books banned by Pakistan are books by Muhammad Saeed Asad, a self-proclaimed Kashmiri nationalist and an employee in the 'Azad' Kashmir Ministry of Social Welfare and Women's Development. In 2002, he was suspended for writing a book on the Mangla Dam that questioned Pakistan's right to water sources originating in Kashmir. Pakistan has banned three of his books for being 'anti-state and an attempt to promote nationalist feelings amongst Kashmiris'.

One of his banned books is called *Shaur-e-Farda*, which comprises letters from Maqbool Butt to his friends and relatives written over a span of two decades.

Human Rights Watch observed that no person in Pak-administered Kashmir can be appointed to any government job, including the judiciary, unless he or she expresses loyalty to the concept of Kashmir's accession to Pakistan. The oath of office for the president, prime minister, speaker, member of the legislative assembly or the 'Azad' Kashmir Council also incorporates the following statement: 'I will remain loyal to the country and the cause of accession of the state of Jammu & Kashmir to Pakistan'.

I wanted to discuss these issues but I knew that as an Indian I would be suspect and I thought it would be wiser to listen and learn.

It was the month of Ramzan and Naeem said that most of the leaders had started keeping fasts recently; when they were in the trade union movement they seldom observed these rules. In his home I was served biryani made by his English wife.

The next day I was invited to an iftar at a newly opened restaurant with absolutely delicious tandoori delicacies. That was to be the venue of the meeting at which I was to speak. I believe most of the people sitting in the audience were happy to hear that Indians had taken up a campaign in solidarity with Kashmiris. Perhaps that is precisely what the ISI did not want.

I returned to India, hopeful that the campaign would save Afzal from the gallows.

The growing appeal of militant Islam and the alliance between sections of it with the West had made the political situation very complex. And Sampat Prakash still talked about Sufism and Kashmiriyat. As a Kashmiri journalist, Tariq Mir, asked: 'How might unorganized believers of Sufi Islam wrestle with foreign cultural practices in an age of satellite television, free media and travel?'[19]

I put the question to Sampat Prakash. How would he organize these people and how would they fight the growing tide of Islamic militancy? He insisted that it could only be through an organization committed to Kashmiri nationalism.

Sampat felt that it was Kashmiri nationalism which had united the men in the trade union movement. During my conversations, I had asked them a question which had been with me for long: Did any of the militant organizations ever object to the Federation joining or affiliating with Indian political parties and Indian trade unions? After all, they were affiliated to Hind Mazdoor Kisan Panchayat (HMKP) and earlier, they were linked to the CPI(M).

Sampat Prakash said that the question had never risen. He admitted that if the militant organizations had ever objected, it would have been impossible to continue with their struggles. And none of the Kashmiri militant organizations had ever raised any objections to the trade union asking for wages at parity with the central employees, or joining all-India trade union confederations.

It was for this reason that they had been able to fight for the implementation of the successive Pay Commissions and continuously improve the condition of the employees, even during the period of insurgency.

Sampat said the only person who ever raised this question was Abdul Rehman Geelani, who had tried to persuade the trade union leaders not to join the New Trade Union Initiative in 2006 because it would link their movement to an Indian trade union.[20] When he told me this, I expressed my surpise because one of Geelani's brothers, a mufti, was a member of the All India Muslim Personal Law Board. Was that not an Indian institution?

I had also had my differences with Geelani because he wanted to conduct the Save Afzal Guru campaign as an anti-India campaign. However, I had argued that the reason he had been acquitted was because I had ensured that our campaign for his acquittal had been in the language of Indian nationalism. The slogan I had come up with was: 'Defend Geelani, defend Indian democracy'. I believed this to be true. Because, to defend the corrupt police officers of the Special Cell who were trying to frame a Kashmiri Muslim would only undermine Indian democratic institutions, the media, the courts and the entire criminal justice system.

Yet, there was no feeling for Indian nationalism among the core group of students and young activists who had helped me in the campaign, and the younger members of the Defence Committee I had set up for Geelani. They thought of it as an issue of human rights, fair trial and the right to life and liberty. Whereas I thought of it as a fight to defend Indian democracy, with the emphasis on 'Indian'. For me, it was not only a tactical question because we were fighting the BJP's Hindu nationalism, but also because I felt a sense of pride in my country. Besides, human rights discourse had itself been used as a tool for US foreign policy; it had a limited use in the fight to expose the injustices being committed in the War on Terror. But the challenge before Sampat Prakash was not militant Islam, but the rise of militant Hinduism.

————

In 2008, Sampat Prakash was faced with the most difficult political challenge of his career when he found himself sandwiched between the forces of Hindu and Islamic fundamentalism.

That was the year when Jammu and Kashmir witnessed a violent clash of religious nationalisms, but this time it was over the administration of a Hindu pilgrimage spot in the Kashmir Valley.

The challenge came in the shape of the controversy over the annual pilgrimage to the Amarnath cave. The Amarnath cave, situated at an altitude of 3,888 metres (12,756 feet), about 141 kilometres from Srinagar, is reached through Pahalgam town. The cave is surrounded by snowy mountains. It is covered with snow most of the year, except for a short period of time in summer when it is open to pilgrims. Before the controversy erupted, it was open for a month in July, but later, the yatra period was extended to two months, between the end of June and August.

Sampat remembered that during his childhood, the pilgrims consisted of sadhus and the occasional adventurous tourist. In those days, it was called Chhari Mubarak rather than Amarnath Yatra, the Sanskritized form that it has taken more recently. Chhari was the name of the saffron-robed silver mace of Lord Shiva. The mahant carried the Chhari from Dashnami Akhara in Srinagar to Pahalgam and then to the Amarnath cave. The state government used to make the arrangements for the pilgrims, and the yatra was a regular part of the Kashmir Valley's cultural life.

Inside the 130-foot high cave, a stalagmite forms every year when melted water falls in drops from the roof of the cave and freezes again. The freezing droplets grow upward in a vertical column. Hindus consider this to be a Shiva lingam, and the main purpose of the annual pilgrimage is the worship of the ice stalagmite, or the Shiva lingam.

For Sampat, the Chhari Mubarak was quintessential to Kashmiriyat. He grew up on the story of how the cave was discovered by Buta Malik, a shepherd. According to legend, the shepherd, while wandering around the mountains, encountered a sadhu who gave him a sack of coal that turned into a precious metal once he reached home. Excited and grateful, Malik rushed to the spot to trace the sadhu to thank him. He did not find the seer, but he found the cave instead. This happened during the Dogra Raj.

The Dogra king was so pleased with the discovery that he honoured Malik. He decreed that a representative of the Malik clan would always be present at the shrine, along with the mahant and priests, during the pilgrimage. Apart from offering the family some estate in Pahalgam and exempting them from land revenue, a part of the offering always went to the clan. Sampat had heard this from Ramzan Malik of Batkoot village, who belonged to the Malik family and had been the president of the ponywala union since 1970.

Sampat said that many a times it would rain or even snow during the pilgrimage and the pilgrims would get wet. Then the local Kashmiri Muslims would take them into their homes, see that they stayed warm, and give them cups of hot tea.

I pointed out to Sampat that the Panun Kashmirwalas emphasized that the Amarnath Cave was known from ancient times and is deeply enshrined in Kashmiri folklore. They claim that for centuries, pilgrims came here from all over India, and in no way is it of a recent origin or a 'show window of so-called Kashmiriat'.[21]

In any case, the association of the Muslim shepherd with the cave ended when the government passed an Act in 2000 to establish a board to supervise the Amarnath Yatra. As a result, the privileges the Dogras had extended to the Maliks were withdrawn. This decision was taken after a tragic incident that occurred in 1996. That year, there was heavy snowfall and more than 200 pilgrims died because of extreme weather conditions and inadequate arrangements for accommodation along the way. The state government stated in a note in 1996 that '...it was necessary to build sufficiently strong structures en route the Holy Shrine which would withstand the fury of the elements if the weather turned hostile during the yatra'. The note states that in order to institutionalize the arrangements for the smooth conduct and management of the pilgrimage to the Holy

Shrine, the State Legislature has passed the Jammu and Kashmir Shri Amarnathji Shrine Act 2000.

In October 2004, the CEO of Shri Amarnathji Shrine Board (SASB) requested the transfer of 3,642 kanals of land to build seven halting places en route to the shrine. In March 2005, the Forest Department granted permission for use of forestland by the Shrine Board. On 3 June 2008, a Raj Bhawan spokesman issued a statement making public the transfer of land to SASB; a few days later the pilgrimage began. The governor's secretary, Arun Kumar, revealed at a press conference in Srinagar that the land diversion was permanent.

The Hurriyat factions led by Syed Ali Shah Geelani and Mirwaiz Umar Farooq issued a joint declaration in Srinagar asking for the revocation of the land deal. Meanwhile, the Amarnath Yatra continued with a record number of pilgrims; more than 50,000 visited the cave. In June 2008, the BJP leader, L.K. Advani, visited the Amarnath Cave. The same month, at a press conference, the state president of the BJP, Ashok Khajuria, threatened an economic blockade in the Kashmir Valley if the land allotment order was revoked. On 23 June 2008, protests against the land transfer began in the Valley; one person was killed and forty were injured when the CRPF fired on protesters at Nowhatta, Srinagar. On 25 June 2008, N.N. Vohra took over as governor and, at a press conference, the chief minister, Ghulam Nabi Azad, blamed PDP ministers Muzaffar Hussain Baig and Qazi Afzal for the land transfer.[22] The protests continued and two more people were killed and 200 injured in Valley-wide protests. Seven people died in eight days of protests.

In the midst of this tense and volatile situation, the Hindu spiritual preacher, Sri Sri Ravi Shankar, stated that the 800 kanals of land transferred to the Shrine Board by then was not enough to accommodate millions of pilgrims. The Shiv Sena leader, Sham Lal Langar, announced at a press conference in Jammu that they would block the national highway as well as the supply of essential commodities to Srinagar if the land diversion order was revoked.

On 29 June 2008, the Shrine Board surrendered its claim over the land and the state government agreed to take over the yatra arrangements. Immediately, Jammu erupted. The BJP, Shiv Sena, VHP and Bajrang Dal activists blocked the Jammu-Lakhanpur National Highway. The BJP and the VHP called for a Bharat Bandh on 3 July. 'If there is no Amarnath yatra, there would be no Haj also,' VHP general secretary, Praveen Togadia, declared in Delhi.[23] The VHP also called for a boycott of all Kashmiri products and goods across India. 'Kashmiri Handicrafts such as carpets, kurtas, scarf, shawls, Kashmiri saffron (kesar), Kashmiri apricots (akhrot) etc, shouldn't be purchased by the people,' Togadia said.[24] The president of the Petrol Tankers Association, Anan Sharma, announced the stoppage of petroleum products to the Kashmir Valley.

The Shri Amarnath Sangarsh Samiti (SASS) was constituted in Jammu with Leela Karan as its convener. The streets of Jammu reverberated with cries of 'Bum bum bole!'

All through those weeks, Sampat Prakash was in Jammu watching the events unfold with growing despondency and helplessness. The Kahsmiri Pandits, especially the supporters of Panun Kashmir, were very active in this agitation. They provided the justification for it and appealed to every Kashmiri Pandit to join the movement. They made a special appeal to Sampat Prakash and his trade union comrades to cooperate. They also demanded that Sampat make a public apology for siding with the JKLF and thereby hurting the sentiments of the nationalist forces of Jammu.[25] They even threatened to stone his house.

When the Panun Kashmir supporters issued this threat, the government employees stood guard, ready to take them on. The trade union had refused to take sides during this agitation to avoid a split between the Jammu and Kashmir units. Sampat phoned Teng and warned him that if his goons tried to attack the house, he would only be harming his own daughter and son-in-law. The house belonged to his son, Ravinder. Perhaps that had a sobering effect on the Panun Kashmirwalas.

The organization even warned those Kashmiri Pandits associated with pro-India parties, such as the National Conference, the PDP and the Congress, to disassociate themselves forthwith and publicly condemn the party leaders for making communal speeches.

When the Amarnath Shrine controversy erupted, Yasin Malik was in Pakistan. On returning, he announced at once that he would sit on a hunger strike until the Shrine Board returned the land. He had expected that Sampat Prakash would support him; after all, he was still a member of the JKLF. However, Yasin was upset because Sampat would not echo the slogan: 'Shrine Board tor do' (Dismantle the Shrine Board). When he phoned Sampat, it was clear that he hadn't understood how the issue had taken on dimensions much beyond the Valley. He had not realized that the intensity of the agitation reflected a genuine grievance of the Hindus and Muslims of Jammu: that Kashmir treated Jammu like its colony.

Sampat could see that the intelligence agencies of both India and Pakistan were trying to take advantage of the volatile situation. The ISI wanted to project it as anti-Muslim, while the Indian intelligence agencies wanted to isolate the separatist leaders by showing that the Muslims of Jammu did not support the Muslims of Kashmir. Sampat did not want to be a part of regional or communal politics; all his life he had tried to build bridges between communities and regions. Although he did not have the power to stop the conflagration, he was not going to feed it even a tiny bit.

Besides, the agitation in Jammu also reflected the very real grievances of the people of the region. Jammu was a much larger area but had far fewer seats in the Legislative Assembly. There were virtually no roads in Doda, Rajouri and Poonch, and while much money had been spent to develop tourism in Kashmir, nothing had been done for Jammu.

Successive Valley-dominated state governments have been blamed for Jammu's poor share in state services; in the civil secretariat, Jammu's representation was less than 10 per cent. All twelve corporations of the Jammu and Kashmir government had their headquarters in Srinagar. The Dogras also felt resentful at the exclusion of their Dogri language from the Eighth Schedule of the Indian Constitution.

In the midst of this mayhem, Sampat helped Balraj Puri organize a seminar on the issue of discrimination against Jammu. There were, broadly, two views on the status of Jammu. The Hindu Right opposed the special status for Jammu and Kashmir and wanted full integration of the state into the Indian Union and full statehood for Jammu. Balraj Puri and the socialists, on the other hand, accepted the special status under Article 370, but wanted devolution of power for all three regions—Jammu, Kashmir and Ladakh. Balraj Puri, with a statement, supported the Shri Amarnath Sangharsh Samiti but Sampat remained silent.

He breathed a sigh of relief when, finally, after sixty-one days of agitation, a settlement was reached on 31 August 2008. Under the Agreement, the Shrine Board could make temporary use of forty acres of land. But the problem could not be wished away. The agitation had exposed the fault lines in the state that would be used by the Hindutva forces to fulfil their own agitation.

By 2011, 650,000 people had visited the Amarnath Cave, and 300 helicopters had whirled, carrying wealthy pilgrims every day for a fee of $200 per return trip. The Shrine Board had ensured that millions of posters were distributed all over India to attract the maximum number of pilgrims to Amarnath.

Due to the increase in pilgrims' footfall, and because of the long duration for which the cave was kept open, the stalagmite, or the Shiva lingam, kept decreasing in size. In fact, it had become so small that the height was artificially increased by adding ice. There was huge public outcry when pilgrims learnt that the lingam which they were worshipping was, in fact, man-made.[26]

Although there was substance in the ecological arguments against the influx of pilgrims for Amarnath Yatra, the Trade Union Centre members were angry because the Shrine Board had, in effect, deprived local Kashmiris of their sources of income. The Shrine Board was organizing the pilgrimage by importing labour from outside the state; as a result, the local Kashmiris, who earned from the annual pilgrimage, had lost their livelihoods. The local people used to set up shops to sell hot tea and snacks to the devotees, the ponywalas took them up to the cave and the pilgrims used local transport to visit other tourism sites. However, at the behest of the Shrine Board, who claimed that terrorists could make use of the local population to disrupt the yatra, jobs were handed over to outsiders.

—

I met Sampat after the Amarnath controversy had died down. He said that he nearly had a heart attack in March 2010 but had managed to avoid surgery. In his inimitable style he had called Baba Ramdev, the international yoga guru, and got one of his yoga experts to come to Jammu to teach him yoga and breathing exercises. After twenty-five days of being disciplined, he claimed he was fit to take up his activities again.

When I asked what he was involved in, he said that he had organized the pensioners in Jammu, Kashmir and Ladakh. He had brought press clips about his association. One of them, published on 9 July 2009 in the *Greater Kashmir*, quoted Sampat: 'We caution the government about the growing social injustices, political uncertainty, crimes against the humanity besides stepmotherly treatment towards the 96,000 gazetted and non-gazetted pensioners associated with the association,' he said, continuing, 'Pensioners constitute a conscientious part of civil society and government can't turn deaf ears towards our pleas...We appeal the pensioners to join the pensioner movement for emerging as a force of senior citizens in the state.'

Sampat had been going around the state organizing district-level committees of the organization. As usual, he masterfully united the economic demands of the pensioners with the wider political agenda of keeping alive the idea of what he still insisted on calling Kashmiriyat; he said he could not think of any other word.

Then I heard that Sampat had suffered a stroke in December 2012. A few months later, we met in Delhi. He looked frail but had lost none of his passion. He still had the temperament of a tiger, as he used to describe himself. I asked him if I could take him out for dinner, and if had to follow any dietary restrictions. He replied: 'I had a stroke in my head, my stomach is fine.' Over unlimited kebabs and a few drinks at Barbeque Nation, he shared his concerns over the rise of the Ahl-e-Hadith's version of Islam.

'Where lies the hope?' Sampat asked me.

I replied: 'Perhaps in a jihad against terrorism.'[27] Several former militants of Al Qaeda and religious teachers had advocated this. And many Islamic scholars from all schools of theology, Deobandi or Salafi, had condemned the mindless violence that really could not be justified by any political or theological doctrines.

I asked Sampat if I could call this present volume *Jihad against Terrorism* because, in many ways, that is what the trade union had really done; they had fought state and non-state terror. He laughed, then said in a serious tone: 'No, it may be misunderstood.'

Sampat wondered why the Communists had never been able to deal with the problem of nationalism and religion; even today, China's biggest political challenge is dealing with the Turkic Uyghur community. From the time the Soviet Union came into existence, the Communists had tried to deal with the Muslims. During the Stalin years, there had even been talk of a Muslim communist party. And there is the International Pan Islamic Communist Party of Proletarian Islam which follows Malcolm X.

But then, by that token, would we have to have a Hindu Communist party? This time Sampat was not amused. He remained silent.

We had no answers, only troubling questions.

DYSTOPIA TO PARADISE

Seven months after Afzal was hanged, a strange report appeared in the newspapers. A militant group had published a book in Urdu: *Shaheed Mohammad Afzal Guru Ka Aakhri Paigam* (The Last Message of Martyr Mohammad Afzal Guru). According to the report, 5,000 copies of the book were being distributed for free. The report claimed that Afzal had written a diary in which he described the slain Jaish-e-Mohammad commander Ghazi Baba, the mastermind of the 2001 Parliament attack, as a 'martyr'. The report went on to say that Guru had called for renewed 'Jihad against India' and had eulogized the Afghan Taliban chief, Mullah Mohammad Umar as 'Ameer-ul-Momineen' (Leader of the Faithful).

The book was released by Nayeem Ahmad Khan of the Jammu and Kashmir National Front. I looked at the website of the party and read that the founder, Nayeem Khan, claimed to have been with Yasin Malik and the original HAJY group. It also claimed that party never resorted to militancy.[1]

I found it stranger that the meeting to release Afzal's jail diaries was attended by his elder brother, Aijaz, who had not bothered to meet his brother in jail until the date of his execution was announced in 2006. And the paper quoted him as saying that Tabassum and Ghalib were media shy so they could not come. But I had seen many photographs of Tabassum when she had given interviews to the press and also attended rallies in Delhi.

Could the intelligence agencies be interested in projecting Afzal as a radical Salafi when he was in fact a disillusioned Kashmiri nationalist?

249

I had got many glimpses into Afzal's mind during my conversations with him and through his letters written to me and his friends.

Afzal did not approve of mindless violence. On 7 September 2011, there was a bomb blast in which thirteen people were killed in the Delhi High Court complex. A militant organization claimed to have carried out the blasts in support of their demand to convert Afzal's death sentence to life imprisonment.

Afzal gave the following statement to the Press:

> This is not for the first time that my name has been dragged by some mischievous persons/groups for such heinous crimes. It has become a routine that whenever such blasts take place, my name is sought to be dragged, in order to de-characterize and malign me to cultivate public opinion against me.
>
> It is a serious matter of concern that some criminal elements and anti-social persons committed that heinous and barbarous crime of bomb blast in the Delhi High Court. It is a cowardly act and must be condemned by all. No religion permits killing of innocent persons.

Afzal also gave this statement to his lawyer, N.D. Pancholi.

On one occasion, he had asked Pancholi and me to try and get a television installed in the high-risk cell. This time I had teased him saying that television would be considered un-Islamic by many of those in the high-risk cell. He had replied, in all seriousness, 'At least it will give them something to do. Otherwise they will become even more radicalized.' Despite being troubled by the radicalization of the youth, Afzal was disillusioned by secular nationalism and had taken refuge in the vision of international Islam.

I have been seriously disturbed by the way in which the very idea of secular nationalism has been devalued and debased in political conversations. I could see that secular nationalism was often preached by the political elites of Third World countries, and secularism often went hand in hand with authoritarian regimes. But I could not dismiss the idea or the ideal as irrelevant. In the course of doing research for this book, I discovered the long history of how Britain and the US had systematically attacked secular nationalists and promoted global Islam.

As far back as in 1962, Crown Prince Faisal of Saudi Arabia had established the Muslim World League, sending out missionaries, printing propaganda material and financing the building of mosques around the globe.[2] Among its first employees were members of the Muslim Brotherhood, and Abdul Ala Maududi, the founder of Jamaat-e-Islami. The League's first proclamation read: 'Those who distort Islam's call under the guise of nationalism are the bitter enemies of the Arabs whose glories are entwined with the glories of Islam'.[3]

After the end of the Cold War, the world's major Islamic groups organizing terrorist activities were allowed to function in London. Millions of pounds were raised in Britain to fund these activities and to recruit militants from around the world. It is estimated that by 2005, 3,000 Britain-based individuals had received training in Al-Qaeda camps.[4]

British authorities not only knew of these activities but actively championed the organizations. This alliance was based on the so-called 'covenant of security' between radical Islamists and the security services; the militants provided information and were told that they were not to cause problems in Britain. A special branch officer told a journalist: 'There was a deal with these guys. We told them that if you don't cause us any problems, then we won't bother you.'[5]

Thousands of Britons of Pakistani origin had joined the jihad in Kashmir since the 1990s; by 2001 around 900 were visiting the Valley for military training every year.[6]

This support for mindless violence to annex Kashmir was a part of the West-supported Pakistani strategy to control the Central Asian Silk Road to China—control over the route would allow Pakistan to act as a strategic power between Iran and China.

A former FBI agent, Sibel Deniz Edmonds,[7] had exposed Operation Gladio B, an FBI code name adopted in 1997 for ongoing relations between US intelligence, the Pentagon, and Al-Qaeda. The name refers to the original Operation Gladio, in which US intelligence had relations with anti-Communist groups in Europe. She also exposed how the US had played on the grievances of the Uyghurs, the Turkic Muslim community living in China's Xinjiang province, and fomented separatist sentiments and radicalism. This has direct bearing on Kashmir because Xinjiang province shares a 2,800-kilometre border with Central Asia. In 2000, four Uyghurs were arrested in Kashmir when they came to fight for the Kashmiris.

If I had known all these facts before, I would certainly have asked Afzal his views on this alliance. Did he think that the West would help the Islamists establish a Caliphate? I knew he considered the Americans to be responsible for the situation. He had written: 'America's arrogance is decivilizing and dehumanizing whole of global value system and societies.' He was referring to the American role in the Palestinian conflict, the invasion of Afghanistan and the occupation of Iraq.

I think Afzal would have pointed out that even if the alliance existed and the Americans used Muslims as agents, the fact remained that the Muslims suffered humiliation and discrimination in the West, as they did in China, India and, of course, in Kashmir. And the War on Terror had made their situation even more vulnerable and precarious.

As he said in his letter to me: 'I don't bother whether Modi and the people of India called me terrorist against those who terrorise and humiliate the common helpless people. I don't have patience to remain mute spectator or silent before the state terror.'

I think Afzal's views reflected the views of many of the Islamic militants. They were fighting against what they knew as injustice; both in the country where they were born in and for their Muslim brothers all over the globe.

It struck me that Sampat and Afzal shared a hatred for imperialism; they both felt that the world's injustice was because of the unequal relations between poor and rich countries. However, Afzal did not have any concrete vision for the future. The real difference was that while Sampat opposed both capitalism and imperialism, Afzal opposed only imperialism and had no critique of capitalist society. Sampat's regret was that his son had not become a Communist; Afzal was afraid that if he was hanged, his son would become a militant. He wanted his son to grow up to be a doctor.

Afzal was caught in the web of international and national machinations—spies and double agents worked with militants and nations, and states backed their intelligence agents while making sworn statements on public forums denying any involvement with wars, conflicts and conspiracies.

———

In the midst of this complex and impossible situation, we continued our campaign to save Afzal Guru from being hanged, and Afzal continued to hope that he would be able to stay alive in prison. He said he had grown used to his cell and had found peace within himself. He continued to read, write and think.

Then, one day in October 2006, I heard on national television that Tihar Jail had fixed a date for the execution: 20 October. The media had already announced that the jail authorities had found a hangman and had bought the special rope needed for the hanging.

Afzal had not filed a mercy petition because he was still waiting for the results of the Curative Petition registered in the Supreme Court, but he agreed to the suggestion that his wife, Tabassum, file a petition on his behalf.[8]

Tabassum had come down to Delhi along with their son, Ghalib, Afzal's mother, Ayesha Begum, and his two brothers, Hilal and Aijaz. I barely had a day to draft the petition. Then we had to make efforts to find out how to file it so that it would reach the President of India. We discovered that there is a counter for such purposes at the Rashtrapati Bhavan. N.D. Pancholi managed to get an appointment with the President and that is how Ghalib found himself walking down the corridors of the Rashtrapati Bhavan. When seven-year-old

Ghalib entered Rashtrapati Bhavan on 5 October 2006, he was awestruck by the structure's grandeur, and exclaimed: 'This is even bigger than the Tihar Jail!' He was accompanied by his mother Tabassum, his grandmother, Ayesha Begum, and his father's two lawyers, N.D. Pancholi and I.

We were escorted into a large room where tea and snacks were served. For a moment I thought the family would refuse to accept the hospitality, especially since it was the month of Ramzan, but they accepted it gracefully.

After the sumptuous tea and snacks, Afzal's family was ushered into the room where the President of India, A.P.J. Abdul Kalam, received them graciously. They greeted him quietly but not once did Tabassum or Ayesha Begum beg for mercy; they did not cry and try to win their case by tears and emotion. All they asked for was justice.

The President turned to Afzal's son and asked him whether he had anything to say. It was then that Tabassum told him that she had found her son with a noose made of her duppatta around his neck. When she asked him what he was doing, he replied: 'I am trying to see how much pain Abba will feel when he is hanged.' Tabbassum told the story in a few words, without any embellishments.

I asked the President whether he had received the mercy petition, filed on behalf of Afzal by Tabassum. The President said he had indeed received the petition, and promised to read it carefully. He also told us that he would even ask for the entire file if he thought it necessary.

Then Afzal's family wished the President of India goodbye and left quietly.

I think it was largely because of the campaign we had been running that the President took the unprecedented step of inviting Afzal's family to Rashtrapati Bhavan.

Later, the Hindutva forces created loud and ugly scenes to protest against the President of India's gesture of inviting Afzal's family. They accused the President of entertaining terrorists in Rashtrapati Bhavan, even insinuating that he had done so because he was a

Muslim. They asked for a public hanging of Afzal Guru and demanded that it be broadcast on national television.

When the Patiala House courts had announced that three Kashmiri men, accused of being part of the conspiracy to attack the Parliament,[9] were sentenced to death, Shiv Sena activists had burst fire crackers within the court premises and danced in glee. Now they went so far as to undermine the office of the President of India. But no one spoke out against this insult.

The BJP and its allies mobilized opinion, demanding the immediate execution of Afzal Guru. They would continue to keep up their campaign for another seven years till they succeeded. In contrast, the campaign to save Afzal Guru from the gallows fizzled out.

The campaign was mired in several unsavoury controversies from the beginning; a large part of the reason was that there was no one leading it. The people who had helped me run the campaign for Geelani's acquittal had moved away and now individuals steered Afzal's case in any direction that they thought best. However, despite these problems, the one thing that our campaign had clearly established was that he had not had a fair trial, and that was mainly because he did not have a lawyer of his choice.

Even so, the campaign could, perhaps, have been effective if the Kashmiri leaders had been united. But from the start, the Hurriyat was divided on the issue; a section of them was even against the idea of India granting pardon to Afzal Guru.[10]

An unnamed Kashmiri leader told an American political officer: 'If someone is a terrorist, they should meet a violent end.'[11]

The so-called hardliners of the Hurriyat were reluctant to take on Afzal's case because he was a surrendered militant and he had told the court that he had been made a SPO for six months. Besides, Afzal Guru had confessed to being involved in the attack on Parliament, even if it had been unintentional and through entrapment. Therefore, to support Afzal would mean justifying the attack.

Syed Abdul Rehman Geelani was keen to take on the leadership of the campaign to save Afzal Guru. He had worked behind the scenes and managed to bring together all the factions of the Kashmiri movement for one day. On 24 September 2005, a meeting was organized by Abdul Rehman Geelani at Taj Hotel, Budshah Chowk, Srinagar, in which all the important Kashmiri leaders came together. These included Syed Ali Shah Geelani, Shabir Ahmad Shah, Mohammad Yasin Malik, Abdul Qayyoom and Nisar Ali Mir representing the Government Servants Federation. I was also asked to speak. The subject of the meeting was political prisoners.

This was the first time I had seen Syed Ali Shah Geelani so closely. Looking at his dignified demeanour, I could see why he was called Bab-e-Qaum (Father of the People). He was admired because of his consistency in advocating that Kashmir belonged to Pakistan, and his unwavering loyalty to Jamaat-e-Islami's ideology, inspite of the serious differences he had with the organization.

I looked at the Kashmiri leaders sitting in the front row and wished that I could have talked to each of them, understood them a little more. I also had political questions which I would have liked to pose.

I knew Geelani had serious differences with Maulana Abbas Ansari[12] who had been elected chairman by the Hurriyat executive council. Ansari was a Shia. This was the first time that the ISI had no role in the election and he had vehemently opposed mediation by the Americans. He had said: 'I am dead against mediation by the United States between India and Pakistan in getting the issue of Kashmir resolved. And if the United States gives a roadmap to resolve the Kashmir issue, it will not be good for India, Pakistan and the people of held Kashmir...'[13]

I would have liked to know Geelani's views on the possible role of America and about his differences with Maulana Abbas. Perhaps ask him why it had been necessary to destroy so much of the cultural heritage of Kashmir; thousands of books on Kashmiri history, culture and heritage had been set on fire. How did he view this destruction?

But when I got up to speak, looking down from the stage, I suddenly felt a humility I do not often feel. As a human rights lawyer I did not see the men waiting patiently and politely for me to speak as enemies, or even opponents. I saw them as people who had been political prisoners, kept in jails, tortured, and kept naked and subjected to humiliation. However much I might disagree with these leaders on their politics, I could not justify the treatment meted out to them. As an Indian, I felt ashamed.

I was brief and gave the facts on why the trial of Afzal Guru had been unfair and why, under the law, he should not have been given a death sentence. Perhaps it was my humility and lack of pretension that prompted Yasin Mailk to stand up and propose that the campaign against the death penalty for Afzal should be coordinated by me and Abdul Qayyoom, the head of the Kashmir Bar Association.

It would have set a precedent in the history of the human rights movement if we had worked together, but Abdul Qayyoom never contacted me, even though he came to Delhi several times and met Abdul Rehman Geelani, who ensured that our meeting never took place.

Qayyoom belonged to the Jamaat-e-Islami, with loyalties to Syed Ali Shah Geelani who had serious differences with Yasin Malik. Moreover, the ideology of that organization would not have allowed him to work with non-believers, especially one not specifically from Kashmir.

But that September day in 2005 all the leaders, including Syed Ali Geelani, Shabir Ahmad Shah, Mohammad Yasin Malik, Mian Abdul Qayyoom and Nisar Ali, signed a joint statement:

The judgement of the Supreme Court states that the attack on the Indian Parliament resulted in heavy casualties and has 'shaken the entire nation and the collective conscience of the society will only be satisfied if capital punishment is awarded to the offender.'

We, the people of Kashmir, ask why the collective conscience of Indians is not shaken by the fact that a Kashmiri has been sentenced to death without a fair trial, without a chance to represent himself? Throughout the trial at the Sessions Court Mohammad Afzal asked the judge to appoint a lawyer. He even named various lawyers but they all refused to represent him. Is it his fault that the Indian lawyers think that it is more patriotic to allow a Kashmiri to die rather than ensure he gets a fair trial?

At the High Court an Indian human rights lawyer who volunteered to represent Afzal actually asked the court that Afzal wanted to be killed by a lethal injection instead of by hanging. Afzal did not know that his lawyer had filed such a petition on his behalf till after the case was over and he had been given three death sentences.

At the Supreme Court the senior lawyer and former Law Minister, Shantibhushanji [Shanti Bhushan], who was representing another co-accused told the court that Afzal was guilty and deserved to die. He made such statements throughout, both inside the court and in the print media.

In Sarabjeet Singh's case the Indian Prime Minister[14] and Indian media have been campaigning with the Pakistan authorities to spare his life. And for the sake of the Indo-Pak friendship process Sarabjeet Singh's life will be spared but is it not a contradiction that the same leaders think that Azal's life needs to be sacrificed at the altar of false notion of national security.

We resolve to launch a Kashmir-wide signature campaign in support of our demand that the death sentence on Afzal be commuted.[15]

It was clear that neither Afzal nor the Kashmiri leaders were claiming that Afzal was innocent. Afzal had never feigned innocence, which was why his story had such poignancy. In a letter sent from Jail No 2 on 26 January 2004, he had written:

The magnitude and gravity of my unknowing, unwilling and unintentional involvement in the parliament attack case was from the beginning emotionalized and magnified by police

through all possible means due to my helplessness and ignorance
and unability to manage the suitable legal aid and the police
made me scapegoat so as to mask their unability and failure and
to make people fool.

In the trial court, Afzal had admitted that he had helped one of the
five militants who attacked the Parliament buy a white Ambassador
car for their mission. But he had not taken part in the actual attack
and was not responsible for any death.

Afzal never had a lawyer to represent him right through the trial
or during the appeal. The court records show that key witnesses
against him were never cross-examined. The reason for this was
largely that he and his family were too poor to engage a lawyer and
the Kashmiri organizations never bothered to help him at that stage.

Could Afzal have been saved from the gallows? I believe he could
have been. There were many sane voices in India who spoke about
the wisdom of not hanging Afzal. Even B. Raman, the former
additional secretary in the Indian intelligence service's Research and
Analysis Wing (RAW), had advised against the hanging of Afzal.[16]
The President of India had expressed his views that the death penalty
should be banned in India and the president of the Congress Party,
Sonia Gandhi, had intervened to save the woman convicted of being
involved in her husband's assassination; Sonia was strongly against
the death penalty.

———

Afzal Guru did not seek martyrdom. This was not a lack of courage.
it was a philosophy that valued life over death.

He did not want to die. In a letter to Abdul Rehman he had
written: 'Indeed you also know that my family needs at least my
being even if it is in jail. After my brother's demise mother would
have broken and if the next episode will take place she will break.'
Afzal was referring to the death of his younger brother, Riyaz, who
had been running a handicrafts shop in Delhi and had died of kidney
failure.

Afzal knew that as long as he lived, even if it was in jail, he would be of some comfort to his wife and son. He was reconciled to living the rest of his life behind bars. But he dreamt of getting a transfer to the jail in Srinagar so they could visit him more often.

The fact that his co-accused had been acquitted and Shaukat's life term had been reduced to ten years had given him hope that his death sentence would be reduced to life imprisonment. The only legal remedy left for Afzal was to file a mercy petition on his own behalf. Afzal asked Pancholi and me to draft the petition. This was sometime in the third week of October 2006.

I drafted the petition and showed it to Pancholi who suggested some changes which were incorporated. Then Pancholi gave the draft to Afzal in jail for him to approve before finalizing it. It was at this stage that something strange happened which was to derail the campaign for Afzal.

Abdul Rehman Geelani expressed his reservations about filing the petition. He told me that it would not go down well with the Hurriyat leaders. It would seem like Afzal was begging for mercy. This was a really odd intervention. The BJP had already started their campaign against Afzal and were baying for his life. One of their arguments was that Afzal himself had never filed a mercy petition. Now Abdul Rehman wanted to deprive Afzal of his last chance to get the death sentence converted to a life sentence.

Besides, the petition was written in the language of a political prisoner—it set out the facts in the background of the movement for Kashmir's freedom. It told Afzal's story and how he was entrapped. It also put down the legal arguments supported by the court records. There was no question of begging for mercy; it was an appeal for justice under Article 72 of the Indian Constitution.

Afzal Guru read through every word of his petition and suggested a few changes; Pancholi incorporated those, finalized the petition and gave it back to Afzal. According to procedure, the condemned prisoner must file the petition himself through the jail.

On 11 November 2006, Afzal carefully signed each page of his petition and handed it over to the authorities of Jail No 3, Tihar Jail.

It was at that time that Abdul Rehman Geelani started a vicious campaign, claiming that Pancholi and I had compelled Afzal Guru to write the petition against his will. He went to the extent of giving a statement to the media in May 2010 that N.D. Pancholi was falsely claiming to be Afzal's lawyer.[17] Geelani claimed that he alone had the authority to represent Afzal.

Pancholi went to meet Afzal and clarify this fact with him. He found Afzal deeply disturbed by the unnecessary controversy created by Geelani and he assured Pancholi that he had no reason for not wanting him to continue as his lawyer.

We could not understand what was driving Geelani to make such a blatantly dishonest statement. Why did he want to deprive Afzal of the only person who could afford him legal assistance during those dark days when he was in solitary confinement on death row? What made him turn against the lawyers who had campaigned for his own acquittal?

Then there were reports in the media that Afzal Guru had written to Syed Ali Shah, apologizing for filing the mercy petition. Portions of that letter were even quoted, but Afzal told Pancholi he never wrote such a letter.

After Afzal was hanged in February 2013, journalists asked Tabassum whether Afzal had indeed written to Syed Ali Shah Geelani apologizing for filing a mercy petition and she replied with anger: 'He never wrote to them. All that has surfaced in his name is nothing but a gimmick created by separatist leaders for their political gains. He never apologized for the mercy petition.'[18]

Afzal's younger brother, Hilal, who worked as a construction labourer in Kashmir, told the journalist: 'No one is telling the real story. It was only Tabassum who fought for her husband. Even I am not in a position to help her. I am a poor man and it is hard to survive here.'[19]

Afzal was deeply pained by another controversy which arose in the course of our campaign to save him from the gallows. He felt that the campaign had resulted in generating distrust and hate between him and his elder brother, Aijaz. Aijaz was deeply disappointed with Afzal for having joined the militancy. But after he surrendered, the brothers maintained their relationship. However, when Afzal was arrested in connection with the Parliament attack, Aijaz was furious. He did not visit his brother in jail, except in October 2006, after the date of his execution was announced—he had come to say goodbye to Afzal.

When he came to Delhi, Aijaz read a pamphlet which carried Afzal's letter in which he had given details about the STF camp. The pamphlet was released by Abdul Rehman Geelani while Aijaz was in Delhi, and he saw it just before he was to pay his last visit to his younger brother.

When he met Afzal, he could not contain his anger and he screamed at his younger brother saying that it was good that Afzal was to be hanged, at least he would not cause any more trouble to the family.

After meeting Afzal, Aijaz came out of the jail and created a scene. He climbed on top of a white Ambassador car which was apparently waiting for him. And in front of thirty to forty media persons, he tore his shirt open and started making a speech; an unidentified man stood behind prompting him. Aijaz told the public that the people involved in the campaign to save Afzal were, in fact, making money from it and on top of the list were Abdul Rehman Geelani and me.

Later, Tabassum told me about the meeting between the two brothers. Aijaz had told Afzal to disown the letter he wrote to his lawyer. He told Afzal that he would die anyway but, by naming the STF in the letter, he was endangering the lives of his wife and son. According to Tabassum, Aijaz said that they would not leave Ghalib and her alive.

I realized that various vested interests were making sure that Afzal did not escape from the gallows. They felt it would be a blot on them if no one was hanged for the attack on the Indian Parliament. Fighting the police or the judiciary was one thing, but it was almost impossible to expose these shadowy powers.

Afzal's family stayed on in Delhi for a few more days. Despite the scene he had created, Aijaz continued to visit me during those days. I did not stop him because I did not wish to cause distress to the family, but his uncouth and rude behaviour was difficult to bear. On one occasion when my husband and I were having our lunch, he shouted: 'What about me?' We had not invited him to join us because it was the month of Ramzan and we had presumed he was fasting. Aijaz announced arrogantly: 'I do not keep roza, I am an Indian.' It was the strangest definition of 'Indian' that I had heard.

The reason the family was virtually staying in my home was because each time they checked into a hotel, they would be thrown out when the manager found out (usually through the police or an intelligence agent) that they were Afzal's family. Finally, I phoned a friend who provided shelter for them in a guest house. But the strange part was that Aijaz had no problem finding a hotel in Jama Masjid.

I had a growing feeling of disquiet.

On 27 November 2006, CNN/IBN conducted a so-called sting operation which they called 'Decoding Afzal'. The programme showed Aijaz sitting in a large empty room saying that many people, including Nandita Haksar, were making money from the Afzal campaign. It was, of course, defamation. I could have proved that I had personally given Rs 100,000 to Tabassum when she could not pay the lawyer in the Supreme Court. As a lawyer, I felt ashamed that an Indian citizen should be sentenced to death without being defended by a lawyer. To sue the media would have undermined the campaign by shifting the focus on me instead of Afzal. For me, it was just another example how the media closes the democratic space by its lack of political understanding.

Later, *Tehelka*[20] exposed how both Aijaz and Shaukat's brother, Yasin, had collected money from the Kashmiri leaders but had not given any to Tabassum to cover legal expenses. The money had been used by Aijaz to buy property. The *Tehelka* reporters said: 'Afzal's wife is now willing to spill the beans when she says, "Aijaz and Yasin have collected five to seven lakh and invested the money in property. Not a paisa has been given to me." None of the money being collected in the name of clemency has been shared with Tabassum who has been fighting the battle, right from the time that the case was being heard in the lower court, until now, when the clemency petition was handed over by her to President Kalam.'

Tabassum had told *Tehelka* that she had discovered the whole business of the Aijaz-Yasin money-collection drive when she made a statement in Kashmir that all those leaders who were now pleading for clemency had not once come forward to help her when she needed it most. This statement from Afzal's wife made headlines in the Valley papers and it was then that the Hurriyat leaders started calling her to say that they had actually helped out and had, in fact, given money to Aijaz and Yasin.

Tabassum told the reporters: 'After my statement, many leaders called me and told that that they all gave money to Yasin. Vo phir nange ho gaye (they then stood exposed). They collected lakhs and kept it. They used this money to buy property.'

_____

By now many controversies had surrounded the campaign to save Afzal, and had jeopardized his chances of reprieve. Once, when I told Afzal that I was upset about being the target of these controversies and that it was not fair, he had smiled and said, 'If you take up my case, you should expect to be a target.' His voice had been ever so gentle. I felt ashamed that I should be seeking comfort from a man condemned in a death cell.

Afzal was deeply distressed by the differences that had cropped up between Geelani and me. He expressed his anguish in a long letter he wrote to me in January 2008:

> There is no doubt that whatever you people did for me I am thankful for that but the differences with SARG disturb me mentally because I never consider you all as members of my campaign but a single indivisible team work.

Then Tehilka episodes, CNN/IBN—various material and state daily newspapers. All these turned the 13 dec episode into family dispute. There were never differences in our family in spite of my brother's indifference and isolation regarding Kashmir conflict. He never share my thoughts, ideas or deeds regarding Kashmir's political conflict but still we always remained as brothers do. But these all things and state terror agencies have created so much differences with my brother he seems to be my most hostile enemy...

As for the controversy of my petition is concerned I want that my petition should not become the subject for debate or controversy. I talked to Mr N.D. Pancholi regarding this issue. Since I have done the formalities regarding constitutional procedure of the petition. It is useless and futile exercise to continue the campaign...

Afzal Guru had decided to stop fighting for justice; that was the only way he could protect his family. After receiving this letter both Pancholi and I ended our involvement in the campaign in accordance with Afzal's wishes, but we did publish his petition to put it on record.[21]

—

Despite myriad controversies, the campaign for the acquittal of Abdul Rehman Geelani and the Save Afzal Guru campaign had opened up a democratic space which could have been used for national debate on many issues, including the Kashmir conflict. For the first time, the media had portrayed the family of a Kashmiri militant with sympathy. Tabassum and Ghalib were visible in the campaign and in the media. But the media still had difficulty portraying human rights activists as Indian nationalists or patriotic citizens.

But I had taken up the case of Abdul Rehman Geelani, and later Afzal Guru's case, precisely because I thought I was defending Indian democracy. Exposing the shoddy investigation by the Special Cell, the undermining of the criminal justice system in the name of fighting terrorism, and revealing the injustice around the decision to hang Afzal, was my way of upholding Indian democracy. But not once did the media ask me to explain my motives for spending four years leading the campaign for justice for Kashmiris.

From 2006, the BJP had made death for Afzal their major political agenda. The Hindutva supporters thought that sending Afzal to the gallows would show that India was a strong country, capable of taking tough decisions. It would help safeguard internal security by showing zero tolerance to terrorism. They were inspired by the US strike in Pakistan against Osama bin Laden.

I had no intention of allowing the BJP the monopoly of holding the national flag. I believed that our work was a contribution to my country. Our campaign had won friends for India, the BJP had made more enemies. We had opened more democratic space, the BJP had closed all space for democratic dialogue with the Kashmiris.

The Congress Party had an eye on the elections. They wanted to take the wind out of the BJP's sails and they thought their one-upmanship would win them the elections. They gave in to the BJP's demand and decided to hang Mohammad Afzal Guru.

—

In the midst of all this ugliness, the one thing that inspired me was Tabassum's love for Afzal. One day when Tabassum and I were returning from a demonstration protesting the death penalty to Afzal, she asked shyly how old Bhagat Singh was when he was hanged. I told her he had been barely twenty-three years old. Then she asked with an unusual brightness in her eyes: How long did it take India to be independent after the hanging of Bhagat Singh? She was trying to calculate how long it would take for Kashmir to be liberated after her husband was hanged. She was so deeply proud of her husband and knew he could be hanged.

But neither she nor Afzal celebrated martyrdom. They hoped against hope that they could both live to see their son grow up, even if they were separated by physical distance and iron bars. On jail visits, she would tell her husband, 'You will be out one day, but you will be an old man by then. Ghalib might be even married by then, but you will be out.'[22]

At night, she would remember all the places where Afzal had taken her for picnics, his loving gestures and the time they had spent together.

It was only once every year that the small family could meet and touch each other, embrace each other and give physical expression to their deep love for each other. The occasion was Rakhi, when the jail authorities allowed the prisoners to receive their sisters so that rakhis could be tied on their wrists. Every year, Tabassum would have to tolerate the lewd remarks made by the jail security force about her being Afzal's 'sister'. She cringed every time she heard those comments, but the thought of how much pleasure she, Afzal and Ghalib got just by being together, helped her bear the insults stoically.

It was after one such visit that she told me how Afzal had cried, with tears flowing down his cheeks. By this time, Geelani had been acquitted and he had told her that she should not tell anyone about Afzal's tears. Implicit in the command was that tears are a reflection of weakness. Tabassum did not reply. She did not think of her husband as a weak man—the tears only made him so much more human.

Tabassum loved Afzal and she was willing to pay the price of being the wife of a man who was to her a freedom fighter. And so she lived, worked and cared for her son and her mother-in-law. She managed to supress the thought that her husband could be executed any day. As long as he was alive, she continued to hope.

And when Shaukat was released from Tihar and came back to Sopore in January 2011, Tabassum could not help but feel if only Afzal, too, could be back home. Shaukat's wife, Navjot, had been released from jail in 2003, but the two had grown apart. When Navjot walked out of jail, there was no one to welcome her back from the hell she had been in. The only person who had cared for her was her father, but he had died and her son, born in prison, had been taken away by the Gurus. His name was Arsalan and he spoke Kashmiri, a language she did not even understand. Tabassum understood some of her pain but she was in no position to offer comfort to the Punjabi woman. The last I heard about Navjot was that she had been admitted into a mental institution. Her suffering would always be invisible. She was a woman who had once defied society; she would pay for it all her life.

———

Having been on death row for nearly a decade, there was hope that Afzal may yet live. That is why Tabassum was not prepared for the news she received on the morning of 9 February 2013.

Mohammad Afzal Guru had been hanged inside Tihar Jail.

He had been denied even a final meeting with his wife and their teenaged son.

I had arrived in Delhi a day before the execution and was woken up by calls from the media, asking for a sound bite on my reaction to the execution. I felt sick in the stomach. Pancholi, too, felt an overwhelming sadness and came over to my home. It was with a sense of deep personal loss that we sat together, wondering what we could do.

Pancholi received a call from Afzal's cousin asking what could be done. We both thought the best thing would be to apply for permission for Tabassum to visit the grave. This would allow Ghalib to see where his father had been buried and help him face the reality of his death. We also wanted to take custody of Afzal's papers; we knew he used to write notes, letters and he also had a collection of books. This would constitute Ghalib's inheritance. Afzal's cousin agreed that this was a good idea.

Pancholi and I went to Tihar Jail and slipped in quietly, without letting the media see us. There was an eerie silence. It was only a few hours after Afzal had been hanged. A jail official, when we met him, said a great wrong had been done. He said he was sorry because Afzal was a gentleman. We made the request for Afzal's papers and left.

In the evening the family members phoned again to ask us to make arrangements for the family to come to Delhi. Our immediate problem then was to find adequate accomodation for them. The last time they had come they could not find a hotel which would give them a room. We decided to contact the concerned member of Parliament and demanded that he make arrangements in Kashmir House.

The liaison officer was not pleased to see us but since he had received the member of Parliament's letter, Kashmir House agreed. It was the only place where the family would be safe and have some privacy as well. We informed Afzal's family members, but each time I asked if I could speak to Tabassum, I was told she was away.

On 12 February, Pancholi and I went to Tihar Jail again and gave a letter to the superintendent asking for an inventory of Afzal's belongings, permission for Afzal's wife to offer prayers at her husband's grave and permission to take Afzal's body back to Kashmir for burial. Each time, the submitted letters were scanned and sent by e-mail to Afzal's family members.

But within two or three days, the controversies began again. The family members started giving statements denying that they had asked to visit the grave; the Kashmir papers carried reports saying that in Islam there was no need to visit a grave to offer prayers for the dead. This, I knew, was a battle of the Salafis to establish their supremacy over the Sufi or Hanafi practice of offering prayers at the grave. Not wanting to be involved in unseemly politico-theological controversies, Pancholi and I resigned. It broke my heart when I read what Tabassum told a journalist: 'It's our religious duty to see the faces of our dead, to bury them properly and to bid them farewell. But my husband was denied all these courtesies because Indian government didn't want us to. It's painful.'[23]

———

Afzal had slowly evolved from a Kashmiri nationalist into an Islamist. I witnessed this change even in his physical appearance.

When he had been arrested he had been clean-shaven, and all the photos I had seen of him as a young man showed that he had never kept a beard. In the course of the trial, I had noticed that he had grown a beard and wore a white cap but later he always wore the keffiyeh. For Sampat Prakash's generation, the keffiyeh represented the Palestinian struggle for statehood; very like the story of Kashmiri nationalism. But now the scarf, made famous by Yasser Arafat, seemed to represent a unity of Muslims.

While Afzal dreamt of a world united by Islamic values, he still did not suffer from blind prejudice or hate. He wrote to me:

> I love and care for my oppressed and helpless people but my love is not at the cost of Indian people. I don't believe in nationalism as political or social philosophy. This planet has got shrinked and condensed through technology. Being a citizen of this planet I believe in universal permanent values, freedom of expression, freedom of faith, freedom from all types of coercion and threat. God has created nothing better than emancipation of slaves (Prophet Mohammad) America's arrogance is decivilizing and dehumanizing whole of global value system and societies.

As the days went by, the newspapers published reports about the last hours Afzal Guru spent on this earth.

On 8 February, at around eight in the night, Afzal was surprised by a visit by the superintendent of prisons and his deputy. They had come to inform him that he was to be hanged the following morning. Afzal was silent. After they left, Afzal asked the security guard whether the news was correct, but the guard said he did not know.

That night, Afzal was shifted to another cell where he could not communicate with any other prisoner. Once in the midst of the controversies, he told me that he had gotten used to his cell. He had felt protected from the disturbing events going on in the outside world; it had been difficult, but now it felt like home. He silently bid goodbye to what had become a kind of a sanctuary.

Early in the morning of 9 February Afzal washed and wore a clean white kurta-pyjama and said his namaaz, his final one on this earth. Then he sat down to write his last words. Even though the letter was addressed to his wife, the words had no emotion. Perhaps he knew that he could not write anything personal because the letter would most certainly become public.

Afzal recorded the time as he wrote his last words. They were in Urdu, not Kashmiri. They were formal and well-rehearsed:

6.25 Subah

Bismillah ir Rehman ir Rahim

9.2.2013

Mohtram Ahle Khan aur Ahle Imaan Aslaam Walekum Allah Paak Ka Lakh Shukriya ki usne mujhe is mukaam ke liye chuna baaki meri taraf se tamaam ahle imam ko bhi mubarakbaad hoki hum sab sachai aur haq ke saath rahen aur haq wa sachai ki khatr akhirat hamara ikhtmaam ho. Ahle khana ko meri taraf se gujarish hai ki mere ikhtaam par afsos ki bajai vo is mukaam ka akhraam kare allah paak aap sab ka hafiz wa nasir hai. Allah hafiz.

Here is the translation of his letter:

I thank Allah the pure a hundred thousand times over for choosing this destiny for me. Rest, I want to congratulate all the believers that we all have stayed on this truthful and righteous path. May truth and righteousness be our destiny in our afterlife. It is my request to my family that instead of grieving at my end, they should respect the stature I have achieved. May God help and protect you.

He wrote in formal Urdu, not Kashmiri. At least one journalist noticed that the letter did not carry an explicit political message for Kashmir or for Kashmiris.[24]

It had been a long journey for the youth who wanted to liberate Kashmir from both India and Pakistan, the man who wanted to be a doctor, the man who found time to read Ismat Chughtai after a day's training in a Pakistani camp and to read Noam Chomsky and M.N. Roy in jail. Even on death row he showed curiosity about the world. He had managed to get a small radio which he hid on the blade of the fan in his cell.

The superintendent of Tihar Jail No. 3, Manoj Dwivedi, was inspired by Afzal and wrote 180 pages on his conversations with his prisoner. They had met when Afzal complained that he was not getting his evening tea. Dwivedi was surprised to discover that it was only in jail that Afzal made a serious study of the Quran. 'I asked him why he used Guru as surname, and he explained that his family had converted to Islam but retained their Brahmin surname. That must have been a few generations before him,' Dwivedi said. The jailor also said Guru had been reading extensively on world religions and wanted to know why young children were buried in Hinduism while adults were cremated.[25]

The government of India prohibited Manoj Dwivedi from publishing his conversations with Afzal and the Hurriyat leaders denied that Afzal had ever said his family converted to Islam or that he had not read the Quran before being imprisoned.

There was a curious convergence of interests by which the BJP, the Congress and the Hurriyat wanted to portray Mohammad Afzal Guru as a hardcore Salafi militant.

———

I believe that Afzal Guru would have walked to the gallows calmly, with dignity. He would have been aware that Maqbool Butt's death anniversary was just two days away.

The last line in Afzal's letter to me said: 'In the end, I request you don't colourize or dress my words in any colour or dress except a purely responsible human concern for humanity.'

He quoted two lines in Urdu and then translated them for me: 'I am in universe in such a way that I am myself universe; I live in a space but I am spaceless.'

———

Ghalib has gone into denial, believing that his father is still in his cell in Tihar Jail. Tabassum works in the Guru nursing home, giving comfort to patients with her cheerful disposition. The pain in her heart is tightly locked inside.

Tabassum has read that soon after her husband's hanging, the Indian Supreme Court had commuted fifteen death sentences to life sentences. These include the seven convicted in the murder of former prime minister Rajiv Gandhi, and Devindar Pal Singh Bhullar, who was convicted for the murder of nine persons and wounding of seventeen others in a bomb attack in Delhi in 1993. She can see a blatant anti-Muslim, anti-Kashmiri bias. She told a journalist: 'They wanted my husband dead. They killed him so that they can later forgive their own.'[26]

Every year, thousands of Kashmiris pour out into the streets to observe the death anniversary of 'Shaheed Mohammad Afzal Guru'. The government tries to restrain them by imposing curfew. Nothing changes.

EPILOGUE

It is June 2015. Sampat Prakash has come to Delhi to have a last look at the manuscript of this book before it goes to print. He has one major objection: the subtitle. I had thought of calling the book *The Many Faces of Kashmiri Nationalism: From the Cold War to the War on Terror*. Sampat says that Kashmiris might feel that I am referring to their resistance as 'terror'.

'But that is not at all what I'm saying,' I tell him. 'I'm referring to America's so-called War on Terror.'

Before we can resolve this issue, Ashwini, a Kashmiri man much younger than us, intervenes: 'What has the Cold War got to do with the Kashmir conflict?' Ashwini is the son of Sampat's friend Jawaharlal Dhar. Dhar died in 1992. He and his family, like many Pandits, had had to leave the Valley in the 1990s. They are now settled in Delhi.

'Had there been no Cold War, the Kashmir conflict would not have become so complex,' I reply. Sampat turns to Ashwini and gives him a quick lesson in twentieth-century history and then turns to me and tells me again that I should seriously consider changing the subtitle of the book (I finally did change it). He also suggests that I write about a possible solution to the Kashmir conflict.

There are three solutions which have traditionally been put forward: One, the integration of Kashmir with Pakistan. Prem Nath Bazaz had argued for this in his brilliant book *The History of the Struggle for Freedom in Kashmir* as far back as in 1954.[1] It is also the solution that many of the Hurriyat leaders still dream of. But knowing that Pakistan has not given the people of what they call Azad

Kashmir or of Gilgit and Baltistan even basic rights, could the people of the Valley still seriously want such integration? Like Afzal Guru, many Kashmiri nationalists feel that Pakistan has betrayed their cause.

But this does not mean that the Kashmiris will agree to full integration with India instead—which is the second solution that is often discussed.

When I ask Ashwini what in his opinion could be a possible way to resolve the conflict, his brother, who has been listening intently, says: 'Remove Article 370 and the problem will be solved.'

Sampat looks at him with impatience and suppresses his anger.

I ask Ashwini's brother how repealing Article 370 can be a solution. He says that it will then be possible for Indians—he means, presumably, Hindus—to settle in the Valley and reduce the Kashmiri Muslims to a minority.

Sampat disagrees strongly—to him, Article 370 is essential because it helps to preserve the composite culture of Kashmir. I ask him how he can still believe in such an idea. Among the many things I have learned through the writing of this book is that Kashmiriyat is a myth; at least Kashmiriyat as defined by official India is. Kashmiri Pandits claim to be the only custodians of the ancient, 'authentic' Kashmiri culture, while Muslims think their history begins with the coming of Islam. Besides, there is so much hatred and mistrust around: between Kashmiri Pandits and Kashmiri Muslims; between Jammu and Kashmir; between India and Pakistan. The only solution that I can think of is to follow the poet Sahir Ludhianvi's advice at the end of love: 'Chalo, ek baar phir se ajnabi ban jayen...' (Come, let us become strangers once more...)

Ashwini says it is true that there is anger and hatred but he himself has been working in Kashmir for the last few years and he finds that the atmosphere is changing. He has been living in the homes of his Muslim friends, and now he's seriously considering buying a home in the Valley.

Ashwini's brother, on the other hand, is working with a

multinational corporation and does not intend to go back to Kashmir. Yet, he wants the repeal of the special status of Kashmir. It does seem ironic.

Sampat asks me: 'So what do *you* think?'

I know that repealing Article 370 would mean that the Kashmiri Muslim would become a minority in Kashmir and he would then be in the same position as those Muslims in India whose minority status has deprived them of full rights as citizens. The Sachar Committee report showed that Muslims have been systematically discriminated against in post-Independence India. They live in fear and insecurity. And now, when India's ruling party is committed to the Hindutva ideology of exclusion, Muslims feel even more besieged.

Sampat says that the Union minister Jitendra Singh, directly responsible to the Prime Minister's Office, has announced that the Amarnath Yatra—when several thousand Hindu pilgrims from outside Kashmir enter the Valley—can carry on throughout the year, instead of being limited, as it has traditionally been, to forty-five days. The minister cites an unspecified geological survey in support of his belief that allowing a round-the-year pilgrimage is feasible and that it will not damage the environment. According to Sampat, this is the Indian government's way of undermining the protection given to Kashmir under Article 370.[2]

Then we discuss the third possible solution, one that, it would appear, the BJP and PDP are working towards: a trifurcation of the state. Over the years many parties have suggested trifurcation of Jammu, Kashmir and Ladakh as a way to resolve the crisis. Balraj Puri had suggested that each province be given autonomy but remain within the same state. Others, however, wanted Jammu and Kashmir to be separate states within the Indian Union and Ladakh to be given the status of a Union Territory. But this does not resolve the problem of the need to protect the Muslims of Jammu who face discrimination both from the Muslims of the Kashmir Valley[3] and the Hindus of Jammu; nor does it satisfy the demands of the Shia Muslims of Kargil who are a minority among the Buddhists of Ladakh and also among the majority Sunnis of the Valley.

These are only the three possible solutions that are most often and most seriously discussed. There are many others. But there must be the political will and the consent of the people of Kashmir. However, even with all the will in the world the obstacle posed by international events is real. An increasing number of Kashmiri youth are attracted by the apparent successes of Islamic organizations in West Asia and elsewhere, and by the dream of the Caliphate; just as they were once inspired by the Naya Kashmir programme.

China, too, will play an important role. As far back as 1967, a general of the Indian army had warned: 'It is, however, the designs of China that will pattern the future for India. China may not be in a position to risk a major war today but confrontation in all its many ways—subversion, tension, border conflicts and aggravating India-Pakistan differences—is to be expected.'[4]

We talk for a long time, and then Sampat asks, 'So what do you think will happen?'

I say I don't know. The Hindus are dreaming of a Hindu Rashtra and the Muslims of a Caliphate—how can the country unite to face challenges, not only in Kashmir but across India?

Sampat says it is not true that all Hindus and all Muslims are dreaming such dangerous dreams; the vast majority of them are just dreaming of peace.

I ask him what could be the path to this elusive peace; especially when official India is celebrating war.[5]

Sampat says it can only be Kashmiriyat.

I say it can only be Insaniyat.

I know we are still a long way from defining Insaniyat or humanism. But, like Sampat, I refuse to stop hoping.

AFTERWORD
November 2016

This book was first published in August 2015. Since then, the reception it has got, especially in Kashmir, has been heartening. One young journalist told me he had not read my first book on Kashmir because of my surname: a Kashmiri Pandit, and daughter of P.N. Haksar. But this time he was ready to have a discussion. Another Kashmiri Muslim student came up to me at the end of my talk on Kashmir in Hyderabad and said: 'I know you don't believe in God, but may Allah bless you.' I felt I had received a genuine blessing. I'm not saying that these readers agreed with my analysis. But they gave me their time, they were willing to consider my analysis, for which I consider myself fortunate.

And I was so happy that Afzal's wife Tabassum came for the release of this book; and I met Ghalib, Afzal's son. He has grown tall and he is determined to fulfil his father's dream by becoming a doctor. He had topped in his class in his final year at school and was in the first year of the MBSS course when I last met him.

Then I heard the news of Burhan Wani's death. I witnessed the turmoil on television; and my thoughts went to Ghalib. I hoped he would be able to continue his studies, as I saw reports of hundreds of students coming out into the streets in protest. A large number were injured in pellet-gun firing; more than a hundred lost their eyesight and many died. So many young dreams destroyed.

The protestors were reacting to the killing of a youth whom they looked upon as an idealist, an icon of Kashmiri nationalism. The

Indian media underestimated the rage that the killing aroused; and the Kashmiris' feeling of alienation became more entrenched.

———

On 8 July 2016, the Indian media reported that a 'Kashmiri terrorist', Burhan Wani, had been killed in an encounter. The immediate concern of the national media was with the 25,000 people waiting in Jammu to go on the Amarnath Yatra; few in the media concerned themselves with the anger of the protestors, many of them very young, who were pouring into the streets of Srinagar. Twenty of them had already been killed within the first few days. The protests continued in defiance of the curfew that had been imposed. It took more than a month for the national media to take serious notice and begin debating the use of pellet guns by the security forces, and discuss the impact the protests were having on the lives of the Kashmiris.

Calling Burhan Muzaffar Wani a pro-Pakistani, anti-Indian terrorist does not explain why thousands and thousands of Kashmiri people, men, women and children, were out on the streets, day after day, facing pellet guns, in protest against his killing by Indian security forces. It does not explain why little boys in Kashmir pretend to be Burhan Muzaffar Wani, the most wanted commander of the Hizbul Mujahideen, while three or four other boys pretend to be soldiers of the Indian army. The objective of the game is for Wani to escape from the clutches of the Indian army.

The continuing demonstrations on the streets of Kashmir are a testimony to the anger of the people towards the Indian state, and its refusal to even acknowledge their very genuine grievances. I think the most powerful articulation of the feelings of the Kashmiri people was by Mahum Shabir, an artist and briefly a patient in a mental health facility: 'The doctor [a psychiatrist] asks if I have witnessed violence. I want to tell him that I have witnessed enough peace to question the distinction in the meaning of these words.'[1]

In contrast to the deep anguish of the Kashmiris is the insensitivity of people like Chetan Bhagat, a popular author. Chetan Bhagat's views on Kashmir would not be of any consequence, except for the fact that he is the idol of millions of Indian youth and his apparent affinity with the kind of Hindu nationalism that is responsible for further alienation of the Kashmiri people in recent years. In a column published in the *Times of India*, he wrote:

> Allow me to tell you how your future will be best, on a practical basis, if the Kashmir Valley integrates and assimilates with India. This is not an emotional, political or historical argument. It is simply more rational for people in the Kashmir Valley who seek a better future to do it with India.
>
> Sure, the experts will jump on me now. Experts who have made the Kashmir problem their fiefdom. However, if the problem were indeed solved, how will these people stay relevant?
>
> The issue is complicated for sure. For those who don't know the Kashmir issue, here it is in a nutshell. India became independent. Princely states were assimilated. Jammu & Kashmir didn't accede. Pakistan attacked Kashmir, took half of it (and still controls it). Kashmir's ruler called India for help. In return for help J&K became part of India, but with riders.
>
> J&K would have its own constitution; have more political independence than other states, while the Centre would handle defence, foreign affairs and communications. In theory, it was a good solution, a sort of one country, two systems approach. In reality, it never worked. Instead of two parents as planned, J&K became nobody's child and an orphan. Pakistan took advantage and used the common factor of Islam to start a militant movement. The Indian army tried to control it. However, it is difficult to control terrorism that co-exists with a civilian population (case in point: even the world's superpowers appear unable to control Islamic State).
>
> Hence the Indian army, and India, only got a bad name in the Valley. Thus the 'we hate India' slogans and perennially unsolved Kashmir problem.[2]

This description does violence to the history of anguish and alienation the Kashmiri people feel, even those among them who would like to be a part of the Indian Union. As this book has tried to show, for a long time after 1947 a significant percentage of the Kashmiri people and many of their leaders supported the idea of Kashmir being a part of India. Without the active support of the Kashmiri people the Pakistani forces could have overrun Kashmir during the tribal raids in 1947, and they could have caused havoc during the Indo-Pakistan war of 1965. And most Kashmiris have often expressed their deep disappointment with the way Pakistan has used the Kashmir issue for its own vested interests.

But the Indian state has trusted neither the leaders nor the people of Kashmir. It has been a long history of broken promises, insensitivity, injustice and brute force as a response to alienation and protest.

———

The Kashmiris know that even if Nawaz Sharif raises the question of Kashmir and Burhan Wani in the United Nations, Pakistan is using Kashmir as a pawn. They see the cynical game for what it is. But when the Indian Prime Minister reacts and raises the Baluchistan issue and the Pakistani government's support for the Kashmiri militants, there is concern that there could be another war.

And this time, the consequences could be extremely serious. It will not be just India and Pakistan at war; China, too, will be involved. China has been backing Pakistan for some time, and this is far more significant than the Western backing of India.

The close relationship between Pakistan and China is a factor that has not been publicly discussed and debated sufficiently in India. As far back as 1965, China had said: 'As long as the Indian Government oppresses the Kashmiri people, China will not cease to support the Kashmiri people in their struggle for self-determination. So long as the Government of India persists in its unbridled aggression towards Pakistan, China will not cease supporting Pakistan in her just struggle against aggression. This stand of ours will never change, however many helpers you may have, such as the US, the modern revisionists and the US-controlled United Nations.'[3]

And true to this promise, China has twice blocked India-sponsored resolutions at the UN declaring the Jaish-e-Mohammad chief Maulana Masood Azhar a terrorist.[4] China has also announced it will open a consulate in Pakistan-occupied Kashmir (PoK), or Azad Kashmir as the Pakistanis call it. An Indian official report warns: 'One should not be surprised by Beijing working on a plan to grab the entire Gilgit-Baltistan along with the 5,000 square kilometre Shaksgam Valley held by China since 1963. Academic writings draw historical antecedent for China's claims over the Hunza Valley.'[5]

India has not paid serious attention to the changing nature of power play that has brought PoK to the forefront of China's geopolitical calculations. The region came in the spotlight after Xi Jinping announced plans to develop the China-Pakistan Economic Corridor (CPEC) and pledged USD 46 billion for building transport and energy connectivity to link Pakistan with China's ambitious 'One Belt, One Road' (OBOR) project. The August 2015 'Karamay Declaration' detailed Pakistan's role in China's global scheme. Lately, even Russia has indicated its interest in joining the bandwagon to prop up Pakistan, which it regards as a country of strategic significance, and facilitate its integration into the Eurasian framework.[6]

There is an urgent need to understand these recent happenings in a historical and political perspective, otherwise we will be falling into the trap of those who are virtually demanding a war. A war between India and Pakistan with China backing Pakistan and perhaps the west backing India—if at all—cannot serve any purpose other than boosting the arms industry and strengthening the right-wing forces that have seen an unprecedented rise in the world, including India.

A section of the Indian media has even tried to hint that the Islamic State could be behind the recent protests in Kashmir, but according to the Institute of Defence Studies and Analysis, an Indian think tank, there is no direct evidence to support such a hypothesis, which it calls 'alarmist'. It goes on to say that such a perception, if it persists, may well become a self-fulfilling prophecy.

With a large section of the media virtually asking for a war with Pakistan, it remains a very real danger. If war breaks out, Kashmir could suffer the same fate as Syria. No one will profit; except for the arms industry.

The US State Department's recent release states that the United States has sold $33 billion worth of weapons to its Gulf allies since May of 2015, with more deals in the works as the business of bombing the Islamic State continues to boom. In the eleven months since, the State Department has helped with the export of everything from attack helicopters to precision guided munitions to the Gulf Cooperation Council states—Bahrain, Kuwait, Oman, Qatar, Saudi Arabia, and the United Arab Emirates.[7]

The cry for war will not make India any safer; just as it did not make the USA or Europe any safer. While military action and intelligence agencies have a role to play, it should be minimal. It is for citizens to inform themselves of the facts.

But facts without a political context do not make sense. This book has argued that while the communists made serious mistakes, they did put forward a vision for Kashmir in their Naya Kashmir programme. There can be a debate on the different visions and political ideas. But first we must equip ourselves with an understanding of Kashmir's tortuous history; we must sincerely acknowledge the fact that the Kashmiris have genuine grievances.

Mohammad Afzal wrote: 'What people need is a political framework in which they don't feel themselves vulnerable, humiliated or terrorized. The people of Kashmir want an honorable space to live on this planet. They are not demanding the stars.'[8]

A Parliamentary delegation visited the Valley more than two months after the people began protesting, after children had been blinded by pellet guns and many had died. The Kashmiri leaders refused to meet them. The leaders had been living under house arrest in a curfew, but the Indian mainstream media debated whether their refusal to welcome the delegation was a violation of Kashmiri hospitality. This was an insult added to the injury already inflicted on Kashmir.

Despite all this provocation the Kashmiri people helped many of the Amarnath pilgrims; they even helped a group of Indian soldiers whose truck had overturned. As I have argued in this book, although Kashmiriyat as a concept is discredited in the eyes of the Kashmiri Muslims, it does not mean that they have taken to being anti-Hindu. A day before Burhan Wani was killed, his six-minute video had gone viral on Facebook, Whatsapp and other social networking sites. In that video he had said that the Kashmiri militants had no plan to and would never attack pilgrims who arrive in Kashmir for the Amarnath Yatra. However he had warned that if there were separate colonies created for Kashmiri pundits, as the present governments at the Centre and in the state have been planning, these would be attacked.

The video was made in response to rumours that the Amarnath yatris would be attacked my militants. Wani had said: 'A BSF officer had recently said militants plan to attack the Amarnath Yatra. His statement is absolutely untrue and false. Let me assure you [pilgrims] that we have no plans to attack Amarnath Yatra. They [Hindu pilgrims] are coming here to fulfil their religious duties and we have nothing to do with it.'

However, after Burhan Wani's killing the Valley witnessed an upsurge of anti-Hindu sentiments. So far the anger of the Kashmiris was against the Indian state, not its citizens or Hindus in general. But on July 10, an enraged mob of Kashmiri Muslims stoned the accommodation complex of Kashmiri Pandits at Haal in Pulwama. The same day, a langar set up for devotees headed to the Amarnath shrine was attacked in Ganeshpora village, en route to Pahalgam. At Srigufwara in Anantnag district, a bus carrying Amarnath Yatra pilgrims was stoned. Ali Shah Geelani condemned the stone pelting in Srigufwara in an article in *Greater Kashmir,*[9] but it is uncertain how long the words of leaders like him will be heeded.

The Hindu nationalists' war mongering has made the situation very volatile. And the lack of viable political alternatives from any of the political parties, which offer only platitudes and empty calls for talks, has encouraged the growth of Islamic ideology.

Many readers of this book have said that they felt dissatisfied because there were no answers in it. This is true. But I do not necessarily have answers, and mine may be irrelevant anyway. However, I do believe we need to have another Reading Room party where we can read, discuss and debate our different visions for Kashmir's future. But Kashmir cannot be understood in isolation; a viable vision for Kashmir will have to include an alternative political vision for the world as a whole.

ACKNOWLEDGEMENTS

Thank you all:

Most of all, the leaders of the Low Paid Government Servants Federation, for their affection, hospitality and trust (I am sorry that I could not include so many of your stories, but perhaps others will be inspired to write a more detailed history of the Federation);

Sampat Prakash, for his time and the energy with which he shared his experience and for all the intense discussions over so many years;

Mohammad Afzal Guru and Tabassum, for their trust, and with the hope that Ghalib will one day read this book;

Bismillah Geelani, who first shared with me the world of Salafis;

Jawaharlal Koul, who lent me his entire library of books on Kashmiri history, culture and politics;

Ashwini Dhar, without whom I would never have completed this book (and he knows what I am talking about!);

My parents, Parmeshwar Narain Haksar and Urmila Haksar, for allowing me to question even their most dearly held ideas and values;

Ravi Singh, for providing a safe harbour for me (and many others) from choppy political waters;

Aruna Ghose, for respecting the author and for the warmth when I needed it most—the book is much better because of you;

To Ulka, she knows why;

And, as always, Sebastian.

APPENDIX 1:
THE NAYA KASHMIR PLAN

The 'Naya Kashmir' plan was submitted by Sheikh Abdullah to Hari Singh, the ruler of Jammu and Kashmir, in 1944. The vision informing Naya Kashmir is still relevant today, especially with the rollback of the welfare state, even as the gap between the poor and the rich is growing.

The full text of Naya Kashmir in Urdu is reprinted in the book *Tehreek-e-Hurriyat-e-Kashmir*. The English translation is available on Wikisource. In this appendix I've included some of the most enlightened parts of the document: 'Article 1', which visualized an inclusive, plural Jammu and Kashmir; and the Charter of Rights for Peasants, Workers and Women.— NH

NAYA KASHMIR (1944)

Future Constitution of The State of Jammu and Kashmir describing Citizenship of the State and Rights and Duties of Citizens and detailing a National Economic Plan for the State

ARTICLE 1

All persons residing in Jammu, Kashmir , Ladakh, Frontier areas, and areas falling under Poonch and Chenini will solely be the residents of the State. In all spheres of National activities, Economic, Political, Cultural or Social the equality of all citizens irrespective of their color, race, religion or heredity would be considered a fundamental and unalienable right of the citizens of this State. Imposing any bar on these rights by direct or indirect means or granting any special privileges to any one citizen or body of citizens on the basis of their descent, family relationship, race or religion as well as demanding special treatment on the basis of heredity, race or religion as well as spreading discord and hatred among the citizens (on abovementioned grounds) would be held to be a punishable criminal offence...

CHARTER OF THE PEASANTS RIGHTS

1. Every peasant would have the right to possess land for tilling till some practical alternative employment is provided to him.
2. All land of which Jagirdars and Chakdars are at present absentee owners would after eradication of this social parasitism be made over to the peasants.
3. In the interim period before the plan is fully implemented all fallow land would be taxed progressively and no land would be exempted from tax even if for some reason it is incapable of being cultivated for some reason. Even before the chakdari system is abolished a strict limit would be imposed on the maximum income that absentee landlords would obtain from their absentee holdings.
4. The right of giving first priority to meeting the requirements of peasants from the produce of a village would be recognized.
5. All feudal impositions, compulsory offering of presents and gifts to feudal lords and begaar (forced labor) would be abolished.
6. It would be the goal of the government to rid the villages of the curse of outstanding loans. It is essential to liberate every peasant from this burden. Hence if the peasant has repaid the principal of the loan to the lender he would be released from the liability of making any additional payments to the lender.
7. Social Insurance would be made available to peasants like other workers.
8. The State would have the duty of taking all necessary steps to protect peasants from natural disasters like floods, hailstorms, crop diseases, diseases of livestock etc.
9. The peasant would have the right to ask the government to provide him assistance based on latest scientific developments in the following matters:

   A. Land use
   B. Grading of foodstuffs
   C. Production of fertilizers from agricultural waste, bones etc
   D. Improving irrigation: Control of water logging and malaria control

(to be done as a village based program along with improving water use)

E. Wetland Preservation

F. Making available labor saving agricultural machines

G. Installing a network of centers where villagers would be provided with knowhow of modern agricultural methods and especially information about varieties of crops and grading of agricultural produce by experts in the field.

H. Establishment of Granaries and Storage facilities by cooperatives to prevent spoilage of agricultural produce

I. Protecting domestic animals from disease and providing assistance in their breeding.

J. Establishment of Poultries

K. Making available improved varieties of grasses and fodders.

L. Improving sanitation in villages.

10. Providing modern fast and efficient means of transport of goods and passengers to the farmers

11. Providing cooperative marketing centers to the farmers so that they get proper value for their produce and thus a proper return for their labor.

12. Giving villagers the right to utilize local produce of adjacent forests and stop their harassment by officials of the forest department.

13. Every farmer will have the right to obtain free medical advice and medicines as per plan.

14. Every farmer will have the right to be provided with clean all weather houses with supply of potable water in villages.

15. Farmers will have the right to have a town hall with a radio set and equipment for indoor and outdoor games so that they can lead a proper social life.

16. Every farmer will have the right to obtain education under the National education Plan and besides basic reading, writing and arithmetic skills be also taught about agricultural subjects and this education be provided to him to as advanced a level as he is capable of.

This abovementioned charter of rights will enable the poor, deprived farmers of Kashmir to attain the status which he deserves and become a prosperous and happy citizen of this beautiful land.

CHARTER OF WORKERS' RIGHTS

1. Every citizen of the Jammu and Kashmir State has the right to be provided employment by the State as per his physical and intellectual capabilities.

2. Every citizen has the right that in an independent democratic State and in a State based on the principle of freedom from exploitation of one person by another to progress according to the above principles and attain a status befitting his pride and self respect as a citizen.

3. Every citizen has the right to have a standard of living much above that of bare existence and this standard of living will have to be attained by the government by following the guidelines laid in the economic plan.

4. Every citizen would have the right to form an association and freely express his views in the same.

5. Every citizen would have the absolute right to leave any trade or profession or join any trade or profession.

6. The government will negotiate all necessary matters regarding artisans, laborers and other workers with the associations and their representatives.

7. In all unresolved disputes arbitration would be resorted to for solving them.

8. Every citizen will be entitled to an eight hour workday.

9. Every worker who is a citizen would receive his wages on a weekly basis.

10. Every worker will have the right of equality of wage with others of the same cadre without discrimination on the basis of caste, color, creed or gender.

11. Every worker will be entitled to leave with full pay for one day a week and also fifteen days after a years service.

12. The State would be responsible for providing pension to the dependents of a worker in the event of his untimely death according to the State Pension Scheme.

13. Every worker would have the right to own a hygienic residence in a healthy environment with proper lighting and clean potable water.

14. The practice of child labor would be stopped and children below the age of 15 years will not be allowed to be employed as laborers.

15. Women workers will be entitled to all rights that are laid out in the Charter of Women's rights.

16. Laborers will be recruited only through their associations.
17. Every laborer will be entitled to use cheap and fast load carriers.
18. Every worker will have the right to have free treatment and care in case of illness.
19. Every worker will have the right to social and cultural advancement.
20. Every worker will have the right to education. This education would not be limited to the 3 R?s but would cover further professional education in his field of interest to the extent he is capable of as laid out in the National educational Plan. The exploited and wretched laboring class of the Jammu and Kashmir State would be enabled by this right to evolve as a perfect and complete human being and play his proper role in the development of the new democratic State of Jammu and Kashmir to the fullest possible extent.

CHARTER OF WOMEN'S RIGHTS

The All Jammu And Kashmir National Conference is committed to fight for the rightful place and status of women in society. The National Conference is of the view that men and women must collaborate with each other in shouldering the weighty responsibility of nation building. With this in view The National Conference takes on itself the giving of the following rights to the women of the State:

1. Universal suffrage for women above the age of 18 years
2. The right to be elected as a member in all institutions whose membership is by election
3. The right to have all matters concerning women that are decided by elected organs of the State to be adopted after due consultation with the representatives of the women.
4. The right to employment in all departments of the State.

The National conference also intends to create a special department for affairs pertaining to women. This department will address the problems of women in general and also look into the problems of the women of the backward classes who are utterly neglected. These include the women of the nomadic tribes, those living in frontier regions, boatwomen and such others. This department will take special steps for their uplift.

ECONOMIC RIGHTS OF WOMEN

The National Conference is of the view that women need to be protected from economic exploitation even more than men. At present women are treated as cheap labour used to do jobs meant for men. The National Conference feels that women have the right to be liberated from heavy physical labor. It is the right of women to obtain state help for their maternal role which entails respect and consideration. A responsible government would be bound to ensure that women have the following rights:

A. Women would get the same wages as men for similar work. The sole criterion for determining wages would be the type of job, its nature and workmanship.

B. Women would have the right to follow any trade or profession that they are capable of according to their will and interest.

C. Women working in industries would be entitled to the same social insurance schemes to which the men would be entitled.

Apart from having the right to avail ordinary holidays like men they will have the following special privileges:

1. No woman will be employed for night shifts in industries.
2. No woman will be obliged to do unsuitable heavy labor during pregnancy

D. Every woman whether living in a village, or a city, a nomad or a boatwoman would be entitled to help and protection in her role as a mother and this would include :

1. Antenatal care
2. Provision of medical help at home or hospital at the time of delivery and special care for complicated cases.
3. Provision of comprehensive post natal patient care.
4. Extending the nursing system on a district by district basis.
5. Paid maternity leave for women six months prior to and six months after delivery.
6. Provision of baby care and kindergarten facility in every place where more than seven women are employed.
7. Every nursing woman would have the right to avail half an hours break after every four hours of work.
8. Women who have a greater number of children would be given a childcare allowance

SOCIAL RIGHTS OF WOMEN

The Jammu and Kashmir national Conference considers the house and the family as the basic social unit and accepts the right of every citizen and every child to enjoy its benefits. This principle demands that:

A. The status of a woman receive legal protection and any offender who is guilty of excesses towards women be awarded deterrent punishment.
B. The women and children of the State be protected from persons indulging in the trafficking of women and children.
C. The economic and physical causes that result in prostitution be addressed and such women brought back into the mainstream by education and persuasion.
D. Special care be taken to address the problems of women belonging to backward tribes and backward regions of the State.

LEGAL RIGHTS OF WOMEN

The Jammu and Kashmir National Conference is committed to the principle of equality of men and women in legal matters. The National Conference recognizes the right of every citizen man or woman to marry according to their custom and religion whether Hindu or Muslim or Buddhist or Sikh or belongs to any other religion. The only requirement would be that the marriage would have to be registered with the Registrar of Marriages of the responsible government of the State. In the interests of women the National Conference desires that:

A. Every woman would have the right to chose her husband according to her will and discretion.
B. Dowry system and the sale of women would be abolished.
C. Women would have the right to obtain divorce or separation.
D. The responsibilities and rights of women will be at par with those of men with regard to the bringing up of children and if the husband and wife get divorced the woman would have the right to custody of the minor child.
E. Women would have the right to own and inherit property and this right will not be affected by marriage.
F. In every dispute where the outcome would have consequences for women and children the judge would have to be a woman.
G. Women prisoners would be treated justly and humanely paying due regard to their physique and gender.

EDUCATIONAL RIGHTS OF WOMEN

Having understood that educational facilities are vital for uplift of women on a large scale the Jammu and Kashmir National Conference takes responsibility for implementing a special scheme for women?s education based on the following principles:

A. Compulsory and free education for all women. Mobile schools would be provided for nomad women and boat schools for boatwomen. For women who are unable to attend ordinary schools special schools will be provided at all levels.

B. The educational rights and facilities for both academic and professional education provided to women would be at par with those provided to men. Women would be given special scholarships at every level to encourage them.

C. Special colleges would be opened to train women in academics, industry and home science. Women would also have the right to study in ordinary colleges along with men.

D. Women would be specially involved in making the syllabi for various courses.

E. Implementation of schemes for adult education among women. This would cover not only instruction in the three R's but also elementary principles of hygiene and the bringing up of children.

CULTURAL RIGHTS OF WOMEN

The National Conference looks forward to the time when women would be playing important and respected roles in the field of science and social life of the future free democratic State of Jammu and Kashmir. With this aim the National Conference takes upon itself the following responsibilities:

A. Encouragement of all women professionals and academicians.

B. Involvement of women in the cultural affairs of the state.

C. Encouragement of different languages spoken in the state.

D. Making special efforts for cultural development of far flung areas of the state.

APPENDIX 2: LETTER FROM AFZAL GURU TO THE AUTHOR

page — ①

Respected Nandita — Adab! Hope you will be fine. The Petition To The President of India being a constitutional Procedure and Simple formality (For me) was never for Publication or campaign. Same happened with my Letters which were personal To the Lawyer or others. This is simply in your own language a breach of Trust. Letters & petition Turned into booklets & became The raw material for all campaign. Since Through due to This my family was Terrorised and Traumatised by state security agencies and also central agencies - in different ways.

There is no doubt That whatever whatever you People did for me I am Thankful for That but The differences with SARG. disturb me mentally because I never consider you all as members of my campaign but are single individule Team-work.

Then Tehleka episodes, CNN-ISB - various national and State daily news papers. All these Turned The 13 Dec. episode into Family dispute. There were never differences in our family inspite of my brother's indifference and isolation regarding Kashmir conflict. He never share my Thoughts, ideas or deeds regarding Kashmir's political conflict but still we always remained as brothers do. But These all Things and State Terror agencies have created so much differences with my brother he seems To be my most hostile enemy.

I am fully aware about The eventualities and consequences regarding my vulnerable family members but The deeper fact about life is That we all are vulnerable when we are a part of sensitive subject

considering all These Facts I stopped ceased To write you and others even I don't

write To my mother as only letters are stopped by
Baramullah so even after passing Through censorship
of Jail authorities.

Please do convey my Thanks To
Amrit for her letters and the visit she paid To
Jail premises. There is no security problem or consideration
it is indeed a communal atmosphere which has created
The Problem for those who want To meet me.
The Jail authorities allow my family just
20 or 30 minutes mulakat time (meeting Time) inspite of
The Fact That They Know That my family comes 2 or 3
Times in a year. The prisoners mostly criminals or cheaters
get 40 to 50 minutes. The reason is They are from Delhi
and They also pay Them just 500Rs. or more orless.

As for The controversy of my petition is
concerned I want That my petition should not become
The subject for debate or controversy. I Talked To
MR. N. D Pancholi regarding This issue. Since I have
done The Formalities regarding constitutional procedure
of petition. It is useless and futile exercise To
continue The Campaign. The decision on my petition
will be Taken on legal grounds for which The concerned
secretary had submitted an affadavit To SC in november 2007.

I don't bother wheather Modi or The people
of india called me Terrorist or criminal. Indeed
I am Terrorist against Those who Terrorise and
humiliate The common helpless people. I don't have
patience To remain mute spectator or silent before
State Terror. On NOV 27,-136 shopes and 50 stores in mahraj
Gunj (SGD). On Dec.2 150 houses in lolab Kupwara, DEC-1
Dangiwacha (BLA) 13 shopes, 14-Dec- 14 shopes in penzgam,
were burnt by security agencies and S.T.F. 2 monthes
back a village of 200 houses in ganderbal and 3 months
back a village in doda were completely devasted by
deliberate fire. In panzgam Four STF men were
caught by villagers. on NOV.10.2007 Boop singh of
18RR resident of sakrar Rajasthan was caught

by Kupwara villagers while setting houses on fire.
He was handed over To Local MLA Jamsheed lone.
Jungles in Dooda, Kupwara etc continued burning for 10days
no forest or govt. official came to stop This devastation
of green wealth—In well-published sex-scandle Top
politicians, security-officials (DIG. BSF) dozens of S.S.P's, Top
Bureaucrats etc were named. They shamelessly said
before The court that the Teenage girls They ~~said~~
~~as~~ ~~raped girls~~ were used for anti-insurgency purposes
and for national security purposes— ~~wheather~~ Burning
of houses- in -7°C cold season or institutionalised moral
& social crimes under the Shadow of AFSPA and policies will
disturbed area Act and other state Terror ~~will~~
~~bleed~~ The present young generation nowhere except the
Push
Towards:
? Radical-Wall. security forces and state security apparatus
under These laws do all This with impunity making
~~national duties have~~ Institutions powerless and mockery.
State courts and other Institutions did not have given a single report regarding burning.
national dailies did not have given a solitary confinement
Respected Nandita;— Being in a solitary confinement
isolated from other Kashmiri prisoners When I know
and feel This in silence. What do you Think about
The ~~burnt houses~~ Those people who houses were
sisters. were ~~raped~~
burnt & whose ~~women had~~ ~~committed with~~
~~committed~~ by state and central agencies? Brute
force & sensless policies will fall under Their own
weight. The constant humiliation and Trauma
will enhance and ignite The heat of conflict.
These policies will cultivate The militant and
radical culture Towards irreversible end. ~~These~~
Police stations have become Terror and slaughter houses.
Families of killed person do not go To police station
because it is police station Which is spreading
The sense of Terror into The hearts and minds
of people. You may be feeling This exaggeration
of State Terror. But This is a bitter fact
of constitutional colony That is called Kashmir.
The worst Part of This ~~in~~ problem is National dailies
never report about These crimes-

I am myself The living epitome of This Terror.

State and stage managed elections will make The ground facts more invisible. These elections will be wastage of Time, energy & resources nothing else. it will only enhance and perpetuate The invisible suppressed anger and alienation of people. These policies are self deception & cultivating radicals unknown to everyone even To The Families They belonged. The closure of all democratic means & vents will naturally push These educated youth Towards radical-walla. Noam Chomsky says, "if we do not believe in Freedom of expression for The people we **despise** we don't believe in it at all." — RSS's philo- -sophy and its political, social & militant offshoots and offsprings are communalising and polarising whole of political and social Fabric and This culture of hatred is penetrating The other local institutions as well and don't exclude Tihar Jail. There is no doubt ISI is also playing its role in This process Through its own devices of hatred. Infact ISI is nurturing on anti-indian ~~this~~ ~~Feeling~~ rhetoric.

Nandita— being a Kashmiri Pandith you may have and naturally should have The deep anger in your mind and heart regarding The Nostalgic existence of Pandith community. it is infact ~~xxxxxxx~~ Jagmohan's communal agenda and policies which is responsible for mass exodus of Kashmiri Pandith community. You ask any non-political Kashmiri Pandith I am 100% sure ~~he~~ will reply you in my words. I don't deny That like SOG/STF men some ~~xxxxxx~~ ~~xxxxxx~~ communal minded people also played Their dirty role in This inhuman dual agenda. Last but not least it is Kashmiri Panditho who left us alone at The mercy of indian security forces and They never condemned or held some mass demonstrations or or ~~xxxxx~~ ⑤

⑤ show some gesture of solidarity for last eighteen (18) years regarding the atrocities and human rights viola-tions committed by security forces or self.

Respected Nandita: When Naga conflict is not Christian. Why conflict in Kashmir is branded as Islamic. Fundamentally it is political, social and historical in nature Robert A Pape's book, DYING TO WIN has given a sophisticated analysis of 300 succide attacks out of which (From 1980-2003) out of which 76 were executed by LTTE. The common cause he says is political & social injustice, oppression and brutal policies of political establisment or occupational powers. Religion gives moral strength but Religion is not basic cause-political injustice, oppression, helplessness and victimization makes death more attractive than life under the shadow of humiliation and submission. It is in the nature of [scribble] living and believing faith that provides the believers a moral and logical force & strength to resist and fight against injustice. Faith does not teaches begging, weakness or to get victimized to its followers. It is in the universal law of nature to make its subjects fit for physical and moral development [scribble] Religion provides strength & universal permanent values To live an honourable life. Jesius [scribble] the son of marry (maryam) (peace be up them) says, "man does not live by bread alone." Economic packages can not bring peace in Kashmir. The people who are constantly living in the flux of humiliation and fear does not need bread for which Allah has given everyperson two hands for single mouth. what people need is a political framework in which they don't feel themselves vulnerable, humiliated or terrorised. The people of Kashmir

Want an honourable space to live on this planet. They are not demanding stars. But if the govt. of india consider that by terrorising, humiliating and subjugating they can silence the will-power of oppressed kashmiris as nation then they should know that ~~they are deceiving~~ they are not deceiving only themselves but to nation as whole. Anger and alienation is dormant not ~~killed~~. Silence does not mean end. Don't let this devastating baby to come out it will be ~~disaster~~. The threat and terror created by media on behalf of political establishment can become reality if the socia-political causes will not be addressed. please don't take my words as hypothetical threat it is human concern for the people irrespective of color, creed or faith we have to live with realities otherwise we ~~will be~~ forced to live with this baby and ~~got~~ will be responsible for this. Kashmir conflict is regional in nature. Neo-cons and zionists who have already pushed the US into desert (Iraq) and mountainous (Khurasan) morass can ~~no go~~ do no good or help to govt. of india by giving their diabolical expertise and weapons of mass destruction. They will only make worlds largest democracy more fragile and soft from the security point of view. Zionists have built strong 1000 miles long 15 x 6 mtrs ~~Apartheid-wall~~ in Isreal and turned whole gaza into virtual prison to save ~~it~~ themselves from helpless plastanians. Does india ~~want~~ same expertise for kashmir valley.?

I love and care for my oppressed & helpless people but my love is not at the cost of indian people. I don't believe in nationalism as political or social philosophy. This planet has got shrinked and condensed through technology. Being a citizen of this planet I believe in universal permanent values, freedom of expression, freedom of faith, freedom from all types coercion & threats. God has created nothing better than the emancipation of slaves— "Prophet Mohammed". Americas arrogance is decivilizing & dehumanising whole of global value system. and societies.

Regarding your book I am unable or rather incapable to write my views. Your book has enclosed almost all subjects. I am the cultivation of misery and state terror and it is my Faith which came to my rescue sustained and supported me to live, think, to feel, to write, to bear ~~xxxxx~~ all that which I receive, I faced and am failing. Intellectual ~~and~~ emotional and intentional honesty with the words is essential & vital that give life & wings to the birds of words. If words are not associated with these, ingradients they turn dry, lifeless and effect~~u~~less. there is no doubt that majority of prisoners who read your book were moved by your untiring efforts for SARE's acquital and your concerns for human rights violations but I have some reservations regarding your analysis and understanding religions and their institutions, even if when you speak through Amina wadood or Turkish poet. Religion is not mere idea, feeling, body or act but whole; organic religion fulfill all the demands and requirements of body and soul. intellectual arrogance darkens our mind & heart to see the finer depths of life. Let me quote few words of Iqbal "wholly overshadowed by his intellectual activity, the modern man has ceased to live soulfully i.e from within. In the domain of thought he is living in open conflict with himself, and in the domain of economic and political life he is in open conflict with others. He finds himself unable to control his ruthless egoism and his infinite gold hunger which is gradually killing all his higher strivings in him and bringing him but life weariness. Absorbed in fact, that is to say, the optically present source of sensation he is entirely cut off from the unplumbed depths of his own being."

Arrogance economic or military or intellectual darkens and blinds the vision of individials as well nations. Learning is process till death not a system of accumulated books. Nature and history are two major sources of learning and understanding life and world and their relationship with their creator.

WEST under the banner of women's liberty is dewomanising the womenhood. Naturally and religiously in West she is known as mother, sister and wife. Now she is known as girl-friend, prostitute or receptionist, giving unwillingly her privacy and smile to unwanted and unknown men. She is sales promoter from shoes to tyres from water to washing machines. This woman (who was called mother & sister) is undressed through Electronic & mass media Just to sell these products. — sheer dewomanisation by West.

Amina wadood is intellectually bankrupt educationally barren and religiously ignorant. Woman while passing through monthly periods, pregnancy pains, and lactation her baby is exempted from obligatory individual prayers and fasting in accordance. How can she be given an duty to lead congregation prayers. It is her Endocrine-glandular changes and her total biology which make women a special status in Islam. Janat (heaven or paradise) lies under the feet of women (mother). Said the prophet of Islam. The prophet (PbUH) said the best among you is who is best with his wife. The putting a bread or food morsal into wife's mouth is act of prayer. One has to understand and differenti-ate the difference between similarity and complementarity. The role of women in Islam is in complementarity with mans role. Ayshia wife of prophet (PbUH) is the first intellectual scholar to whom prophet's companions resort for social and religious teachings. We should not mix culture and ethos with religion. Afganistan is not Islam. but a country we also need to separate a religious Islam from historical Islam. While dealing a subject we should be intellectually, emotionally and scientifically honest. Too much intellectualism spoils faith. It is Faith which gives meaning and sense to this world. We are indeed in embroynic stage as for our consciousness is concerned. Due to this divine energy for individually for all are responsible and accountable individually for our thoughts, intentions and deeds. as mystic Rumi says. "Don't remain unmindful of retribution for your deeds—as wheat springs from wheat and barely from barely

⑨

Your book reflects one thing very clear you are very much patriot than anyone like modi. Since modi's nationalism is devastating but your patriotism is logical. I am not against your patriotic feelings but I can not remain indifferent and feelingless regarding 40,000 widows and 8 their 80,000 orphans while Talking the 9 widows of 13 Dec. and Their children. We must restrain and balance our feelings and not to succumb to Rhetoric and emotionalism. who needs Forgiveness and compassion (page 208) is a debatable matter. Personally I am morally obligated to you But that my personality belonges not to me only. Indeed I have no personal misery, pains or pinches. My personality has got dissolved rather my misery has dissolved into misery of Kashmiri people so I don't feel misery. Since charity starts from home otherwise ideologically skin politically I am citizen of this planet I don't believe in choosen land & choosen race concepts which are diabolical and devastating and disastrous in their consequences and results. There is only one way to comeout of these devasting concepts and policies of nationalism That is we must believe and practise The universal permanent values. Professor Amrityasen says Honesty is first a value Then it becomes the best policy in economics. Us and its silent followers have detonated and Fragmantized the whole value based policies & programmes of entire world governments and this Godzella is eating up all finer and nobles things around the world. Every responsible citizen of this planet must stand against this neo-colonialism of humanity, cultures & universal values. It is Terrible Threat To human civilization. The so called International community by is euphemism for the united states furthering its interests through consumerism and materialism associated directly or indirectly with armed occupations under The Flag of globalization. Francis Fukuyoma's liberal democracy is not The end of history rather The political philosophy Towards end of all human moral values. In This neo-colonialism ~~was~~ we are prisoners but unaware about the prison cell in which we are caught. Our Tastes, desires and imagination are all imprisoned & This is where the greatest danger lies.

my ideas may ~~seem~~ more utopian and larger Than life. But one should never escape from individual responsibility. Every person has special & vital role to play, in This world, Everyone is accountable for This personal individual deeds. No one can share The burden of other soul. It is our sincere deeds which will go with us. Everyone comes alone and goes alone. We can develop ourselves only when we develop our concerned socities and humanity as whole. Humanity will develop only on The basement and foundation of universal permanent values. Let The noble Thoughts come from everyside. In The end I request you don't colourize or dress my words in any colour or dress except a purely responsible Human concern for humanity. جیسا کہ میں اپنے آپ کو سمجھتا ہوں

کائنات میں اپنے آپ کو ایسے سمجھتا ہوں کہ میں

[I am in universe in such a way That I am myself universe — I live in a space but I am spaceless]—

With. Regards. and Respect,

MOHAMMAD AFZAL GURU
High security Ward
C. Jail No— 1— Tihar
N. DELHI

Received from Afzal
on 8th January 2008
8-1-08

NOTES

PREFACE TO THE REVISED EDITION

1. Devinder Bhullar, a Khalistani convicted in a bomb blast case that killed nine people and sentenced to death three years before Afzal Guru, had his sentence commuted in 2014.
2. Shujaat Bukhari (1968-2018) was the editor of Srinagar-based *Rising Kashmir* and known for his outspoken views. He was assassinated on 14 June 2018 in Srinagar by militants.
3. Institute of Peace and Conflict Studies Special Report #204, 'Article 370 and the Reorganization of Jammu and Kashmir', New Delhi: August 2019.
4. Ibid.
5. https://www.thehindu.com/opinion/lead/understanding-article-370/article11640894.ece1
6. http://phdcci.in/file/state%20profiepdf/J&K-The%20State%20Profile.pdf
7. Pallavi Sareen, 'The Constitution is Allowing the Continued Discrimination of Valmikis in J&K' https://thewire.in/rights/jammu-and-kashmir-article-35a-valmikis

INTRODUCTION

1. Chitralekha Zutshi, *Languages of Belonging: Islam, Regional Identity and the Making of Kashmir*, (Permanent Black, 2003), 310.
2. The Jammu and Kashmir People's Democratic Party (PDP) and the Bharatiya Janata Party (BJP) forged an alliance based on a common minimum programme and PDP leader Mufti Mohammad Sayeed was sworn in as chief minister in March 2015. The Valley-based PDP emerged as the single largest party with twenty-eight seats; BJP's support came entirely from Hindu-dominated Jammu where it won twenty-five seats.

3. Overall, the Hindus form a majority in Jammu province which accounts for around 45 per cent of the total population of Jammu and Kashmir. Jammu consists of six districts: Doda, Poonch, Rajouri, Udhampur, Jammu and Kathua. Muslims are in a majority in the first three districts.

4. K.M. Panikkar, *Gulab Singh 1792-1858: The Founder of Kashmir*, (London: Martin Hopkinson, 1930), http://archive.org/stream/gulabsingh.

5. Dorothy Woodman, *Himalayan Frontiers*, (London: Barrie and Rockliff, The Cresset Press, 1969), 351.

6. K. Warikoo, 'Geo-Strategic Importance of Gilgit-Baltistan', in *The Other Kashmir*, K. Warikoo, ed., (New Delhi: IDSA, 2014).

7. For a description of the communities living in the Indian state of Jammu, Kashmir and Ladakh see K.S. Singh, 'People of India Jammu and Kashmir', *Anthropological Survey of India & Manohar*, 2003, Vol. XXV, New Delhi.

8. P.N.K. Bamzai, *Culture and Political History of Kashmir*, Vol. 3, (New Delhi: MD House, 1994,) 723.

9. Praveen Swami, 'Silk, Wool and Workers' Blood', *Frontline*, Vol. 23 Issue 9, 6-19 May 2006.

10. Balraj Puri (1928-2014), director, Institute of Jammu and Kashmir Affairs based in Jammu; he had taken part in the movement against Dogra oppression led by Sheikh Abdullah. He was the author of more than thirty-five books.

11. Aksai Chin and Trans-Karakoram were given by Pakistan to China in 1963.

12. Azad Jammu and Kashmir and Gilgit-Balstistan; Gilgit-Baltistan is an amalgamation of Gilgit Agency, Baltistan and the princely states of Humza and Nagar. It was known as the Northern Areas till August 2009. For a history of Azad Kashmir see Christopher Snedden, *Kashmir: The Unwritten History*, (Noida: HarperCollins, 2013); 'Pakistan Occupied Kashmir: Changing the Discourse', IDSA PoK Project Report, May 2011.

13. Jammu, Kashmir Valley and Ladakh.

BORN IN THE ERA OF KASHMIRIYAT

1. The political idea of Kashmiriyat signifies Kashmir as a land of communal amity where Hindus and Muslims have lived in harmony from times immemorial. It is not a Kashmiri term and emerged as a concept in the post-1947 years; some scholars have said the term

gained currency only after the 1980s. See Toru Tak, 'The Term Kashmiriyat: Kashmiri Nationalism of the 1970s', in *Economic and Political Weekly*, Vol. XLVIII No 16 (20 April, 2013); also see Chitralekha Zutshi (2003) and Mridu Rai (2004).The chapter heading reflects Sampat Prakash's perceptions.

2. C.E. Tyndale Biscoe, *Fifty Years against the Stream* (Srinagar: Gulshan Books, 2013 (original 1930), 21.

3. Ibid.

4. I was referring to Kashmiri families like mine who came to the plains of Uttar Pradesh from Kashmir in the beginning of the nineteenth century and no longer speak Kashmiri.

5. The RSS is a Right-wing Hindu nationalist organization founded in 1925. Their firm stand has been that Jammu should be a separate state since it is a Hindu-majority area, but they discount the fact that Poonch, Rajouri and Doda are Muslim-majority districts within Jammu.

6. Historians cannot say who laid the garden but they say it existed even before the rule of Sultan Zain-ul-Abidin in the fourteenth century. The bloom on the almond trees heralded the spring and marked the New Year for Kashmiris.

7. Dayanand Anglo-Vedic or the DAV public schools were based on the teachings of religious and social reformer, Swami Dayanand Saraswati, the founder of the Arya Samaj. The Arya Samaj was founded in 1892 and was responsible for communal tensions between Hindus and Muslims. The DAV schools attracted the Punjabi Hindu community which ensured that Kashmiri Pandits had little sympathy for the Arya Samaj.

8. Ded was Sampat's grandfather's first wife's daughter-in-law.

9. Yusuf Shah Chak (1579-1586) was exiled to Bihar where he died and was buried in a village called Biswak in the Nalanda district. His wife was the legendary Kashmiri poet, Habba Khatoon (1554-1609) who is popularly known as Zoon.

10. Fida Hussnain, 'The Genesis of the Reading Room Party', in *Greater Kashmir*, 11 August 2009, http://www.greaterkashmir.com/news/2009/Aug/11/the-genesis-of-the-reading-room-party-29

11. Chaudhry Ghulam Abbas (1904–1967) reorganized the socio-political organization, the Young Men's Muslim Association, which had been established earlier in 1909. Abbas, a Gujjar from Jammu, later supported the affiliation of Kashmir with Pakistan and became head of the government of Azad Kashmir.

12. The Khanqah-i-Moula is the shrine of Mir Saiyid Ali Hamdani, a Sufi saint credited with bringing Islam to Kashmir in the fourteenth century. There were growing tensions between the mirwaiz of Khanqah-

i-Moula and the mirwaiz of Jama Masjid. The followers of the latter included the more conservative, elite Sunni Muslims turning towards Wahhabi doctrines. The Dogra rulers patronized the Jama Masjid mirwaiz as did the Kashmri Pandits who even wrote petitions on his behalf. See Mridu Rai, Op. cit, 268.

13. Saima Bhat, 'The Hero of 13 July 1931', 7 July 2011, www.thekashmirwala.com

14. Fida Hussnain, Abdul Qadeer Khan, 'Ghazi Hero of 1931 Uprising', *Greater Kashmir*, 13 July 2007, www.greaterkashmir.com

15. Ibid.

16. There is still controversy over who Abdul Qadeer Khan really was. Some writers have said he was a servant of Colonel Alfred Butt who instigated him to make the speech; others believe that he was really a disciple of Maulana Jamal-ud-din Afghani, one of the foremost Muslim philosophers; and still others believe that he was from a Pathan family of Rampur and was involved in a pan-Islamic movement begun by Jamal-ud-din Astrabadi and came disguised as a servant of a British tourist. No one knows what happened to the Pathan after his sentence; it is believed that he was murdered in the prison by the Maharaja.

17. Fida Hussnain, 'The Genesis of the Reading Room Party', Op. cit.

18. P.N.K. Bamzai, *Culture and Political History of Kashmir*, Vol. 3, (New Delhi: MD Publications, 1994) 732.

19. Maharaja Hari Singh was born in 1895, ascended the throne in 1925 and remained maharaja till 1951 when the monarchy was abolished.

20. Prem Nath Bazaz (1905–84) was the president of the Sanatan Dharma Yuvak Sabha which represented Kashmiri Pandit interests to the Dogra rulers; later, he became a close associate of Sheikh Abdullah and played a large part in convincing him to rename the Jammu and Kashmir Muslim Conference as the National Conference. Bazaz was very critical of the Indian National Congress. In 1942 he became a follower of M.N. Roy and started the Kashmir Socialist Party. He is the author of several books on the history of Kashmir's freedom struggle.

21. Prem Nath Bazaz, *The History of Struggle for Freedom in Kashmir*, (New Delhi: Kashmir Publishing Company, 1954), 162.

22. Mridu Rai, *Hindu Rulers, Muslim Subjects: Islam, Rights and the History of Kashmir*, (Ranikhet: Permanent Black, 2004 (2012), 273.

23. Sheikh Abdullah, *Flames of the Chinar*, trans. Khushwant Singh, (Delhi: Vikas, 1993), 12-13.

24. Mridu Rai, *Hindu Rulers, Muslim Subjects*, (Ranikhet: Permanent Black, 2004), 271-72.

25. Quoted in Ajit Bhattacharjea, *Sheikh Mohammad Abdullah: Tragic Hero of Kashmir*, (New Delhi: Roli Books, 2008), 20.

26. Ab Qayoom Khan, 'Sheikh Abdullah: A Political Sufferer', *Kashmir Observer*, 10 September, 2012.

27. Quoted in Prem Nath Bazaz, *The History of Struggle for Freedom in Kashmir Cultural and Political*, (New Delhi: Kashmir Publishing Company, 1954).

28. Alys Faiz reflects on her marriage to Faiz Ahmad Faiz in an interview uploaded by Radiance Urdu on YouTube on 5 April 2009.

29. N.N. Raina, *Kashmir Politics and Imperialist Manoeuvres 1846-1980*, (New Delhi: Patriot Publishers, 1988), 124-25.

30. Ibid.

31. Freda Bedi (1911–77) later worked with Tibetan refugees and took on a new name, Gelongma Karma Kechog Palmo after she became the first Western woman to take ordination in Tibetan Buddhism; Baba Pyare Lal Bedi (1909–93) claimed to be a direct descendant of Guru Nanak and took refuge in Sikhism.

32. Andrew Whitehead's blog www.andrewwhitehead.net/kashmir has a lot of material on the Communists of Kashmir, including the cover of the Naya Kashmir manifesto.

33. Pandit Kashyap Bandhu (1899–1985) was a Kashmiri Pandit called Tara Chand. He joined the Arya Samaj in Lahore and was given the name Kashyap Bandhu. He organized the Kashmiri Labour Board and was associated with Bhagat Singh's party. In Kashmir, he, along with Prem Nath Bazaz, started the Sanatan Dharma Young Men's Association, also known as the Yuvak Sabha. He initiated social reforms in the Kashmiri Pandit community, especially in the area of women's education.

34. Chitralekha Zutshi, *Languages of Belonging*, (New Delhi: Permanent Black, 2003), 297.

35. Rajani Palme Dutt (1896-1974) was a journalist and theoretician in the Communist Party of Great Britain. He founded the *Monthly Review* and was editor of the CPGB's *The Workers' Weekly*.

36. Andrew Whitehead, 'The People's Militia: Communists and Kashmiri Nationalists in the 1940s', *Twentieth Century Communism: A Journal of International History*, 2, 2010, 141-168, www.andrewwhitehead.net/kashmir.

37. Christopher Snedden, *Kashmir*, (Noida: HarperCollins, 2013), Chapters 2 and 3.

38. See also Yoginder Sikand, *The Muslims of Jammu*. The Muslims of Jammu town lead a somewhat ghettoized existence. Most of them live in the town's two almost entirely Muslim localities. Jammu province

accounts for around 45 per cent of the total population of Jammu and Kashmir. The province consists of six districts: Doda, Poonch, Rajouri, Udhampur, Jammu and Kathua. Muslims form the majority of the population in the first three districts, and Hindus in the remaining three. Overall, the Hindus form a majority in the province, with Muslims accounting for around a third of the population. Other communities living in the province include Christians and Sikhs. Of the Hindu population, around a third belong to the Scheduled Castes. http://jammuregionalmuslims.wordpress.com/

39. Vinayak Razdan, 'Short Story of Bira' in www.searchkashmir.org.
40. One Kashmir writer has argued that Kashmiriyat is a figment of Pandit imagination. Ashiq Hussain Bhat, *Jammu and Kashmir Conflict or the Great Game*, 2004 (2007), 496-499.
41. Quoted by A.G. Noorani, *The Kashmir Dispute 1947–2012*, Vol. 2, (New Delhi: Tulika Books, 2013), 5.
42. N.N. Raina, *Kashmir Politics and Imperialist Manoeuvres 1846-1980*, (New Delhi: Patriot Publishers, 1988), 152.
43. Andrew Whitehead, Op. cit.
44. The term J&K refers to: the India-controlled Jammu, Kashmir and Ladakh; the Pakistan-controlled area known as Azad Kashmir (full name: Azad Jammu and Kashmir) and Northern Area (renamed by Pakistan in 2009 as Gilgit-Balstistan); India stakes a claim on the entire region.
45. The government of Narendra Modi told the UNMOGIP in July 2014 to vacate its office in Delhi on the grounds that it has outlived its mandate.
46. Article 370 in the Indian Constitution is based on the Hereditary State Subject Order of 1927, amended in 1932, by which state subjects had rights to government office, land use and ownership and non-state subjects did not.
47. The Praja Parishad was founded in November 1947 by Balraj Madhok on the existing organizational base of the Rashtriya Swayamsewak Sangh (RSS) in Jammu. It accused Sheikh Abdullah of trying to Islamicize the administration. The Sheikh had broken up the Hindu-majority district of Udhampur and closed down the Sanskrit Research Department. The study of Urdu was made compulsory for all. Navnita Chadha Behera, 'A Signal from Jammu', *Frontline*, Vol. 19, Issue 22, 26 October-08 November 2002. http://www.frontline.in/static/html/fl1922/stories/20021108006002000.htm.
48. Syama Prasad Mukherjee (1901–53) returned from London after being called to the Bar and became vice chancellor of Calcutta

University. He left the Congress Party and started the Bharatiya Jana Sangh in 1951, the precursor of the Bharatiya Janata Party.

49. More recently, Narendra Modi, then the prime ministerial candidate of the BJP, called for a national debate on Article 370 at his Lalkar Rally in Jammu in December 2013. However, after having formed a government along with the Valley-based People's Democratic Party, the BJP has agreed to maintain status quo on Article 370.

50. See, for example, Josef Korbel, *Danger in Kashmir*, Princeton University Press, 1954, for the Western point of view, and N.N. Raina, *Kashmir Politics and Imperialist Manoeuvres 1846–1980*, (New Delhi: Patriot Publishers, 1988) for the Communist viewpoint.

SEASON OF BETRAYALS

1. Sheikh Abdullah's wife, Akbar Jehan, popularly called Madar-i-Meherban, or gracious mother, was the daughter of Michael Harry Nedou, owner of a hotel in Srinagar. The Pakistani scholar has said on the basis of a report published in a Calcutta newspaper that Akbar Jehan was married in 1928 to Karam Shah, while she was studying in a convent in Muree. Karam Shah was none other than the British agent known as Colonel T.E. Lawrence of 'Lawrence of Arabia' fame.

2. Pervez Majid, 'The Moment of History', *Greater Kashmir*, 15 August 2011, www.greaterkashmir.com

3. However, we still do not know the real reasons behind his sudden arrest because the papers relating to this period have not been opened to the public. Ramachandra Guha, 'A Fateful Arrest', *The Hindu*, 3 August 2008, www.thehindu.com/thehindu/mag/2008/08/03/stories

4. An eyewitness account can be found in *Chicago Tribune* of 26 September 1949, http://archives.chicagotribune.com/1949; and photos of the procession are available on www.searchkashmir.org

5. Mohammad Ashraf, 'Lal Chowk Freed', 31 January 2010, www.kashmirfirst.com/articles

6. A.G. Noorani, 'Nehru and the Cold Wars', *Frontline*, Vol. 21, Issue 04, 14–24 February 2004, www.frontline.in

7. M.J. Akbar, *Kashmir: Behind the Vale*, (New Delhi: Viking, 1991), 141.

8. M.J. Akbar, Op. cit. 142

9. Ibid.

10. Sheikh Abdullah, *Flames of the Chinar: An Autobiography*, abridged, translated from the Urdu and introduced by Khushwant Singh, (Delhi: Penguin Books, 1995), 12–13.

11. Syed Junaid Hashmi, 'Jammu and Kashmir's National Song', published in the *Kashmir Times* and reproduced by www.countercurreents.org

12. Bruce Riedel, *Deadly Embrace Pakistan: America and the Future of the Global Jihad*, (New Delhi: HarperCollins, 2011), 13.

13. Bruce Riedel, ibid.

14. Ibid. The Cold War began after the Second World War and lasted until the dissolution of the Union of Soviet Socialist Republics (USSR) in December 1991.

15. Saroja Sundarajan, *Kashmir Crisis: Unholy Anglo-Pak Nexus*, (New Delhi: Kalpaz Publications, 2010) quoted by Praveen Swami, 'Kashmir and Great Power Geopolitics', review in *The Hindu*, 29 June 2010, www.thehindu.com

16. Mark Curtis, *Secret Affairs: Britain's Collusion with Radical Islam* (London: Serpent's Tail, 2012) and other recent authors about how the US and Britain continue their collusion with radical Islam and have nurtured global terrorism.

17. Sir Francis Ivans Simms Tucker (1894–1967).

18. Quotes are from Saroja Sundarajan. Op. cit.

19. Mihir Bose, 'Legacy of the Raj', *New Statesman*, 23 April 2009, http://www.newstatesman.com/asia/2009/04/india-british-raj-pakistan

20. Ibid. See also http://dilipsimeon.blogspot.in?2013/09/history-arc for more documents and discussion.

21. Escott Reid, *Envoy to Nehru*, (Oxford University Press, 1981). Quoted in D.N. Panigrahi, *Jammu and Kashmir: The Cold War and the West*, (New Delhi: Routledge, 2009).

22. Motilal Kemmu, 'Bumbro, Bumbroo: My Recollections', *Kashmir Herald*, Vol. 1 No 4, September 2001, www.kashmirherald.com/artandculture/

23. Mohammad Ishaq Khan, *Evolution of My Identity vis a vis Islam and Kashmir* in Nyla Ali Khan, ed., *The Parchment of Kashmiri History, Society and Polity*, (New York: Plagrave Macmillan, 2012).

24. Ibid, 201.

25. Ashutosh Varshney, 'Three Compromised Nationalisms: Why Kashmir Has Been a Problem', in Raju G.C. Thomas, *Perspectives on Kashmir: The Roots of Conflict in South Asia*, (Colorado: Westview Press, 1993).

26. The Plebiscite Front was finally merged into the National Conference after Sheikh Abdullah became chief minister of Jammu and Kashmir in 1975.

27. 'Keesing's Record of World Events 1931–2006', Vol. 7, 18, 290, www.stanford.ed/group/tomzgroup/pmwiki

28. Dhanwantri (1902–53) was a freedom fighter who had accompanied

Shaheed Bhagat Singh when he shot the British officer who killed Lajpat Rai. Dhanwantri was sent to jail in the Andaman Islands. After spending ten years, he was released and Sheikh Abdullah had welcomed him back. When he returned to Jammu, he guided movements for farmers, youth and students. Jammu celebrated the memory of Comrade Dhanwantri by naming the University Library after the revolutionary and his statue stands in the Jammu Development Park in Trikuta Nagar.

29. Justice Jia Lal Kilam, *A History of Kashmiri Pandits*, (Delhi: Utpal Publications, 2003), 227.

30. Hazaratbal is one of the two most important mosques in Kashmir; first is the Jami Masjid and the other is Hazaratbal where a hair of the Prophet Mohammad was installed by Emperor Aurangzeb in 1699.

31. A.B. Qayoom Khan, 'Sheikh Abdullah: Political Sufferer-II', *Kashmir Observer*, 10 September 2012. www.kashmirobserver.net/news/opinion

32. Keesings's Worldwide, Op. cit.

33. Sadiq Ali was a poet and later became a MLA. He was the author of a report on Self Rule which was acceptable to both India and Pakistan, and even today it is said that his was the most workable solution. He also suggested ways to save the Dal Lake. He died in April 2011. See http://syedalisafvi.blogspot.in/2011

34. For Bakshi's achievements, see www.kashmirnetwork.com/bgm/achievementfull.htm

35. Bakshi Ghulam Mohammad was eased out of office during the Kamraj Plan in 1964 and a Commission of Enquiry was set up to look into charges of corruption headed by Justice Iyengar.

36. M. Ashraf, 'Outsourcing Kashmir', *Greater Kashmir*, 27 July 2013, www.greaterkashmir.com/news.

37. M.J. Akbar, *Kashmir: Behind the Vale*, (New Delhi: Viking, 1991), 159

38. A.G. Noorani, 'Electoral Fraud', *Frontline*, Vol. 28, Issue 24, 2011.

39. Balraj Puri, *Kashmir Towards Insurgency*, (Hyderabad: Orient Longman, 1993) (reprint 1995), 48.

40. A faction of the Plebiscite Front appropriated the name National Conference and this was the party which Sheikh Abdullah worked with when he became chief minister in 1975.

41. Balraj Puri, 'Budh Singh is a Unique Symbol of Inter-regional and Inter-religious Unity of the State', *Greater Kashmir*, 6 June 2010, www.greaterkashmir.com

42. G.N. Gauhar, *Hazaratbal: The Centre Stage of Kashmir Politcs*, (Srinagar: Gulshan Books, 1998), 98.

43. Maulana Masoodi quit teaching Arabic at the Prince of Wales College, Jammu, and joined the Quit Kashmir movement; he was the co-founder of the Muslim Conference and the National Conference and later the first Member of Parliament from Srinagar. Known for his simple lifestyle and personal integrity, the Maulana was shot dead at the age of eighty-seven on 13 December 1990 by Islamic militants.

44. The other charges levelled against him were: being the brain behind the conversion of the Muslim Conference to the National Conference; fighting against Pakistani Mujahideens and helping in their arrest in 1947; informing Indian intelligence about the Pakistani infiltration in 1965. 'Kashmir Under Seige', *Human Rights Watch*, May 1991, 195.

45. The Awami Action Committee was formed to lead the Moi-e-Muqaddas movement. Sayyid Mir Qasim, in his autobiography, *My Life and Times*, says that the committee was formed at the instance of Pakistan and a call for jihad was given against 'the Hindu rulers of India, who outraged Islam' (page 95). But Sampat described the committee as being 'moderate'.

46. For a detailed version of the incident from the point of view of the Kashmiri Pandits read M.L. Koul, 'Loot of Kashmiri Pandit Girl in Kashmir', *Kashmir Information Network*, www.kashmir-information.com

47. Sadiq was the prime minister of Jammu and Kashmir between 1964–65. When the post of prime minister was abolished, he became the chief minister till 1971.

48. Praveen Swami, *India, Pakistan, and the Secret Jihad: The Covert Was in Kashmir (1947–2004)*, (London: Routledge, 2007; Indian reprint 2011), 90.

49. Navnita Chadha Behara, 'Autonomy in J&K: The Forgotten Identities of Ladakh', 2001, www.satp.org

50. The Jana Sangh sees this story of how the Kashmiri Pandits betrayed the Hindus; Balraj Madhok, *Kashmir: The Storm Centre of the World*, http://www.kashmir-information.com/storm

51. M.L. Koul, *Kashmir Past and Present: Unravelling the Mystique*, http://www-kashmir-information.com/storm

52. Mridu Rai, *Hindu Rulers, Muslim Subjects*, (Ranikhet: Permanent Black), 285.

53. Ashiq Hussain Bhat, *Jammu Kashmir Conflict, or, The Great Game Part I, 1707–1990*, (Srinagar: Media Book Service, 2004, 2007).

54. Ibid. 496–497.

RAGE AGAINST THE DYING OF THE LIGHT

1. Land from 9,000 landowners was taken by the government and 220,000 acres was transferred to tenants during the land reform programme. Of the thirty biggest landowners, six belonged to the Valley, two Muslim shrines and three were gompas in Ladakh. All others were non-Kashmiris, including Muslims. N.N. Raina, *Kashmir Politics and Imperialist Manoeuvers 1846–1980*, (New Delhi: Patriot Publishers, 1988), 208-9.

2. Abul Ala Maududi (1903–77) founded the Jamaat-e-Islami in Lahore in 1941. Subsequently, in 1953, the organization was reorganized and the Jamaat-e-Islami in India, Pakistan and Kashmir were separated. The organization had little influence in Kashmir till the late 1970s. A part of the reason for Maududi to establish his exclusive organization was anti-Muslim violence perpetuated by the Arya Samaj.

   In the Pakistan of that time, there was little room for such extremist views and Maududi was charged with sedition; but the charge was for excluding a Muslim community, not for his views of jihad in Kashmir. In any case he was released in 1955. Ayesha Jalal, *Partisans of Allah: Jihad in South Asia*, (Ranikhet: Permanent Black, 2009), 260.

   In Pakistan, Maududi is mostly remembered by the Left and liberal segments as the man who let the Americans use his organization to undermine Leftist and progressive politics during the Cold War. He laid the foundations of what came to be known as 'Islamism'—a theory that advocated the formation of an Islamic state by first 'Islamising' various sections of the economy and politics so that a fully Islamized polity could be built to launch the final Islamic revolution.

3. Sampat pointed out that at the time most of the Islamic world was under the influence of Communism, including Indonesia, which had the largest non-ruling communist party in the world till it was decimated in 1965 when upwards of 500,000 members and sympathizers of the party were murdered.

4. Prem Nath Bazaz organized the Kisan Mazdoor Sabha under the leadership of Salam Yatoo but Afzal Beg thought it was a challenge to the Plebiscite Front and attacked it. It did not last long. The Kisan Sabha that Bhat is referring to was the Peasant Front of the Democratic National Conference (the name under which the Communist Party functioned).

5. Navnita Chadha Behera, *State Identity and Violence: Jammu Kashmir and Ladakh*, (New Delhi: Centre for Policy Research, 2000), 49.

6. Ghulam Mohammad Sadiq, the man who had been in the Democratic

National Conference and then rejoined the National Conference, and then merged with the Indian National Congress, was the prime minister of Kashmir from 1964 to 1965. He then became the first chief minister after the post of prime minister was abolished and remained so till his death in 1971.

7. Since government servants are not allowed to form trade unions, the organization is called an association; whereas in factories, the organization is called a trade union.

8. Abdul Majid and Sampat Prakash later split. Abdul Majid continues to be active in the trade union movement but has not been involved in the movement for self-determination in Kashmir, which is the subject of this book.

9. The affiliated trade union of the Communist Party of India (Marxist), the CITU, had not been formed then.

10. These shepherds were not the traditional shepherd-nomads but government employees looking after sheep on government farms.

11. Bhaderwahi was born in 1920 and died in 2010. Sheikh Nasir, 'Ghulam Mohammad Bhaderwahi Is No More', *Greater Kashmir*, 3 September 2010, www.greaterkashmir.com.

12. Haider Naqvi, 'Natwarlal Leaves 'Em Guessing Even in Death', *Hindustan Times*, 29 July 2009, www.hindustantimes.com. Faizan Ahmed, 'Nuts about Natwarlal', *Times of India*, 23 April 2011, quoted in Wikipedia.

13. Sampat Prakash versus State of Jammu and Kashmir 1969 SCC (1) 562.

14. Sampat Prakash left the CPI(M) and joined the Naxalites, but there too the party had split, leaving the trade union without the backing of any political party.

15. The Civil Secretariat of the state government functions in the summer capital, Srinagar, for six months and moves to Jammu at the onset of winter. This bi-annual practice was introduced in 1882 by the then maharaja, Pratap Singh.

16. Ghulam Ahmad Mahjoor (1885-1952).

17. Jamaat-e-Islami is dedicated to spreading Islamic values and practices and for working towards the goal of an Islamic state which it distinguishes from a Muslim state like Pakistan.

18. Doda was the third largest district after Leh and Kargil; in 2006, two more districts, Ramban and Kishtwar, were carved out of Doda.

19. Some people claim that he was murdered by pro-government elements.

20. During Sadiq's time there were demands for autonomy in Jammu and Ladakh which he undermined by polarizing communities along

communal lines; it was during this time that a Ladakhi Buddhist identity emerged (with the centre at Leh) as well as a Ladakhi Muslim identity (with its centre in Shia-dominated Kargil). In 1969, there were incidents of tensions between these two communities.

DARK SIDE OF THE MOON

1. The Indian Emergency (25 June 1975–21 March 1977) was a twenty-one month period when President Fakhruddin Ali Ahmed, upon advice from Prime Minister Indira Gandhi, declared a state of Emergency under Article 352 of the Constitution of India, effectively bestowing on her the power to rule by decree, suspending elections and the fundamental rights of citizens. The Emergency was in part a response to the movement by Jayaprakash Narayan demanding the resignation of the prime minister after the Allahabad High Court passed a verdict against her for election malpractices.

2. The Simla Agreement was signed on 2 July 1972 between the president of Pakistan, Zulfiqar Ali Bhutto, and the prime minister of India, Indira Gandhi. The two agreed that the differences between them would be settled through bilateral negotiations.

3. Victoria Schofield, *Kashmir in Conflict: India, Pakistan and the Unending War*, (London: I.B. Tauris, 2000 (2003), 123.

4. Under the Rules, deprivation of life or personal liberty could not be questioned in a court; in other words, the fundamental rights guaranteed under the Constitution were suspended. It is interesting that the PDP party has asked for the repeal of the Armed Forces (Special Powers) Act but has not repealed any of the detention laws applicable in Jammu and Kashmir itself, such as the controversial Public Safety Act.

5. Madras became Chennai in July 1996.

6. Mohammad Yusuf Chapri later became head of the Environment Cell of the Jammu and Kashmir Liberation Council in 1992.

7. P.N.K. Bamzai (1994) writes that the houseboat was invented by a Kashmiri Hindu, Pandit Naraindas, and used by Europeans who were banned from settling down in Kashmir by the maharaja: P.N.K. Bamzai, *Cultural and Political History of Kashmir*, Vol. 3, 710.

8. Elder mother would be the senior wife of his father; his own mother would be mother and junior wife and would be referred to as younger mother.

9. A Kashmiri feast which could have as many as thirty-six courses of which thirty are different kinds of mutton dishes, each cooked according to different recipes.

10. I confirmed the story from Arif Shafi Wani, 'Neil Armstrong's Dal Connection', *Greater Kashmir*, 11 September 2012, www.greaterkashmir.com

11. Sir Owen Dixon, an Australian judge, represented the United Nations pursuant to the UN Security Council Resolution on Kashmir in 1950. His Plan envisaged giving Ladakh to India; Northern Areas and Azad Kashmir to Pakistan; splitting Jammu between India and Pakistan and a plebiscite in Kashmir.

12. This practice continues even today. Some 5,000 state employees of the Secretariat (Darbar) travel 300 kilometres from Jammu to Srinagar, and vice versa, taking all the government records packed in boxes and jute bags. There has always been criticism of the expenditure this bi-annual move entails.

13. Watali was known to catch political activists and leaders. Later, on 18 September 1988, an attempt was made on his life by militants; some say that this was the first armed action carried out by the JKLF.

14. Website of the Maqbool Butt Foundation, http://maqboolbutt.com

15. www.maqboolbutt.com

16. Neelkanth Ganjoo was assassinated on 4 October 1989 by Kashmiri militants for handing out the death sentence to Maqbool Butt.

17. Praveen Swami, *India Pakistan and the Secret Jihad*, (New Delhi: Routledge, 2011), 117.

18. Amanullah Khan was born in the Astore area of Gilgit in 1934. He, along with Maqbool Butt, formed the Jammu and Kashmir National Liberation Front (JKNLF). He was in Gilgit prison in 1970–72, accused of being an Indian agent; he was tried in absentia in Srinagar for being a Pakistani agent. His only daughter, Asma, is married to Sajjad Lone, member of the Hurriyat. Both of them supported Narendra Modi in the 2014 elections.

19. Shams Rehman, *Maqbool Butt: The Life and Struggle of an Imprisoned Kashmiri Martyr*, 1 February 2012, www.dayal.com.pk, Amanullah Khan quoted from his biography in Urdu which was published in 1992, 112.

20. Janata Party was an amalgamation of political parties opposed to the Emergency. The Left parties did not join.

21. George Fernandes (born in 1930) was trained to be a priest. He became active in the socialist trade union movement, led the 1974 railway strike, was accused in the Baroda dynamite case, held ministerial portfolios including industry, railways and, finally, defence. The Kissinger cables revealed he sought CIA funds during the Emergency. 'Fernandes Sought CIA Funding During Emergency', *The Hindu*, 8 April 2013, www.thehindu.com

22. Jyoti Basu (1914-2010) was chief minister of West Bengal from 1977 to 2000 and member of the Politburo of the Communist Party of India (Marxist) from the time the Party emerged in 1964 till 2008.

23. Yusuf Tarigami was born in 1947 and has been involved in politics from his youth. He first went to jail in 1967 for his involvement in the peasant movement; in 1971, when he was in jail, his daughter was born and his wife died; he was not allowed to attend her funeral. He is still in an active member of the CPI(M). Tarigami won his seat in the 2014 elections as well. I asked Sampat how that happened given the overwhelming support for the PDP. According to Sampat, 'Tarigami won by a margin of 262 votes against the PDP candidate. He and his party very efficiently and systematically mobilized nearly 5,000 Kashmiri Pandit migrant votes for his Kulgam constituency in Kashmir and also managed 70 per cent postal ballot votes. He had very good relations with migrants from his constituency who were living in Jammu and outside the state.' Sampat Prakash remained in the CPI(M) from 1979 to 1987.

24. Navnita Chadha Behera, *State Identity and Violence: Jammu Kashmir and Ladakh*, (New Delhi: Centre for Policy Research, 2000), 142.

25. Syed Ali Shah Geelani initially formed the Tehreek-e-Hurriyat-e-Islami in the early days of his political career, but then abandoned the platform to join the more established Jamaat-e-Islami (Jammu and Kashmir). He now uses the name of his original party (re-formed in 2003) for his faction of the APHC, in contrast to the one led by Mirwaiz Umar Farooq, which is known as the 'moderate' APHC.

26. D.N. Dhar, *Dynamics of Political Change in Kashmir: From Ancient to Modern Times*, (New Delhi: Kaniska Publishers, 2001), 203.

27. Praveen Swami, *India, Pakistan and the Secret Jihad: The Covert War in Kashmir, 1947–2004*, (Routledge, 2011), 125.

28. News report in Greater Kashmir on 13 July 2009, www.greaterkashmir.com/news/2009

29. Mridu Rai, *Hindu Rulers, Muslim Subjects*, (New Delhi: Permanent Black, 2004).

30. Chitralekha Zutshi, *Languages of Belonging*, (New Delhi: Permanent Black, 2003).

31. Ayesha Jalal, *Partisans of Allah*, (Ranikhet: Permanent Black, 2009), Op. cit., 272.

32. The Jamaat-e-Islami exists in six different regions in South Asia: Pakistan, India, India-administered Jammu and Kashmir, Pakistan-administered Azad Kashmir, in Bangladesh and in Sri Lanka. Frederic Grare, *Political Islam in the Indian Subcontinent: The Jamaat-e-Islami*, (New Delhi: Manohar, 2001).

33. Ayesha Jalal, Op. cit., 260.
34. Paul Todd, Jonathan Bloch and Patrick Fitzgerald, *Spies, Lies and the War on Terror*, (London: Zed Books, 2009).
35. Ayesha Jalal, *Partisans of Allah*, (Ranikhet: Permanent Black, 2009), 274.
36. Paul Todd et al, Op. cit., 13.
37. Yusuf Tarigami finally won the elections in 1996 and since then he has been a permanent face in the Legislative Assembly; the CPI(M) is committed to maximum autonomy for Kashmir.
38. In fact, twelve MLAs of the National Conference defected to the Congress on 2 July 1984, and joined hands with their twenty-six MLAs to form a government.
39. Farooq Abdullah, *My Dismissal*, (New Delhi: Vikas Publishing House, 1985).
40. Balraj Puri, *Kashmir Towards Insurgency*, (Delhi: Orient Longman, 1993 (1995), 36.

GATHERING OF THE STORM

1. Since then it has been renamed the National Institute of Technology.
2. The account of Afzal's early life is based on 'Tariq Bhat, Afzal Guru: Ghazals, Guns and Gallows', cover story in *The Week*, 9 February 2013, http://week.manoramaonline.com; Sameer Yasir, 'The Grieving Gurus', *Kashmir Life*, 18 February 2013, www.kashmirlife.net; Javed Iqbal, 'Cross Currents: A Visit to Guru Abode: Tale Continues', *Kashmir Times*, online edition, www.kashmirtimes.in
3. Muzamil Jaleel, 'Afzal Loved Poetry and Discussed Books', *The Indian Express*, 27 September, 2006, http://expressindia.indianexpress.com/news/fullstory.php?newsid=74516
4. Muammar Gaddafi was a Libyan revolutionary who governed Libya from 1969 to 2011, when he was killed. He was an Islamic socialist; he believed in Pan Africanism and was the president of the African Union from 2009 to 2010.
5. The website of the Guru Charitable Foundation has photographs and material on Dr Guru. http://gurufoundation.org
6. Javed Iqbal, 'Cross Currents: A Visit to the Guru Abode: Tale Continues', www.kashmirtimes.com
7. Rubaiya Sayeed was kidnapped from Lal Ded Hospital on 8 December 1989, and released on 13 December, in exchange for five militants who were in jail.
8. See http://www.maqboolbutt.com

9. Navnita Chadha Behera, *Demystifying Kashmir*, (Washington: Brookings Institutional Press, 2006), 45.

10. 'CIA, ISI Encouraged Sikh Terrorism: Ex-R&AW Official', http://www.rediff.com/news/2007/jul/26raw.htm

11. Farooq Abdullah, *My Dismissal*, (New Delhi: Vikas Publishing House, 1985).

12. Ibid, 678.

13. Balraj Puri, *Kashmir: Towards Insurgency*, (New Delhi: Orient Longman, 1993 (revised 1995), 41.

14. The organizations included the Jamaat-e-Islami, the Ummat-e-Islami, Anjumane Ittehad-ul-Musalmeen, the People's Conference, and several social and religious organizations affiliated to the Jamaat-e-Islami.

15. Quoted in Navnita Chadha Behera (2000).

16. Ashiq Hussain, *Jammu Kashmir Conflict*, (Srinagar: Media Book House, 2007 (2004) 676-680.

17. Praveen Swamy, *India, Pakistan, and the Secret Jihad*, (New York: Routledge, 2007 (Indian edition, 2011), 159.

18. Analysts say that even if the elections had not been rigged, the MUF would have won only between ten to twenty seats, not enough to dislodge Farooq Abdullah. However, due to blatant rigging, the allegations that the MUF would have won appeared credible, eliciting popular sympathy. Navnita Chadha Behera, Op. cit., 159

19. Ibid. 686–87.

20. See Navnita Chadha Behera Op. cit., 159.

21. 'Freedom Fighter Awaken'.

22. Hilal Ahmad, 'I Am Not a Product of 1987 Elections: Salahuddin', *Greater Kashmir*, 14 April 2008, http://greaterkashmir.com/news/2008/April/14

23. Ahmed Rashid, 'The Taliban: Exporting Extremism', *Foreign Affairs*, November-December 1999. 'In 1988, Al Qaeda is formed at a meeting attended by Bin Laden, Zawahiri and Dr Fadl in Peshawar, Pakistan.' Quoted by Michel Chossudovsky, Al Qaeda and the 'War on Terrorism' in http://globalresearch.ca

24. Praveen Swami, *India Pakistan and the Secret Jihad*, (London: Routledge, 2011), 164.

25. Hameed Sheikh was killed by security forces in November 1992. Some say he was killed while crossing the Jhelum river and was shot at by the Indian army, while others have said he was captured by the Indian army, tortured and given a lethal injection. He has been called Abu Jihad or the Father of Jihad.

26. Sameer Yasir, 'With Grieving Gurus', Op. cit.

27. Manoj Joshi, *The Lost Rebellion: Kashmir in the Nineties*, (New Delhi: Penguin, 1999), 47.

28. Ayesha Jalal, Op. cit., 280.

29. Ibid. 288.

30. Gyan Varma, 'Between the Devil and Deep Blue Sea: The Story of Afzal Guru', 9 February 2013, www.business-standard.com

31. 'The Human Rights Crisis in Kashmir: A Pattern of Impunity', *Asia Watch* (A Division of the Human Rights Watch) and *Physicians for Human Rights*, 1993.

32. Wajahat Habibullah, *My Kashmir: The Dying of the Light*, (New Delhi: Penguin, 2011), 96.

33. The Delhi Agreement was an Agreement between Nehru and Sheikh Abdullah by which the government of India agreed to give wide-ranging powers to Jammu and Kashmir, including special status to its residents.

34. Mirwaiz Maulvi Farooq, founder of the Awami Action Committee, was killed in his home on 21 May 1990. Mohammad Ayub Dar of the Hizbul Mujahideen was convicted of the murder and the Supreme Court confirmed the life sentence in July 2010.

35. There are many excellent reports by Indian, Kashmiri and international human rights organizations on the extent of human rights violations that were committed by the Indian armed forces. These violations took place in the context of the struggle of the Kashmiri people for the right to self-determination which is the basic human right guaranteed under international human rights law. India does not recognize the right to self-determination within borders of sovereign states as a human right.

36. Narasimha Rao was prime minister from 1991 to 1996.

37. Harjinder Baweja, 'A Calculated Gamble', 15 June 1994, http://indiatoday.in/story.

38. Sampat Prakash seems to be ignorant about the fact that George had close links with the RSS; while he was the defence minister, the RSS infiltrated the highest levels of the Army's apparatus. Fernandes opposed Narasimha Rao's 80th Amendment to the Constitution which sought to delink religion from politics. See A.G. Noorani, 'The Meaning of George Fernandes', *Frontline*, Vol. 16, Issue 22, Oct 23 – Nov 5, 1999.

39. Muheet ul Islam, 'JKLF Ceasefire in 1994 Was Brokered by US, UK: Yasin Malik', 16 January, 2013. www.thekashmirwala.com/2013/01/jklf

40. Faisal Yaseen, 'Giving Up Arms Proving Costly for Former Militants', *Rising Kashmir*, www.risingkashmir.com/giving-up-arms

41. HAJY was formed from the first letter of their names: Hamid, Ashfaq, Javed and Yasin.

42. Dukhtaran-e-Millat or Daughters of the Faith is an all-woman organization set up in 1987 with the aim of establishing Islamic law in Kashmir. It supports Kashmir's accession to Pakistan and the Islamization of Kashmiri society. This was the organization which has tried to impose the burqa on Kashmiri women. It is headed by Asiya Andrabi.

43. Ishtiaq Qadri moved on to join the PDP and was later threatened by the militants and had to take shelter with the Indian security forces.

IN THE EYE OF THE STORM

1. Shishupal Sharma was a Communist leader from Jammu. He joined the Government Press in 1958 and worked with the union from its inception. He, along with other leaders, was jailed and dismissed after the 1967 strike. He was the editor of *Sandesh*, a weekly. He died in 1990. His elder brother, Vaid Paul Deep, is a well-known Dogri poet.

2. Ishwaq Majid: 'The Raw Clay of Resistance', 30 March 2011, *Kashmir Dispatch*, www.kashmirdispatch.com

3. Ibid.

4. Ibid.

5. Mehrzad Boroujerdi, professor of political science at Syracuse, said the following were the five most important geopolitical events related to the Iranian Revolution: (1) The emergence of Hezbollah in Lebanon, (2) The moral boost provided to Shia forces in Iraq, (3) The regional cold war against Saudi Arabia and Israel, (4) Lending an Islamic flavour to the anti-imperialist, anti-American sentiment in the Middle East, and (5) Inadvertently widening the Sunni-Shia cleavage. 'Iran 1979: A Revolution That Shook the World', http://www.aljazeera.com/indepth/features/2014/01/iran

6. Sati Sahni, *Kashmir Underground*, (New Delhi: Har Anand, 1999), 151.

7. For a full account of the case read Nandita Haksar and Sebastian Hongray, *The Judgement That Never Came: Army Rule in North East India*, (New Delhi: Chicken Neck Publications, 2011).

8. Quoted in *Kashmir Imprisoned*, (New Delhi: Committee for Initiative on Kashmir), July 1990, 30.

9. Quoted in *Kashmir Imprisoned*, (New Delhi: Committee for Initiative on Kashmir), July 1990, 3.

10. Ibid.

11. Wajahat Habibullah, *My Kashmir*, (New Delhi: Viking, 2011), 89.
12. Ibid.
13. The USIP is an instrument of American foreign policy; it came into existence by an Act of the US Congress. The US Congress funds the Institute without being answerable to the US President.
14. Another reason for the Shias not buying properties belonging to Kashmiri Pandits was that they live in their own neighbourhoods since they themselves are in a minority.
15. After getting empowered as prime minister, Sheikh Abdullah immediately wanted to fulfil his promised policy of 'Land to the Tillers' and do away with 'Jagirdarana System'. The government enacted the Big Landlords Estates Abolition Act in 1950 which did not allow landlords to keep more than twenty acres of agricultural land and one acre of residential land. The land in excess of the ceiling was transferred to the tillers and subsequently, on 26 March 1952, the Constituent Assembly passed a resolution that the tillers would not pay compensation to the landlords. A.B. Qayoom Khan, 'Sheikh Abdullah: the Political Sufferer-II', *Kashmir Observer*, 10 September 2012, www.kashmirobserver.net/news
16. The Gawkadal massacre, named after the Gawkadal bridge over the Jhelum, took place on 21 January 1990. People had gathered to protest against the wide-scale search and seizure operations, especially in Chota Bazar where women had been molested the previous evening. The Central Reserve Police Force fired on the protestors a day after Jagmohan took over as governor on 20 January; at least thirty-five died instantaneously. Later, others succumbed to injuries and some drowned as they were pushed into the river. This was the one event which acted as a catalyst for the mass upsurge. More than fifty people died.
17. Mohammad Ashraf, *Reviving the Central Asian Links* in www.kashmirfirst.com/articles
18. Manoj Joshi, *The Lost Rebellion*, (New Delhi: Penguin, 1999), 56.
19. At a two-day international conference in July 1990, the Kashmiri Pandits demanded a secure zone with a concentrated Hindu population in the Valley consisting of parts of Anantnag, Baramullah, Srinagar and Pulwama districts.
20. 'Panun Kashmir, Why Homeland? For Kashmiri Pandits in Kashmir'; date and place of publication not given. It is interesting that the Kashmiri Pandits did not try to forge any solidarity with the Hindus of Jammu or the Buddhists of Ladakh.
21. Umar Manzoor Shah, 'Gawkadal Massacre Through the Eyes of a Kashmiri Pandit', 20 January 2014, www.kashmirdispatch.com

22. Mridu Rai observes: 'This frame of mind was conditioned largely by the history of the community and its memory preserved collectively by Kashmiri Pandits. As they remember it, their survival as a community was due in large measure to their indispensation to the administrative machinery of the various rulers of the Valley.' *Hindu Rulers, Muslim Subjects*, Op. cit., 245.

23. M.K. Teng and C.L. Gadoo, *Kashmir Militancy and Human Rights*, (New Delhi: Anmol Publications, 1998), 103.

24. Report in the *Economic Times*, 19 June 2011.

25. 'Kashmir: The Pandit Question', Azad Essa interviews Mridu Rai for *Al Jazeera*, 1 August 2011.

26. Ibid.

27. For a moving and poignant description see Rahul Pandita, *Our Moon Has Blood Clots: The Exodus of Kashmiri Pandits*, (Noida: Random House, 2013).

28. K.S. Singh ed. 'People of India', Vol. XXV, *Jammu and Kashmir* (New Delhi: Manohar, 2003), 394; and C.E. Tyndale Biscoe, *Fifty Years Against the Stream*, (Srinagar: Gulshan Books, 2013 (original: 1930), 15.

29. The film was released in 1965; the director asked the scriptwriter, Brij Katyal, to which religion Raja belonged and Katyal replied he had not thought of it. There are no Hindu shikarawalas in Kashmir.

A FOREST OF DEAD LEAVES

1. The description of Parray has been taken from Sati Sahini, *Kashmir Underground*, (New Delhi: Har-Anand, 1999), 348-351. While he won in the 1996 elections, he lost in 2000 and in September 2003 he was assassinated by militants.

2. One of these pro-India militias was involved in kidnapping foreign tourists in 1995 in an attempt to discredit Pakistan.

3. The SOG was set up in June 1994 in Srinagar under the Jammu and Kashmir Police but it was coordinated by the G Branch, an intelligence organization set up by the then inspector general of the Border Security Force, Ashok Patel. The task of G Branch was to turn captured militants into informers or renegades. Prem Mahadevan, *Politics of Counterterrorism*, (London: I.B. Tauris, 2012) 138, 169.

4. Javed Hussain Shah was a police constable but during the insurgency he went across the border and got arms training in Pakistan and returned to be a top-ranking commander of a militant group; he joined Kuka Parray's group.

5. Many years later the people of Pampore filed a case against Papa Kishtwari in the National Human Rights Commission. Arif Shafi Wani, 'Papa Kishtwari Murdered 150 civilians in Pampore', *Greater Kashmir*, 10 May 2007.

6. Farooq Wani, 'Bhoots Appear in Chenab Valley', 12 August 2013, www.brighterkashmir.com/home

7. Durga Prasad Dhar (1918–75) was involved in the Quit India movement in 1946 and played an important role during the tribal invasion in 1947. He was a member of the State Constituent Assembly and later, Ambassador to the USSR during the Bangladesh liberation war and subsequently, he and my father P.N. Haksar were involved in the negotiations that led to the signing of the Simla Agreement.

8. The director general of the Border Security Force, D.K. Arya, said in February 1994 at a press conference in New Delhi that there were an estimated 3,000 foreign militants operating in the Kashmir Valley, mostly of Afghani, Pakistani, Sudanese, Lebanese and Egyptian origin. Sati Sahini, *Kashmiri Underground*, Op. cit., 401.

9. K.S. Singh, 'People of India', *Jammu and Kashmir* Vol. XXV, (New Delhi: Manohar, 2003), xivii

10. Dr S.N. Dhar, *Eighty-three Days: The Story of a Frozen River*, (New Delhi: Infuse, Inc. 2000).

11. Round white balls made of boiled sugar.

12. Sati Sahini, 'The Birth of the Hizbul Mujahideen', http://www.rediff.com/news/2000/jul/31hizb.htm; later, in 2010, some Hurriyat leaders admitted that the mirwaiz and other Kashmiri separatist leaders had been killed by the pro-Pakistan militant groups.

13. I was told that this was the proposal that Saraf had sent to General Musharraf who had put it forward during the Agra Summit.

14. The *Times of India* survey of twenty-one years, from January 1990 to April 2011, revealed the following: 43,460 people have been killed in the Kashmir insurgency. Of these, 21,323 were militants; 13,226 civilians killed by militants; 3,642 civilians killed by security forces; and 5,369 policemen killed by militants. Randeep Singh Nandal, 'State Data Refutes Claim of One Lakh Killed in Kashmir', *Times of India*, 20 June 2011, http://timesofindia.indiatimes.com. Kashmiris claim many more have been killed and disappeared than is reflected in this survey.

15. After winning the elections of 1996, Farooq Abdullah's government set up the Regional Autonomy Committee. At that time there were demands for autonomy for Zanskar, Doda, Jammu, Rajouri. The discussion on these demands is well beyond the scope of this book, but central to any discussion on the construction of Kashmiri nationalism.

16. Irfan Mehraj, 'The Story of Tabassum Guru', 8 February 2014, https://www.authintmail.com/article/reportage/story-tabassum-guru
17. Ibid.
18. The Special Police Officer was usually a renegade attached to the police and his job was to spy on civilians and report on their connections with militants.
19. In a written reply to a question from Congress legislator, Bashir Ahmad Magray, in the Legislative Council here, Chief Minister Omar Abdullah stated that 25,474 SPOs are presently working in different units of the Jammu and Kashmir Police (JKP). He added that so far 1,852 SPOs have been regularized as constables. http://zeenews.india.com/news
20. The details of the torture were written in a letter by Afzal to his lawyer in the Supreme Court, Sushil Kumar, and the letter was later published in a pamphlet, http://www.sacw.net/hrights/AfzalBooklet.pdf. Davinder Singh later admitted to torturing Afzal Guru in an interview to CNN/IBN: http://ibnlive.in.com/news/tortured-but-kept-alive-for-a-deal/27164-3.html
21. This certificate was never produced in the court, nor was the surrendered militant certificate.
22. Under the circumstances, if he thought Afzal was involved with militants, he would have hardly asked him to teach his sons.
23. The five were killed by the Indian security forces soon after they entered the Parliament. The Indian government gave no information about the men except to say that Afzal identified them as: Mohammad, Raja, Rana, Hamza and Haider. However, Afzal denied knowing the slain men.
24. The prosecution witnesses told the court different and contradictory stories about the arrests and the court observed in its judgement that the prosecution stories about the arrests did not seem to be truthful.
25. For details of the legal anomalies and inconsistencies read *The Afzal Petition: A Quest for Justice*, (New Delhi: Bibliophile South Asia, 2007).

AMONG A CARAVAN OF BELIEVERS

1. See Nyla Ali Khan's blog where she writes that Abdul Ghani Lone was assassinated by the Lashkar-e-Taiba.
2. Yoginder Sikand, 'The Face Of "Azadi"', *Outlook*, 26 September 2010, http://www.outlook.com/article
3. The Ahl-e-Hadith school of thought is a reformist Islamic movement that had its origins in early nineteenth-century north India. The

founders of the Ahl-e-Hadith, men such as Maulana Nazir Husain (1805–1902) and Maulana Sanaullah Amritsari (1870–1943), believed that they were charged with the divine responsibility of purging popular Muslim practice of what they saw as 'un-Islamic' accretions and borrowings from their Hindu neighbours. They insisted that Muslims must go back to the original sources of their faith, the Quran and the Hadith, the Traditions of the Prophet. The Ahl-e-Hadith saw themselves as carrying on in the long tradition of jihad, which they accused other Muslims of having abandoned. Besides attacking the Hanafi ulama, the Ahl-e-Hadith are bitterly critical of Sufism, which they see as a 'wrongful innovation', which has no sanction in the practice of the Prophet and his Companions. They stiffly oppose the devotion given to the saints and the cults centered on their shrines, which are such an integral part of popular Sufi tradition in South Asia in general and Kashmir in particular. Yoginder Sikand, 'Islamic Militancy in Kashmir', www.sacw.net/DC/CommunalismCollection/Articles. It is important to remember that Ahl-e-Hadith scholars have condemned the Lashkar-e-Taiba for giving the ideology a bad name by spreading hatred against other communities.

4. Harindar Baweja, 'Portrait of a Suicide Bomber', *Outlook*, 31 December 2001.
5. Manisha Sobhrajani, 'Women's Role in the post-1989 Insurgency', *Faultlines*, Vol. 19, April 2008.
6. Mohammad Shehzad, 'Suicide Bombing Is the Best Form of Jihad', 17 April 2003, quoted in Ahmed Rashid, *Descent into Chaos*, (London: Penguin, 2008).
7. Ayesha Jalal, *Partisans of Allah Jihad in South Asia*, (Ranikhet: Permanent Black, 2008) 291 and 292.
8. 'Prof of Hate: Why Hafiz Saeed is Mad at India', *Hindustan Times*, 4 April 2012, www.hindustantimes.com
9. Praveen Swami, *India Pakistan and the Secret Jihad: The Covert War in Kashmir, 1947–2004*, (New Delhi: Routledge, 2007), 181.
10. Ibid and Lashkar-e-Taiba at www.satp.org
11. Lashkar-e-Taiba at www.satp.org
12. Praveen Swami, *India, Pakistan and the Secret Jihad*, (New Delhi: Routledge, 2007), 181.
13. Testimony of Ashley J. Tellis in a US Congressional Hearing on 11 March 2010.
14. Reports suggest that some of the mass killings of Hindu villagers in Doda and Rajouri have been the Lashkar's handiwork, with the aim of engineering an exodus of the Hindu population from these areas so as to make its task easier. By mid-2001, the Lashkar claimed it had killed

14,369 Indian soldiers in Kashmir, losing in the process 1,016 of its own men. Yoginder Sikand, 'Islamic Militancy in Kashmir', 20 November 2003, http://www.sacw.net/DC/CommunalismCollection/ArticlesArchive/

15. 'Ex-ISI Head Accepts Jaish Hand in Parliament Attack', www.rediff.com/news

16. The Deobandi school made a sharp distinction between 'revealed' or sacred knowledge, and 'human' or secular knowledge. The school excluded all learning that was not obviously Islamic by firmly rejecting other religious traditions and forbidding Western-style education and the study of any subjects not directly related to the study of the Quran. They were strict adherents of the Hanafi school of Islamic jurisprudence. There are many Deobandi scholars who have condemned the militants and the use of jihad for terrorist activities.

17. The official name of the madrassa is Jamia Uloom-e-Islamia. It has been described by the International Crisis Group as the fountainhead of Deobandi militancy in Pakistan, due to the madrassa playing a major role in helping establish and sustain a number of militant organizations, including Harkat-ul-Mujahideen (HUM), Jaish-e-Mohammed (JeM), and Sipah-e-Sahaba Pakistan (SSP).

18. Harkat-ul-Ansar set up in 1980 in Karachi to send volunteers to Afghanistan.

19. Ahmed Rashid, *Descent into Chaos*, (London: Penguin, 2008), 113.

20. Ibid. 113–114.

21. Ibid., 113, footnote 10.

22. Rohit Honawar, *Jaish-e-Mohammad*, (New Delhi: Institute of Peace and Conflict, November 2005).

23. Hemendra Sharma's blog: http:/ibn.inlive/blogs; Siddhartha Gautam of CNN/IBN claims that it was Afzal's elder brother who identified Ghazi Baba when he was killed because he had seen him at Afzal's place, http://ibnlive.in.com/news/tortured-but-kept-alive-for-a-deal/27164-3.html

24. I have written extensively about the trial and campaign for both Geelani and Afzal in my book, *Framing Geelani, Hanging Afzal Patriotism in Time of Terror*, (New Delhi: Bibliophile South Asia, 2009).

25. Parmeshwar Narain Haksar (1913–98) was a Communist and well-acquainted with the Communists in Kashmir. He was respected for his integrity and nationalism. He was close to Jawaharlal Nehru who brought him into foreign service; he supported the liberation movement for Bangladesh and was part of the team that negotiated the Simla Agreement in 1972.

26. These statements were widely reported in the papers and television in the first week of January 2011.

27. The entire story of the trial and the campaign for his acquittal has been documented in Nandita Haksar, *Framing Geelani, Hanging Afzal Patriotism in Time of Terror*, (New Delhi: Bibliophile South Asia, 2007).

28. Quoted in Sati Sahini, *Kashmir Underground*, (New Delhi: Har-Anand, 1999), 172–73.

29. Ibid.

30. Praveen Swami, 'The Autumn of Kashmir's Islamist Patriarch?' *The Hindu*, 10 August 2010, http://www.thehindu.com/todays-paper/tp-opinion/the-autumn-of-kashmirs-islamist-patriarch/article582923.ece

31. Irfan Ahmad, *Isalmism and Democracy in India: The Transformation of Jammat-e-Islam*, (Ranikhet: Permanent Black, 2010).

32. Ibid.

33. Harinder Baweja, 'Kashmir: People Turning against Militants', *India Today*, 31 May 1992.

34. I have dealt with the conversations between Bismillah and myself in a chapter entitled 'In Celebration of an Impossible Friendship' in my book *Framing Geelani, Hanging Afzal: Terrorism in Time of Terror*, (New Delhi: Bibliophile South Asia, 2009).

35. Syed Bismillah Geelani, *Manufacturing Terrorism: Kashmiri Encounters with Media and the Law*, (New Delhi: Bibliophile South Asia, 2006), also reproduced by Balraj Puri in his publication.

36. 'Fighting for an Independent Kashmir', *International Socialist Review* Issue 37, September-October 2004, online edition.

37. Chaplin's brother was called Charlie.

38. Arif Jamal, *Shadow War: The Untold Story of Jihad in Kashmir*, (New Delhi: Vij Books, 2005), 252.

39. Peerzada Ashiq, '45% Militants in Kashmir Belong to Foreign Origin', *Hindustan Times*, http://www.hindustantimes.com/jandk/45-militants-in-kashmir-belong-to-foreign-origin-let-tops-list/article1-1307250.aspx

40. Parvaiz Bukhari, 'The Eerie NGO Phenomenon in Kashmir', *The Honour Magazine*, April 2010, 16-20, http://pulsemedia.org

41. Aman Sharma, 'ISI Funded US-based NGO $4 Million for Its Kashmir Cause', *India Today*, 20 July 2011, http://indiatoday.intoday.in/story/isi-funded-$4-million-to-us-based-ngo-for-kashmir-cause/1/145524.html

42. Salla Allahu Alaihe wa Salaam (May Allah's peace and blessings be upon him) or the English version, PBUH (Peace be upon Him)

43. 'JKLF Launches All-out Attack on Geelani', 16 October 2012, http://kashmirwatch.com

KASHMIR AND THE WAR ON TERROR

1. http://indiatoday.intoday.in/story/2008-mumbai-attacks-a-book-describes-how-david-headley-bragged-in-emails/1/320488.html
2. Asit Jolly, 'The Wahhabi Invasion', *India Today*, 2 January 2012, http://indiatoday.intoday.in/story/saudi-charities-pump-in-funds-through-hawala-channels-to-radicalise-kashmir-valley/1/165660.html
3. The followers of Sunni Islam follow the four Sunni schools of Fiqh, i.e. the Hanafi, Maliki, Shafi'i and Hanbali schools. The Ahl-e-Hadith group, an Islamic movement that emerged in the nineteenth century in South Asia, reject the view that Muslims should blindly follow these four Schools of Law, they believe that Muslims should seek to follow the religious opinions which are closest to the original principles of Islam. The Salafis are Sunnis who have tried to modernize Islam by dropping the traditional law schools and reading scripture directly instead. In this sense, they are the Muslim equivalent of Protestants. Like some Protestants, some Salafis justify militancy and terrorism from their non-traditional readings of scripture. The term 'Wahhabi' denotes this kind of extremist tendency among Salafist followers of the Arabian reformer, Ibn Abdul-Wahhab. There are many Islamic scholars, Sunni as well as Ahl-e-Hadith, who condemn jihadi militancy. Sufis are the mystics.
4. Riyaz Wani, 'The Fight for Kashmir's Soul', *Tehelka*, 31 March 2012, http://archive.tehelka.com/story_main52.asp?filename=Ne3 10312Fight.asp
5. Afzal mentioned the Naga conflict because he knew I had been involved in the Indo-Naga talks, but he did not know the extent to which the Naga national movement was influenced by the Christian fundamentalism of the Baptist Church and the sharp conflict between the Catholics and Baptists in Naga villages.
6. According to Wikipedia, Robert Pape compiled a database on suicides as a part of his project on 'Security and Terrorism' at the University of Chicago. Pape claims to have compiled the world's first 'database of every suicide bombing and attack around the globe from 1980 through 2003—315 attacks in all' (3). 'The data show that there is little connection between suicide terrorism and Islamic fundamentalism, or any one of the world's religions…Rather, what nearly all suicide terrorist attacks have in common is a specific secular and strategic goal: to compel modern democracies to withdraw military forces from territory that the terrorists consider to be their homeland.'
7. Graham E. Fuller, *A World Without Islam*, (New York: Back Bay Books, 2010), 343.

8. Syed Abdul Rehman Geelani.

9. Amina Wadud is an Afro-American Islamic scholar and feminist theologist and co-founder of the Sisters in Islam. In August 1994, Wadud delivered a Friday sermon on 'Islam as Engaged Surrender' at a mosque in South Africa; and more than a decade later, on Friday 18 March 2005, Wadud acted as imam for a congregation of about sixty women and forty men seated together, without any gender separation. Her book, *Inside the Gender Jihad: Women's Reform in Islam*, discusses the textual foundations of the feminist movement in Islam. The Turkish poet is Nazim Hikmet (1902–63) who was a Communist and spent much of his adult life either in exile or in jail. In my book I have discussed the uneasy relationship between Communists, and their definitions of secularism and Islam.

10. Narendra Damodardas Modi became the fifteenth prime minister of India on 26 May 2014. He was a member of RSS since the age of eight.

11. Amrit Wilson, one of the founders of the South Asian Solidarity Group, has been active on issues of gender and race. She is the author of several books, including: *The Threat of Liberation: Imperialism and Revolution in Zanzibar* (2013) and *Dreams, Questions, Struggles: South Asian Women in Britain* (2006). I had known her parents, Amiya and B.G. Rao, whose flat in Delhi's Nizammudin East was a refuge for activists of all hues.

12. Nandita Haksar, *Human Rights Lawyering: A Feminist Perspective* in Amita Dhanda, Archana Parashar eds. *Engendering Law*, (Lucknow: Eastern Book Company, 1999).

13. Moazzam Begg, *Enemy Combatant: My Imprisonnment at Guantanamo, Bagam and Kandahar*, (New Press, 2007).

14. The entire debate can be found on the Internet so I will not reproduce it here. However, it is relevant to point out how feminists often land up taking up stands which are opposed to principles of human rights.

15. Richard Norton-Taylor, 'The Strange Case of Moazzam Begg', http://www.theguardian.com/world/defence-and-security-blog/2014/oct/07/moazzam-begg-mi5-syria#comments

16. Dhiren Barot was born in Baroda, Gujarat, into a Hindu family. His parents moved to the UK from Kenya in 1973 to escape violence and discrimination, when Barot was only one year old. In the UK, his father, a banker in Kenya, supported his family by working in a factory. Barot converted to Islam when he was twenty in the UK. In 2006, he pleaded guilty to planning a dirty-bomb attack on London.

17. Mark Curtis, *Secret Affairs: Britain's Collusion with Radical Islam* (London: Serpent's Tail, 2012), 284.

18. '"With Friends Like These..." Human Rights Violations in Azad Kashmir', September 2006, www.hrw.org/reports/2006/pakistan0906/

19. Tariq Mir, 'Kashmir: From Sufi to Salafi', Pulitzer Centre, http://pulitzercentre.org/reporting/kashmir

20. This was an initiative of trade unions who were not affiliated to any of the political parties and many were more in the nature of NGOs.

21. As listed on this blog: http://thekashmir.wordpress.com/2008/07/05/amarnath/

22. 'Amarnath Land Row-Chronology of Events', http://www.greaterkashmir.com/news/gk-magazine/amarnath-land-row-chronology-of-events/38658.html.

23. On 4 July 2008, the Supreme Court refused to intervene.

24. Union minister of state in the Prime Minister's Office, Jitendra Singh, stated that geological surveys had indicated that the Amarnath Yatra could take place throughout the year. He said this in June 2015.

25. Panun Kashmir advice to Kashmiri Pandits, Greater Kashmir, 1 August 2008.

26. This was reported in newspapers, such as a report by Arun Joshi, 'Amarnath Shivling Man-made?', *Hindustan Times*, 17 June 2006.

27. Pakistani cleric Tahir ul Qadri declared a jihad against terrorism in his 600-page fatwa issued in 2010. Quoted in Robin Wright, *Rock the Casbah: Rage and Rebellion across the Islamic World*, (New York: Simon and Schuster, 2011).

DYSTOPIA TO PARADISE

1. As listed on the website of Jammu Kashmir National Front, http://www.jknf.org

2. Mark Curtis, *Secret Affairs: Britain's Collusion with Radical Islam* (London: Serpent's Tail, 2012), 85.

3. Ibid. p. 86.

4. Ibid. p. 256.

5. Ibid. p. 257.

6. Ibid p. 191.

7. Sibel Deniz Edmonds is a former Federal Bureau of Investigation (FBI) translator and founder of the National Security Whistleblowers Coalition. She has been described as 'the most gagged person in American history' by the American Civil Liberties Union. Edmonds testified before the 9/11 Commission, but her testimony was excluded from the official 567-page 9/11 Commission Report. She is the

founder and publisher of the *Boiling Frogs Post*, an online media site that aims to offer non-partisan investigative journalism.

8. After the Supreme Court has passed its judgement, the petitioner can file a review petition to point out any errors in the judgement. A Curative Petition can also be filed, but only by a Senior Counsel Court, to point out a violation of the law or provisions of the Constitution which may have gone unnoticed. In this case, Indira Jaising filed a Curative Petition to point out that Afzal did not receive the legal assistance he was entitled to. The final appeal of a condemned petitioner is to the President of India for reprieve; the mercy petition.

9. Syed Abdul Rehman Geelani, Shaukat Guru and Mohammad Afzal Guru.

10. Wikileaks quoted by the media, including *Greater Kashmir*, 17 March 2011, http://www.greaterkashmir.com

11. Ibid. The Hurriyat, led by Mirwaiz Umar Farooq, denied that anyone had said it and claimed the statement was made to defame the Hurriyat.

12. Abbas was born on 18 August 1936, in Srinagar. After graduating from Srinagar, he went for further studies to Lucknow, the centre of Islamic theological education in India; and then for higher studies to Najaf, Iraq. He majored in Arabic literature, Philosophy, Hadith and Tafseer, Islamic Jurisprudence and Political Science. After eight years of study in Iraq, he returned to Kashmir and launched a religio-political monthly magazine named *Safeena*. He emerged as a leader during the Holy Relic movement and was active in the Plebiscite Front, and later in the Muslim United Front.

13. Arif Jamal, *Shadow War: The Untold Story of Jihad in Kashmir*, (New Delhi: Vij Books, 2009)

14. Sarabjit Singh (1964–2013) was an Indian intelligence agent convicted in Pakistan for bomb blasts in Lahore in 1990; a campaign for his release ran almost parallel with the campaign for reprieve for Afzal. The prime minister at the time was Manmohan Singh of the Congress Party.

15. *Hanging Afzal Would be a Stigma on Indian Democracy*, (New Delhi: SPDPR pamphlet, October 2006).

16. B. Raman, 'Afzal Guru's Execution: Possible Security Implications', South Asia Analysis Group, Paper 5385, (9 February 2013), www.southasiaanalysis.org/node/1154

17. 'NGO, Lawyer Fight Over Death Row Convict Afzal Guru', *The Indian Express*, 27 May 2010, http://archive.indianexpress.com/news/ngo-lawyer-fight-over-death-row-convict-afzal-guru/624540/; 'In Defence of N.D. Pancholi's Legal Representation of Mohammad Afzal Guru', *Mainstream*, Vol. XLVIII No 24 (5 June 2010), http://www.mainstream weekly.net/article2115.html

18. Panini Anand, 'A Town Comes to Mourn', *Outlook*, March 4 2013, http://www.outlookindia.com/article/a-town-comes-to-mourn/284014.

19. Ibid.

20. Mihir Srivastava and Harinder Baweja, 'Blood Brothers, Blood Money', *Tehelka*, Vol. 4 Issue 4, 3 February 2007.

21. 'The Afzal Petition: A Quest for Justice', *South Asia Bibliophile*, New Delhi, 2007.

22. Irfan Mehraj, 'The Story of Tabassum Guru', February 8 2014, https://www.authintmail.com/article/reportage/story-tabassum-guru

23. Irfan Mehraj, Op. cit.

24. Riyaz Wani, 'Afzal Guru's Last Letter to Wife', *Tehelka*, 18 February 2013, www.tehelka.com/afzal-gurus-last-letter-to-wife.

25. Chinki Sinha, 'I Asked Afzal Guru What If He Dies. He Said Book Will Tell How I Lived', *The Indian Express*, 9 February 2013, http://archive.indianexpress.com/news/-i-asked-afzal-guru-what-if-he-dies.-he-said-book-will-tell-how-i-lived-/832394/ also http://www.kashmirglobal.com

26. Irfan Mehraj, 'The Story of Tabassum Guru', 8 February 2014, https://www.authintmail.com/article/reportage/story-tabassum-guru.

EPILOGUE

1. Prem Nath Bazaz, *The History of the Struggle for Freedom in Kashmir: From the Earliest Times to the Present Day*, (New Delhi: Kashmir Publishing House, 1954).

2. The Rajinder Sachar Committee, appointed in 2005 by the then prime minister Manmohan Singh, was commissioned to prepare a report on the latest social, economic and educational condition of the Muslim community of India. The report was the first of its kind and revealed the alarming backward status of Indian Muslims. According to the report, some of the major concerns are: The social and economic condition of India's Muslims is worse than other suppressed and disadvantaged groups like the Scheduled Castes and Scheduled Tribes; the overall percentage of Muslims in the bureaucracy is just 2.5% whereas Muslims constitute above 14% of India's population.

3. See Zafar Choudhury, 'Kashmir Conflict and Muslims of Jammu', *The Hindu*, 20 June 2015.

4. Lt Gen P.S. Bhagat, *The Shield and the Sword: India 1965 and After*, *The Statesman*, 1967

5. In the summer of 2015 the Indian government announced that it would celebrate India's victory over Pakistan in the 1965 war.

AFTERWORD

1. Mahum Shabir in the *Scroll.in* August 31, 2016.
2. The full letter was originally published in *Times of India* and reproduced here with a reply from a Kashmiri woman: http://www.thecitizen.in/index.php/NewsDetail/index/8/7457/Kashmiri-Woman-Pens-Powerful-Response-To-Chetan-Bhagats-Open-Letter-To-Kashmiri-Youth.
3. Quoted by Andrew Small p. 47.
4. See *Among the Caravan of Believers* pp. 195-6 for a brief background
5. P. Stopdan, *The Need for Haste on Pakistan-occupied Kashmir: China Pakistan Economic Corridor Needs a Counter Strategy*, New Delhi: IDSA October 07, 2015.
6. Ibid.
7. http://fortune.com/2016/03/28/u-s-arms-sales-gulf/
8. See Afzal's letter annexed.
9. Rajni Shaleen Chopra http://www.dailyo.in/politics/burhan-wani-kashmir-hizbul-mujahideen-azadi-omar-abdullah/story/1/11697.html

INDEX